D0207711

PUBLIC PROBLEMS

PUBLIC PROBLEMS
The Management of Urban Distress

CHRISTOPHER J. SMITH
Department of Geography and Regional Planning
State University of New York at Albany

THE GUILFORD PRESS
New York   London

© 1988 The Guilford Press
A Division of Guilford Publications, Inc.
72 Spring Street, New York, NY 10012

Printed in the United States of America

Last digit is print number: 9 8 7 6 5 4 3 2 1

Library of Congress Cataloging in Publication Data

Smith, Christopher J.
    Public problems.

    Bibliography: p.
    Includes index.
    1. City and town life—Case studies.   2. Sociology,
Urban—Case studies.   I. Title.
HT151.S525   1988   307.7′6   87-17815
ISBN 0-89862-782-6
ISBN 0-89862-924-1 pbk.

Acknowledgments

It is almost impossible to thank all the people who have made contributions to this book, and I must apologize in advance to those who are inadvertently left out. My friend and former colleague, Bob Hanham, played a major role in helping me with the alcohol and mental health research in the late 1970s and early 1980s, both before and after we left Oklahoma. From those days I also owe a lot to Jim Bohland, yet another of the many Oklahomans who left the plains at about the same time in search of greener pastures.

In the northeast my work has benefited greatly from my association with Phil Brown. Although Phil and I have never actually met, he has provided great inspiration and support over the last few years. Joe Morrissey's work at the New York State Office of Mental Health was also a consistent source of help as I was writing the book, and his move to North Carolina represents a great loss, both to myself and to the state of New York.

The person to whom I owe the most is, of course, Carolyn Smith. Many people ask me how a geographer became interested in such topics as mental illness, alcohol abuse, and crime. The answer is quite simple. Carolyn, who is a clinical social worker, has been involved in these three areas during the last two decades. Whenever she began a new job, she started to read about the issues involved. She left her books lying around the house, I picked them up, and before I knew it, I found myself following a new lead.

I would also like to thank the people at Guilford Publications for providing the support I needed to finish the book. Janet Crane, with her unflagging energy and enthusiasm, has been marvelous from start to finish. Nancy Worman provided some of the most thorough editing I have ever seen. I only wish she were available to edit all of my work.

Contents

PART I. INTRODUCTION

1. *Public Problems in the Modern City* 3

   Introduction, 3
   The Unifying Characteristics of Public Problems, 4
   The Epidemiology of Public Problems, 7
   Theoretical Approaches to Public Problems, 13
   Public Problems: An Outline of the Book, 16

PART II. THE ETIOLOGY AND SOCIAL GEOGRAPHY OF PUBLIC PROBLEMS

2. *The Experience of City Living* 21

   Introduction: The City in History, 21
   Spatial Patterns and Public Problems, 25
   Spatial Processes and Public Problems, 37

3. *A Contextual Account of Public Problems* 51

   Introduction, 51
   Neighborhood Effects on Human Outcomes, 52
   Social Contexts: The Network Approach, 59
   Social Networks and the Decision to Seek Treatment, 68
   Creating Social Support Networks: The Community Support
     Program, 73

4. *The Environmental Context of Public Problems* 78

   Introduction, 78
   Well-Being and Mental Health: The Residential Dimension, 82
   The Behavioral Ecology of Drinking, 90

PART III. SERVICE DELIVERY AND THE MANAGEMENT OF PUBLIC
        PROBLEMS

5. *Deinstitutionalization of the Mentally Ill* 105

   Introduction, 105
   The Shift from Indoor to Outdoor Relief, 106

Deinstitutionalization: Moving the Mentally Ill onto the Streets, 110

6. *Decriminalization of Public Drunkenness*   120

   Introduction, 120
   Evaluating the Impact of the Uniform Intoxication Act, 124

7. *Diversion of Youthful Offenders*   133

   Introduction: Finding Alternatives for Youthful Offenders, 133
   The History of Juvenile Diversion, 134
   Evaluating Diversion, 136

PART IV. THE POLITICAL CONTEXT OF PUBLIC PROBLEMS

8. *Structural Accounts of Public Problems*   145

   Introduction, 145
   The Positivist Account of Public Problems, 145
   The Interactionist Account of Public Problems, 147
   Conflict Accounts of Public Problems, 150
   Mental Disorders, 160
   Alcoholism and Problem Drinking, 165
   Conclusion, 172

9. *Arena Building and the Social Construction of Public Problems*   174

   Introduction, 174
   The "Facts" About Public Problems, 175
   The Mechanisms for Constructing Public Problems, 179
   Problem Drinking and the Designation of Special
      Populations, 181
   The War on Heroin, 188
   Community Mental Health: The "Bold New Approach," 195
   Conclusion, 204

10. *The Social Control of Public Problems*   205

   Introduction, 205
   The Great Society: A Case Study in Social Control, 206
   Models of Social Control, 208
   Conclusion, 222

11. *Home and Homelessness in the Postindustrial City*   225

   Introduction, 225
   The Homelessness Phenomenon, 226
   Conclusion: Home and Homelessness in Historical Context, 235

Bibliography   239
Index   265

PART ONE

INTRODUCTION

1

Public Problems in the Modern City

INTRODUCTION

One of the most distressing features of the contemporary city is the persistence of social problems. These problems are sources of distress in two ways: They create trouble for the people involved and those around them, and they frustrate those who genuinely want to diminish the overall level of human suffering. As incomes rise and the quality of life improves for the majority of city dwellers, many people are left behind. In addition to the absolute level of distress that is generally more prevalent among those "left behind," they experience relative distress. They are unhappy about missing out on the good life, but they feel helpless when it comes to doing something to change their situation. Their distress is manifested in many ways: Some commit crimes, some drink too much, others experience difficulties that are diagnosed as mental disorders. This book is concerned with a subsample of these problems—the ones that become serious enough to be defined as "public problems."

Public problems are issues that have become matters of controversy in the public arena, and for which official actions are judged to be necessary. In response to these problems public agencies are required to take action, either by providing services for those experiencing the problems or by removing them from the mainstream of society. There are at least two categories of problems that could concern us here. The first is a group of issues in which illegal behavior is involved, such as drug abuse, crime, delinquency, and family violence. The second category includes a variety of situations in which there is a significant but not illegal deviation from societal norms. This includes such issues as mental disorders, problem drinking and alcoholism, and the wide range of health and welfare concerns associated with poverty, old age, and various forms of inequality.

To keep this book to a manageable size without compromising the need to cover the field as broadly as possible, it is necessary to sample from the wide array of public problems. Most of the case studies in the book will come from three broad areas: substance use and abuse, including both alcohol and drugs; mental disorder; and crime and delinquency.

In many cases the individuals involved do not agree that their behavior or their condition represents a public problem. It follows from this that in such cases there will be no consensus about the actions taken. It is also evident that the problems to be discussed here are only problems because they have an impact on others, in other words, because they are inherently social in nature. On the other hand, not all social problems become concerns in the public domain. It is difficult to predict what issues will become defined as public problems in the future. An example of this, as Gusfield (1982a) has observed, is that by the end of this century sexual inadequacy may be defined as a public problem. As farfetched as this may seem, it is probably no more outlandish than the prospect of government-funded programs to treat alcoholics would have appeared to an observer in the early 1940s.

THE UNIFYING CHARACTERISTICS OF PUBLIC PROBLEMS

Although public problems manifest themselves in many ways, they share some common traits. In the first place they are, by definition, problems that have become "public," that is, an official attempt has been made to provide services for the persons in question. The responses have been made by public agencies using public monies, which implies that the problems have come under the umbrella of the welfare state. Some of the individuals experiencing public problems are referred to as "service dependent," which suggests that without interventions by the state on their behalf, their problems would be even more serious.

A second common characteristic is that most public problems involve some degree of stigma. The affected individuals are likely to be downgraded socially, either because of the characteristics associated with the problems themselves, or because of the inherently degraded status associated with being dependent on the welfare state. The degree of stigma varies from one problem category to another. Those involving crime and violence or the use of dangerous substances are generally the most feared and avoided. However, it is evident that the level of stigma associated with a specific problem rises and falls over time. Before the use of cocaine was made illegal in the United States it was considered appropriate for use by respectable citizens, many of whom were doctors (Reinarman, 1979). Today cocaine is illegal and its presence in the community is considered to be a significant public problem. Alcohol, on the other hand, was legalized in the 1930s, and for the majority of the population, using alcohol is not considered publicly problematic.

A third characteristic of public problems is that they are relative. What is defined as a problem depends on where and when it occurs, as well as on the status of the individual in question. In most cases a behavior is not defined as a problem until it reaches an extreme level. In fact, the nonextreme behavior itself is often evidence of "normality." It is acceptable for adults to drink moderately, and unremarkable for college students or servicemen to drink heavily. Similarly, it is normal to discipline one's children and to feel anxious and depressed at times. Only when these behaviors pass beyond a certain point, or when they occur at the "wrong" times or in the "wrong" places, are public responses considered to be necessary.

Recent history also shows that definitions of public problems are likely to change frequently as a result of greater public awareness and legislation. An example of this is the phenomenon of "driving while intoxicated" (DWI), which has become increasingly prevalent during the 1970s and 1980s. No doubt some of this increase is the result of heavier drinking among relatively inexperienced young drivers, but it is difficult to assess what proportion of the rising prevalence has resulted from artifactual variables such as increased police vigilance (Ross, 1982). In roughly the same period arrests for public drunkenness have fallen sharply, largely because of the implementation of new state laws decriminalizing public drunkenness (Regier, 1977). As these examples indicate, within a relatively short period there have been two opposite trends in alcohol-related crime rates, both of which have been influenced by changes in the law and the way it is interpreted.

Opinions about the relative seriousness of different public problems vary considerably over time. When members of the public are asked what they consider to be the most serious public issues, their responses depend largely on whatever happens to be topical. In the 1970s such issues as the energy crisis, wrong-doing by public officials, and drug abuse were considered to be the most pressing problems; in the 1980s unemployment and the threat of war have dominated, while concerns about such issues as inflation, crime, and the courts have remained at about the same level (Table 1.1).

Table 1.1. Respondents Concerns About Public Issues in the United States, Selected Years 1974–1982

Issues	Percent[a]						
	1974	1975	1976	1977	1979	1981	1982
Inflation and Prices	56	58	44	48	63	56	53
Crime and Lawlessness	30	34	40	40	31	35	37
Having Enough Money	25	30	26	28	33	31	29
The Energy Crisis	46	27	22	31	25	30	17
The Courts	20	22	30	27	23	24	25
Unemployment and Recession	15	13	20	19	20	24	34
Relations with Foreign Countries	18	10	13	9	15	19	21
Wrongdoings by Government Officials	40	26	32	22	24	18	17
Getting into Another War	7	11	10	8	9	18	16
Drug Abuse	23	20	24	21	14	16	17
The Way Young People Act	10	14	15	17	14	14	12
Pollution	12	11	11	13	10	10	7
Alcoholism	—	—	6	7	6	7	7

[a]Respondents could list more than one issue as a major concern.
Source. Brown, Flanagan, and McCleod (1984).

Opinions about how to deal with public problems also vary significantly over time. The general trend toward liberalizing drug and alcohol laws provides an example. The proportion of the population interviewed in Gallup polls who agree that the use of marijuana should be legalized increased from about 12% in 1969 to 30% by 1980, while the proportion favoring the prohibition of alcohol fell from more than 40% in 1936 to 17% in 1981. By comparison public attitudes toward crime and criminals have become significantly less liberal. When respondents were asked in 1970 what they thought the major role of prisons should be, 73% of them said "rehabilitation," 8% said "punishment," and 12% said "to protect society." When asked the same question in 1982, 44% of the respondents considered the role of prisons to be rehabilitation, 19% punishment, and 32% the protection of society (Harris, 1982).

Another characteristic of public problems is their remarkable persistence over time. Even with the best intentions and the expenditure of vast amounts of public funds, the incidence rates of most public problems have continued to rise. The empirical evidence can be interpreted in sharply divergent ways. It has been suggested that problems have at least partly been "manufactured" or "socially constructed" (Conrad & Schneider, 1980), which implies that the supply of services has risen independently of the demand for them, usually as a result of professional expansionism and "arena building." In recent years this argument has been at the center of a politically heated debate, with calls for cutbacks on potentially wasteful social services. Another interpretation of the rising incidence rates is the argument that public problems are an accurate reflection of the stresses endemic to modern urban living. Whatever the cause, the empirical evidence demonstrates that in recent years the prevalence of public problems has persisted. As gallant as the attempts to "do something" about these problems have been, they have done little more than scratch the surface of the underlying causes.

A further common characteristic of public problems is that etiological explanations for many of the conditions associated with such problems were until relatively recently thought to be primarily located within the individual. It was generally understood that a person experienced mental disorders or became a thief or a problem drinker mainly as a result of some unfortunate combination of personal characteristics. Theories about the nature of these characteristics have changed considerably over time, ranging from moral failings to genetic defects, psychological dispositions, and physical incapacities. There is no doubt that individual etiological explanations are important, but the focus in this book is on social and ecological accounts of public problems—not as competition with but as a complement to individual accounts.

A final attribute of public problems is that they are highly interrelated, both in terms of their etiology, and in the types of individuals likely to encounter them. It is no surprise to anyone to find that problems are most often concentrated in a few urban locations, or that they are most prevalent among particular subgroups of the population.

One of the most important features of the study of public problems as presented in this book is its interdisciplinary nature. The work of sociologists and anthropologists is clearly central in a study of human problems, but such problems also need to be viewed in their historical, political, and economic context. What sets this book apart from others dealing with similar issues is the explicit recognition that there is also a social geography of public problems. Most problems have a clearly identifiable spatial pattern that can contribute to hypotheses about etiology. In addition, the public responses to such problems and the outcomes of those responses are influenced by geographical factors.

Most of the investigations conducted by sociologists or other social scientists are fragmented and microscopic in their approaches to public problems. Many impressive ethnographic studies of specific social control agencies have been conducted, but they tend to be epiphenomenal in nature, and suspended in space and time. As Cohen (1979) has pointed out, these studies are "abstracted from the density of urban life in which social control is embedded. It is not so much that these agencies often have no history: they also have little sense of place . . ." (p. 340).

A major goal of this book is to inject a sense of place into the study of public problems. This does not imply that a disciplinary approach will be adopted, neither does it suggest that there is an independent and self-contained "geography of public problems." The work that is geographical in this area can best be viewed as contributing to and complementing an interdisciplinary orientation to the understanding of public problems.

THE EPIDEMIOLOGY OF PUBLIC PROBLEMS

Although this book is concerned with a largely nonmedical approach to public problems, it has been useful to borrow some of the methods used in epidemiology, one of medicine's subfields. Epidemiology has been broadly defined as "the study of the frequency, distribution, and determination of disease in groups" (Schwab & Schwab, 1978, p. 28). What makes epidemiology distinctive and also applicable to the study of public problems is its concern with geographically defined populations. Epidemiologists attempt to estimate incidence and prevalence rates for a specific population in a prescribed location at a given time. They study the rise or fall in prevalence rates, and attempt to match such events with spatial variations in a set of potentially influential environmental variables.

Borrowing from epidemiology involves more than a set of strategies, it also provides a consistent and coherent mode of operation in the conduct of social science. As Lilienfeld and Lilienfeld (1980) have commented "epidemiology can be regarded as a sequence of reasoning concerned with . . . inferences derived from disease occurrence and related phenomena in human population groups" (p. 4). It is obvious, therefore, that to use epidemiological methods successfully in the study of public problems it will be necessary to reach far beyond the boundaries of individual academic disciplines. This was in fact anticipated by the Lilienfelds, who concluded that epidemiology is "an integrative, eclectic discipline deriving concepts and methods from other disciplines such as statistics, sociology, and biology . . ." (p. 4).

The general goals of epidemiology also provide some useful insights for this book. In applying the epidemiological method to psychiatry, for example, Hinsie and Campbell (1970) defined their task as the study of the occurrence of mental disorders within a specified population. As they saw it, this would involve three major components: identifying the patterns of occurrence of mental disorders; accounting for the ecological and human factors associated with these patterns; and studying the outcome of attempts to modify or alter these factors (Gruenberg, Terns, & Pepper, 1976). As this definition illustrates, epidemiologists are concerned not only with the measurement and etiology of problems such as mental disorders, but also with the way services are provided and how they are used.

It is also clear, however, that most epidemiologists rarely consider the structural forces that influence both the etiology of public problems and the delivery of services. In this sense epidemiology has guided the organization of this book in both a positive and a negative way. The major goals of the book are to go beyond the traditional concerns of the epidemiologist with measurement, etiology, and service delivery; to examine the social and spatial context of public problems; and to consider the political, economic, and organizational barriers to the provision of equitable services.

Etiology and the Social Geography of Public Problems

The chapters in the first part of the book examine some of the more plausible etiological explanations for variations in the prevalence rates. The major premise here is that social, cultural, and ecological variables should be considered on a par with the traditional individual explanations from medicine or psychology. For a number of problems there is evidence that in recent years the stranglehold of the "medical model" is being relaxed, at least enough to allow alternative accounts to be heard. Proponents of the medical model assume that explanations for pathological behavior are primarily to be found within the individual, with only a glancing reference made to his or her sociocultural milieu. The recent history of the treatment of alcoholism provides a useful example of the supremacy of the medical model, as well as the subsequent challenges to that supremacy.

In the latter part of the 19th century and during the years of Prohibition, there was a consensus that the major cause of alcohol problems was the alcohol itself, or rather the industry that was producing and supplying alcohol (the "liquor trade"). After the repeal of Prohibition in 1933, there was a major shift of attention away from the substance and toward the drinking problems of individuals. The "alcohol problem" increasingly became defined as the problems encountered by a minority of drinkers who, for unknown medical or psychological reasons, could not control their drinking or its effects. By the middle decades of this century the medical model of alcoholism had finally established itself as the major paradigm within the field (Beauchamp, 1980; Gusfield, 1982b; Room, 1983). From this perspective it was considered pointless to try to limit the supply of alcohol, because would-be alcoholics could always find a way to drink. Similarly, it seemed a waste of time to consider the social and cultural circumstances in which people drank, because those with alcoholic tendencies would probably not be influenced by changes in such factors.

In recent years, largely as a result of the epidemiological studies of drinking behavior conducted by social scientists, there has been a major shift in the way of thinking about the problem of alcoholism (Cahalan, Cisin, & Crossley, 1969; Cahalan & Room, 1974). Nationwide probability surveys showed dramatic differences in the alcohol-related problems experienced by individuals in different cultural, demographic, and geographic subgroups of the population. It was felt that these variations could offer some useful insights into the etiology of what had become known as "problem drinking," and that they should be considered at least as important as the more traditional individual explanations for heavy drinking.

Another important conclusion was that the times, places, and circumstances in which drinking occurs can predict problem drinking as effectively as individual variables (Harford, 1979, 1984; Braucht, 1983). One of the observations made possible by the new survey data, for example, was that as drinkers get older the social geography of their drinking changes; they tend to drink in different places, with different and usually fewer people, and for shorter periods. Changes like this could have a major impact on how older people are affected by their drinking. These findings would open up a whole new range of possibilities for researchers interested in understanding the nature of alcohol-related problems and developing strategies to help prevent the incidence of such problems.

Service Delivery and the Management of Public Problems

The distribution of public problems is influenced significantly by the provision of services. It is evident that major changes in public policies can influence both the level and the distribution of services, and this in turn can have an impact on the individuals experiencing different problems. Of particular importance in this respect are two phenomena: the dispersion of public services, and the tendency for services to be distributed inequitably. In the last 2 to 3 decades many of the services provided for people experiencing public problems have been spread more evenly across the urban landscape. As we shall see in several of the chapters in this book, the tendency to provide services "in the community" rather than centrally is a key feature of the contemporary urban world. In spite of this the distribution of services is rarely consistent with the demand for them. Services often appear to be located where they are least needed.

Most of the existing research on this topic has concentrated on the distribution of health care facilities. In almost all cases it is assumed that the existence and use of services in a specific location produces some major benefits for the recipients; in other words, it is taken for granted that the services "work" as long as they are located in the "right" places. It follows from such an assumption that most of the problems can be solved simply by finding out where needs are greatest, providing the necessary services, and then making sure that those in need make use of the services. The logic behind this assumption is based on the use of services rather than on a consideration of their usefulness. It is unfortunate that we know much more about the number of people who use services than we do about how well those services actually work.

Because of the difficulties involved in evaluating the effectiveness of services, relatively few outcome studies are available to provide barometers for the success of different service strategies. In the field of health care we have some indications that more is not necessarily better. Countries with the highest per capita spending on health care and the highest ratio of doctors to patients tend to have the highest rates of perinatal mortality (Eyles & Woods, 1983). Although this is probably not a causal relationship, it makes us question our traditional assumptions about the provision of services. In the case of mental health services, the dispersal phenomenon was accompanied by a giant leap in the use of services. This suggests that the prevalence of mental disorder is at least partly a function of the supply and location of services, rather than the need for such services. From that perspective it is reasonable to expect that in times of fiscal austerity, the welfare state will take a hard look at the level of service provision in a search for excess capacity with which it can dispense.

The Political Context of Public Problems

Even if the social and ecological characteristics associated with particular problems remained constant, prevalence rates would still tend to fluctuate in response to political forces. The trend in recent years has been for the prevalence rates of most public problems to increase, but there have been great variations among the different problem categories. Some problems have proliferated, at least in terms of their prevalence rates and the resources allocated for their treatment; while others have stabilized or diminished. Political forces of two basic types are important in explaining such variations in the prevalence of public problems. The first involves the outcome of legislation. Laws to create new mental health facilities in the 1960s resulted not only in an increase in the overall prevalence of mental illness, but also a shift between the different categories of mental disorders (Table 1.2). Since the passage of the Community Mental Health Centers (CMHC) Act in 1963, "episodes" of mental illness increased from 1.7 million in 1955, to 6.9 million in 1977 (Witkin, 1980). After controlling for population increases during these 2 decades, this amounted to an increase from 1,028 to 2,964 episodes per 100,000 people (Figure 1.1). The ratio of inpatients to outpatients shifted from 3.4:1 in 1955 in favor of inpatients, to 2.5:1 in favor of outpatients in 1977. The new facilities were selective about their clients, and they were justifiably criticized for this. In relative terms they failed to expand the availability of services for chronically mentally ill patients, and chose instead to treat patients who were not previously receiving services.

A second category of political processes operates in a less obvious way to influence the prevalence rates of public problems. Official agencies are to some extent able to manipulate the demand for the services they offer, and even on occasion to create new categories of public problems. Although there may be no official legislation involved, such actions are political events because they are distributional in nature, in other words they help to answer such questions as who gets what, when, how, and where (D. M. Smith, 1977). These distributional processes occur at three different levels:

1. Situations in which certain individuals are entered into discredited categories that can be used as the basis for treating them in an exclusionary or discriminatory fashion. These are what Schur (1980) referred to as "deviantizing" processes;

2. Organized attempts by individuals in such stigmatized categories to object to the way they are treated (or not treated). As Schur notes, in both circumstances, the issue centers on the relative distribution of social power: "What is most essentially at stake in such situations is the power or resources of moral standing or acceptability . . . all those who have been designated deviant comprise, by virtue of such treatment, some kind of have-not class" (pp. 6–7);

Table 1.2. Patients in Care in Community Mental Health Centers 1968–1976 (Percentages)

Diagnostic Category	1968	1969	1970	1971	1972	1973	1974	1975	1976
Alcoholism	—	—	7.5	8.8	8.7	8.4	9.4	9.7	11.1
Drug Abuse	—	—	3.9	4.4	4.2	3.5	3.3	3.1	3.7
Mental Retardation	—	—	3.8	4.6	4.2	3.5	3.7	3.4	2.8
Depression	—	—	19.9	18.4	15.8	15.1	12.9	13.4	13.8
Schizophrenia	—	—	19.1	15.9	13.6	12.4	11.2	10.5	10.5
All Other Mental Disorders	—	—	41.2	40.2	42.2	43.2	39.2	38.6	38.4
Social Maladjustment (No Mental Disorder)	—	—	4.6	7.7	11.3	13.9	20.3	21.8	19.7
No. of CMHCs	165	205	255	295	325	400	434	528	548
Total No. of Patients	180510	254855	334760	432640	511706	652652	771821	919037	1016113

Source. Adapted from Goldman, Regier, Taube, Redick, and Bass (1980, p. 85).

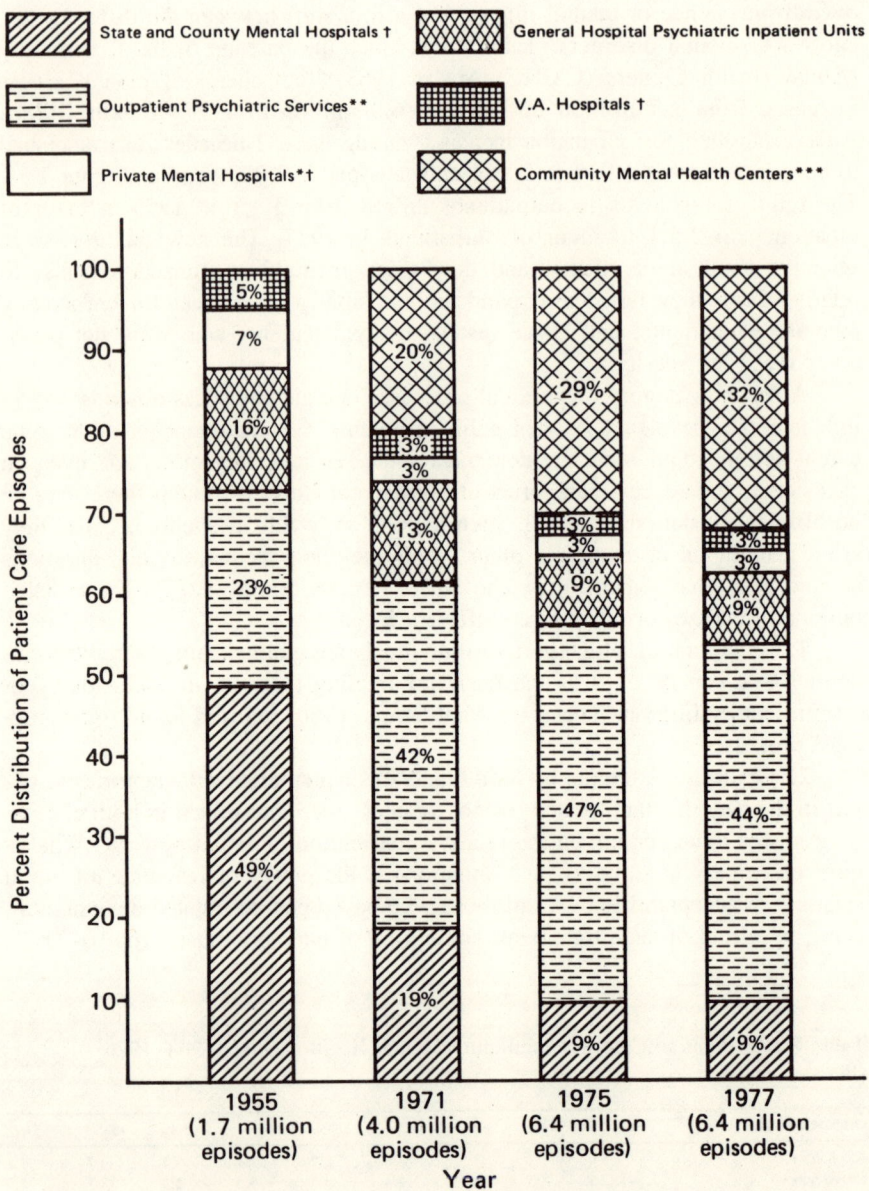

Figure 1.1. Percent distribution of inpatient and outpatient care episodes in mental health facilities by type of facility: United States, 1955, 1971, 1975, 1977.

Source. Witkin (1980, p. 5).

3. At the agency or institutional level, the tendency for the distribution of resources between different problem categories to reflect institutional goals rather than the "true" demand for services. Agencies that receive government funding and certification often find themselves in a situation that is "enrollment-driven," and in which they have to compete with other agencies for credibility and resources, and ultimately even for clients. For examples we need look no further than the "wars" waged on drugs, crime, alcoholism, and mental disorder in recent decades, all of which have contributed to the vast growth of professional groups and the bureaucracies organized to administer and deliver the appropriate services (Wiener, 1981).

As these examples illustrate, political forces influence both the overall prevalence of a particular problem and the eventual provision of services. In addition, there are likely to be some interactions between these two processes. If a problem becomes increasingly prevalent shortly after a new law comes into effect, the provision of services will increase. This may in turn call forth an even greater demand for services by creating more public awareness about the problem in question.

The importance of political forces in the epidemiology of public problems is essential precisely because they are public problems. They occur in the public domain, they cause public concern, and public funds have to be spent to deal with them. For all of these reasons public problems are controversial. They are also inherently political issues because in many cases they call forth what Schur (1980) refers to as "stigma contests"—battles over rights and entitlements that are fought out in the public arena.

Many of the problems dealt with in this book have traditionally been public health concerns. The usual public health strategy is to determine the extent to which populations are exposed to potential hazards, and then design interventions that can have positive outcomes. This traditional concern has become increasingly politicized in recent years (Brownlea, 1981). One reason for this is the rising public awareness about potential problem areas, which is largely a result of greater media involvement. Another reason is that dealing with such issues involves the distribution of social justice and the need to make difficult social choices, many of which ultimately have to be made in the public arena. Moreover, the increasing competition for scarce resources dictates political solutions. In this sense the study of public problems is a part of what Brownlea refers to as "political epidemiology," which is inseparable from the complex of corporate economic and political life.

THEORETICAL APPROACHES TO PUBLIC PROBLEMS

Studies of public problems have tried to explain how certain behaviors have been defined as problems, and also how the problems have traditionally been dealt with in different societies. From the many different perspectives described in the literature, a fairly small number of overlapping theoretical models has emerged. The first of these is the medical model, which is obviously not appropriate for all public problems but which has until fairly recently dominated the areas of mental disorder and substance abuse, as well as other problems in which health issues are a major concern. The medical model locates the source of the problem in the individual, and postulates a physiological, organic, or psychological agent that is assumed to have precipitated the problem.

The medical model usually mandates intervention by medical personnel, and the problem is considered to be a disease that can be treated within the traditional medical milieu (Conrad & Schneider, 1980, p. 35). One of the most effective ways to ensure that a certain behavior is defined as a problem has been to gather evidence on its adverse medical consequences. This was a major feature in the campaigns against drugs and alcohol in the first decades of the 20th century (Boyer, 1978; Duster, 1970; Helmer, 1975), as well as in the battle against smoking in the middle of this century.

In spite of the apparent success of these campaigns, the medical model provides only a partial explanation for how certain behaviors become defined as problems. There has been a consistent effort in recent years to educate the public about the health hazards associated with such common substances as sugar, salt, and caffeine. Although consumption of these items has declined, there is little chance that the use of any of them will be prohibited by law. This illustrates that the medical model alone is not a sufficient condition for the designation of certain behaviors as problems; neither does the model account for the prohibitive actions that are taken at particular times rather than at others. In the case of smoking, for example, medical evidence was available for many years before any official actions were taken to control the supply of tobacco or to warn the public of its hazards (Troyer & Markle, 1983).

The assumptions underlying the medical model are not appropriate when considering many of the behaviors associated with public problems (Mishler, 1981). In the first place the medical model assumes a specific etiological pattern of cause and effect that is rarely evident in social behavior. It is often difficult to set the standards for "normality" against which problematic or pathological behavior can be assessed. The medical view of public problems also tends to divorce such issues from their social, economic, and political contexts, by focusing on the scientific evidence of individual malfunctioning (Stark, Flitcraft, & Frazier, 1979).

The medical model approach to public problems is an "objectivist" view of social phenomena (Gusfield, 1984), in which certain objective conditions are implicated as the major cause of specific problems. Social scientists working from this perspective try to isolate specific environmental or social events that result in a higher prevalence of certain behaviors. In other words, some degree of disequilibrium or strain occurs, and the individual responds by behaving in ways that are subsequently defined as problems. To define a behavior as a problem involves the evaluation of a specific event (the social facts) and a comparison with the currently acceptable norms for behavior. Most of the criticism of this objectivist view focuses on the difficulty of defining norms for behavior, and on the lack of concern with the processes that are involved (Conrad & Schneider, 1980).

Partly as a response to criticisms of this sort, sociologists have refined a "labeling" or interactionist view of social phenomena. From this perspective "a particular act is deviant if and only if it is reacted to distinctively or 'so labeled' by at least one member of the social unit in question" (Gibbs, 1981, p. 25). In other words, instead of assuming that problems have an objective life of their own that will generate collective actions, it is hypothesized that problems are "created" or exacerbated by such actions. Some proponents of this view have concluded that it is unproductive to conceptualize social phenomena in functional terms (Etzioni, 1976; Liska, 1981). Instead, they urge a concentration on the more fluid concepts of interactions between individuals and groups. They thus consider that instead of talking about the "facts," we ought to consider the processes by which social problems are continually labeled and sustained.

Beyond these two basic approaches—the medical model and the labeling theories—there are other approaches to public problems that have been built on conflict within society rather than consensus. Such approaches generally focus on a specific source of conflict, which is most often a pervasive condition such as capitalism (Etzioni, 1976, p. 9). For most conflict theorists class rather than society is the central fact of life; they recognize no society-wide collective conscience as Durkheim would have described it, only the interests of different classes conflicting with each other.

From the conflict perspective public problems are not necessarily thought of as "deviance," but as the product of an unequal distribution of power in society. Similarly, problems are not necessarily things about which something should be done because they are considered to be "wrong" on moral grounds, but because their very existence threatens the interests of particular classes in society. From this perspective the search for the causes of public problems cannot be conducted at the level of individual or group behaviors, but should focus on the larger political, economic, and cultural contexts in which such behaviors occur. A criminal act, for example, is thus not seen to be caused by the individual in question, but by the society that has deprived that individual of any viable alternatives to crime. Similarly, public responses to problems and the development of services are not so much intended to reduce the overall amount of suffering as to pave the way for a more orderly and efficient workforce (Ralph, 1983).

None of these perspectives is above criticism, and none is able to provide completely satisfactory explanations for specific problem behaviors. It is difficult to deny, however, that at least some part of the overall prevalence of public problems results from the way society deals with such problems. In this sense the proponents of the labeling and the conflict approaches are in general agreement that official interventions tend to exacerbate the existing problems in a number of ways:

1. Through the enactment of the laws and rules that regulate social behavior and establish a set of definitions of what is right and wrong. These rules generate what sociologists refer to as "secondary deviance," such as the crimes resorted to by drug addicts to pay for their indulgence in an illegal and therefore expensive activity.

2. Through the bureaucratic and profession-building actions of the rule enforcers, who are often accused of expanding their activities and increasing their clientele for essentially survival-oriented purposes rather than as a result of a real concern for the human suffering that is involved.

3. Through the official use of labels to describe specific behaviors that were formerly acceptable but are now perceived by the general public to be "symptoms" of a "problem." The labels are also responsible for the "self-fulfilling prophecy," in which either friends and relatives or the official control agents help the rule breaker to "learn" the behavior required by the labels.

PUBLIC PROBLEMS: AN OUTLINE OF THE BOOK

The second part of the book is concerned with the etiology and social geography of public problems, focusing on the social and spatial contexts in which such problems occur. Chapter 2 looks in some detail at the relationship between city living and public problems; Chapter 3 considers the importance of social contexts in the prevalence and location of public problems; and Chapter 4 assesses the role of the physical environment and the contribution of "environment and behavior" studies to the field of public problems.

The third part of the book looks at the attempts that have been made to provide services for the people experiencing public problems. The first three chapters are case studies, included to illustrate the problems associated with implementing social policies and delivering services. Chapter 5 focuses on the different cycles of reform that have evolved to deal with the problem of mental disorder. This chapter considers in some detail the policies that were intended to deinstitutionalize the residents of state mental hospitals and the provision of alternative services "in the community." Chapter 6 deals with public inebriates and the policies implemented to redefine such behavior as the responsibility of the welfare state rather than the criminal justice system; and Chapter 7 extends this discussion to include the policies intended to "divert" youthful offenders away from the criminal justice system.

Each of these three chapters paints a gloomy picture of the attempts to implement new social policies. After a promising beginning the new strategies have largely failed to do what they set out to do. At the same time there has been a vast expansion in the delivery systems, and the management of public problems has become a major growth industry. The chapters in the last (fourth) section of the book provide some different but complementary ways to account for the failure of the policies designed to deal with the public problems discussed here. Chapter 8 presents an overview of the structural/Marxist accounts of public problems, using as case studies the treatment of mental disorders and alcohol abuse. As this chapter illustrates, it is impossible to evaluate the attempts to provide services without taking into consideration the structural forces and contexts within which such policies are developed. Chapter 9 describes some of the processes involved in the "construction" of public problems, focusing on the issue of "arena building" and the expansionism of professional caregiving groups and service delivery agencies. Chapter 10 investigates the issue of "social control" as it has been applied to a range of different public problems, revealing that the desire to do something about public problems is not always based on a humanitarian concern for the sufferers, and that the type of services provided are strongly determined by the social class of the recipients.

The book concludes with a discussion of one of the most topical issues of the 1980s—the problem of homelessness. The choice of homelessness in this context is not meant to imply that it is the most important problem in the modern city, or that it is the most distressing. It is, on the other hand, a problem that overlaps considerably with the other problems discussed in the book, both in terms of its etiology and its location. It has proved extremely difficult to provide accurate estimates of the incidence and prevalence of homelessness, and we have only the vaguest ideas about why the numbers have increased so much in recent years. We have also witnessed the rapid expansion of services for homeless people, and it is evident that homelessness has a political significance that is far greater than a simple attempt to do something about the problem.

PART TWO

THE ETIOLOGY AND SOCIAL GEOGRAPHY OF PUBLIC PROBLEMS

2

The Experience of City Living

INTRODUCTION: THE CITY IN HISTORY

A dominant theme in Western culture over the last 2 centuries has been the general distaste for city living. In the latter part of the 19th century what had been a trickle of antiurban sentiment developed into a torrent, fueled by the writings of literary figures and intellectuals. The negative view of the city has most often been directed against the morphology of the city rather than against the underlying social forces at work. This has reinforced the belief that the city's ills can most easily be rectified by environmental manipulation. As Ley (1983) has observed, "A preoccupation with the city as a spatial object may divert analysis from the city as the home of man, that is, as a complex of interest groups, value systems, routines, and activities set in the built environment and situated within a broader range of contexts" (p. 369).

Much of this antiurbanism has remained at the level of sentiment and has not had a major influence on behavior. Most people continue to live in cities even though they may express a desire to live somewhere else. There is, in other words, an ambivalence toward cities. In a 1973 nationwide survey of residential preferences, 53% of the respondents expressed a desire to live in a rural area or a small town, and only 33% preferred a large city (Maizie & Rawlings, 1973). Obviously these preferences are inversely correlated with actual residential patterns: nearly two-thirds of the respondents said they would prefer to live in a town smaller than the one in which they currently lived (Dicken & Lloyd, 1981, p. 297).

On the other hand there is evidence that, in the twentieth century at least, many people do act on their desire to leave the city. Suburbanization can be interpreted as, among other things, a compromise between the desire to live in a small town and the need to live close to a large city (Jackson, 1985; Binford, 1985). In recent years the "population turnaround" has also demonstrated that many people have acted out their dreams about living in the rural and small-town areas of America.

At the regional level it appears that many of the people who say they want to live elsewhere actually follow through on their desires. In a study conducted in the early 1970s, D. J. Morgan (1976) calculated the net population changes that would occur in American regions if people moved to where they said they wanted to move. The theoretical results would have produced a major change in the population geography of the United States (Table 2.1). Nothing quite so dramatic actually occurred, but the 1980 census data shows that although Morgan's results overestimated the absolute amount of movement, with the exception of one region (New England), his rank ordering of residential preferences matches what actually happened during the 1970s. A large part of this population reshuffling can be interpreted as antiurbanism. We know, for example, from the residential preference studies that many urban dwellers are unhappy about their continued residence in the city. Quality of life studies have also demonstrated this, showing that overall life satisfaction among the residents of large cities is lower than that of those living in smaller communities (Campbell, Converse, & Rodgers, 1976).

The ambivalence toward cities among noncity dwellers and city dwellers alike is by no means a new sentiment. In the United States it can be traced back to the early national period. Some Americans took a dislike to the rapidly growing cities, but others considered them to be a great source of pride; still a third group was apprehensive about cities, which had come to represent symbols of rapid change and unlimited growth (Rothman, 1971). These anxieties were reflected in sermons, speeches, and periodicals warning about the evils associated with city life, including drunkenness, gambling, and sexual immorality (Pivar, 1973). Cities were considered to be both the result of and the cause of the massive upheavals in the social order that were occurring. The contemporary reformers were looking back longingly to a past they felt was more simple and more moral.

Three aspects of city living seemed to upset the reformers most. One was

Table 2.1. A Comparison of Potential and Actual Population Shifts in the United States

Region	Proportional Changes (percent) in Population (by region) If People Desiring to Live Elsewhere Moved to Their Region of Preference[a]	Net Migration 1970–1979 (percent)[b]
Mid-Atlantic	−27	−4.4
East North Central	−25	−3.7
West North Central	−21	−0.6
New England	15	0
East South Central	0	2.9
West South Central	1.3	7.2
South Atlantic	11	7.8
Pacific	41	7.3
Mountain	124	16.6

[a]Morgan (1976).
[b]U.S. Department of the Census.

the unfamiliarity of life at high densities, for which most people were totally unprepared. Most of the "vices" in the big cities had existed in the smaller communities of colonial America, but in this new setting they were much more menacing:

> The bawdy servant girl was transformed into the painted prostitute soliciting on the street. The village tavern became a beer cellar in the slum; the neighborly wager on a horse race . . . the organized gambling of the city. (Boyer, 1978, p. 5)

The crusades to overthrow the urban menace were usually led by a well-educated and vociferous minority, many of whom based their arguments on idealistic views of the "way things used to be." Although the city's evils were clearly interrelated, the single issue campaigns were the most successful. Probably the most worrisome issue of all in the middle decades of the 19th century was prostitution, which was closely followed by and associated with the problem of drunkenness.

Here we encounter the second disturbing aspect of city living. Cities provided an arena in which sin and vice not only flourished, but flourished in public, in full view of anyone who wanted to look. It was not so much the problems themselves that caused outrage, but the fact that they occurred so visibly. It is not surprising that for many the solution to the city's problems was not to try to cure or prevent them, but to hide them, or even to hide from them. The problems could be hidden from view in institutions such as prisons, mental hospitals, and almshouses; at the same time the people most likely to be offended could hide themselves, at first in the newly emerging middle-class neighborhoods, and later on in the suburbs (Binford, 1985).

The issue of drunkenness provides a useful example of late-19th-century attitudes towards pervasive social problems. There was no overwhelming evidence that city living caused people to drink more heavily (N. H. Clark, 1976), but the switch from drinking at home and in the workplace to drinking in the city saloon (literally, the "public" house) was at least partly responsible for the belief that more drinking and more drunkenness were occurring (Johnson, 1978; Duis, 1983). The antidrink crusaders wanted to close down the public drinking places and force the drinkers back into their homes with their families, where the crusaders felt they belonged.

The third disturbing aspect of the city was that it clearly segregated the population into its component categories. The earliest categorization was the haves and the have-nots, followed by the natives and the immigrants, and finally by the racial majorities and the minorities. At the large scale the city became more heterogenous, as increasing numbers of different people jammed themselves into fiercely guarded territories. At the local scale this meant intense parochialism and homogeneity, which created obvious difficulties in cultural communication. The city was a melting pot, but for many of its inhabitants there was little crosstown neighboring or cultural mixing between diverse groups.

The proximity of rich and poor did little to ease the burden: The rich feared the poor; the poor envied the rich.

One of the prevailing themes that began in the 19th century and reached its climax in this century was the belief that life in the sort of city described here was psychologically debilitating. Many of the prominent early psychiatrists subscribed to the view that urbanized humanity had fallen from its earlier grace. This has been referred to as the "paradise lost" doctrine:

> This retrospective vision harks back to the innocence of Scriptural Eden, to serenity in the golden Age of Hellenic mythology, then to chivalric security in the medieval literature, to quintessential harmony in the Rousseauian "state of nature," and to the earthy wholesomeness of our more recent agrarian past. (Srole & Fischer, 1980, p. 209)

One exponent of this nostalgic view of the past and the jaundiced view of the present is Erich Fromm, who has argued that mental health in the population at large has deteriorated so rapidly that it is now "legitimate to speak of an 'insane society' . . . in which modern man has lost the capacity for subjective experience" (Srole & Fischer, 1980, p. 210).

In the remainder of this chapter this rather sweeping statement will be examined in depth, with particular reference to the experiences associated with city life. Before that, however, it is important to note that the view of the city as a place in urgent need of social reform was not shared by all who lived there, and in fact it may have been a distinct minority who held this view. Most of the captains of industry and commerce were more interested in making a living than in making the city more liveable. For them the city was economically rational: It provided huge markets for their goods and services and gave them access to vast supplies of cheap and eager workers, who would not only sell their labor but would also pay back their wages for sustenance and a place to live (Perry & Watkins, 1977). As long as the 19th century city "worked," in the sense of generating profits, its social problems could be largely overlooked. There would be many attempts at reform, but arguably the purpose of such reforms was not to redistribute wealth, but to help the city to work even more effectively (Gordon, 1977; Boyer, 1978). The methods that were adopted included attempts to demonstrate to the urban masses that their ways of life could be improved.

Many of these masses were recent immigrants; a second strategy was thus to argue for a reduction in the flow of immigrants. This had been a fairly consistent theme throughout the 19th century, and one that often had a decidedly nativist and often racist tone (Higham, 1978), although it would not be fully successful on the level of policy making until the immigration laws of the 1920s. These two strategies involved "blaming the victims" for their poverty, but a third strategy also emerged. It was evident to many that the major social problems could be solved by "regulation," such as the adoption of higher standards for public health conditions. It was clear to such strategists that the lower classes needed to adopt the middle-class standards of decency. This was not seen as coercive repression, or even necessarily as reform, but as "the preservation of the moral order amid vastly altered social conditions" (Boyer, 1978, p. 58).

Responses to the prevalence of disorder, distress, and degeneracy in the city took two basic forms. One was "positive environmentalism," which included attempts to raise the moral tone of the city by making it a more wholesome place in which to live (Boyer, 1978). This would include attempts to clean up the city; to maintain public health standards in the workplace; to provide building codes and standards for homes; to build parks, playgrounds, and public baths; and to provide recreational outlets other than the saloon and the whorehouse (Rosenzweig, 1983). The other response to urban disorder was "negative environmentalism," the default stance to be adopted after all else had failed. The assumption was that human behavior had deteriorated too far to be influenced indirectly by making the city more liveable. Direct action involving coercion and prohibition were required to rid the city of the major threats to morality, particularly drunkenness and prostitution.

Although the positive and negative forms of environmentalism were quite different, both sought to elevate the human character, to inhibit private desires, and to re-form the urban masses in the image of the reformers. Even for the reformers, then, the city was not seen as the source of social problems, but as the source of moral problems—the solutions for which appeared to be far more straightforward.

SPATIAL PATTERNS AND PUBLIC PROBLEMS

The effect of urban living on human well-being has been studied in two ways, one looking at the contrasts between urban and rural environments and the other investigating the spatial variations in the rates of problems within a particular city. In the urban–rural comparison studies the differences, if identifiable at all, appear to be minor; in fact the available evidence suggests that there may be higher rates of mental disorder in rural areas (Fischer, 1976; Srole & Fischer, 1978, 1980). The other type of urban study has attempted to identify the social and ecological variables that are associated with excessive prevalence rates of public problems.

There is a long tradition of ecological studies in which aggregated rates of a particular problem such as mental illness are related to aggregated sociodemographic measures collected for different areas of the city (Faris & Dunham, 1939; Levy & Rowitz, 1973). In spite of the many criticisms of this approach, it has not disappeared from the literature; in fact, improvements in methodology that have been made possible by computer technology have resulted in more studies rather than less in recent years (Eyles & Woods, 1983; Giggs, 1979; Kasl & Harburg, 1975). In addition to the well-known problems with "ecological fallacy," it has proved difficult to disentangle the individual effects of highly correlated independent variables. This issue has been dealt with at least in part by collecting data from more than one source and at smaller scales (C. J. Smith, 1977) and by constructing orthogonal factors or dimensions of environmental variables instead of using individual variables (Fischer, 1978). The major question, however, is not methodological but inferential: What do the results of ecological studies tell us about the effect of urban living on individual measures of mental health? In most cases ecological studies are unable to answer such questions, so it appears that the only appropriate use of ecological data is in conjunction with individual observations. One strategy involves assessing the extent to which individuals living in certain localities "fit" or do not fit with their local context. As we shall see in Chapter 4, this approach has been used successfully in a number of studies. The major advantage is that it allows survey data collected from individual households to be used in combination with the ecological data that is available for surrounding localities.

Much of the theory behind ecological studies was developed by individuals in the human ecology school at the University of Chicago, and the more specifically deterministic hypotheses developed by Wirth (1938). To summarize Wirth's position, it is sufficient to note that social problems are assumed to be the outcome of individual and group adjustments to the conditions prevailing in certain parts of the city:

> The aloofness and impersonality which are developed in response to the competing stimuli and conflicting demands of different social situations are felt to lead to a breakdown of interpersonal relationships and social order and to an increase in social isolation, which in turn facilitates the emergence of ego-centered unconventional behavior and precipitates various kinds of deviant behavior. (Knox, 1982, p. 49)

Wirth attributed the social and psychological consequences of urbanism to the combined influence of three sets of factors that he felt were the products of increasing urbanization: (1) the greater size of the population; (2) the greater densities at which people are forced to live and work; and (3) the greater levels of segregation that occur between different segments of the population.

City Size and Cultural Heterogeneity

One of the most frequent observations made about cities is that they provide shelter for a disproportionately large number of individuals who experience serious problems or who act unconventionally. The major problem associated with cities is crime, and from most empirical accounts this concern is real. In England and Wales, for example, there has long been a strong positive relationship between city size and crime rates: The largest cities reported crime rates 90% higher than the rural areas (in 1965), and 168% higher for "major crimes'' (those committed against persons, plus breaking-in offenses, robbery, and larceny (see McClintock & Avison, 1968). In the United States a similar relationship exists (Table 2.2): In general, arrest rates are higher in the cities than in the suburbs or the rural areas, but the decline is not linear—in fact there is relatively little difference between the arrest rates in cities with populations below 100,000. The largest cities (250,000 plus) have considerably higher rates of violent crime than all other cities, but this difference is not so clear-cut for property crimes.

The latest data indicates that the city–noncity difference between crime rates has been declining in recent years. In 1973 arrest rates in the suburbs were 66.2% of those in cities and the rates in rural areas were 49.5%; by 1978 these two percentages were 87.8% and 63.5%. This convergence trend slowed somewhat after 1978, so that in 1981 the proportions were 77.3% in the sub-

Table 2.2. Number and Rate (per 100,000) of Arrests by Size of Place (United States, 1981)

	Cities Over 250,000	100,000 249,999	50,000 99,999	25,000 49,999	10,000 24,999	<10,000
All Offenses						
Number	2,754,171	955,407	926,099	998,723	1,120,655	1,121,436
Rate	6,816	5,818	4,647	4,806	4,588	4,956
Violent Crimes[a]						
Number	172,237	44,499	41,887	35,921	34,677	30,502
Rate	426.2	271	210	173	142	135
Property Crimes[b]						
Number	461,649	200,583	211,828	215,775	217,256	165,106
Rate	1,143	1,222	1,063	1,038	889	730

	All Cities	Rural Areas	Suburbs	TOTAL
All Offenses				
Number	7,876,491	942,242	3,475,442	10,278,107
Rate	5,447	3,229	3,994	4,795
Violent Crimes[a]				
Number	359,723	36,348	136,413	464,826
Rate	249	125	157	217
Property Crimes[b]				
Number	1,472,197	113,020	639,254	1,828,928
Rate	1,018	387	735	853

[a]Violent crimes are murder, forcible rape, robbery, and aggravated assault.
[b]Property crimes are burglary, larceny/theft, motor vehicle theft, and arson.
Source. Federal Bureau of Investigation. (1982). *Crime in the United States 1981* (pp. 163–164). Washington, DC: U.S. Government Printing Office.

urbs, and 59.3% in rural areas. The general trend across this time period was for crime rates to increase in all areas. In 1973 the rates (per 100,000 inhabitants) were 4781 in cities, 3165 in the suburbs, and 2370 in rural areas; by 1981 the rates were 5447, 3994, and 3229. As this indicates, the largest rate of increase was in the nation's rural areas rather than in its cities.

There are some significant regional differences in crime rates in the United States, especially the well-known tendency for cities in the south to have the highest rates of violent crimes (Harries, 1980; Herbert, 1982). The most important question to be asked about the empirical evidence linking high prevalence rates of public problems to urbanization concerns the causal mechanisms involved. There is no doubt that city dwellers tend to be more offbeat and unconventional than the norm, but this may imply only that the larger cities attract the most unorthodox people (Fischer, 1976, 1982). A more deterministic explanation is an outgrowth from spatial diffusion theories, namely that in the largest settlements any individual runs a greater risk of being exposed to and attracted toward nonnormative behaviors. This has been used to explain why the prevalence of drug abuse is initially highest in the largest cities, only later diffusing downwards (or "trickling down") to smaller cities (Hunt & Chambers, 1976).

The most comprehensive discussion of these alternative accounts has been provided by Fischer (1976), who suggests that the largest cities provide room for a wide variety of subcultures. This is an optimistic view of the city, one that regards it not as an evil place where social worlds are broken down, but as a place that is large enough to provide a threshold level of support for subcultural variations. Some of these subcultures include obvious rule-breakers, and many will find themselves in conflict not only with other subcultures, but with the dominant culture. In the biggest cities we may find homosexuals battling on the street with hard-hats. Their violently opposite views of the world have not resulted from the alienating experiences of living in the city, but because both groups often live in cities they are more likely to encounter each other's opposition. Similarly, criminals are not produced by the harshness of city life. In Fischer's words, "Criminals are found everywhere, but cities permit them a full-time specialization and provide them with helpful associates" (Fischer, 1976, p. 199).

To help support this hypothesis, Fischer (1978, 1982) has reviewed the literature and gathered his own data from household surveys conducted in communities of varying size. This data has allowed him to evaluate the "mental paradise lost" doctrine, which implies that mental health has deteriorated as a result of life in the city. Fischer was not the first to challenge this doctrine: In the Midtown Manhattan Study (Srole, Langner, Michael, Opler, & Rennie, 1962) and its follow-up (Srole and Fischer, 1978), researchers have confronted it with the arch-villain, New York City. The results show that the doctrine cannot be defended (see also Fischer, 1976; Webb, 1978). Respondents in the Midtown Study, after living in the city for at least 20 years, show no significant changes in their mental health, and this holds across all decades of birth cohorts. The survey data show in fact that the respondents were more healthy in the 1970s than in the 1950s (Table 2.3).

In Fischer's survey of communities in northern California (1982) the results also challenge the paradise lost doctrine. Although larger cities are home to many more unconventional people than smaller cities, there is no evidence that psychological disorders are significantly more prevalent in larger cities. Cities have fewer people adhering to traditional beliefs about such things as sex and drugs, but the urban–rural differences are largely a result of personal traits, suggesting that nonconformists choose to live in larger cities (self-selection).

The Effects of Urban Density

One aspect of urban living that has received more than its share of research attention in recent years is the effect of high density and crowding on human behavior. Taking into account the considerable methodological problems in density

Table 2.3. General Mental Health Scores, Mid-Town Manhattan Study, 1954 and 1974 Comparisons

Birth Cohorts	1954 Age Group	Rate of Impairment	1974 Age Group	Rate of Impairment
+1900	50–59	22%	70–79	18% *
($n = 134$)				
+1910	40–49	16%	60–69	12% *
($n = 199$)				
+1920	30–39	14%	50–59	10% *
($n = 195$)				
+1930	20–29	7%	40–49	8% *
($n = 167$)				
Categories on the General Mental Health Scale[a]				
Well	21.9%		25.0%	
Mild	42.6		42.0	
Moderate	21.3		21.1	
Marked	9.3		7.5	
Severe	4.3		3.5	
Incapacitated	0.6		0.9	

* = differences not significant

[a]Categories 4, 5, and 6 on the General Mental Health Scale represent impaired cases. The evaluations were made by psychiatrists, who considered each individual's response on the 83-item scale.

Source. Adapted from Srole and Fischer (1980, p. 214).

studies, and recognizing that the results of such studies need to be evaluated with great caution, there are some conclusions that make sense intuitively. There is considerable evidence of territorial behavior among urban dwellers (Knox, 1982), and the "territorial imperative" in humans appears to be at least as diverse as it is among animals. For some, territory involves the notion of a secure home and a haven, for others it is an extension of themselves, and for still others it is a piece of "turf" that will be marked and defended as ferociously as any cat's territory.

In traditional ecological studies, living at high density has been shown to be at least moderately related to numerous indicators of social and psychological problems, although the evidence remains ambiguous. Some of the major issues are illustrated in the study of Chicago census tracts conducted by Galle, Gove, & McPherson (1972). They identified five indicators of "pathology" that were related to the problems usually observed among laboratory animals. These were: (1) increased fertility; (2) increased mortality; (3) inadequate care of the young; (4) aggressive social behavior; and (5) psychological disorders. Using the number of persons per acre as the independent variable, Galle's team found modest but significantly positive correlations between density and all of the pathology indicators, but the correlations disappeared when controlled for social class and ethnicity. By using different measures of density (eg. persons per room), the correlations remained significant even when controlling for class and ethnicity (Table 2.4).

Table 2.4. Correlations Between Density and Social Pathology Measures

Dependent Variables	Pathologies (Independent Variables)				
Density/Social Class Measures	Mortality	Fertility	Public Assistance	Juvenile Delinquency	Admissions to Mental Hospitals
Population Density (persons per acre)	.28	.37	.34	.49	.35
Population Density (controlling for social class and ethnicity)	−.18*	−.02*	−.12*	0.23*	0.14*
Social Class and Ethnicity	.83	.85	.89	.93	.55
Four Alternative Measures of Density (persons per room, rooms per house, houses per structure, structures per acre)	.48	.37	.58	.50	.51

 * = not significant
 Source. Galle, Gove, and McPherson (1972, p. 26).

The most important conclusion to be drawn from such studies is what it can tell us about the processes involved and the experiences associated with life at high densities. The relationship between persons per room and the pathology indicators suggests that the greater levels of social interaction at higher densities provide more chances for arguments, greater irritability, and an increased need to withdraw. These relationships remain elusive; as Ley (1983) has observed, "The correlation between density and pathology is unambiguous, what is controversial is its interpretation" (p. 348). Most observers agree that high density is a necessary but not a sufficient condition for the onset of pathology. This explains why in places like Hong Kong, extraordinarily high densities appear to be related to mental health only in extreme cases, such as where a family's normal patterns of social interaction are intruded upon by other households (Loring, 1977; R. E. Mitchell, 1971). The epidemiologist John Cassel (1970) has argued that the density–pathology relationship is only observed among lower status individuals, and in situations of extreme disruption, such as unemployment or divorce. Most individuals are able to avoid the worst effects of high density living through the use of social networks that provide a source of psychological and material support (Lin, Ensel, Simeone, & Kuo, 1979). Thus we are likely to find that individuals whose life-styles are transient and who are socially isolated are the most vulnerable to density-related stresses (Freeman, 1978; Levy & Herzog, 1974).

In a comprehensive review of the literature, Gove and Hughes (1983) have identified some general theoretical and methodological conclusions about the effects of density:

1. Crowding at the microlevel (persons per room) appears to be a more threatening condition than at the macrolevel (e.g., persons per acre);
2. Most studies conducted in laboratories show that crowding has negative effects on both adults and children;
3. Studies conducted on individuals living in institutional settings such as college student dormitories show that crowding is related to residential satisfaction and a number of indicators of physical and mental health;
4. In some studies the effect of crowding has been shown to be independent of social structure variables, but in most cases collinearity between the two sets of independent variables invalidates the conclusions;
5. Many survey-based studies have unusual or poorly drawn samples, and inadequate measures to assess the long-term effects of high density.

Refusing to let the density issue die a natural death, Gove and Hughes (1983) conducted yet another study in Chicago, but one that was designed to overcome these major methodological problems. To minimize the collinearity between social status, race, and crowding, they selected 20 census tracts in each of four social-status–crowding categories (low status, low crowding; low status, high crowding; high status, high crowding; high status, low crowding).

In each category 5 of the 20 tracts were predominantly black (over 90%); 10 were predominantly white; and 5 were mixed (10% to 90% black).

The density variable was made operational by including the objective measure (number of persons per room) and two subjective measures: a three-item scale measuring the lack of privacy; and a four-item scale measuring the "felt demands" that might result from living at a high density. Gove and Hughes found that the scores on these two subjective scales were strongly related to the number of persons per room, and on this basis they provide the most accurate picture of the actual experience of personal overcrowding. The strength of this study in comparison to most others is that it is based on a theoretical model of the actual impacts of overcrowding within the household. The persons-per-room measure was significantly related to all but two of the mental health scales used in the survey, even controlling for age, sex, income, education, race, and marital status (Table 2.5). Other results showed that overcrowding is associated with physical withdrawal from the home, psychological withdrawal in the home (ignoring others), a lack of planning, and a feeling of being physically and psychologically "washed out." In most cases, when the subjective measures of crowding (the two scales) were added to the predictive models, the relationship between persons per room and mental health is greatly reduced, which suggests that the experience of crowding acts as an intermediating variable.

Some researchers have tired of the debate over density; others like Fischer (1975) have argued that the effects of crowding are "trivial compared to race, sex, education, income and the like . . ." (1975, p. 415). In view of Gove and Hughes' (1983) findings it may be necessary to reopen this debate.

Table 2.5. Zero Order Correlations (r) and Standardized Regression Coefficients (β) Showing the Relationship Between Crowding (Persons per Room) and Eight Mental Health Scales

Scales	r	β	% Variance Explained by Crowding Variables	% Variance Explained by Demographic Variables
Positive Affect	−.093	−.134[a]	31.7	73.0
Psychiatric Symptoms	−.167	.058[c]	37.6	39.4
Mental Health Balance	−.180	.131[a]	31.7	54.2
Self-Esteem	.135	−.084[b]	28.1	52.1
Nervous Breakdown	.094	.057[c]	60.4	20.8
Normlessness	.187	.160[a]	21.6	72.5
Happiness	−.110	−.089[a]	49.3	40.8
Manifest Irritation	.192	.066[b]	34.4	33.9

[a] $p < .001$
[b] $p < .01$
[c] $p < .05$
Source. Adapted from Gove and Hughes (1983, pp. 76–77).

Differentiation and Segregation in the City

One of the major theoretical tenets of the human ecology school of thought was the analogy of the city with a living organism, in which individuals and groups struggled to survive. Many of the Chicago studies were "natural histories" that examined the processes of competition, dominance, and succession among different sectors of the population. A key concept in all of this was the competition between individuals and groups who were searching for optimal locations within the city. In most instances the struggles were resolved in the marketplace, with the outcomes determined by who could pay most for the desirable locations. One group would become dominant in a specific part of the city, but over time the characteristic land uses would change as some groups filtered "upward" and others "downward" through the city's sociospatial hierarchy. One group would start to nibble away at another's territory, this group would move elsewhere, eventually the invasion would be complete, and the process would start all over again. These ecological concepts were used to explain the social geography of cities like Chicago in the first few decades of the 20th century.

As some groups gained in wealth and power, and as transportation allowed people to be less tied to the inner city, further spatial sorting and segregation occurred. In 19th-century industrial cities, segregation was first noticed along class or occupational lines. In industrial Manchester, for example, Engels (1958) noted that the poor were squeezed into certain shabby neighborhoods in the city's industrial core. It is important not to overstress the degree of segregation in the early industrial cities in Britain and the United States (Dennis, 1984; Pack, 1984; Ward, 1980). By modern standards, most of them were extremely small, and the different classes and ethnic groups lived in close proximity to each other. Empirical studies show that the amount of segregation by class in 19th-century English cities was not as great as the literature would lead us to believe, with the exception of the "professional" classes (Dennis, 1984, p. 217). This suggests that the upper classes often managed to segregate themselves successfully from the rest of the population. As this example illustrates, segregation, where it existed, occurred at the microlevel; in fact, in European cities, the classes were often segregated vertically, with the lower-status groups at the top of large tenement buildings (White, 1984).

In the United States, segregation by the end of the 19th century occurred mainly along ethnic lines, and this would become a recurring theme in the urban literature. One of the most useful ways to assess segregation proved to be the index of dissimilarity, which is a measure of the spatial separation between different groups (the greater the score on a 1–100 scale, the greater the spatial dissimilarity between any two groups).

With the segregation index it has been possible to quantify the social cleavages based on all sorts of phenomena, including life-style, occupation, religion, and age (Dicken & Lloyd, 1981), but the most dramatic observations were produced in studies of racial segregation. Using data from the 1960 census, Taeuber (1965) reported that in 207 American cities the median segregation index for blacks was 87.8 (ranging from 60.4 in San Jose to 98.1 in Fort Lauderdale).

From the scattered and methodologically confusing evidence that is available, it appears that black–white segregation in American cities has increased since the 19th century. Lieberson (1963) has shown evidence of considerable increases in the indices for American cities between 1910 and 1950, but as a result of the different methods used to calculate the indices at different times, these conclusions should be viewed cautiously. In Boston, however, Lieberson shows that the index increased steadily from 51.2 in 1850, to 65.3 in 1920, using the same methods of calculation. The level of segregation of blacks has changed little during the last several decades. Winsborough, Taeuber, & Sorensen (1975) found that the median index in 109 cities was 85 in 1940, and 82 in 1970, with a slight increase in southern cities, and a decrease in northern cities (Table 2.6). In the late 1970s, Van Valey, Roof, & Wilcox (1977) found a median dissimilarity score of 70 in a study of 237 cities, with many having a score higher than 90 (e.g., Chicago, Dallas, and some smaller cities such as Oklahoma City). In comparison, the segregation of foreign-born groups in American cities is considerably lower than for blacks: Lieberson (1963), for example, found a range of segregation scores between 35 and 40 using 1950 census data.[1]

The levels of ethnic and racial segregation can only be partly explained by the socioeconomic status of the groups involved (Knox, 1982). Thus in Chicago, Lieberson (1963) found that on the basis of income distribution alone, the segregation index for blacks should have been 10, instead of which it was 83 (in 1960). It appears that the continued spatial separation of one group is a function of how different they are perceived to be from the majority or "charter" group.

A new phenomenon has been evident in British and North American cities in recent years: the segregation of "service-dependent" groups such as the

Table 2.6. Indices of Residential Segregation Between White and Nonwhite Households for Selected Cities (United States, 1940–1970)

Date	All Cities	Southern Cities	Non-Southern Cities
1940	85	85	85
1950	87	89	86
1960	86	91	83
1970	82	88	87

Source. Yeates and Garner (1980, p. 27).

mentally ill, the elderly, and the homeless. A popular image is that of a grow-ing army of dependents, most of whom are minorities, unemployed, often el-derly, sometimes intoxicated, and occasionally bizarre in appearance. Although it has been difficult to document the growth of urban dependents, the notion of a "public city" has captured the attention of some academics (Dear, 1980; Wolch, 1979). An increasing proportion of the population in the inner city is dependent on the welfare state for its shelter and well-being. Until fairly re-cently the most publicized occupants of the public city have been the mentally ill (Bloom, 1975a; C. J. Smith, 1976; Wolpert & Wolpert, 1976).[2]

Another recent concern has been for the elderly, who appear to have be-come increasingly segregated in the inner city. As the 1980 census tract maps for most of the major metropolitan areas illustrate, the inner city areas usually have considerably higher proportions of elderly residents, though the degree of segregation is nowhere near as high as it is for blacks (Figure 2.1). According to B. W. Smith and Hiltner (1975), for example, the segregation index for the elderly rarely reaches one-quarter of the level for blacks.[3]

Distance and Locational Effects

The effect of urban living on human outcomes can be disaggregated into the separate but overlapping influences of city size, density, and segregation (het-erogeneity). A final variable—one that is most often considered to be a surro-gate for numerous urban characteristics—is location. Many ecological studies have included locational measures as independent variables, expressing them either numerically (e.g., distance from the downtown area) or categorically (e.g., urban vs. surburban vs. rural). In one of the earliest and probably the most famous of these studies in Chicago, Faris and Dunham (1939) showed that the pattern of treated mental illness could be fitted into the ecological structure of the city. Admission rates to mental hospitals fell as distance from the city center increased, and these observations suggested either that certain locations "caused" mental illness, or that mentally ill people "drifted" into such locations. These areas were characterized by:

> [a] social life which is terrifically harsh, intensely individualistic, highly competi-tive, extremely crude, and often violently brutal . . . one's chances of growing up and developing a personality which can adjust in some fashion to our cultural life are less than in those communities at the periphery of the city (Schwab & Schwab, 1978, p. 159).

In testing these competing hypotheses, researchers are often hampered by the absence of geographical data in the survey responses, or the failure to ag-gregate the responses at levels that correspond to the levels for which census data are available. These problems were partly overcome with survey data col-lected in Chicago and used by Daiches (1981). A scale measuring psychologi-

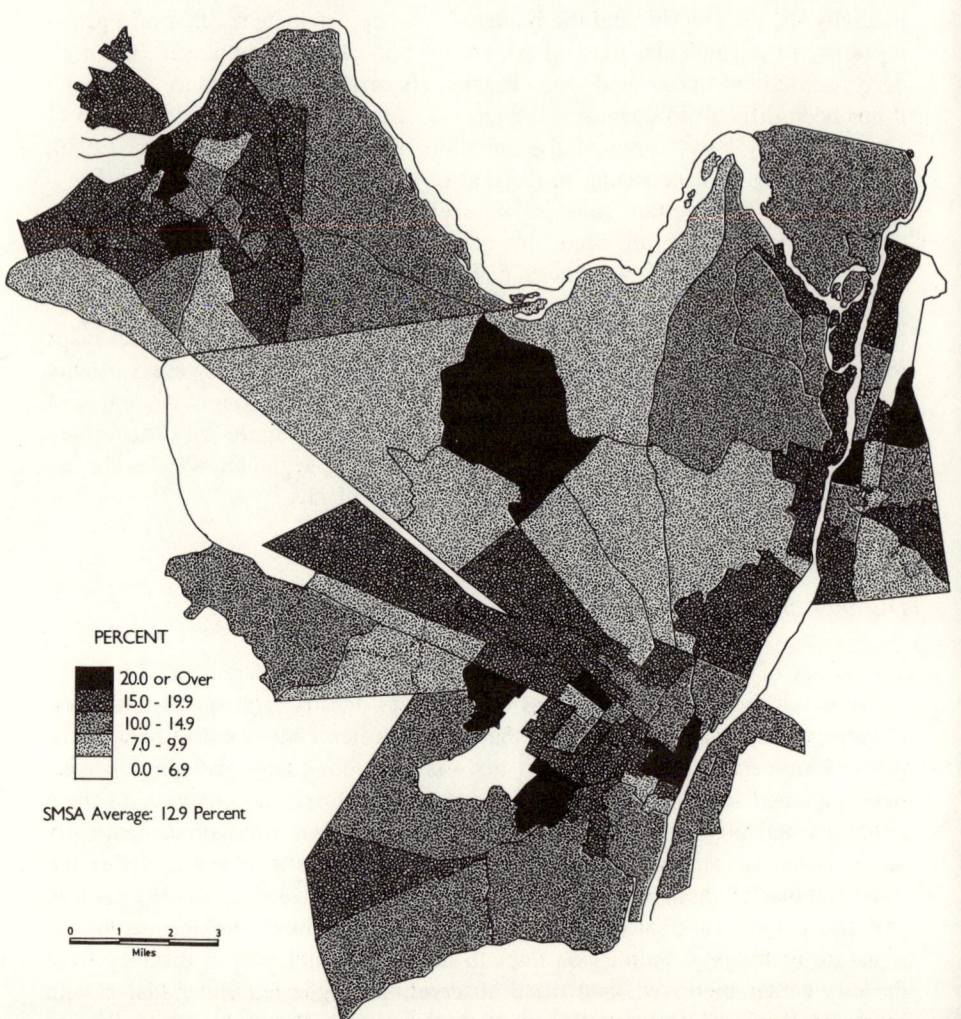

PERCENT

	20.0 or Over
	15.0 - 19.9
	10.0 - 14.9
	7.0 - 9.9
	0.0 - 6.9

SMSA Average: 12.9 Percent

0   1   2   3
Miles

Figure 2.1. Albany–Schenectady–Troy, New York standard metropolitan statistical area: Percentage of the total population 65 years of age or older.

cal well-being was included in the survey, so that it was not necessary to use in-treatment rates as the dependent variable. In addition, data were collected on a range of socioeconomic background characteristics of the respondents, which could be matched with the corresponding aggregated data available for each of the census tracts. About half of the respondents were reinterviewed 4 years after the initial survey, which provided a unique opportunity to assess the direction of causality in some of the traditional ecological hypotheses, and to answer the following questions: (1) to what extent are mental illness prevalence rates a function of relative location within the city and spatial variations in social and ecological characteristics associated with mental illness; and (2) to what extent does the contextual effect of living in a particular area influence an individual's mental health, regardless of his or her personal attributes—in other words, is it possible to isolate any independent ecological effects.

The survey results cast considerable light on each of these issues. The locational variable appeared to be significant, in that the psychological distress scores were significantly and negatively related to distance from downtown Chicago. The geographical effect remained significant when controlling for the effect of social and demographic variables, but it was insignificant when the respondents income was entered into the explanatory model. The contextual effect of living in a particular area was also significant, at least in the case of the social isolation hypothesis. The only census tract variable that was significantly correlated with psychological distress when the respondents' personal characteristics were taken into account was the proportion of divorced and separated individuals (Table 2.7). This suggests the existence of a true contextual effect, implying that the type of neighborhood one lives in has an important influence that cannot be attributed to the respondent's own marital status, race, or income.

SPATIAL PROCESSES AND PUBLIC PROBLEMS

The ecological variations within the city have been implicated, although rather weakly, in the onset of public problems like mental disorder. It should be recognized, however, that the city is a dynamic entity, and that changes are continually occurring that can influence human outcomes. Clearly there are almost infinite possibilities here for evaluating the extent to which processes of urban change are related to the prevalence of public problems. To make a discussion of these possibilities manageable, processes occurring at three levels will be discussed: (1) individual decision making that results in residential change; (2) neighborhood processes that may influence individual well-being; and (3) macrolevel structural forces that produce significant economic and social changes.

Residential Mobility and the Search for the Perfect Place

Much of the research conducted on the issue of residential mobility has adopted some variation of a generalized stress model (W. A. V. Clark, 1981). It is assumed that stress is created when a change occurs in the relationship between a family's housing needs and the perceived character of the existing housing

Table 2.7. Variables Associated with Psychological Distress
Scores (Chicago)

Predictor Attributes	Zero Order Correlations	β Weights
Locational		
Distance	−.067[b]	−.059
Background		
Sex of Respondent	.232[c]	.201[c]
Age of Respondent	−.086[c]	−.066[b]
Race of Respondent	−.004	−.097[c]
Childhood Socio/Economic		
Status	−.037	.004
Race x Childhood	−.045[a]	−.087[c]
Social Relations		
Widowed	.047[a]	.037
Single	.065[b]	.050[a]
Divorced/Separated	.165[c]	.116[c]
Friends (within one hour's		
drive)	−.114[c]	−.077[c]
Moved (within 5 years of		
interview)	.086[c]	.043[a]
Family Income		
Income	−.172[c]	−.097[c]
Census Tract Variables		
% Female	.031	.034
% Divorced/Separated	.088[c]	.078[c]
% Movers	.063[b]	.003

[a] $p < .05$
[b] $p < .01$
[c] $p < .001$
Source. Daiches (1981, p. 99).

environment. The mismatch may occur for several reasons, some of which are internal to the decision-making unit, while others are the result of external forces. In response to the stress, the family has a number of options: They may try to adjust to their new situation, they may make additions to their home, or they may decide to move.

The decision to move can have a significant bearing on an individual's overall well-being, both in positive and negative terms. Life in the old house can be stressful, but the move itself may be more traumatic, at least in the short term. The residential location decision becomes of even greater significance when the individuals involved are excessively constrained, either by a lack of resources and mobility, or by the reactions of a potentially hostile community. One such group is the elderly.[4]

The elderly experience considerable problems when the time comes for them to look for new places to live. Residential mobility has traditionally been lower for the elderly than for all other age groups (Wiseman, 1978), but in recent years mobility among the elderly has been increasing. In the United States this phenomenon has been referred to as a retirement "bulge" consisting of two distinct components: the relatively long moves made by the recently retired (the "young old"); and the shorter moves associated with the loss of mobility and the need to be close to medical and personal help (the "old old"). Empirical studies reveal some major differences between the motivations of younger and older movers: Economic (job) variables are much less important than temperature differentials, recreational opportunities, and the availability of medical care. The elderly are also involved in more "return" migrations to states in which they used to live and as a result are more likely to move greater distances than younger migrants. In New York State, for example, in spite of the loss of 1.7 million outmigrants, 1.1 million people entered the state between 1975 and 1980. Of these, 20% had been born in the state of New York and were returning there to live. The same data also shows that the outflow of persons over 65 years of age between the years 1975 and 1980 was 170,600, which represented about 10% of the total migrants from the state. Among the elderly emigrants, almost half moved to Florida (Alba & Batutis, 1984). Although the movement of New Yorkers to Florida is generally characterized in the media as being dominated by elderly persons, it is important to note that the elderly were in fact less than one quarter of the 373,000 New Yorkers who moved to Florida in this 5-year period.

The geography of elderly migration in other parts of the United States and elsewhere in the world reveals a strong desire to leave the urban areas for more remote regions. The trend in New York State·is replicated in other northeastern states, from which there are major flows of migrants to more rural areas of Sunbelt and western states like Florida, Arizona, Oregon, California, Texas, and Arkansas. Together these six states accounted for more than half of the elderly interstate migrants between 1965 and 1970 (see R. F. Wiseman, 1978). The anti-urban bias is evident in Figure 2.2, which identifies eight "elderly net migration regions" that had a surplus of elderly persons as a result of migration patterns between 1960 and 1970 (Bohland & Treps, 1982).[5]

The region selected by retirement-age migrants is only one of their important decisions. Another is the decision about the type of living situation (Golant, 1980). Some elderly people prefer relatively age-concentrated locations because they want to live close to other elderly persons, or because they have always been used to living within an active social network and think of themselves as highly sociable (Heintz, 1976; Sherman, 1971).

A critical issue for the elderly is how well they are able to adjust to their new lives after moving. One of the most important variables in this respect is whether the move is made voluntarily or involuntarily. In general we know that people who move voluntarily tend to adjust much better to their new situations than involuntary movers, even if they have moved frequently (Fischer, 1978). It follows that the most serious adjustment problems will be among those peo-

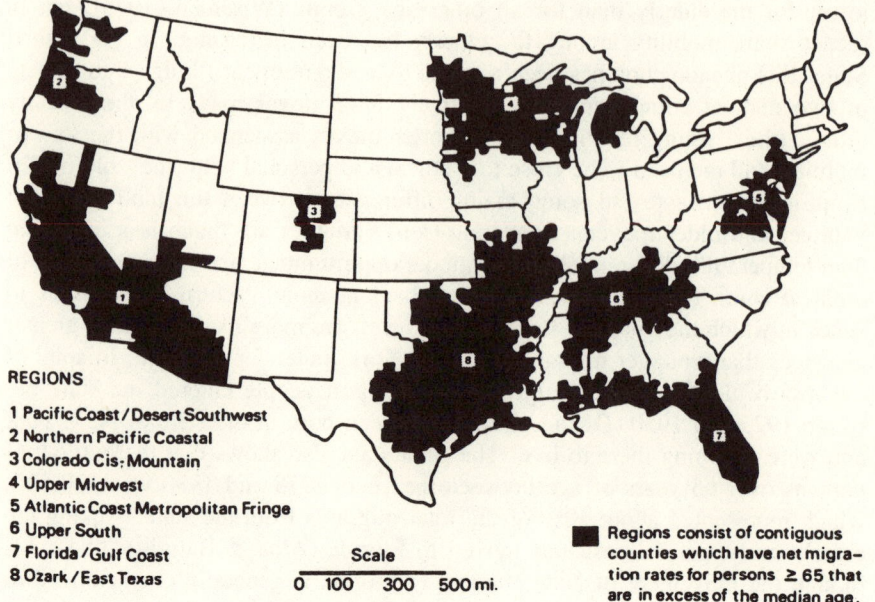

REGIONS

1 Pacific Coast / Desert Southwest
2 Northern Pacific Coastal
3 Colorado Cis-Mountain
4 Upper Midwest
5 Atlantic Coast Metropolitan Fringe
6 Upper South
7 Florida / Gulf Coast
8 Ozark / East Texas

Scale

0   100   300   500 mi.

■ Regions consist of contiguous counties which have net migration rates for persons ≥ 65 that are in excess of the median age.

Figure 2.2. Elderly net migration regions: United States, 1960–1970.[1]

1. Regions are based on county elderly net migration rates for the decade 1960–1970. The regions constitute contiguous counties which have net migration rates for persons aged 65 years or more that are in excess of the median.

Source. Bohland and Treps (1982, p. 151).

ple who do not move out of choice, for example, nonworking women, children, the elderly, and the poor.[6]

Among the elderly voluntary movers, the consensus of studies conducted in a variety of residential settings is that the migrants are reasonably satisfied with their new locations, and their morale is high (Golant, 1980). This is probably because for many the move was a result of self-selection, and in most cases the new housing is clearly an improvement on their previous situations. In addition, many old people evaluate their housing positively, in spite of relatively negative assessments made by objective evaluators (Stevens, 1976; Stutz, 1976). There are dissatisfied elderly migrants, but many of these tend to be involuntary movers (Sherman, 1971). On the other hand, there is little evidence that residential mobility contributes significantly to the mental health of the elderly (Golant, 1980). The major exception in this case is the well-known Victoria Plaza study (Carp, 1977), in which the residents were happier, more sociable, felt better about themselves, and were more satisfied with their housing and their neighborhood than elderly persons not living in the Plaza. It seems likely, however, that this study was not representative. Over and above being more satisfied with their new housing, the majority of elderly migrants reported few if any cognitive or behavioral advantages from their voluntary relocation.

Involuntary or unplanned moves tend to be associated with a range of negative outcomes, and as Fischer and his colleagues (1978) have observed for all age groups, the consequences are worse if the individuals have no choices about where to move, if their new living environment is unpredictable, or if the amount of change they have to deal with is significant. The major problem associated with involuntary relocation is the disruption of social networks, although the network issue is complicated. People who have few friends before they move may find themselves unable to draw on the resources that could help them cope with the associated problems. On the other hand, people with strong and active social networks may have more to lose as a result of their move, and thus may be more disrupted. As this suggests, the line between voluntary and involuntary moving is ill defined, because many of the individuals who have to move are in fact ready and willing to do so.

Neighborhood Character, Neighborhood Change, and the Portability of Urban Ties

At the aggregate level the sum total of inward and outward moves in the city produces a mosaic of neighborhood types, ranging from the most transient to the most stable. Many city neighborhoods pass through a series of life cycles (Bourne, 1976), and at any point in time along a transect from the city center, we could observe some of this variety. A tract at the edge of the city would begin with new suburban growth, in the early years would be characterized by homogeneity in terms of social status and ethnicity, and the landscape would be dominated by single-family dwellings. In later years this neighborhood might experience "in-filling" of the vacant land by nonresidential land uses and conversions to multifamily dwellings, both of which would result in increasing levels of heterogeneity. An end stage might be reached with the demolition of existing housing units to make way for new buildings, for either public or private housing (Bourne, 1976). Each stage in this gradual process of change will be associated with distinctive transformations in social and demographic characteristics, and although the possible permutations are almost infinite, it is possible to identify some of the more common neighborhood types simply by considering two ingredients: mobility rates and sociodemographic characteristics (E. G. Moore, 1972; see Figure 2.3).

As a result of these variations between neighborhoods, the residential experience in each area will be different. Some neighborhoods provide a solid base for social interaction and neighboring in spite of a deteriorated physical environment. Others, particularly those in the suburbs, are satisfactory as places to live, but do not foster much reciprocity among neighbors. Going back to the deterministic tradition, we might expect that the ecological characteristics of

	Change in Selected Sociodemographic Characteristics	Stability in Selected Sociodemographic Characteristics
Neighborhoods Experiencing *High* Mobility	*Type A* 1. Rapid change areas where one ethnic or racial group "invades" the territory of existing occupants 2. Gentrified and revitalized neighborhoods 3. Abandoned and undesirable neighborhoods, concentrated with "noxious" facilities and controversial land use—the "public city"	*Type B* 1. Transient, largely rental inner-city neighborhoods 2. Stepping-stone suburbs for incoming middle-class residents
Neighborhoods Experiencing *Low* Mobility	*Type C* 1. Slow aging of the population and out-migration of younger families 2. Deteriorated housing with selective in-migration, e.g. by ethnic minorities and newly arrived immigrants	*Type D* 1. Tightly structured, stable neighborhoods; strong local ties; often ethnic "villages" (inner city) 2. Some affluent white suburbs

Figure 2.3. A typology of neighborhood change.
Source. See Knox (1982, p. 137).

neighborhoods will result in significant differences in: (1) patterns of social interaction within the area; (2) feelings of attachment and belonging to specific places; and (3) overall social well-being and mental health.

It is also possible to construct neighborhood typologies that are largely independent of ecological characteristics, and are based on existing patterns of social interaction. One such strategy was used by D. I. Warren (1978), who defined neighborhood types based on the responses to a household survey. Neighborhoods were classified according to: (1) the extent to which individuals identify with their neighborhoods; (2) the level of neighboring and social interaction; and (3) the linkages between neighborhood residents and individuals or organizations within the larger community. Using the survey data, Warren identified six broad neighborhood types (see Table 2.8), and he noted some significant variations in the patterns of social support that were typically available in each category. The results implied that in the structurally "weaker" neighborhoods ("Stepping Stone," "Transient," and "Ordinary Anomic"), if any mutual help was available it tended to be in the more "passive" mode (e.g., "just listening" or "asking questions"). In most cases this sort of help is considered less useful than more action-oriented help.

In some of the neighborhoods Warren observed that the respondents were willing to seek help from neighbors when dealing with life-crisis events, in addition to the more mundane everyday problems usually associated with neighboring. This was particularly the case in the Integral, Stepping Stone, and Diffuse neighborhoods, and it suggests that even for serious problems access to "weak" neighborhood ties might provide a swift source of help, (Granovetter, 1973; C. J. Smith, 1980).

These findings demonstrate that neighborhood characteristics influence the type and the effectiveness of the help that is provided locally, but Warren's results preclude any simple deterministic conclusion that the most closely knit neighborhoods are always the most mutually supportive. Similarly, there is no

Table 2.8. A Classification of Neighborhoods

Neighborhood type and description	Identity	Interaction	Linkages
Integral			
A cosmopolitan and a local center. Residents interact strongly, share concerns, and are linked to the larger community.	+	+	+
Parochial			
Strong ethnic identity or socioeconomic homogeneity. Self-contained, not linked strongly to the larger community.	+	+	−
Diffuse			
Largely homogeneous setting with which residents identify, but internal interaction is low, and ties to the larger community are weak.	+	−	−
Stepping-Stone			
An active neighborhood in which people interact with each other and are also linked to the outside. Low identification and high residential turnover ("musical chairs").	−	+	+
Transitory			
Low identity and internal interaction. Residents are in clusters, and demographic structure is continually changing. Collective action is external to the neighborhood.	−	−	+
Anomic			
No internal cohesion or interaction, no collective action by residents either internally or externally.			
Two sub-groups, Ordinary and Mosaic.	−	−	−

Source. Adapted from Warren, R.B., and Warren, D.I. (1977).

consensus about the effect of city size on the effectiveness of social networks. Fischer's (1982) survey data shows that respondents living in cities tend to have smaller social networks than small town and rural residents, and that their networks are likely to include more acquaintances ("just friends") and fewer kin members.

On the other hand, there is evidence that city dwellers have more flexible and broadly based social networks than people who live in smaller towns (Wellman & Leighton, 1979). As Leighton (1979) has observed, city dwellers constantly lose friends and network members as a result of their higher levels of mobility, but they can respond effectively to such losses in two ways: firstly, they are often able to make their ties "portable" by keeping in touch with old friends even though they are far-removed; and secondly, they have more opportunities to replace their old ties in the richer urban social landscape. This empirical observation has been forged into a theoretical proposition: Urbanism does not "destroy" community, as the determinists would argue, but in fact "liberates" community by providing an almost infinite variety of social and cultural opportunities.

On the issue of attachment to neighborhoods, the determinist argument implies that in modern cities there is no longer any desire or need for strong local ties. Empirical studies of attachment have, however, shown that attachment to place is a complex and multidimensional phenomenon. Fischer (1978), for example, found that neighborhood attachment could be measured in many different ways: Social ties to local organizations and individuals was the most dominant dimension, while feelings about the place itself was a separate and independent measure.

In a more recent study using telephone survey data, Riger and Lavrakas (1981) identified two independent dimensions of community attachment: one that they referred to as "social bonding" and the other as "physical rootedness." Based on the respondents' scores on these two dimensions, Riger and Lavarakas identified four groups of residents who have significantly different attitudes toward their neighborhood, and whose behavior reflected such differences (Table 2.9). The young mobiles, who are "low bonded" and "low rooted," live where they do purely on a temporary basis; the young participants ("high bonded, low rooted") are mainly working-class and middle-status adults who are new to the neighborhood but have selected it as a permanent home and have begun to involve themselves in its social and organizational life. The isolates ("low bonded, high rooted") are the stable but socially inactive residents of the neighborhood; the established participants ("high bonded, high rooted") tend to be the neighborhood's oldest and most involved citizens. This last group, identifying most strongly with the neighborhood, try to look after its interests, subscribe to its newspaper, belong to its organizations, and socialize with its residents (Table 2.9).[7]

Table 2.9. Mean Behavioral and Attitudinal Values by
Neighborhood Attachment Type

Variables	Young Mobiles	Young Participants	Isolates	Elderly Participants	F Ratio[a]
Type of residential unit (Single; 2–6 units; 7 + units)	2.28	1.96	1.52	1.25	132.46
Proportion who usually try to keep an eye on the street in front of their home	.52	.68	.53	.79	18.91
Proportion who gather with neighbors to discuss or do something about local problems	.23	.42	.31	.52	18.39
Proportion who regularly read a community newspaper	.42	.51	.58	.65	11.64
Proportion who are members of neighborhood community groups	.12	.26	.19	.30	10.33
Number of visits to neighbors' homes in past 2 weeks	1.89	2.96	1.00	2.65	8.74
Extent of personal fear when out alone at night in the neighborhood	2.23	2.12	2.43	2.04	4.96
Number of times out in neighborhood for evening entertainment (past 2 weeks)	1.78	1.75	1.00	1.39	3.48

[a]F ratios all significant at the .05 level ($n = 905$)
Source. Riger and Lavrakas (1981, p. 62).

Structural Change and City Life

The economic and demographic fate of individual neighborhoods within a city is often determined by forces operating at a scale significantly larger than the city itself. One such force is the widespread residential abandonment of many urban areas in the northeastern and midwestern United States. One explanation for abandonment is the reduced flow of immigrants to the inner city, which has allowed many of the city's residents to "filter" upwards and outwards without being replaced by new waves of immigrants (Ley, 1983). For many cities a better explanation is the overall loss of jobs and the general economic decline of the inner city, which has been particularly virulent in the old industrial core regions. As the demand for housing in the inner city has fallen, the properties deteriorate, and ultimately landlords in search of more lucrative investments take them off the market because the "ground rent" falls to an unacceptably low level (N. Smith, 1983).

It has also been suggested that the process of abandonment is at least partly contagious (Dear, 1976) in that it seems to spread from block to block and from street to street. Eventually the abandonment itself becomes a major reason for its spread: The more abandoned property there is in a neighborhood, the more likely it is that a property owner facing important reinvestment decisions will decide to cut his or her losses and abandon the property. In this way the abandonment of huge tracts of the inner city becomes an almost self-fulfilling prophecy.

From a deterministic perspective, the effect of processes like abandonment on the prevalence of public problems is fairly obvious. Abandoned areas are likely to become prime targets for crime and vandalism (Herbert, 1982), which will in turn work to hasten the spread of abandonment. The long-term effects of living in largely abandoned and deteriorated sections of the city are unknown, but it seems likely that such effects would be negative. A more tangible outcome of abandonment is the large-scale displacement of urban populations, and the rising phenomenon of homelessness in urban areas (Appleby & Desai, 1985; Bassuk, 1984).

Residential and commercial abandonment has had some positive effects; it has, for example, allowed the inner city to accommodate many of society's marginal groups that would otherwise have been squeezed out in the normal marketplace for urban land uses. Although the places available in the abandoned inner city are often not highly desirable, the concatenation of events leading to abandonment was fortunate. Urban abandonment became widespread at roughly the same time that many service-dependent individuals were looking for homes in the inner city, including the mentally ill (Dear, 1980), the poor and the homeless (Wolch, 1979), the drunks and derelicts (R. J. Miller, 1982), and even to some extent the elderly (Golant, 1980).

Concentrations of these groups are only partly the result of individual decisions about where to live. At a much broader level, the "ghettoization" process can be interpreted as the outcome of two sets of forces: one operating in the marketplace to cause abandonment, and another operating in the corridors of state government to dictate public policies for dealing with dependent populations (Lamb, 1984). Partly in response to the growing concentrations of such dependents in the inner city, the agencies providing public services have also sought out central locations. This has been the case for community mental health clinics, welfare offices, residential and treatment centers for substance abusers, hostels, rooming houses, and nursing homes.

All of this helps to create the impression of an increasingly "public" city that is sharply differentiated from the private suburbs. The co-location of service-dependent individuals and the facilities providing their services may be a marriage of convenience, based on the realization that in few other areas outside the abandoned inner city is it likely that such nontraditional and nonprofitable land uses would be tolerated without intense resistance from local residential and commercial interests. Dear (1980) has argued that neither residential abandonment nor deinstitutionalization policies provide a full explanation for the growth in recent years of the "public city." He suggests that the ghettoization of service dependents is simply a new and highly specialized form of the residential segregation that has always been a major feature of the capitalist city (Gordon, 1978; R. A. Walker, 1981). The major difference is that the growth of the public city of the 1980s has not been dictated by market forces, but by patterns of community exclusion, in which residential opposition to groups like the mentally ill has effectively prevented their assimilation throughout the city. In many ways the processes involved were similar to those that have segregated ethnic and racial minorities in the 19th- and 20th-century city. It is also evident that the state has contributed to the "ghettoization" process, partly through its decisions about where to locate facilities and programs for service dependents, and partly through its decisions to favor community care and deinstitutionalization as ways to ease the fiscal burden of the welfare state (Scull, 1977). As Dear (1980) argues:

> Locational choice tends to be pre-empted by one's service-dependent status, however, the state is responding to those groups who have the most to contribute toward easing the crises of capitalism; those whose problems have few ramifications for the social order tend to receive little, if any, attention. (p. 237–238)

The dying city has thus found itself to be a haven for all types of service dependent people. They have been able to move into once grand but now ramshackle buildings, they can walk along streets that used to be prosperous but which are now lined with small stores, hotels, bars, barber shops, and cheap cafés, all within a stone's throw of the central business district. In these locations they may be able to find what they need easily, and perhaps most importantly, they are judged to be acceptable as neighbors.

The architects of the community mental health movement and other Great Society programs no doubt envisioned something a little more elegant, a little nicer, for the people discharged from state hospitals or released from jails and drug treatment centers. But it probably would not have worked to try to place such individuals in middle-class suburban surroundings. Life in the inner city has many advantages for the people who live at the social and economic margins, not the least of which is the opportunity to live close to others who have needs that are similar to their own. It is usually considered to be desirable to be surrounded by other people who are like oneself. Proximity and similarity help people to feel at home, and there is considerable evidence that people in similar life situations are more likely to be helpful in times of need. In the face of considerable opposition from academics, this was one of the major arguments favoring uniform housing projects for the elderly (Caplan & Killilea, 1976).

In mental patient "ghettos" the same advantages may be present. Although the chronically mentally ill person may have few friends, the people who are important in his or her life are likely to be individuals who have experienced similar problems (Pattison, 1975; Sokolovsky, Cohen, Berger, & Geiger, 1978). On the other hand, life in such areas may expose individuals to a range of unwholesome and none-too-therapeutic influences, and could increase the possibility of further deterioration. As we shall see in Chapter 11, the concentration of former mental patients in the inner city may have also played a role in the development of the homelessness problem that has dominated the media in the mid-1980s.

NOTES

1. In comparison to American cities, ethnic segregation in European cities is considerably lower, but as P. N. Jones (1979) has demonstrated in England, segregation varies considerably by city and also by ethnic group. The segregation of Pakistanis in Coventry, for example, is significantly higher than for other immigrant groups. In Brussels, segregation rates by nationality are also highly variable, with the highest rates for the smallest population groups (Turkish and American), as well as for larger groups with generally low status, such as the Spanish, Greek, and Moroccan populations (De Lannoy, 1975)

2. In the city of Hamilton, Ontario, for example, Dear (1977a) found that 61% of all patients admitted to the regional mental hospital came from the core area of the city, and 70% of the patients discharged returned to live in the core. Dear (1980) uses this evidence to describe a now familiar development in North American cities:

> [A] new "asylum without walls" seems to be developing in downtown Hamilton. Since the operation of the formal institution has been diminished, its population has transferred itself to the inner city. . . . [T]he growth of service agencies to aid the discharged patients intensifies the attractive qualities of the core, and a self-reinforcing cycle is thus initiated, intensifying the growth of the "public city."

3. The average age of the population of many inner-city neighborhoods increased as many younger families departed for the suburbs, but the idea that the elderly have been banished to "geriatric ghettos" is clearly stretching the truth. The extent to which elderly people are segregated and isolated depends much more on their personal and social characteristics than on their degree of spatial concentration (Golant, 1980). Thus, although segregation indices for the elderly are not high, many old people are "place-bound" by illness or lack of mobility (Rathbone-McCuan & Hashimi, 1982). An individual with a narrow circle of friends is more likely to experience age segregation negatively, in comparison to one who still maintains an active social calendar. It is also difficult to quantify segregation for the elderly because of the relatively small-scale nature of many age-segregated areas. An age-segregated apartment building, or even a city block in which there are many old people, may be located within a census tract that is generally much more age-integrated. All of this helps to explain why the segregation index for the elderly in American cities in low: Golant (1980) shows that the index ranged from 10.8 to 37.7 in 72 central city areas and from 15.2 to 44.4 in 241 metropolitan areas (using 1970 census data). The elderly are also more concentrated in the inner-city areas of states and regions that are experiencing overall population decline and economic stagnation (J. M. Kennedy & DeJong, 1977), which is part of a more general trend usually referred to as "aging-in-place" (Graff & Wiseman, 1978).

4. In the last 2 or 3 decades, the problem of where to find homes for the mentally ill has become a major public policy issue, largely because of the release of significant numbers of patients from mental hospitals (Bachrach, 1976; P. Brown, 1985). Many of the patients need to look for a new place to live in the community. Although there have been many approaches to the question of residential mobility (Adams & Gilder, 1976; W. A. V. Clark, 1981) because of the particular needs of the mentally ill and their relatively low occupational and social status, traditional models of locational decision making are not appropriate. Discharged mental patients are at a considerable disadvantage in the housing market; many need to look for a new home as an alternative to returning to hospital or living with their families, while others who have no families may have had to give up their old dwellings on admission. The champions of deinstitutionalization gave little thought to the magnitude of the housing problem they would create, but at a conservative estimate more than 5 million people have left institutions in the United States since 1955 (Bassuk & Gerson, 1978). In central Oklahoma, for example, 90 to 100 patients were released from the regional mental hospital every week in 1979, most of them returning to live in nearby Oklahoma City. This trend has continued in many states in the 1980s, especially with the climate of fiscal austerity that has been sweeping the country.

5. Most of these regions are in parts of the country that have experienced high rates of population growth for all age groups, although there were three exceptions: (1) the upper midwest region, where positive rates of increase were the result of a slowing down of the emigration rate of the elderly (aging-in-place); (2) the Ozark/East Texas region, which appears to be an important new destination region for elderly migrants; (3) the Atlantic coast metropolitan fringe, made up mainly of suburban counties in which the elderly have become an increasingly large sector of the population.

The bias against cities in the pattern of elderly migration is also evident in Britain, where a significant growth in the elderly population has occurred in the favored retirement areas along the south coast of England, in East Anglia, the Lake District, North Wales, and various places along the East coast (Law & Warnes, 1980, 1982).

6. Considering how much has been written about residential mobility, it is surprising that so little is known about post-migration adjustment. The Chicago mental health study described earlier in this chapter has some interesting light to shed on the topic (Daiches, 1981). Just over 10% of the sample respondents ($N = 268$) had moved after the first interview, but could still be located at the time of the follow-up. The survey results show that changes in location were associated with modest increases in psychological distress symptoms at the time of the follow-up interview, even when controlling for age, race, marital status, and distress at the first interview. People who had moved closer to the center of Chicago became more distressed, and vice versa. The results suggested that the changes in census tract characteristics associated with these moves were not significantly related to the distress symptoms at the follow-up, which reinforces the suggestion that residential mobility per se has an independent effect on psychological distress. It should be noted, however, that this effect was relatively minor in comparison to the individual social isolation and social class variables. In addition, these results still do not tell us whether mobility is the "cause" of psychological distress or the outcome. The longitudinal data shows that distressed individuals at the first interview were more likely to move, but the mean direction of the moves could not be determined significantly. In other words, it was not clear that the psychologically distressed respondents were more likely to "drift" downtown than others, although they did appear more likely

to select transient neighborhoods. It seems that distressed residents in the inner city had either originated there, or had become distressed after (and perhaps as a result of) moving there. The results are far from unequivocal, but Daiches' conclusions provide some support for the suggestion that urban living has an independent effect on mental health.

7. From studies like this, it is but a small step to consider how the neighborhood characteristics contribute to the well-being and mental health of its residents (C. J. Smith, 1980a). Some population subgroups such as young people without children and old people remain outside the local networks of social interaction. Individuals in such groups could be targeted in attempts to enhance the overall level of social cohesiveness in the neighborhood. One of the major difficulties is to identify neighborhood characteristics that make a significant contribution to mental health that is independent of the contribution made by personal and purely social characteristics. This problem is confounded by Fischer's (1981) observation that the so-called "urban effect" appears to be contradictory. As he notes, urbanism is clearly associated with a general lack of helpfulness, and a perception that in comparison to city dwellers, small town dwellers tend to be friendlier. There is no doubt, as we saw earlier in this chapter, that social conflict and crime is more prevalent in cities than in smaller towns. On the other hand, there is little evidence that the quality of social relationships in cities is lower than it is elsewhere, or that city life "produces" significantly higher prevalence rates of psychological disorder. These apparently contradictory findings can be reconciled by acknowledging that city dwellers operate in two distinct social and spatial spheres; the public and the private. Fischer's (1982) survey data collected in northern California communities of varying sizes supports his general argument. In larger cities, the respondents' public activities increasingly bring them into contact with unfamiliar, annoying, and threatening people. They may respond by avoiding or publicly opposing members of these foreign subcultures. However, urbanism does not necessarily estrange individuals from familiar and similar people.

Consistent with this hypothesis, Fischer's survey data shows that although big city dwellers were initially less likely than others to allow interviewers into their homes (mainly as a result of their fear of crime), those who did were as cooperative as others. The data indicated that urbanism did not impair personal relationships, nor does it appear to be related to higher rates of psychological distress. Fischer concludes that if there is an urban effect, it occurs largely in the public domain. Urbanism tends to produce estrangement from and possibly even conflict with the unknown, distant, and potentially threatening "world of strangers" that is more evident in large as opposed to smaller cities. In other words, in the face of the city's bewildering array of subcultures, city residents may come to rely almost exclusively on the private worlds of friends and kin, effectively excluding the fast and fearful public territory of the city at large.

3

A Contextual Account of Public Problems

INTRODUCTION

It was suggested in Chapter 2 that a particularly useful type of ecological study would consider the extent to which an individual fits into his or her larger social and geographical context. In most cases individual characteristics are consistent with contextual characteristics. So we find that a former mental patient is likely to live in a neighborhood where there are many mental patients and a person who is a Democrat often lives in an area where many vote on that ticket. Others are not so fortunate. They may find themselves living where there are few mental patients or Democrats to talk to. As these simple cases illustrate, both individual and aggregate effects can influence the ultimate outcome of adjustment patterns. If they operate in the same direction, they will presumably reinforce each other, and the dominant trait will be amplified. The neighborhoods will become more homogenous and "safer" for Democrats and for mental patients. If the individual and the aggregate effects work in opposite directions, the outcome could be less than satisfactory. An individual may find that fitting in with the neighborhood is no longer possible. In this situation there are two obvious choices: trying to conform to neighborhood standards, or moving out of the area.

In a contextual analysis it is possible to assess the relative influence of grouped and individual variables on a specific outcome measure. As the examples above illustrate, there are in theory many situations in which the group effect works in a way that is contradictory to the individual effect. Some of the earliest work conducted by sociologists in this area was conducted in military establishments (J. A. Davis, Spaeth, & Huson, 1961). Soldiers who are not promoted tend to behave differently from soldiers who are promoted, but some of the individual differences disappear when outfits with low overall promotion rates are compared to those with significantly higher promotion rates. The "unpromotable" soldier may find him- or herself in a situation where his or her overall performance improves as a result of the group effect.

In a similar fashion political geographers have observed a contextual effect on individual voting behavior (Taylor & Johnston, 1979). The major determinant of voting behavior is parental influence, but it has been shown that the political "climate of opinion" in different communities can in many cases out-weigh the effect of parental influence. In the following discussion contextual effects are dealt with in two categories: those that occur within a defined geographic space such as a neighborhood or a region, and those that are more social in nature and can not be spatially delimited.

NEIGHBORHOOD EFFECTS ON HUMAN OUTCOMES

It is evident that a study of contextual effects is relevant not only to the etiology of public problems but also to the way services are provided to respond to such problems. To begin with a mental health example: Urban neighborhoods differ dramatically in the extent to which they help to provide a local climate of opinion that is conducive to the provision and local use of mental health services. Individuals in certain neighborhoods may be more inclined than others to report their problems and seek help, from either within or without the neighborhood. If a person knows that resources are available locally and are being used, it can be helpful to have his or her particular problems put in a healthier perspective. The knowledge that help can be provided might make him or her willing to discuss these problems with others and look for solutions.

This observation raises what can be referred to as the "human service paradox." In most cases healthy neighborhoods are defined as places with a low prevalence rate of mental health problems (C. J. Smith, 1980). Yet as the previous discussion suggests, areas where many residents are willing and able to seek out help for their problems, should perhaps not be thought of as "pathological." Although it is probably unwise to suggest that areas with the highest use of formal and informal mental health services are the "healthiest" in the city, it is possible that a high incidence of help-seeking behavior indicates a healthy attitude to the solution of mental health problems. It is a sign, at least, that viable helping services are being provided within the neighborhood. Areas reporting low levels of problems and help-seeking behavior may be places where individuals either feel isolated from potential sources of help, or where very little mutual helping is actually available.

The perceived and actual level of informal help provided at the local level can be used to clarify the meanings of the terms "neighborhood" and "community" (D. I. Warren, 1978). Most people think of a neighborhood as a spatially defined unit that contains a population and a set of resources; while the notion of community implies that there are meaningful ties between the residents. The ties may or may not exist in any given neighborhood, but if people believe they exist, a neighborhood is considered to have a "sense of community." The difference between the two notions becomes important when we consider an individual's perceptions and behaviors in response to his or her own mental health problems. A decision to seek help depends partly on the neighborhood's ability to provide help, and partly on the individual's perception of whether any suitable help is available. If a woman thinks that her neighbors do not care about her or her problems, then she lacks a sense of community. On the other hand if she believes that her neighbors do care, she may be willing to reach out and ask for help. In some cases her perceptions may not coincide with the actual ability and willingness of her neighbors to provide informal mental health services.

According to Warren a neighborhood is only a community in mental health terms if the actual ability of its residents to provide help coincides with their perception of that ability. Thus it is possible to identify four broad groups of neighborhood residents:

1. *Resource Identifiers* identify strongly with their neighborhood and correctly perceive that substantial helping resources are available. Typically these people seek to expand their social networks, and their efforts often extend the overall helping capabilities of the neighborhood. These persons have been referred to in the literature as "natural neighbors" (Collins & Pancoast, 1976; C. A. Smith & C. J. Smith, 1978).

2. *Resource Exploiters* perceive their neighborhood as a community with ample common ties and linkages, but the actual resources and human helping skills are poorly developed. If their perceptions lead them to seek out local help, they may soon exhaust the pool of scarce resources. This occurs frequently in neighborhoods where the same few people are continually called on for a variety of purposes. Eventually these individuals will become jaded and ineffective.

3. *Resource Underutilizers* have no sense of community and do not believe that local resources can be usefully exploited. If there are too many of them, the services and access points that are available in the neighborhood may atrophy from lack of use.

4. *Resource Isolates* do not believe they live in a community, but their perception is warranted because few significant ties between the residents can be observed. Feeling this way they have little incentive to develop and extend their neighborhood's resources. Consequently, residents are forced to seek help from outside the neighborhood, either from professionals or from relatives.

This simple schema provides some insight into the intervention strategies for enhancing preventive mental health capabilities at the neighborhood level (Andrews, 1985). In addition to studying the geographical pattern of problems and help-seeking behavior, it is important to consider how people perceive the "climate" in their neighborhood for providing and seeking help. Some neighborhoods may have resources and informal facilities available that remain underutilized. In this case the solution may not be to provide more resources but to convince the residents that informal help is already available and that it can be useful. Warren warns against a too literal interpretation of this notion, because in neighborhoods where a meager supply of helping resources is already being overused, it may not be helpful to encourage residents to improve their sense of community. Without an extended resource base, this might only result in even greater frustration.

Turning now to look at contextual effects on the demand for mental health services, it is obvious that in some situations individual effects and aggregate conditions can work in opposite ways. This is well illustrated by Rabkin's (1979) study of first admission rates to mental hospitals in New York City. For 338 areas within the city, Rabkin examined admission rates for whites, blacks, and Puerto Ricans. For the city as a whole the data show that per capita admissions rates are significantly higher for blacks and Puerto Ricans than for whites. Being black or Puerto Rican thus appears to involve a higher risk for mental illness. It was anticipated that the effect of race would be nullified when the overall ethnic characteristics of the neighborhood were considered. Rabkin's data show that admission rates for each of the three groups decline as the "ethnic density" of the neighborhood increases in favor of that group (Figure 3.1). In largely black areas the admission rates for blacks are lower than they are for whites and Puerto Ricans, the same is true for the other two groups. It appears that being part of an ethnic majority in a specific locality (the contextual effect) results in a lower rate of admission to mental hospitals.

This observation can be interpreted in a number of ways. One possibility is the "breeder" hypothesis: Individuals in the ethnic minority in a particular area may feel alienated and isolated in times of need, and are more likely to be admitted to mental hospitals. Another explanation is "drift" or sociospatial selection, in which people in better mental health move out of areas with high concentrations of ethnic minorities, thereby making room for people in worse mental health. Yet another interpretation comes from community labeling theory (Dohrenwend & Chin-Shong, 1969). There is some evidence that black community leaders define deviance differently from their white counterparts, and the norms for admission to a mental hospital may reflect such differences. Thus, in a largely black or Puerto Rican community, psychiatric illness may be defined more rigorously for purposes of admission to mental hospitals. In predominantly white communities, the symptoms of psychiatric illness among members of other ethnic groups may be more noticeable and thus more likely to lead to hospitalization than the same symptoms among members of the majority group. Theoretically, this explanation may also hold for whites living in predominantly nonwhite areas.

Another possibility, also related to labeling theory, is that the higher rate of admissions for minorities in largely white areas is an artifact of the behavioral response to the treatment of psychiatric illness. In a predominantly white area, blacks may feel there is less stigma attached to seeking out psychiatric care, or they may simply find there are more services available to them. As this example illustrates, there is some overlap between the factors that influence the prevalence rates of mental disorders and the factors that influence the rate at which individuals experiencing such disorders present themselves for treat-

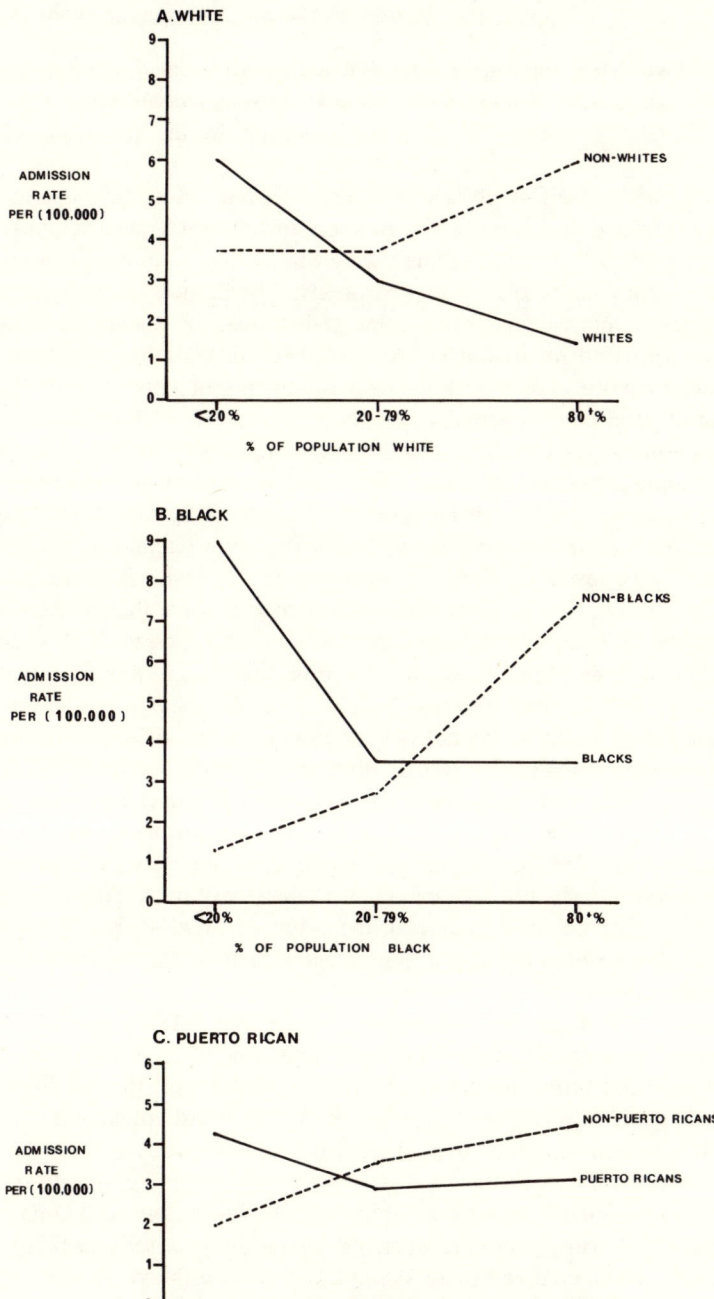

Figure 3.1. Ethnic density and mental hospital admissions.
Source. Adapted from data in Rabkin (1979).

ment. As we have seen here, the prevalence of treated mental disorders varies geographically. Some of the same factors that contribute to an area's overall prevalence rates may also be important in the provision of local services.

The contextual effect of race was also observed in a study conducted in Baltimore (Huffine & Craig, 1973). In some racially integrated neighborhoods prevalence rates of psychiatric illness were higher than in either predominantly white or predominantly black neighborhoods. The authors suggested that this may be because individuals living in integrated areas are somewhat hesitant to articulate their need for treatment. Again we see that the neighborhood effect may result in more people seeking help for their problems, even though the real level of need has not actually increased.[1]

A continued lack of fit between the individual and his or her larger context can have some important outcomes. To illustrate some of the possibilities it is useful to consider drinking behaviors at a variety of scales. At the regional level it is obvious that in the United States there are significant geographical differences in the levels of alcohol consumption (C. J. Smith & Hanham, 1982). Per capita consumption is lower in the southern and Great Plains states, which have persistently been referred to as the nation's "dry" areas. It is no surprise to find that in these regions there are more abstainers and more negative attitudes toward alcohol and drinking. Similarly, at the local level, in the driest communities (those where alcohol is least available), the majority attitudes and behaviors toward drinking are largely abstinent. In these communities approximately 65% of the adult population are abstainers, and only 6% are defined as "heavy" drinkers (Cahalan *et al.,* 1969). In comparison, in the "wettest" communities only 28% are abstainers, while 13% are heavy drinkers. Thus, although alcohol is always available even in the driest areas (either illegally or by travelling to neighboring counties), the evidence suggests that the local context of alcohol availability has a significant effect on the drinking habits of individual residents.

In spite of this general observation, the people who do drink in the dry states and communities tend to drink more and experience a higher prevalence of alcohol-related problems than those from wetter areas (Room, 1983). It is possible that this results from the lack of fit between individual and contextual effects. It has been suggested that where drinking is not fully acceptable behavior, the people who break the local norms tend to do so excessively (Cahalan & Room, 1974). One explanation is that alcohol is viewed in such communities as a "forbidden fruit," so that when the opportunity arises, drinking events may be more protracted and more alcohol may be consumed. At the neighborhood level the lack of fit between an individual's drinking behavior and the local norms toward drinking has also been associated with a high degree of prevalence of alcohol-related problems. The household survey data collected by Cahalan and Room are used to illustrate this situation in Figure 3.2. Contrary to expectations, the ratio of problem drinking to drinking is higher among

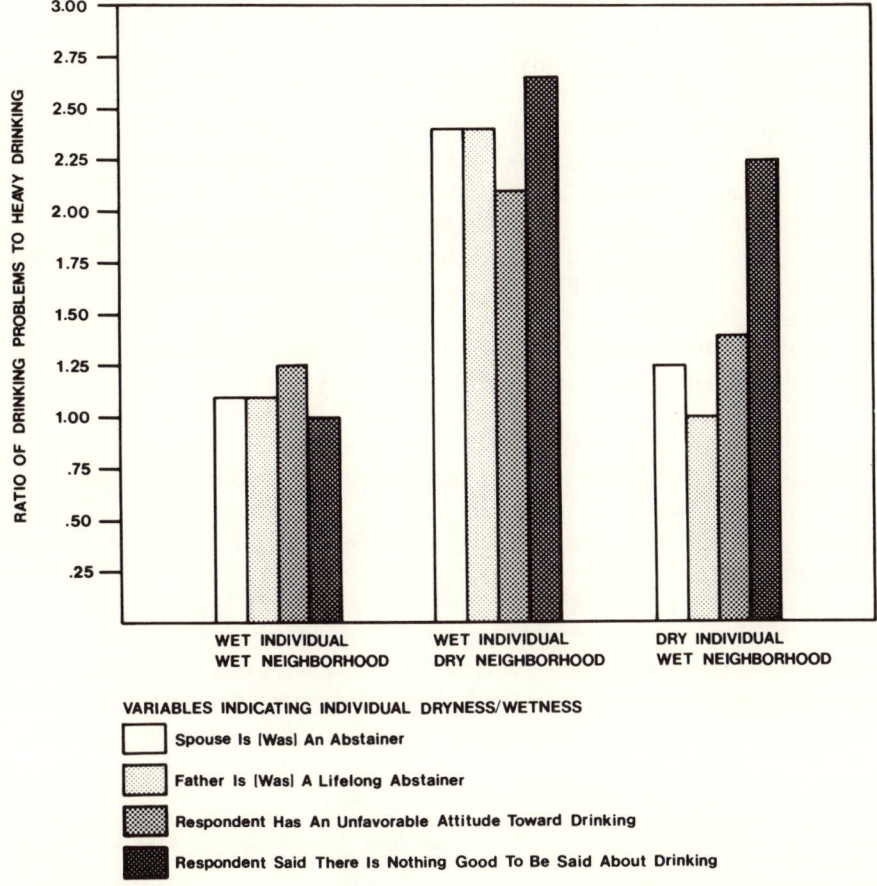

Figure 3.2. Ratio of drinking problems to heavy drinking in different neighborhood categories.
Source. Smith and Hanham (1982).

wet individuals who live in dry neighborhoods than among wet individuals who live in wet neighborhoods (C. J. Smith & Hanham, 1982).

No fully convincing explanations are available for these observations, but it seems that the prevalence of problem drinking is often higher in areas where there is ambiguity about the norms related to drinking. Whatever the explanation, it is clear that the prevalence of problems associated with drinking is not a direct function of how much alcohol is consumed in a locality. It appears to be influenced in some way by the degree of fit between the drinking behavior and the prevailing local attitudes toward drinking.

Further insight into this issue comes from a study of the effect of contextual variables on the drinking habits of teenagers in three American counties that differed significantly in their relative wetness, which was determined by the local availability of alcohol (Harford, 1984). The three counties were (1) Spartanburg, South Carolina, the driest; (2) Pima, Arizona (Tuscon and its suburbs), the wettest; and (3) Allegheny, Pennsylvania (Pittsburgh and its suburbs), which was roughly midway between the two extremes.

The survey data showed, not surprisingly, that the proportion of abstainers was significantly related to the overall availability of alcohol (61% in Spartanburg, 37% in Pima, and 43% in Allegheny). Of greater significance, however, was the observation that differences in availability influence the context and location of teenage drinking (Table 3.1). Although in Spartanburg county 32% of the teens drank at unsupervised teen parties, which is somewhat lower than in the two wetter counties (42% and 50%), significantly fewer teenagers in Spartanburg county drank at parties supervised by adults (16% as opposed to 34% in Allegheny and 42% in Pima). Fewer teenagers drank at unsupervised parties in the driest county, but the gap between the supervised and unsupervised parties is higher than in the wetter counties. The higher ratio of unsupervised to supervised drinking probably reflects the higher proportion of nondrinking adults in Spartanburg County, and the greater likelihood of parental sanctions against drinking.

When only the male drinkers among the sample are considered, the data show that in the driest county teenagers are more likely to drink in secretive contexts, particularly in cars and bars (Table 3.2). It appears that within the overall context of lower alcohol availability, teenagers who want to drink are likely to do so without parental sanction or supervision, and in clandestine

Table 3.1. Drinking Contexts among a Sample of Teenagers, in Percentages[a]

Drinking Contexts	Relative Wetness		
	Spartanburg Co. (driest)	Alleghany Co. (middle)	Pima Co. (wettest)
Supervised			
Teen Parties	16	34	42
Special Occasions	22	46	50
At Dinner	8	22	24
Unsupervised			
Teen Parties	32	42	50
In Bars	15	16	24
In Cars	20	19	25
Out of Doors	15	26	31
Total Sample Size	561	653	594
(Overall % of abstainers)	(61)	(43)	(37)

[a]Percentages represent percent of the total sample of teenagers who drink in the contexts listed.

Source. Adapted from Harford (1984, p. 136).

Table 3.2. Drinking Contexts among Male Teenage Drinkers, in Percentages

	Relative Wetness		
Drinking Contexts	Spartanburg Co. (driest)	Alleghany Co. (middle)	Pima Co. (wettest)
Supervised			
Teen Parties			
Do Not Drink	57	44	32
Drink	43	56	68
Special Occasions			
Do Not Drink	40	23	25
Drink	60	77	75
At Dinner			
Do Not Drink	81	65	61
Drink	19	35	39
Unsupervised			
Teen Parties			
Do Not Drink	21	25	19
Drink	79	75	81
In Bars			
Do Not Drink	60	74	71
Drink	40	26	29
In Cars			
Do Not Drink	48	65	55
Drink	52	35	45
Out of Doors			
Do Not Drink	59	50	48
Drink	41	50	52
Total Sample Size	117	195	174
(% of abstainers)	(57)	(39)	(35)

Source. Adapted from Harford (1984, p. 138).

locations. These results indicate that the contextual effect of different levels of availability at the county level influence where, when, with whom, and how much teenagers drink. As we shall see at various times throughout this book, all of these variables have an important influence on the outcome of drinking (Harford, 1979; Snow, 1984; Wittman, 1982).

SOCIAL CONTEXTS: THE NETWORK APPROACH

The consideration of structural or contextual effects on human behavior has in recent years ascended to a prominent position in the social sciences, with much of the work falling under the heading of "social networks." In the early 1970s it was suggested that "networks will probably become as important to sociology as Euclidean space and its generalizations are to physics" (Lorrain & White,

1971, p. 77). Although this has probably not yet come about, there is no doubt that social network approaches have contributed significantly to the social sciences in general, and to the study of public problems in particular.

The simplest definition of a social network describes it as "a device for representing social structure which depicts persons as points and relations as connecting lines" (Granovetter, 1976). The units linked together may be groups or individuals, with their interrelationships represented either by lines (as in graph theory) or by numbers (as in matrices). A review of the social network literature suggests they are being used in at least three different ways: as metaphors, as models, and as methods (C. J. Smith, 1980b). In the first usage, the term social network has been used rather loosely as a general metaphor to describe a contextual approach to social situations. We tend to hear about the importance of the subject's social network, but in such instances the term is most often being confused with the more general term "group" to indicate that an individual or a group is embedded in a wider social or spatial structure.

Social networks have also been used as conceptual models for guiding theoretical research, but to date, very few social scientists have treated social networks as theory, perhaps because there have been so many challenging empirical issues to grapple with. The third and most popular application of social networks is in the realm of methodology. The methods used to investigate social networks are as numerous as the properties of the networks themselves, and Figure 3.3 illustrates some of this diversity. The structural or morphological network features are shown on one side of the illustration, and the characteristics of the interactions are on the other side.

The term social network was used in the metaphorical sense by sociologists in the early decades of the 20th century, but the first empirical applications were not made until the 1950s by social anthropologists in the "Manchester School" (Barnes, 1954; Bott, 1957; J. C. Mitchell, 1969). This early work was paralleled in the United States by a number of Harvard-based sociologists in the structuralist school, which included Harrison White, Charles Tilly, and several of their students (eg. Barry Wellman and Claude Fischer), who spread the social network approach to other universities in North America (Mullins, 1973).

In the 1960s social networks became a regular feature in the anthropology and sociology literature, but much of the work was still conducted under the more traditional academic labels such as class, community, and kinship. Although many studies in this period included the term social network in their titles, the work appeared haphazardly, and it spread to other disciplines only slowly. In the late 1960s and early 1970s this situation changed rapidly, and social networks became familiar to a wide range of social scientists. One of the most important contributions was the publication of J. Clyde Mitchell's book, *Social Networks and Urban Situations* (1969), although social networks had already been introduced to social psychologists by Stanley Milgram's "small-world" research. The message was also spread to clinical psychologists and others in the helping professions by Speck and Attneave's book *Family Networks* (1973), which described a "retribalization" therapy based on the concepts of social networks. In 1976 the helping professionals were introduced more formally to the theory and practice of network analysis by Collins and Pancoast's influential book *Natural Helping Networks*.

In the meantime, Craven and Wellman's (1973) article "The Network City" had demonstrated the potential usefulness of social network concepts for the study of urban and community issues. This paper also provided a theoretical underpinning for some of the emerging views of city living that were challenging the social ecology determinism that had long pervaded these fields (see Chapter 2). In the same year Granovetter's (1973) influential article "The Strength of Weak Ties" demonstrated the importance of uniplex or single-stranded relationships between urban dwellers. Granovetter provided a theoretical explanation for what many urbanists had already observed—the phenomenon of "loose coupling" between urban dwellers, which appeared to be neither residentially based nor multistranded by nature. Instead of belonging to one closely knit homogeneous social network, as had been the case in the old "natural areas" and neighborhoods of the 19th-century cities, the modern city dweller appears to dabble in several networks, but he or she remains only loosely connected to the other members (Fischer, 1976).

Later in the 1970s Sarason, Carroll, Matton, Cohen, and Lorentz (1977) demonstrated that a number of key works in social science disciplines—notably political science, organizational relations, and community development—had provided an impetus for the adoption of the social network approach. Although these were not always the original works in their field, each one acted as a catalyst and an inspiration for other researchers to review critically their own discipline's intellectual history, and to suggest social networks as a major new approach.

The Function of Social Networks

The network approach has brought to the study of social problems a more realistic and less biased view than was possible with the already-existing paradigms. Networks are a suitable analogue for the social and psychological complexities of large systems such as cities. Social network analysis begins with a clean slate, in that no a priori assumptions are made about human behavior. An individual may belong to many groups or to none; similarly, he or she may live in a particular neighborhood, but his or her ties may be city-wide. As Barnes (1954) had shown in the early 1950s, even in a remote Norwegian fishing village important social behavior could not be explained by location or occupation alone. He saw the need for a "third social field with no units or boundaries" (p. 43), and he was perhaps the first person to call this field a social network.

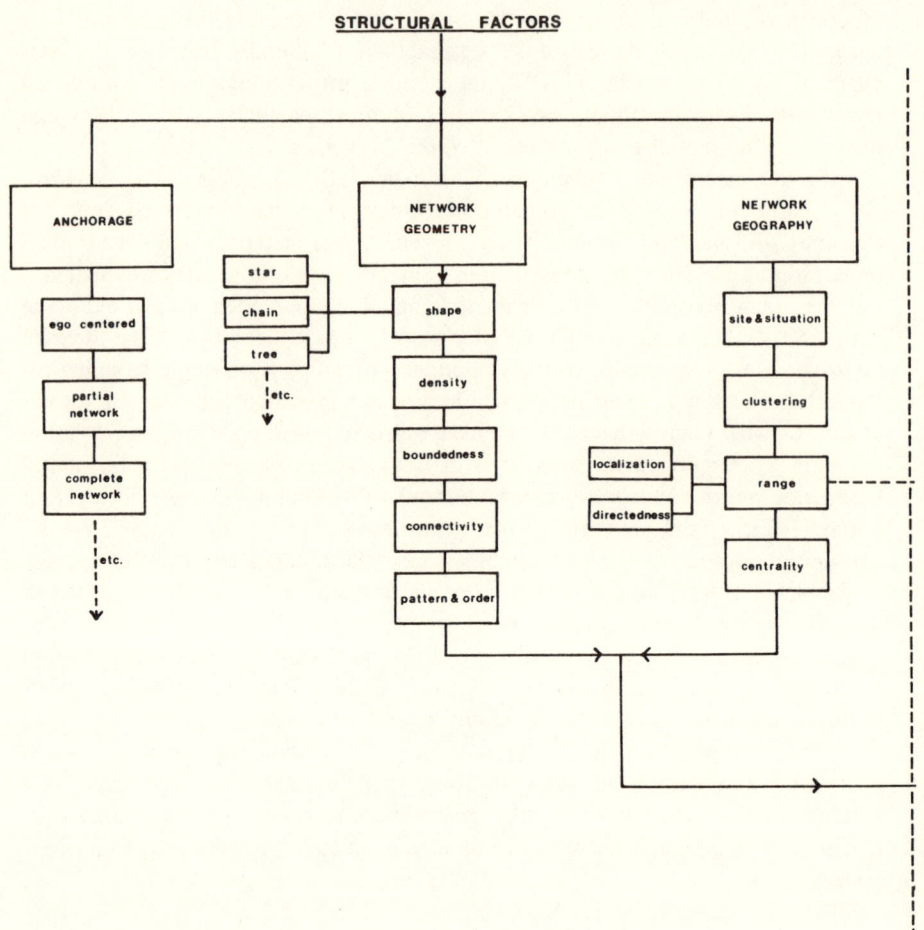

Figure 3.3. Network characteristics: Interactional and structural factors.
Source. Smith (1980).

A second advantage is that networks allow the investigator to consider only those persons directly involved in any situation, rather than ascribing a blanket actor status based on common group attributes. A good example of this is provided by neighborhood action studies. In most neighborhoods relatively few people are actively involved in bringing about change, but traditional ecological studies use aggregated residential characteristics as independent variables, which runs the risk of misclassifying many of the residents. This can be avoided by studying only the neighborhood change agents and their social networks.

A third advantage of social networks is that they represent an optimistic view of human nature. Networks can be thought of as theoretical counterparts

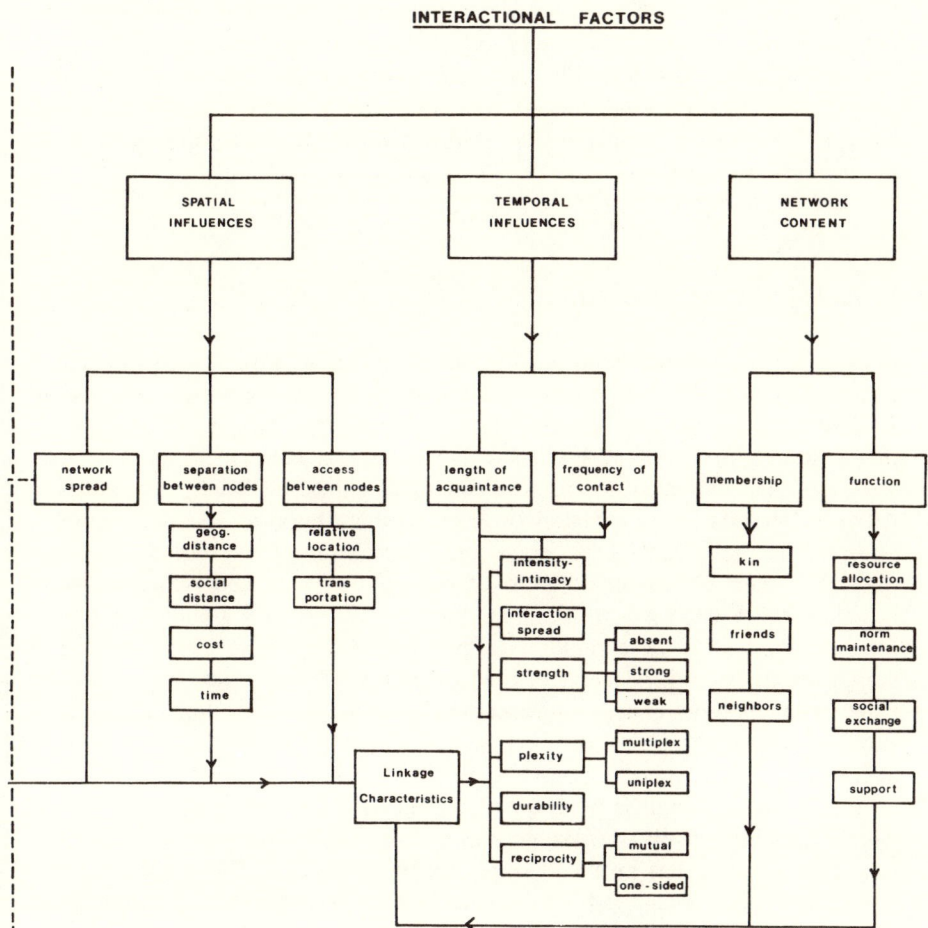

Figure 3.3 (continued).

to the so-called "mutual aid" movement because a network by definition involves potentially unlimited interaction. The prospect of helping networks, with nodes located almost ubiquitously throughout the city, is a viable alternative to the narcissism of many popular psychotherapies, which espouse a "you can do it on your own" philosophy (M. L. Gross, 1978; Marin, 1975). A network links people together, so it has the potential to expand their mutual resources exponentially, through the "friends of friends of friends" mechanism (Boissevain, 1974). Because people interact with each other for any number of reasons, social networks can also help to solve one of the perennial problems facing the providers of human services, which is the chronic lack of resources. As Naparstek, Biegel, and Spiro (1982) have argued, a social network is a human resource in itself, and one that is potentially capable of mobilizing significant resources in the community that traditionally remain untapped.

Social networks can also be used as important analytical tools in the study of social and public problems. As illustrated earlier in Figure 3.3, there are basically two sorts of measures: one associated with the structural properties of the networks themselves, and the other with the character of the interactions between the network members.[2]

Social Supports and Mental Health

In recent years the importance of an individual's social support network to his or her mental health has been well documented in the literature. One reason for this has been the growing emphasis on community care. Outside the hospital people with mental health problems have to rely much more on their own resources, and they need to be more actively involved in their own treatment. As mental hospitals have increasingly become the last resort for long-term chronic patients, the individuals experiencing less serious mental disorders have remained in their communities. Most of the patients who are discharged from hospitals will probably never be readmitted, at least not for a lengthy stay, so for them a return to the community implies either a return to their family or a search for a new and independent life in the city. In some cases the individual experiences multiple entries into and exits from the hospital, with intermittent stays in community-based facilities such as half-way houses, and numerous attempts to live at home. One of the best documented examples of this is the case of Sylvia Frumkin, a pseudonym chosen by Susan Sheehan (1982) in her widely acclaimed book *Is There no Place on Earth for Me?*

This situation has provided some unique opportunities to investigate the importance of social supports in the maintenance of mental health. Among the most interesting issues raised are the following: (1) what the role of the family is in the former patient's recovery process in the community; (2) how the family copes with the burden of having a former patient return to live with them (or having a person stay with them who otherwise would have been institutionalized); and (3) how the family members cope with their new situation.

In the community mental health literature of the 1960s and 1970s, relatively little emphasis was placed on the role of the family. Most of the deinstitutionalization studies were concerned with the attempts to establish a continuum of care outside the hospital (Bachrach, 1976) or with the community's willingness to accept mental patients after they were discharged (P. Brown, 1985; Dear & Taylor, 1982). During all of this activity researchers lost sight of the fact that in the majority of cases deinstitutionalized patients returned to live with their families. It has been estimated that as many as two thirds of the patients discharged from public mental hospitals rejoined their families (Minkoff, 1979); among a sample of young chronic patients, Pepper, Kirshner, and Ryglewicz (1981) have found an even higher percentage living at home. Researchers at the National Institute of Mental Health estimated that in the late 1970s as many as 650,000 patients returned each year to their families from inpatient settings (Goldman, 1980, 1982). Most of the treatment these individuals receive, if they receive any at all, is located in community-based outpatient settings. This implies that the bulk of their supervision and round-the-clock care is provided by family members.

For most people who experience mental illness, the family is the primary source of companionship, and often family members provide the only source of assistance for coping with everyday problems (Boyd, McGill, & Falloon, 1981). Although the locus of treatment has clearly been shifted to the community in recent years, only in a few model programs are families identified as an integral part of the treatment and rehabilitation team, and only rarely are they trained for their role as caretakers of the mentally ill (Hatfield, 1979). In addition to the overall lack of program coordination, some recent economic and demographic trends will result in families being less able than ever before to provide support for their dependent members. One of these is the reduction in family size, another is the increasing proportion of women leaving the home to work on a daily basis, and a third is the absence of kin living nearby—a result of higher levels of geographic mobility (Miles, 1981). In spite of the stresses made inevitable by these trends families still provide most of the support for society's dependent members; in a great many cases there are simply no alternatives (Goldman, 1982; Moroney, 1976; Zimmerman, 1978). In most communities family members have no choice but to care for their relatives themselves because there are no suitable after-care or residential facilities available for the patients (Betts, Moore, & Reynolds, 1981; C. J. Smith & Hanham, 1981a).

In addition to the discharge of persons from state and county hospitals, an important goal of the deinstitutionalization process was to provide community care alternatives for individuals who experience mental disorder but have never been hospitalized (Bachrach, 1976). It is difficult to estimate the size of this population because the true prevalence of mental disorder is unknown. The best estimates for the United States indicate that between 16% and 25% of the population is in need of mental health services (Ashbaugh & Manderscheid, 1985; Dohrenwend *et al.*, 1980). It has been estimated that approximately 32 million Americans experience mental disorders at any point in time, but only about a quarter of them receive services within the specialty mental health care sector, and only 1.5 million receive inpatient services (Goldberg, Regier, & Taube, 1978). As the focus of treatment has shifted increasingly over to the community, families have had to shoulder the burden of keeping at home people they would rather have seen enter formal treatment facilities. In most states it is now difficult for an individual to be committed to a mental hospital for anything other than acute drug or alcohol abuse or a suicide attempt, and even then the average length of stay is less than 3 weeks (Boyd *et al.*, 1981; C. J. Smith & Hanham, 1981a).

Mental Disorder and the Family Burden

In spite of the circumstantial evidence that the family bears the brunt of dein-stitutionalization, it is surprising that so few studies of the impact of mental disorder on family life have been conducted (Kreisman & Joy, 1974). The studies that have been carried out indicate that the presence of mental disorder in the home is likely to increase the level of stress and reduce the quality of life within the family (Doll, 1976; Goldman, 1982). In a review of the litera-ture, Segal (1979) concluded that having a mentally ill person living at home places a substantial burden on the rest of the family (see also Creer & Wing, 1974; Hatfield, 1978, 1979; Miles, 1981). Segal's observation was consistent with the studies that have investigated the impact on families of having some-one with a chronic physical illness living at home (Satterwhite, 1978).

The term "burden" in this context has been defined as "the load or stress on the family system resulting from the behavior and the care of the mentally ill family member" (Hoenig & Hamilton, 1969). Most researchers agree that the burden is made up of a set of objective circumstances—the behavior of the individual that adversely affects the family—and a set of subjective feelings about the disabling condition of the individual in question. In most cases family members are unable to differentiate clearly between the objective and subjec-tive elements because the perception of burden will be determined both by the actual problems encountered and by the meanings that they assign to them. Although objective problems such as the disruption of household activities and the additional expenses of having the person living at home (Hatfield, 1979) are consistently reported, it is likely that the heaviest burden results from the patient's impact on the "emotional climate" of the household (Miles, 1981).

One of the most influential studies of family burden compared two com-munities that offered different types of psychiatric services (Grad & Sainsbury, 1966). In one community, community care was the norm and only a small proportion of patients were admitted to the mental hospital; in the other com-munity only hospital-based services were available. Over a 2-year period the study revealed that the continued presence of the patient in the home was as-sociated with an ongoing burden, whereas the families that had patients hospi-talized more often reported a reduction in the burden. The researchers noted, however, that in spite of the additional burden encountered, most of the fami-lies said they preferred to have the person in question living at home rather than in other residential settings. In a study of 125 deinstitutionalized patients living with their families, Doll (1980) also reported that the families generally did not reject their kin unless they were grossly disturbed. Doll noted, however, that beneath a superficial acceptance of the patients, substantial adjustment problems often existed, although in most cases these did not result in the patient being rehospitalized.

These conclusions are consistent with those reported by Vanicelli, Washburn, and Scheff (1980), who found that family attitudes toward the mentally disordered change very little over time, and they are not likely to deteriorate when the patients leave the hospital to come home, or even when their condition worsens. All of these studies suggest that even under extremely difficult circumstances, most families manage to cope with the extra burden. We can also assume that in the process they accumulate a wealth of experience, mostly gained by trial and error, that helps them solve both the patient's problems and their own. This does not mean that such families do not need any outside help. Hatfield (1979), for example, found that although the family's coping mechanisms were impressive, they benefited significantly from professionals working with them to provide supportive services such as education about mental disorder, training and communication skills, problem-solving abilities, and information about referral sources for crisis situations.

These sorts of strategies were advocated by Segal (1979) to help lessen the burden experienced by families that had mental patients returning home from hospitals. Segal suggested that social workers and other professionals should actively begin to identify and strengthen the family's support systems as a way of helping them cope with the additional burden. This is consistent with Grad and Sainsbury's (1966) observation that although having patients living at home was associated with a greater burden, the actual experience of the burden, both in objective and subjective terms, was largely a function of how much external support the family had received. This observation has been repeated numerous times in subsequent studies (C. J. Smith, 1976; Stein, Test, & Marx, 1975).

Empirical observations unfortunately demonstrate that the support systems described by Grad and Sainsbury (1966) and by Segal (1979) are rarely provided formally. For this reason it was necessary to explore informal alternatives to the establishment of formal support systems. In what rapidly became a major part of the mental health literature, there were numerous descriptions of successful attempts to develop effective community-based support systems that use informal or ''natural'' sources, including relatives, friends, and neighbors (Collins & Pancoast, 1976; Kahn & Antonucci, 1980; C. J. Smith, 1978). Although it is not practical to suggest that informal supports should completely replace formal services, it makes sense to suggest that when the supply of professional help is limited by financial or geographic constraints, a partial solution is to turn to one's social network for support. For some problems, particularly those that are associated with everyday living, professional help may actually be less useful than help from a neighbor or an empathetic peer (Borman, 1976; Katz & Bender, 1976).

There is considerable evidence that individuals suffer less serious effects in a wide range of problem situations if they have an extensive and well-functioning social support system (for reviews see Dean & Lin, 1977; Evans & Northwood, 1979; Froland, Pancoast, Chapman, & Kimboko, 1981). Although it is difficult to ascertain exactly what is meant by the term "social support" from one study to the next, a generally accepted definition has been offered by Lin and his colleagues (1979), in which "support networks" are defined as the "support accessible to an individual through social ties to other individuals, groups and the larger community" (p. 109). Subsequently, Thoits (1982) has noted the need to distinguish between two forms of social support: instrumental support, which includes information and assistance with tasks; and expressive support, which includes affection and understanding. Although this is still vague as an operational definition, the evidence from a wide range of studies demonstrates that the severity of physical and psychological symptoms is negatively related to the amount of social support an individual receives (Pilisuk & Froland, 1978). It is not known exactly why social supports have this effect, but Lin and his colleagues (1979) have suggested two alternative hypotheses. The first implies prevention: Other individuals and groups present the individual in question with a wide range of norms, some of which may differ substantially from his or her own. When problems surface, normative pressures or guidance from network members might help to suggest solutions or alternative courses of action. This hypothesis necessarily implies comparisons between group members and pressures toward conformity within the network. The second hypothesis is that social supports play a buffering role. After the onset of problems, individuals within the social network may provide help by offering emotional support, suggesting strategies, providing information, or actually donating useful goods and services. In other words, social supports may help the individual to cope with his or her problems more effectively, even after they have become serious.

An additional perspective on the role of social supports was offered in a study conducted by Berkman and Syme (1979), who demonstrated that people lacking social and community ties have a significantly higher risk of mortality than those who have extensive social supports. They thus suggested that isolation may be associated not only with higher rates of mortality, but also with pathologies such as mental disorder, in at least three ways: (1) isolated individuals may choose damaging or even self-destructive health practices; (2) people with few social contacts may become depressed and feel more hopeless about their lives; and (3) the absence of social networks may be associated with some physiological changes, presumably in individuals' nervous or hormonal systems, that somehow make isolated individuals more susceptible to a wider range of physical and emotional illnesses.

SOCIAL NETWORKS AND THE DECISION TO SEEK TREATMENT

How do social network members respond when their friends and relatives first exhibit symptoms of mental disorder? To answer this question Perucci and Targ

(1982) interviewed a total of 321 network members of 47 mental patients (an average of 6.8 persons per network). The respondents were asked to describe the first time they had observed any "unusual" behaviors exhibited by the individual in question. Perucci and Targ presented the respondents with a list of 19 unusual behaviors and grouped them into two broad categories: (1) those indicating medical or psychiatric problems (these included physical problems, interpersonal problems, and "unusual ideas"); and (2) those indicating deviations from acceptable norms for behavior, but with no obvious medical or psychiatric symptoms (eg. role failures, aggression, and norm violations). The results showed that some network members tended to "medicalize" the problems; they described the problems mainly in medical or psychiatric terms and advocated professional help. Others preferred to "normalize" the problem behaviors, defining them as part of the individual's behavioral repertoire and tending not to see them as problems for which medical or psychiatric care was immediately necessary. The results suggested that it was neither the severity of the individual's symptoms (the medical model) nor the status resources of the patients (the societal reaction model) that accounted for the different definitions, but the properties of their social networks. In comparison to the "normalizers" the "medicalizers" were in social networks that were larger and denser, were more open to nonfamily members, had stronger ties both to the patient and among other members, and were better able to achieve instrumental goals by identifying leaders who were willing and able to make decisions when necessary. We can assume that on the basis of their evaluations of the patient's symptoms, network members respond differently to the situations that precede hospitalization.

On the basis of such results it would be reasonable to expect that the nature of a patient's social network also plays a key role in the decision-making process involved in hospitalization. Some network members decide to hospitalize (or to encourage hospitalization) after years of knowing about the individual's problem, so the important question is how such decisions are reached. In this respect Perucci and Targ's (1982) work was anticipated by A. V. Horwitz (1977), although their conclusions are somewhat different. Horwitz assessed the influence of two network structure variables on the decision to seek psychiatric help: One was a measure of cohesiveness and the degree of contact within the kinship network and the second was the openness of the friendship network, which was an indication of ease of access into the network. Horwitz hypothesized that high scores on the cohesiveness measure would indicate a strong informal service element and mutual supportiveness, while high scores on the openness measure would indicate high access and linkages to external resources. He demonstrated that persons with cohesive kin networks and close friendships (strong ties) were less likely to have their problems formally labeled as psychiatric problems and were more hesitant to seek formal psychiatric help. Consequently, those who sought help in this category typically waited longer after they had first encountered the problems, and usually had more serious symptoms. Individuals with weaker kinship networks and more open networks were more likely to have had their problems labeled at an earlier stage and had a better chance of being referred for treatment before their problems became too serious. Horwitz's findings could be interpreted as a mixed blessing, because although close kinship ties can provide a supportive environment, they may also allow problems to compound until treatment becomes very difficult. People without close kinship networks may enter formal treatment too soon, but the advantage may be that their problems will be less severe and perhaps more easily treated.

A study of community recuperation among discharged mental patients sheds further light on this issue (C. J. Smith, 1976). The results suggested that the optimum community setting for discharged patients involves living with a close and supportive family, but that it may be better not to live with the family at all if they are not supportive. Trute and Segal's (1976) study of social integration among discharged patients further supports this notion. They found that patients could integrate more effectively in communities that were neither highly socially cohesive (strong ties) nor completely socially disorganized (nonexistent ties). the optimum setting was a neighborhood with a substantial proportion of socially detached, non-family-oriented residents (weak ties). This was an optimistic note for the study of mental patients living in the community, both because after a lengthy stay in the hospital so many of them tend to have weak and disrupted family networks, and because most of them live in neighborhoods that are socially disorganized (Dear, 1977a). As a strategy to accompany deinstitutionalization policies, it might be advisable for community workers to help patients develop their weak ties to neighbors and acquaintances, rather than attempting to restructure and solidify their strong (family) ties, which is a lengthy and often a distressingly difficult procedure.

It is interesting to note that Perucci and Targ's (1982) observations are not consistent with those reported by Horwitz (1977). They found that the patients who were committed relatively soon after their unusual behaviors were observed tended to have network members who focused on the medical and/or psychiatric character of their symptoms. In addition to the differences in network characteristics that were mentioned earlier, the networks were more likely to include people of higher socioeconomic standing, with more favorable attitudes and more knowledge about mental disorder and a greater tolerance for deviance. The patients whose behavior had been normalized by network members tended to have been exhibiting symptoms for a much longer period, and hospitalization had been delayed. According to Perucci and Targ, the eventual decision about hospitalization is generally precipitated by "some change in the structure of the network that reduces its ability to cope with a problem member" (p. 132). Among the most important changes that had this effect were: (1) a worsening of the stresses experienced by network members; (2) a loss of economic or emotional support within the network, which often resulted from the loss of a member, usually through death or illness; and (3) the intervention of professionals or law enforcement personnel in network affairs. Until such events forced the network members to consider hospitalization, they generally tended to define the patient's problems in nonmedical terms, for example, as aggression, problem drinking, or spouse abuse. When they finally agreed to hospitalization, it was often interpreted more as a way of removing the person from the community than as an opportunity to receive treatment for a psychiatric problem.

Perucci and Targ's (1982) findings suggest that the characteristics of the patient's social network strongly influence community reactions to their symptoms, and influence the decision-making involved in hospitalization. They also showed that patients in closely knit social networks were more likely to accept both their mental disorder and the need to be hospitalized (see Table 3.3). It was not surprising to find that these patients also had a better prognosis in the hospital: They received more varied treatment, they had more contact with friends and relatives, and they were released sooner than patients with less dense networks. The overall conclusion was that patients whose social network ties are strong and multistranded have the best prognosis for recuperation:

> Networks influence the way in which the problem behaviors of members are defined and dealt with. They also have different kinds of social and emotional resources—that is, capabilities for supporting members in times of need. (p. 138)

From their empirical observations, Perucci and Targ were able to reach two general conclusions:

1. In multiplex networks the problems of any one member are more likely to have greater consequences for the other members because they can affect a

Table 3.3. Strength of Ties between Network Members and Patients: Reactions to Their Illness and Need for Hospitalization

Patients' Reactions	Close-Tie Networks		Weak-Tie Networks	
	#	%	#	%
Patient accepts his or her mental illness	20	67	6	35
Patient does not accept his or her mental illness	10	33	11	65
Total	30		17	
Patient accepts need for hospitalization	22	73	7	41
Patient does not accept need for hospitalization	8	27	10	59
Total	30		17	

Source. Adapted from Perucci and Targ (1982, p. 87).

larger number of network members in a broader range of contexts (eg., disrupting kinships, friendships, and work ties);

2. Dense networks are more likely to have a consensus on expectations about their members' behavior, presumably as a result of the greater frequency of social interaction.

Perhaps the most significant achievement of this work is the contribution it can make to the ongoing debate between the proponents of the medical model and the social reaction perspectives on mental disorder (Gove, 1982). Perucci and Targ do not suggest that a social network perspective is the only way to study this issue, simply that it offers a new way of thinking about how community members respond to the presence of disordered behavior in their midst. A social network view provides some important missing links between the dominant models. According to the medical model, an individual's symptoms are important determinants of a mental patient's career. From Perucci and Targ's vantage point, this is not because the symptoms are objective facts, but because they are used by network members to define problem behaviors, and to suggest broad avenues for treatment. Different types of networks produce different types of labels for symptoms. Some of these are no doubt based at least partly on differences in actually observed behavior, but this is complemented by the network member's cognitive and attitudinal constructs about mental disorder and how it should be treated:

> Having chosen medical-psychiatric symptoms to make sense of observed problem behaviors, the network has automatically adopted an illness model that has built-in expectations of treatment and cure. When the network decides upon hospitalization, it does so with an expectation that the patient will be cured and eventually released from hospital. (p. 136)

According to the societal reaction perspective the patient's lack of status resources are more important than his or her symptoms in determining when and under what circumstances hospitalization will occur. The network perspective strengthens this argument by demonstrating that it is not so much the resources of individual patients that determine their subsequent careers, but the resources of the social networks within which they are situated. This reinforces the suggestion made in the previous chapter that neighborhoods can function in much the same way as networks by not only providing actual resources, but also by providing access to resources, and helping to create a local "climate of opinion" that is favorable to seeking help. The resources of a network are not just its tangible features; they also include those network characteristics that facilitate the flow of resources through the network. In the words of Perucci and Targ, "Some networks were more capable than others of acting in concert, of transmitting information, and of providing emotional support" (p. 137).

The patient's social network continues to be important even after the decision to hospitalize. Perucci and Targ's data show, for example, that if a patient had a supportive social network, this would be articulated in the hospital records and would subsequently influence both the treatment received and its outcome. As they note, "Negative comments (in the patient's hospital records) about a patient's family may adversely affect chances for week-end home leaves and may discourage staff from thinking about early release from the hospital" (p. 134). In comparison, the records of patients who have strongly tied and multiplex social networks were almost universally positive about the patient's kith and kin, and the net effect was that these patients were much more likely than others to be released from the hospital within their first year.[3]

CREATING SOCIAL SUPPORT NETWORKS: THE COMMUNITY SUPPORT PROGRAM

By the middle of the 1970s it was evident that the policies designed to deal with mental disorder had caused some new and unanticipated problems. Most states had sharply reduced their resident populations to the point where only the most disturbed patients remained hospitalized (C. J. Smith & Hanham, 1981a). This achievement was in itself a step in the right direction, but it soon became clear that in most communities very few of the components of a coordinated system of care were available to individuals who experienced mental disorders (Bachrach, 1976; Brown, 1985). These individuals would fall between the cracks of the existing service delivery system unless they had a strongly supportive family and social network. However, as we have seen, many of them did not have such advantages, and in fact the lack of a viable support system was often their major problem once they left the hospital.

From a policy perspective it was time for a new set of strategies, a new initiative to provide long-term care for the noninstitutionalized mentally disordered. The optimistic literature describing the merits of social support systems suggested that formal service agencies ought to try to develop a coordinated and supportive array of services for each individual. With this in mind the National Institute of Mental Health (NIMH) announced the Community Support Program (CSP) in 1978. The goal of the program was to develop a Community Support System (CSS) for individuals in need. In the official announcement, the CSS concept was described as "a network of caring and responsible people committed to assisting a vulnerable population to meet their needs and develop their potential without being unnecessarily isolated or excluded from the community" (NIMH, 1977, p. 1).

The target population was the nonhospitalized chronically mentally ill, who were defined as those "adult psychiatric patients whose disabilities are severe and persistent but for whom longer term skilled . . . nursing is inappropriate" (Turner & TenHoor, 1978, p. 319). Although estimates have varied, there is a general consensus that this population may range from 800,000 to 1.5 million in the United States (Ashbaugh, Leaf, Manderscheid, & Eaton, 1983).

The CSS concept was developed from the research that had demonstrated the importance of social support networks in the community adjustment of the mentally ill. It was hoped that an individual's natural supports could be utilized as much as possible but that whenever necessary they would be reinforced by strategic interventions made by representatives of the official service agencies. Where no such supports were in existence, the goal would be to establish a viable network of care within which the individual could gradually develop the confidence and skills needed to function relatively independently in the community.

The philosophy behind the new program was not one that involved sweeping changes or the establishment of new facilities on a large scale. Its major purpose was to build from what was already in existence, combining the best of both the formal and the informal service networks. The goals of the program did not call for any major changes in the pattern of service delivery, neither were any major new facilities to be built. There was, however, an expectation that the states involved would try to foster an ideological commitment to the development of informal support systems at the local level. Reading between the lines written by the program planners makes it clear that the CSP was the first official recognition that the only way to provide long-term community care was to coordinate formal services with the extensive array of services already being provided by friends, neighbors, relatives, and volunteers (C. J. Smith, 1980a).

To launch the program 19 states were awarded demonstration grants to implement the CSS concept. It was hoped that through the development of a few model programs, general guidelines could be established for later use in the areas that were not initially awarded contracts. In comparison to previous federal outlays in the mental health area, the initial investment was modest: $3.5 million in fiscal year 1978, and $5.0 million in 1979, compared to $135 million for Community Mental Health Centers (CMHCs). Unlike its predecessors, this program was not specifically intended to provide any direct client services. A reasonable goal was for the CSP to be a "program of influence, one that could stimulate further changes in the system of care" (Tessler & Goldman, 1982, p. 43). According to the program guidelines, a CSS would need at least ten essential service components (see Table 3.4) More important than the existence of these services, however, was the requirement that the components be integrated into a system of interconnected services that could, in concert, meet the needs of the chronically mentally ill. In other words, the most important long-term goal was system building. To determine the extent to which this had occurred, evaluators would later use some of the social network methodologies discussed earlier in this chapter (Morrissey, 1982).

To ensure that the system of care would function in the best interests of its clients, the states with the demonstration grants had to follow a set of rigid guidelines (Tessler & Goldman, 1982, p. 17):

1. The comprehensive needs of the population at risk must be thoroughly assessed;

Table 3.4. National Institute of Mental Health Principles for Community Support Systems (1980)

1. *Locate CSS clients, reach out to inform them of available services,* and assure their access to needed services and community resources by arranging for transportation, if necessary, or by taking the services to clients.
2. *Help CSS clients meet basic human needs* for food, clothing, shelter, personal safety, general medical and dental care, and assist them to apply for income, medical, housing and/or other benefits that they may need and to which they are entitled.
3. *Provide adequate mental health care,* including (1) diagnostic evaluation; (2) prescription, periodic review, and regulation of psychotropic drugs, as needed; and (3) community-based psychiatric, psychological and/or counseling and treatment services.
4. *Provide 24-hour, quick response crisis assistance,* directed toward enabling both the client and involved family and friends to cope with emergencies, while maintaining the client's status as a functioning community member to the greatest extent possible. This should include round-the-clock telephone service, on-call trained personnel, and options for either short-term or partial hospitalization or temporary supervised community housing arrangements.
5. *Provide comprehensive psychosocial services* that include a continuum of high to low expectation services and environments designed to improve or maintain clients' abilities to function in normal social roles. Some of these services should be available on an indefinite duration basis, and should include but need not be limited to services that:
    a. *Help clients evaluate their strengths and weaknesses* and participate in setting their own goals and planning for appropriate services.
    b. *Train clients in daily and community living skills* such as medication use, diet, exercise, personal hygiene, shopping, cooking, budgeting, housekeeping, use of transportation, and other community resources. Whenever possible, these should be taught in the natural setting.
    c. *Help clients develop social skills, interests, and leisure time activities* to provide a sense of participation and personal worth, including opportunities for age-appropriate, culturally appropriate daytime and evening activities.
    d. *Help clients find and make use of appropriate employment opportunities,* vocational rehabilitation services, or other supported or sheltered work environments. Provision must also be made for people who may not be able to use these opportunities and services, but who need a chance to be useful and a meaningful way to structure their time.
6. *Provide a range of rehabilitative and supportive housing options* for persons not in crisis who need a special living arrangement. The choices should be broad enough to allow each client an opportunity to live in an atmosphere offering the degree of support necessary while also providing incentives and encouragement for clients to assume increasing responsibility for their lives. Some supportive living arrangements must be available on an indefinite duration basis.
7. *Offer backup support, assistance, consultation, and education* to families, friends, landlords, employers, community agencies, and others who come in frequent contact with mentally disabled persons, to maximize benefits and minimize problems associated with the presence of these persons in the community.
8. *Recognize natural support systems,* such as neighborhood networks, churches, community organizations, commerce, and industry, and encourage them to increase opportunities for mentally disabled persons to participate in community life.
9. *Establish grievance procedures and mechanisms to protect client rights,* both inside and outside of mental health or residential facilities.
10. *Facilitate effective use by clients of formal and informal helping systems* by designating a single person or team responsible for helping the client make informed choices about opportunities and services, assuring timely access to needed assistance, providing opportunities and encouragement for self-help activities, and coordinating all services to meet the client's goals.

Source. Tessler and Goldman (1982, pp. 47–49).

2. There should be legislative, administrative, and financial arrangements to guarantee that adequate resources are available to meet those needs;

3. There should be a core services agency in the community that is committed to helping their severely mentally disabled clients to improve the quality of their lives;

4. A case manager must be responsible for staying in touch with the client, regardless of how many different agencies are involved.

The demonstration projects were funded for 4 years, and in 1981 NIMH provided modest grants to 20 previously unfunded states. Unfortunately for the CSP experiment, the steady withdrawal of federal involvement in health and welfare services during this period means that it will probably never expand into a major mental health program, although a number of states have followed the federal "seed" money with their own CSP plans. The lessons learned from the model programs and the publicity associated with the CSS concept has, however, helped to reinforce efforts to provide comprehensive care for the chronically mentally ill, even in states where there was no CSP funding. In other words, "The CSS has become a generic concept; the ten components, in one form or another, have become commonplace in the mental health vocabulary" (Tessler & Goldman, 1982, p. 194). Whether this will continue to be the case with diminished federal funding remains in question. It is a great irony that the CSP, which is a categorical program, was developed at precisely the time when the federal government was trying to turn over the responsibility for such programs to states and localities. The program was in fact an anachronism, but it differs from other mental health programs in that its influence probably exceeded its actual accomplishments.

NOTES

1. The importance of minority status within a particular neighborhood has also been investigated in studies of residential satisfaction. The general consensus is that blacks tend to be less satisfied with their neighborhoods than whites (Campbell *et al.*, 1976), but when the amount of racial integration in the neighborhood is considered as a contextual variable, there are some important variations in the level of satisfaction. The data from a quality of life survey conducted in Oklahoma shows that whites living in integrated neighborhoods are significantly less satisfied with their neighborhoods than whites who live in all or mostly white neighborhoods (C. J. Smith, 1980a). It is interesting to note that although blacks were less satisfied than whites in all four of the domains shown in the illustration, blacks living in integrated neighborhoods appeared to be more satisfied than whites. The survey results suggested that satisfaction for blacks living in mostly black neighborhoods is slightly higher than it is for those in all-black neighborhoods. These observations support the assumption that nonwhite urban resi-

dents tolerate and perhaps even enjoy some diversity in their neighborhoods (Durand & Eckart, 1973).

2. The interactional characteristics of social networks are illustrated by the concept of directionality, which refers to the direction of the interaction between two nodes in the network. Many of the links in a network are undirected or reciprocal. Shulman (1976), for example, found that among 149 individuals who where named as "intimates," only 54 (36.2%) reciprocated by naming the person who had named them. In most cases the probability of reciprocation increases with familiarity, which implies that reciprocity is most likely between people who are close acquaintances. It follows that reciprocity is much greater in friendship networks than in functional groupings like neighborhood associations, or in professional helping networks.

The most commonly investigated structural characteristic of social networks has been density. High density describes a situation in which most of the possible contacts are actually made, while low density implies that very few of the possible contacts are made. The traditional measure of density is the number of actual relationships expressed as a percentage of the total possible relationships within the group. In a study comparing social networks in Hull (England) and Orange Country (California), Irving (1977) investigated the relationships between network density and other measures of social interaction. His results, not unexpectedly, showed that density is significantly related to residential proximity, and specifically that low density networks are typically nonlocalized. Loose networks are also less intense in terms of the frequency and duration of the interactions. Irving's results provide further evidence that closely tied webs of friendship do still exist in urban areas in spite of the widespread view of the city as a highly impersonal place (Fischer, 1982).

3. The importance of an individual's social network in determining both the type of treatment selected and its outcome has also been demonstrated among alcoholics (Strug & Hyman, 1981). Two groups of alcoholics were compared: In one, the individuals had only attended a county detoxication unit, but in the other they were being treated at an inpatient rehabilitation center. The survey data showed that the social networks of individuals in the two groups were significantly different. Those who had decided to go beyond detoxication and seek long-term treatment tended to have larger, denser, and more closely knit networks. They were also more likely to be in frequent contact with network members, and perhaps most importantly, their networks contained members who discouraged drinking. As we shall see in Chapter 6, one of the major hopes expressed for the decriminalization of public drunkenness was that repeat offenders would seek treatment and long-term rehabilitation. The empirical evidence suggests that in most cases public drunks have been unwilling to submit to the "patient role" and put an end to a lifetime of drinking on skid row. Strug and Hyman's observations suggest that the chances of alcoholics choosing treatment over continued rounds of detoxication followed by release depend on their social networks. The question still to be answered, of course, is how some alcoholics come to be embedded in "therapeutic" social networks in the first place. After a lengthy period as a heavy drinker an individual runs a serious risk of cutting him- or herself off socially, until eventually he or she either has no friends left, or all his or her friends are also heavy drinkers. To alter this pattern before it is too late is clearly one route toward prevention, but it is obviously one that is extremely difficult to achieve.

4

The Environmental Context of Public Problems

INTRODUCTION

The 1960s and 1970s witnessed a dramatic growth in awareness of the importance of environmental influences on human behavior. This was an era of advancing technology, expanding populations, crumbling cities, energy shortages, and environmental pollution. These developments helped an initially skeptical public to realize that the environment was no longer just something to use at will without thought for the future (S. Kaplan, 1972a). The new level of concern was expressed in political activism, which was largely responsible for the drafting of laws passed at the local, state, and federal levels—laws that served either to protect the environment or to control human behavior in specific environments.

The new awareness also demonstrated that we knew relatively little about the complex relationships between environments and people. This vacuum encouraged researchers from a number of academic disciplines to begin exploring specific person–environment situations. In such fields as geography, sociology, psychology, architecture, city planning, and forestry, the environment had been an important but easy-to-overlook variable. New subdisciplines emerged in universities to focus on the environmental issue and the new level of interest in human–environmental interactions. New names were found for these areas of study, such as "behavioral geography," "social ecology," "ecological psychology," "architectural psychology," and "environmental psychology" (Mercer, 1975). In a relatively short time an impressive academic infrastructure was created, including textbooks, journals, newsletters, annual reviews, research monographs, symposia, and degree programs (T. R. Lee, 1976). In a 5-year period (1972–1977) one reviewer found that ten new textbooks had been written, six edited readers, 30 "state of the art" monographs, and literally hundreds of journal articles (Stokols, 1978).

Much of the work being fitted into the new corpus of environment and behavior studies was by no means new. Many pioneers who had been scratching along in relative obscurity now found themselves in the warm glow of academic respectability, visibility, and best of all, "relevance." Others who had grown disillusioned with their old disciplines could now jump ship and experience an about-face in their careers. Work in this area began to take on a truly interdisciplinary character (Downs & Stea, 1973; G. T. Moore & Golledge 1976; Spencer & Blades, 1986).

The new field of environment and behavior studies was a "multi-paradigm affair" (Craik, 1976), a respectable way of saying it was an academic hodgepodge. Researchers had entered the field from many different routes, but in spite of the apparent confusion a small number of themes emerged (Craik, 1973). Some people had been arguing that human beings could become emotionally attached to the physical environment. Geographers, for example, had emphasized the peculiarly strong "sense of place" that people develop for their homes, no matter how humble they may be (Relph, 1976; Tuan, 1974). Sociologists had noticed how some people felt lost and genuinely grieved for these old homes when they were lost to urban renewal. Some psychologists and even the occasional psychiatrist had argued that the physical environment had an important role to play in human development (S. Kaplan, 1972a; Searles, 1960). Something this important needed to be studied in earnest, particularly after having been so long neglected.

One of the most interesting questions being asked at the time was how we had allowed our environment to reach a crisis state without any serious plans for the future. This raised the crucial issues of perception and cognition: How did people develop imagery about their environments? This was a question that had long been asked by psychologists, but rarely with the everyday physical environment acting as the stimulus. How do individuals gather, store, and use environmental information? It was fashionable in the 1960s and 1970s to ask how city dwellers were able to tolerate living in such obviously stressful and noxious environments. What were the "human costs" of visual blight, noise pollution, economic stagnation, rampaging crime rates, and cognitive overload (Milgram, 1970)? How did we manage to adapt to such "unnatural" environmental circumstances? And most importantly, what did we have in our minds as solutions for the future (S. Kaplan, 1972b)?

To begin answering such questions many of the new practitioners were developing the skills to help them quantify the vast array of environmental experiences human beings reported. Using and modifying the familiar tools of the testing trades, they started to develop scales to measure environmental attitudes and orientations. Discriminations were possible along a "Person–Thing" scale, and an "Environmental Response Inventory" (McKechnie, 1974) allowed one to construe the dimensions of human responses to the physical world. In countless studies such scales would prove useful in predicting environmentally critical behaviors (e.g., who the activists and who the spoilers are). In addition to the study of environmental personalities (P-Assessment), efforts were made to quantify the psychological or human-oriented characteristics of environments (E-Assessment). It proved possible to characterize residential neighborhoods and other physical settings with a parsimonious and orthogonal set of dimensions (R. Kaplan, 1977; C. J. Smith, 1976) and even to measure the psychological "atmosphere" of such milieux as hospital wards, universities, classrooms, and prisons (Moos, 1973). By combining their P- and E-Assessment tools, researchers could now begin to tackle the mysteries of person–environment interactions in terms of fit and "congruence," in an attempt to determine how well specific environments cater to individual needs.

Researchers in numerous disciplines had already demonstrated the influence of space on human behavior, focusing on the interrelated issues of personal space, territoriality, and crowding (Altman, 1975). A popular issue was the study of high-density locations and the impact of crowding on human health and welfare (see Chapter 2). Many of these studies were conducted at the microlevel (rooms and buildings), but others took the work out into the field to inspect neighborhoods and everyday "behavior settings" (Barker, 1968).

One of the major intellectual contributions to the growth of these new subdisciplines was the knowledge that environmental factors had been implicated in the etiology and distribution of pathological human behavior. At the macrolevel this had been demonstrated by the Chicago school of social ecologists and their followers, who had correlated urban characteristics with virtually all forms of public problems (Faris & Dunham, 1939; Reckless, 1933; C. R. Shaw & McKay, 1969). At the microlevel it had been possible to identify even more explicit links between physical features and adverse behavioral outcomes, such as in the studies conducted in mental hospitals (Ittelson, Rivlin, & Proshansky, 1970) and other physical spaces such as schools and libraries (Sommer, 1969). In response to such studies it seemed more than reasonable to ask how the knowledge being generated could be used to produce more positive outcomes:

> If environments can have negative effects like these, then surely, if we could understand the processes involved, we could create environments that had positive effects. The underlying assumption is that the physical form of the enclosure itself can be an influential factor in promoting behavior changes and human growth in the widest possible sense. (Mercer, 1975, p. 17)

The two questions asked most frequently by the new environment and behavior practitioners were, firstly, what the everyday physical environment does to people and secondly, what people do to the everyday physical environment. To these Craik (1976) added an obvious third question, one that probably explains why the new fields of study were so often grouped under the heading of "environmental psychology." This question, concerning how people comprehend the everyday physical environment, had rarely been asked. Although some psychologists thought they could identify clusters of interpersonal interactions, they were strangely quiet when asked whether people had similarly enduring orientations to buildings, neighborhoods, and cities. If they did, then how were such orientations constructed? Did they differ from one group to another? And most importantly, how could they be altered to help the individual cope with drastic environmental changes like urban renewal and migration?

When they spoke of the environment, the new practitioners were speaking not just about the physical environment that was "natural" or "built." In almost all cases other people were present in the environments being studied, and their presence complicated the transactions between the individuals and their immediate environment. Perhaps they were not the "right" people or there were too many or too few of them, or their characteristics were undesirable. To the outsider, and to the skeptic, this new area of study appeared to have no boundaries. If all environments were environments, nothing could be excluded from legitimate study. By multiplying all the possible environments by all the possible human behaviors and attitudes, we would have an almost infinite set of possible areas for study. As early as 1973, Craik was able to identify 12 broad categories of research in the field: environmental assessment; environmental perception; cognitive representation of the environment; personality and the environment; environmental decision making; public attitudes to the environment; the quality of the sensory environment; ecological psychology and behavior settings; human spatial behavior; behavioral effects of density; behavioral factors in residential and institutional environments; and outdoor recreation and responses to the landscape.

In a review of the field 5 years later, Stokols (1978) decided that instead of producing an even longer list, with major categories and subcategories, a simple two-by-two classification could be used (Figure 4.1). By drawing somewhat artificial boundaries, Stokols classified environment and behavior studies

TYPE OF TRANSACTION

	Cognitive	Behavioral	
PHASE OF TRANSACTION	INTERPRETIVE Cognitive representation of neighborhoods Neighborhoods and personality development	OPERATIVE Experimental studies Spatial behavioral studies Proxemics	Active
	EVALUATIVE Neighborhood satisfaction and quality of life estimation Environmental attitudes and awareness	RESPONSIVE Impact of physical/ecological characteristics on behavior and outwardly manifested responses	Reactive

Figure 4.1. Transactions between the individual and the environment.
Source. Smith (1980a, p. 378).

along two major dimensions: (1) the phase of the transaction, which could be either active (the person influences the environment) or reactive (the person is influenced by the environment); and (2) the form of the transaction, which could be either cognitive or behavioral. This produces four general modes of human–environmental transactions:

1. Interpretive: cognitive representations of the environment;
2. Evaluative: cognitive reactions to the environment;
3. Operative: active behaviors within the environment;
4. Responsive: reactive behaviors that are the outcome of environmental influences.

As we shall see in this chapter, there are numerous examples of research studies in which public problems have been examined from the environment and behavior perspective (Russell & Ward, 1982). In what follows we shall sample from this literature in two areas that are particularly appropriate to the study of public problems: (1) mental health and "quality of life" studies, and (2) the study of drinking and problem drinking.

WELL-BEING AND MENTAL HEALTH:
THE RESIDENTIAL DIMENSION

In recent years numerous studies of satisfaction with neighborhood and community life have been conducted, and several extensive reviews of this literature have been written (Fischer, 1975; Marans & Rodgers, 1975). Although it is debatable whether environmental satisfaction is a useful indicator of overall mental health, the evidence indicates that residential satisfaction can contribute significantly to an individual's overall life satisfaction and general well-being (Angrist, 1974; C. J. Smith, 1976).

Questions about residence, neighborhood, and community are included in most quality of life studies. One of the most consistent results from such studies is that place satisfaction is age dependent; the physical environment appears to be more important to older residents than to younger residents (Golant, 1984). Subjective evaluations of housing and neighborhood characteristics also appear to be inconsistent with supposedly objective evaluations of the same characteristics (Struyk & Soldo, 1980). Many older persons report that they are reasonably satisfied living in places that are judged to be threatening to their physical and mental health (Lawton, 1978). Similarly, old persons living in places considered to be physically similar report wide variations in their levels of satisfaction. It appears that "The dwelling assessments of old people may be as much a product of their perceived life situations as it is a product of a dwelling's observable, objective conditions" (Golant, 1982, p. 132). To investigate the relationship between perceptions and residential conditions among the elderly, Golant conducted a household survey among 400 persons over 60 years of age in Evanston, Illinois. The results of the survey allowed Golant to generate some conclusions:

1. Being unhappy with one's life in general may produce dissatisfaction with dwellings that by objective standards are viewed as satisfactory. (In this sense overall life satisfaction can be thought of as an independent variable rather than a dependent variable; it is not necessarily a result of residential satisfaction, but a contributor to it);
2. Individuals who are more active and more favorably inclined toward novel and stimulating environments are less satisfied with their dwellings, perhaps because the home is not their sole source of satisfaction;
3. Individuals who have lived longer in the same place and who own their homes are more satisfied, presumably because they have a stronger feeling of attachment to their residence.

These observations helped Golant (1982) to conclude that assessments of the living environment are multifaceted. They occur because older persons

> create, select, and maintain environments that have physical and social properties consistent with their own diverse thoughts, motives, and behaviors. Environments thereby become instilled with qualities that are consistent with the characteristics of their inhabitants. Viewed in this way, the dwelling becomes an inseparable part of the individual's total life situation. (p. 122)

Characteristics of the physical environment at the neighborhood level also appear to contribute to an individual's mental health and life satisfaction. Most researchers agree that the physical environment can best be interpreted as having a facilitative role: It allows certain outcomes to take place, but it does not initiate them or "cause" them to happen. It is also generally accepted that physical variables become more significant in extreme situations, as is the case during periods of great physical upheaval that require relocation and the disruption of existing social networks (eg., urban renewal, highway construction). Under such extreme conditions individuals may for a time be unusually susceptible to environmental circumstances.

The effect of physical factors in the residential environment should be studied in conjunction with social and psychological factors. It appears that such variables interact with each other in two major ways: (1) the effect of physical variables may be different for some subgroups of the population, particularly those such as the elderly who have specific needs and desires; and (2) the effect of a particular physical variable is contingent on how the individual responds to it, both cognitively and behaviorally. To explore these interactions, Bohland and Davis (1978) tested a model of neighborhood satisfaction, using data collected from 900 urban families in Oklahoma. The model assumed that: (1) satisfaction with one's neighborhood is a summary response in which a variety of different attributes (physical and social) are perceived, evaluated, and compared with expectations; (2) a lack of fit or dissatisfaction occurs when the combined set of neighborhood characteristics are perceived to fall short of the individual's needs, aspirations, or expectations; (3) individual circumstances, and particularly life-cycle differences, will result in different combinations of both perceptions and evaluations. The model was able to explain slightly more than one third of the variance in satisfaction, with the most significant predictors being "perceived neighborliness" and "perceived condition" of the neighborhood. (The other two exogenous dimensions in the model were "perceived safety" and "perceived convenience" of the neighborhood.)

Somewhat surprisingly, the perceived safety of the neighborhood was not significantly related to overall residential satisfaction among the elderly respondents in the survey. Although there has been a lot written about the fear of crime among the elderly (A. H. Patterson, 1978; Skogan & Maxfield, 1981); some of the available evidence supports the conclusion reached by Bohland and Davis (1978). Many elderly persons live in central city areas where crime rates are high, but in general, people over the age of 65 do not appear to be that much more concerned about being the victims of crime than other age groups. The data in Table 4.1 illustrate that the among a nationwide sample, the elderly were actually slightly less concerned about vandalism, burglary, and being the victims of serious crimes than were the younger respondents (E. J. Brown, Flanagan, & McCleod, 1984). This should not be interpreted as a sign that older people are not worried about crime, just that they may not be much more worried about it than any other group (Conklin, 1976).

The fear of crime issue has also been considered as a major determinant of satisfaction at the community level. In a study in Detroit, Kasl and Harburg (1975) investigated the effect of perceptions and evaluations of the residential environment on well-being and mental health measures. Four census tracts were selected for study, two with predominantly black and two with predominantly white populations. Among each pair one was assessed as a "high stress" area

Table 4.1. Respondents Worrying About Being the Victim of a Crime By Age and Type of Crime—1982 (Percentages)

Age Group	Property Vandalism	Burglary	Street Robbery	Street Injury	Injured at Home	Murder	Chances of Being Victim of a Violent Crime			
							Very Likely	Somewhat Likely	Somewhat Unlikely	Very Unlikely
18–24	59	50	31	30	33	28	6	31	40	22
25–39	45	44	30	26	29	21	4	31	38	25
40–49	42	44	28	27	28	20	6	28	35	30
50–64	44	47	33	31	32	19	6	23	32	35
65+	38	43	36	33	35	20	6	16	27	43

Source. Adapted from Brown, Flanagan, & McCleod (Eds.). (1984, pp. 200–202).

Table 4.2. Perceptions of the Neighborhood Environment, by Sex, Race, and Area "Stress" Level (Detroit)

Group Means (Z scores)

	Men				Women			
	Black		White		Black		White	
	High Stress	Low Stress	High Stress	Low Stress	High Stress	Low Stress	High Stress	Low Stress
1. *Danger from Crime* (The sum of 5 items on perceptions of crime prevalence in the area)	.87	−.34	−.02	−.76	1.02	−.27	.13	−.62
2. *Perceived Lack of Safety* ("Thinking about the neighborhood you live in, how safe would you say it is?")	.88	−.31	.05	−.73	.84	−.29	.21	−.64
3. *Poor Facilities* (Evaluation of schools, entertainment facilities, and readiness of the city to improve the area)	.71	−.16	.06	−.44	.51	−.26	.00	−.41
4. *Dislike for Neighborhood* ("On the whole these days, how do you feel about living in this neighborhood?")	.89	−.42	.14	−.57	.94	−.50	.14	−.57
5. *Dissatisfaction with Dwelling* ("In general how satisfied or dissatisfied are you with your house/apartment as a place to live?")	.63	−.40	.09	−.24	.52	−.48	.13	−.20
6. *Crowded Dwelling* (Ratio of persons in household to rooms in dwelling)	.25	−.68	.31	.50	.21	−.79	−.02	.19
7. *Desire to Move* ("Right now, if you had your way about it, how much would you want to move to a different neighborhood?")	.76	−.39	.10	−.42	.76	−.49	.14	−.43

Source. Adapted from Kasl and Harburg (1975, p. 274).

(with low socioeconomic indicators, high rates of marital and residential instability, and high rates of crime) and the other was assessed as a "low stress" area. Residents of the high stress area evaluated their communities negatively (Table 4.2). This was the case regardless of the sex and race of the respondents, although the perceptions of blacks living in high stress areas were the most negative. In spite of these differences in perception, indicators of well-being and mental health among the survey respondents showed few significant differences between the high and low stress areas, and those that did exist were primarily among the women respondents (on "unhappiness" and "marital dissatisfaction" measures). Correlations of the neighborhood perception scores with various indicators of well-being demonstrated that variations in neighborhood stress and perceptions of neighborhoods are only weakly related to well-being (Table 4.3).

As the data in Table 4.3 illustrates, the correlations were generally highest for white men living in high stress neighborhoods, which is somewhat contrary to expectations. Kasl and Harburg note that their results should be interpreted cautiously, but they make some tentative conclusions about the relationships between environmental variables and measures of mental health:

Table 4.3. Correlations of Indicators of Mental Health and Well-Being with Perceptions of the Residential Environment, by Sex, Race, and Area 'Stress' Level (Detroit)

	Men				Women			
	Black		White		Black		White	
	High Stress	Low Stress	High Stress	Low Stress	High Stress	Low Stress	High Stress	Low Stress
	Correlations with Fear of Crime							
SMHI[a]	.09	.04	.24	.15	.21	−.03	.15	.11
Unhappiness	.04	.14	.27	.03	.14	−.04	.05	.08
Low Self-Esteem	.13	.05	.34	.11	.20	−.09	−.01	.01
Marital Dissatisfaction	.02	.08	.27	.04	.21	.12	.13	.09
	Correlations with Dislike of Neighborhood							
SMHI	.05	.16	.14	−.02	.08	.02	.10	.02
Unhappiness	.21	.34	.46	.20	.16	.28	−.04	.21
Low Self-Esteem	.04	.10	.39	.16	.06	.20	.12	.30
Marital Dissatisfaction	−.02	.23	.41	.17	.12	.21	−.04	.22
	Correlations with Dissatisfaction with Dwelling							
SMHI	−.10	.21	.09	.06	−.08	.08	.07	−.08
Unhappiness	.28	.28	.36	.21	.19	.42	.09	.10
Low Self-Esteem	.19	.19	.29	.24	.26	.42	.08	.18
Marital Dissatisfaction	.05	.27	.22	.27	.15	.37	.07	.13
	Correlations with Desire to Move							
SMHI	−.10	.09	.08	.04	.05	.08	.18	.06
Unhappiness	.30	.35	.29	.19	.10	.23	−.04	.22
Low Self-Esteem	.08	.00	.25	.06	−.13	.17	−.03	.25
Marital Dissatisfaction	.07	.20	.29	.22	.16	.27	−.03	.22

[a] Summary Mental Health Index
Source. Adapted from Kasl and Harburg (1975, p. 277).

1. Fear of crime is associated with poorer mental health among white men and black women living in high stress neighborhoods;
2. Dislike of the neighborhood and a desire to move are associated with avowed unhappiness, low self-esteem, and marital dissatisfaction among high stress men and with unhappiness for most of the other groups;
3. Dissatisfaction with one's dwelling is associated with unhappiness, low self-esteem, and marital dissatisfaction for most of the groups.

In addition to the studies of residential, neighborhood, and community satisfaction in cities, a number of researchers have assessed the role of city living in an individual's overall quality of life. This has been attempted by the use of two sets of indicators, objective and subjective (D. M. Smith, 1977). In the objective studies attempts are made to measure some of the generally agreed-upon components of the "good life" in cities, using official sources of data such as the census and agency statistics on the prevalence of public problems. In a study of 109 Standard Metropolitan Statistical Areas (SMSAs) larger than 250,000, D. M. Smith (1973) collected data on 31 indicator variables in five categories: material living standards, welfare, health, education, and social disorder (crime). The data were collapsed into a general index of social well-being, one that presumably categorizes cities according to their overall "liveability." When the results were mapped a clear regional pattern emerged, with cities in the West and the Northeast having positive scores on the index, and cities in the South and Southwest having negative scores. Smith's research also identified two other dimensions, measuring affluence and crime, which again varied by region. One of the most interesting observations Smith made from his results is that cities in the west tended to score highly on both the affluence and the crime indices. He suggests that the affluence is:

> achieved at the price of greater tensions than in cities in most other parts of the country and higher incidence of physical and mental stress-induced illness. Poor performance on the pathology dimension (crime) also reflects the instability of a population with many immigrants, some of whom are Chicanos and Blacks, subject to the usual abuses and deprivations of racial minorities. (p. 119)

Perhaps stepping completely beyond the bounds of his data, Smith goes on to conclude that

> The perpetuation of something of the hustling, anxiety, and violence of the frontier days in this region of ethnic and socio-economic heterogeneity thus produces distinctive cities. With its extremes of conspicuous material affluence and untreated social degradation the urban West may still be considered "wild." (p. 119)

As farfetched as this conclusion sounds, there is some support for the suggestion that stress at the community level is higher in western states than elsewhere in the country. Linsky, Straus, and Colby (1985) calculated a stress index using data collected at the state level. To construct the index they con-

Table 4.4. State Stress Index (SSI) Scores, by Region

Census Regions	SSI Score	Ranking by Region
Pacific	71	1
Oregon	78	
Washington	80	
California	76	
Hawaii	42	
Alaska	87	
East South Central	69	2
Tennessee	71	
Kentucky	52	
Alabama	78	
Mississippi	74	
Mountain	57	3
Idaho	57	
Montana	33	
Utah	26	
Nevada	104	
Arizona	74	
New Mexico	47	
Colorado	65	
Wyoming	35	
South Atlantic	56	4
Florida	61	
Georgia	82	
S. Carolina	61	
N. Carolina	48	
Virginia	54	
Maryland	50	
Delaware	50	

(continued)

sidered the items used in the scales to measure stressful life events at the individual level (see, e.g., Rabkin & Struening, 1976). At the aggregate level Linksy's group collected data on variables that as far as possible matched the individual items: the prevalence of business failures, unemployment claims, workers involved in strikes, bankruptcy cases, mortgage foreclosures, divorces, abortions, illegitimate births, infant deaths, fetal deaths, families receiving disaster assistance, mobility rates, new house building activity, welfare recipients, and high school dropouts. The variables were combined into an overall stress score that ranged from 104 (Nevada), to 16 (Nebraska), and as Table 4.4 shows, states in the Pacific region (California, Oregon, Washington, and Alaska) had the highest overall mean stress levels, followed by states in the southern regions. As provocative as these results appear to be, it is important to remember the significant problems associated with making any inferences about indi-

Table 4.4. (continued)

W. Virginia	44	
West South Central	52	5
Texas	47	
Oklahoma	62	
Louisiana	51	
Arkansas	47	
Middle Atlantic	51	6
New Jersey	49	
Pennsylvania	46	
New York	59	
East North Central	46	7
Wisconsin	20	
Michigan	59	
Illinois	59	
Indiana	40	
Ohio	51	
New England	34	8
Maine	35	
New Hampshire	26	
Vermont	34	
Massachusetts	34	
Connecticut	35	
Rhode Island	37	
West North Central	26	9
N. Dakota	19	
S. Dakota	17	
Nebraska	16	
Kansas	42	
Missouri	40	
Iowa	17	
Minnesota	28	

Source. Adapted from Linsky *et al.* (1985, p. 76).

vidual behavior using data collected at the aggregate level. In addition, there is some evidence that the sort of community-level stresses identified by Smith and by Linsky's team are not locationally unique, but are the result of more general forces such as population growth or economic decline (C. J. Smith & Hanham, 1984)

Some cities appear to provide better living environments than others (Cutter, 1985), although it is probably more accurate to say that some cities have a better mix of factors considered by the researchers to be desirable, because the residents of the cities in question are rarely asked for their opinions. On the other hand, there is no consistent evidence from the objective indicators that large cities are significantly worse as places in which to live than smaller cities. In Canada, for example, Ley (1983) has reported that only 9 of the 32 indicators he investigated were significantly correlated with city size, and some of these were variables probably unrelated to quality of life concerns, such as the percent of the population living in their province of birth and the percent Canadian born.

Correlations with rates of growth also suggested that educational achievements were lower in the cities growing most rapidly, and housing shortages were more likely. On the other hand larger cities are obviously places where incomes are highest and where occupational opportunities are greatest. None of the social pathology variables (crime rates, illegitimate births, etc.) was correlated significantly with either city size or growth rates. This is a sharp contrast with United States cities, which generally have far higher rates of crime (Ley, 1983).

The subjective studies of quality of life and social well-being make use of survey data collected from individual households. The respondents are asked how satisfied they are with life in general, and with various "domains" of their lives. In one such study conducted in Oklahoma, C. J. Smith (1980a) showed that there was no clear linear relationship between city size and any of the satisfaction measures, in fact the worst assessments tended to be from the residents of medium-sized towns. At the national level the survey data suggest that satisfaction appears to be related to community size, but on most of the domains the maximum level of satisfaction is in the suburbs and the small towns, rather than in the rural areas (Campbell, Converse, & Rodgers, 1976). It is important to note that city size may be only a surrogate for the city characteristics that are causally related to individual satisfaction levels. As Campbell and his colleagues found, most of the variance in levels of satisfaction can be accounted for by community attributes such as the quality of the public schools, the climate, road conditions, local taxes, parks and playgrounds, and the level of police provision. When the effect of these variables was controlled, the influence of community size all but disappeared. Again it appears that ecological factors play at most a secondary role in the development of human well-being.

THE BEHAVIORAL ECOLOGY OF DRINKING

In the last 2 decades a sizeable literature has documented the influence of social, cultural, and environmental factors on the use and abuse of alcohol (Harford & Gaines, 1981; C. J. Smith & Hanham, 1982). There are several possible explanations for this trend. One is the empirical evidence generated to refute or at least question the major assumptions of the medical model of alcohol abuse. For many of the individuals who experience problems as a result of excessive drinking but who are not alcoholics, there are no satisfactory psychological or medical predictors of their behavior. It seemed reasonable, therefore, to explore the social, demographic, and cultural factors associated with their drinking. This began with the large epidemiological surveys of drinking habits in the 1960s and 1970s (Cahalan, 1970; Cahalan, Cisin, & Crossley, 1969; W. B. Clark & Midanik, 1982). The major question asked in these studies was not why people drank heavily, but where they drank, with whom, under what circumstances, and with what consequences.

Another impetus to the environmental study of drinking was the desire to generate information that could be useful in shaping public policy (Gerstein, 1984; M. H. Moore & Gerstein, 1981). Although this certainly did not mean that research on the individual antecedents of drinking would become less important, it did encourage the development of social science studies of drinking (Levine, 1984). The goal of these studies was to generate information that could be used to build up a body of prevention strategies. As Gerstein (1984) has observed, this effort can be subdivided into three specific areas: (1) the availability of alcohol—how easy and convenient it is for people to gain access to alcohol; (2) what can be done to "teach" people how to drink safely and responsibly; and (3) whether it is possible to make the environment safer for those who are drunk, (eg., whether people can get home easily after drinking in public places).

The epidemiological studies demonstrated that there is a social geography of drinking, and to understand the outcome of a drinking event, it is important to consider where and under what circumstances it occurred. One of the major proponents of this view has provided some illustrations:

> drinking . . . settings organize groups of people into groups of drinkers, creating social occasions predicated on the use of alcohol. Bars in particular create social conditions in which the consumption of alcohol underlies all contacts between people. Homes, through the simple device of setting out bottles, putting up decorations, and playing music, are made to accomplish the same purpose for parties. Offices are made to do the same for celebrating the signing of the big contract. . . . At the community level, the mix of "watering holes" in relation to other places of entertainment, recreation, and civic activity provides tangible evidence of the extent to which the town organizes its life around drinking. (Wittman, 1983, p. 135)

To put these environmental influences into perspective, it is useful to outline a model of drinking behavior (Figure 4.2). As suggested in the illustration, the groups of factors likely to influence drinking behaviors are interrelated, and no attempt is made here to identify the most significant factors. In addition to a range of individual influences, the model shows that drinking practices are shaped by interpersonal variables, spatial context variables, and situational variables.

Interpersonal influence on drinking. An important influence on drinking habits and attitudes toward drinking derives from an individual's primary and secondary group members. This includes the family of birth as the primary agent of socialization, which influences drinking behavior both directly (by introducing the individual to drinking and defining what is and what is not

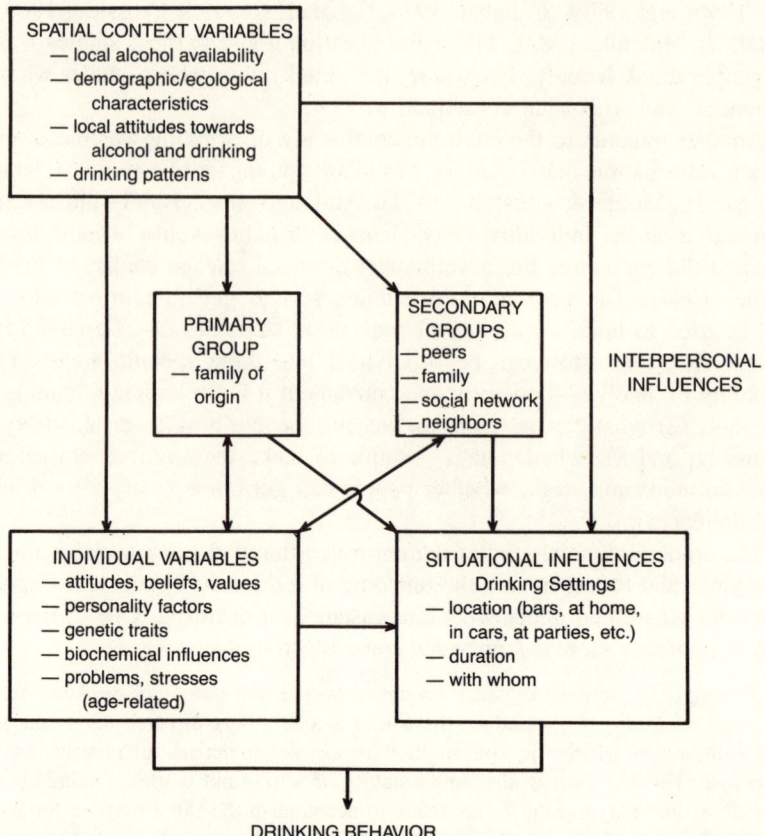

Figure 4.2. A model of drinking behavior: Interpersonal variables, spatial context variables, and situational variables.

acceptable drinking behavior) and indirectly, through parental modeling of their own alcohol use and through communication about acceptable behavior in general (Zucker, 1979). The secondary groups that have an effect on individual drinking behaviors include friends and other significant social network members (Harford & Spiegler, 1982).

Situational influences on drinking. Until recently the consideration of situational influences such as where, with whom, and for how long a person drinks, were considered to be epiphenomenal to the outcome of drinking. However, as Wittman (1983) has observed, there is now considerable evidence that drinking settings not only contain, but also help to shape and give meaning to drinking occasions, as well as determining an individual's choices about whether to approach or avoid settings in which alcohol is present (Harford, 1979, 1984; Braucht, 1982).

Spatial Context Variables. It has been established by using both survey data and mortality rates from liver cirrhosis, that a clear link exists between the per capita consumption of alcohol in a population and the prevalence of heavy drinking (Popham, Schmidt, & deLint, 1975). Interest in this issue has generated a number of studies examining the relationship between average consumption levels and the environmental variables that influence alcohol availability (Rabow & Watts, 1983). Most of these studies have been focused at the macrolevel, with relatively little emphasis on the specific relationship between local availability factors and individual decisions about where, what, when, and how much to drink. The relationship between availability and consumption patterns is also presumably mediated by the influence of local attitudes. Thus in areas where alcohol is more easily available, we would expect the residents to adopt a more favorable stance toward drinking.

The importance of this was stressed by the results of the nationwide surveys of drinking practices. One of the significant antecedents of heavy and problem drinking was shown to be environmental support for heavy drinking within an individual's social and physical milieu (Cahalan *et al.,* 1969). Using the survey data, Cahalan and Room (1974) showed that an individual's opinions about drinking and his or her subsequent drinking behaviors are influenced both by the extent to which drinking occurs within the neighborhood and by local attitudes toward alcohol.

Situational Influences on Drinking and Drinking Outcomes

The situations in which drinking occurs can be thought of as "behavior settings" (Harford, 1979). This is a term first used by ecological psychologist Roger Barker to describe the settings in which a specific type of behavior is observed (Barker, 1968). The advantage of the behavior setting approach is that it allows the researcher to focus on both the physical characteristics of the environment and the social/behavioral characteristics at the same time. As one of Barker's followers has observed, a behavior setting has the following characteristics:

> a) one or more regularly occurring or standing patterns of behavior (for example, lecturing, listening in an academic class), b) behavior patterns which are compatible with and closely related to the physical characteristics of the place in which the behaviors occur (for example, chairs in a classroom all face the front, the blackboard used by the lecturer is in a location readily visible from the chairs), and c) temporal and physical boundaries (for example, class begins at 8:00 and ends at 8:50; it occurs within an area bounded by four walls; the behaviors in the class are different from those in the hall, just outside the boundaries). (Wicker, 1972, p. 269)

By observing what takes place in numerous different behavior settings, the ecological psychologists have concluded that "both overt behaviors and psychological states are affected as socio-physical environments change. A corollary to this conclusion is that most of the time, most people behave in ways that are compatible with or adaptive to their immediate socio-physical environments'' (Wicker, 1972, p. 269).

The implication of this is that predictable patterns of behavior can be observed within the boundaries of a given behavior setting. The limits of what is acceptable in a setting will be established by the individuals involved and by the physical features of the setting. When people move from one setting to another, or when the physical characteristics of a setting change, the observed behavior will also change.

Much of this work has been written off as trivial and atheoretical (Downs, 1981), but studies conducted in this genre have generated some illuminating descriptions of drinking behavior. It is evident that the tempo of drinking, the amount consumed, and perhaps even the effects of the alcohol vary from one setting to another (Harford, 1979). Drinking in a bar is clearly a different phenomenon than drinking at home or at a party, but there is probably as much variation within settings in the same category as there is between them. There are, for example, many different types of bars, and they vary by location, by physical characteristics, and in their clientele (Cavan, 1966; Cutler & Storm, 1975; Gusfield, 1981). It is reasonable to expect that some of these differences will result in different types of drinking and drunken comportment. In a study of 185 bars in Vancouver, Graham, La Rocque, Yefman, Ross, and Guistra (1980) identified numerous situational variables, both social and physical, that were correlated positively and negatively with observed aggressiveness (Table 4.5). As a result they were able to describe a typically aggressive bar in the following way:

> [it] . . . tends to be a haven for those who are not often accepted elsewhere. There are few limits on acceptable behavior and little pressure for patrons to behave ''normally.'' This accepting attitude seems to be combined with suspicion and hostility. . . . Most of the barworkers are not friendly . . . [and] the bar tends to be physically unattractive with a shabby, run-down decor, tables close together in rows and poor ventilation. (Graham *et al.*, 1980, p. 290)

Opponents of a strictly deterministic viewpoint might argue that the clientele of the bar and its general location in the city would be better predictors of its overall ''aggressiveness,'' but these results confirmed some of Cavan's (1966) observations about the physical arrangements inside bars. By influencing the amount of mobility and social interaction between the patrons, the layout of a bar can have a significant influence on the level of drunkenness and aggression that occurs.

Out of necessity much of this work has been conducted by observing specific settings in which drinking occurs (Cavan, 1966; Sommer, 1965). In recent years these studies have been complemented by survey research data, where the respondents were asked about their drinking settings (W. B. Clark, 1981;

Table 4.5. Variables Correlated Significantly with Aggressive Behavior in Vancouver Bars[a]

Situation Variables	Physical Aggression[b]	Nonphysical Aggression
Social		
Sobriety of patrons (%)	−.36	−.32
Drunkenness of patrons (%)	.44	.28
White patrons (%)	−.37	−.36
Indian patrons (%)	.41	.39
Unkempt patrons (%)	.19	.34
High turnover rate	−.21	−.16
Lots of table hopping	.31	.21
Physical		
Ventilation	−.40	−.40
Decor	−.24	−.26
Noise level	.28	.09
Dancing	.32	.12
Pool playing	.17	.19
Location (downtown vs. suburban)	.13	.19
Cleanliness	.40	.40
Tables in rows	.27	.20
Tables spaced, lounge style	−.19	−.19

[a]Significance level was $r = .19$ ($p < .0005$, $N = 303$).
[b]Physical aggression was defined as physical violence (punching, kicking); aggressive physical contact (grabbing, pushing); and physical incidents such as threats and challenges to fight where no contact occurred.
Source. Adapted from Graham *et al.* (1980, p. 286).

Fisher, 1981). Of particular concern has been the situational influences on adolescent drinking patterns (Harford, 1979, 1984; Harford & Spiegler, 1982; Zucker, 1979). The focus of this research has been on the situations in which teenage drinking occurs: Where does the drinking take place? Who is involved? When does it take place? How long does it last? As the ecological psychologists have noted, most of these factors are interrelated. Obviously a teenager is more likely to be with his or her peers when drinking occurs at teen parties or in bars, in comparison to when it occurs at home.

The data that have been collected in nationwide surveys of adolescent drinking behavior (Rachal, Maisto, Guess, & Hubbard, 1982) have shown that the settings in which drinking occurs appear to be related to how much alcohol is consumed and to its consequences (frequency of drunkenness). Obviously it is difficult to determine from this data whether such relationships are causal. It is possible, for example, that teenagers who drink more heavily and are more likely to get drunk may be drawn to specific settings to do their drinking (Skog, 1981).

From the survey data, Harford and Spiegler (1982) have investigated drinking levels among teenagers and cross-tabulated the data with the frequency of drinking in three different settings: unsupervised teen parties; at home on special occasions; and parties supervised by adults. The data show that teenagers (both boys and girls) who drink frequently and heavily do the majority of their drinking at parties where adults are not present (Table 4.6). Among the frequent/heavy drinkers only 2% never drink at unsupervised parties, while 75% drink "most of the time" at such parties. In comparison, 19% of this group never drink at adult parties and 17% never drink at home; and only 25% and 27% said they drink most of the time in these supervised settings. Although these results are hardly suprising, it is important to note that even the teenagers who drink less and less frequently tend to do most of their drinking at unsupervised parties. Among the infrequent drinkers, 21% drink most of the time at teen parties, as opposed to 4% and 15% in the supervised settings. Among the intermittent drinkers the difference is even more marked: 45% drink most of the time at teen parties, compared to 8% and 19% in the other settings.

The survey data also shows that where teenagers do most of their drinking is related to the frequency with which they get drunk. Among the boys who say they get drunk at least once a week, 75% drink most of the time at teen-only parties, but among those who were never drunk in the previous year, 39% said they never drank at teen parties. The implication here is that without the modifying influence of parental or adult supervision, teenage drinkers are more likely to be frequently drunk. To take the analysis one step further, Harford and Spiegler disaggregated the responses into four mutually exclusive groups:

Table 4.6. The Distribution of Drinking Context Frequency for High School Boys, by Drinking Frequency and Quantity of Overall Drinking

	Rare			Intermittent			Frequent		
Drinking Location	Light	Medium	Heavy	Light	Medium	Heavy	Light	Medium	Heavy
Unsupervised Teen Parties									
Never	44	18	6	34	8	3	46	8	2
Most of the time	4	21	45	8	45	66	17	55	75
Adult Parties									
Never	62	45	50	58	37	38	39	27	19
Most of the time	2	4	8	3	8	14	8	15	25
At Home									
Never	22	29	36	15	24	23	4	16	17
Most of the time	18	15	13	21	19	18	42	35	27
N	121	277	145	38	176	189	24	238	464

Rare drinking is defined as once a month at most; intermittent = three to four times a month; and frequent = at least once a week.

Heavy drinking is defined as more than 2.7 ounces of ethanol per drinking occasion (about 5 or more drinks); medium = .68 − 2.7 ounces; and light = less than .68 ounces (about one drink or less).

Source. Adapted from Harford and Spiegler (1982, p. 174).

(1) those who drink only at home; (2) those who drink at adult parties but not at home; (3) those who drink at teen parties but not at home; and (4) those who drink at teen parties and at home. The results showed that 72% of the boys and 76% of the girls in the first group said they were never drunk in the year before the survey. Teenagers who drink in both supervised and unsupervised settings (the fourth group) reported the highest frequency of drunkenness (41% of the boys and 31% of the girls in this group reported being drunk at least once a month). The implication that unsupervised settings are related to heavier and more frequent drinking and to higher levels of drunkenness needs to be explored further with observational studies. The survey data have provided an important focus for future research, but the next phase requires a much more finely grained analysis of unsupervised teenage drinking settings.

An intriguing research possibility is the indication that situational influences on drinking and problem drinking are age dependent. Using survey data collected in Boston, Harford (1979) found some significant differences in the drinking settings of 18- to 25-year-olds, as opposed to people in their 60s and older. Older persons drink in far fewer contexts than younger ones; they drink mostly in private (at home) and for shorter periods of time. Only 6% of the 18- to 25-year-olds drink on weekdays in private, and with two or fewer persons present, as opposed to 35% of the older drinkers.

If we pursue this line of thought, it is reasonable to suggest that in addition to the changes in drinking settings, the mix of variables influencing drinking and problem drinking will also vary by age. Adolescents, for example, are more likely than their elders to respond to "external" (environmental) influences than older drinkers (Harford, 1979). Adolescent drinking practices may be strongly determined by peer pressure and models for drinking established by peers, but in comparison, adult and elderly drinking patterns may be much more the result of "internal" needs or stresses. Thus we would expect that for different age groups some variables would play a crucial role, but others would be inconsequential. Some of the possibilities are illustrated in Figure 4.3.

The Social Geography of Drinking

In addition to the specific settings in which drinking occurs, a number of other environmental factors have a significant influence on drinking behavior. The investigation of geographical variations in these factors has produced some interesting and useful results. In the case of adolescents Harford (1984) and Harford and Spiegler (1982) have shown that drinking behavior varies significantly by region and by community size (urban vs. rural). The major underlying dimension here is not the geographical characteristics of different localities, but the way those characteristics combine to make alcohol more or less easily available and accessible to drinkers.

Many researchers, policy makers, and care providers believe that manip-

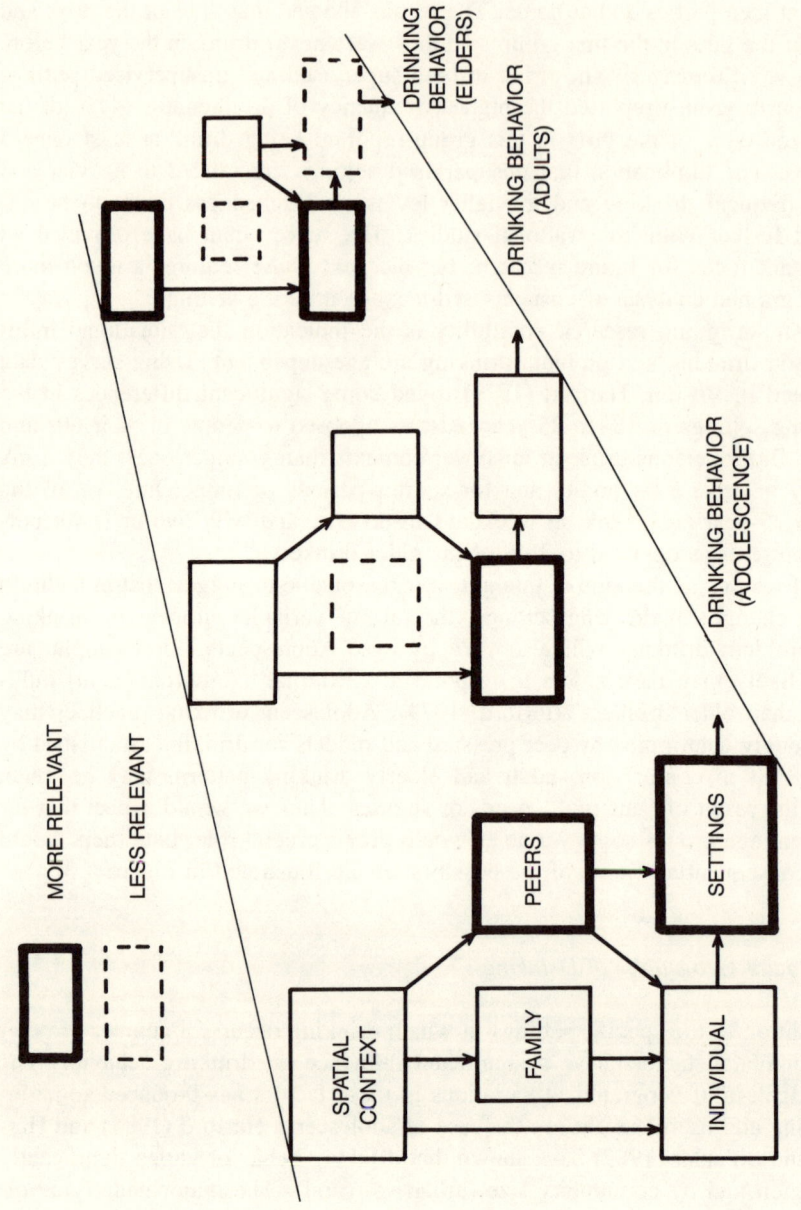

Figure 4.3. Influence of external and internal variables on drinking behavior among different age groups.

ulating the availability of alcohol is the most effective strategy to help prevent alcohol abuse (Gerstein, 1984). Theoretical support for the availability argument has come mainly from the "distribution of consumption" model of alcohol use and abuse (Rabow & Watts, 1983; Room, 1984). Stated in its most simple form, this model accounts for variations in the prevalence of alcohol-related problems (particularly medical problems such as cirrhosis of the liver) in terms of the mean level of per capita alcohol consumption. As the level of consumption rises, the percentage of the population that drinks heavily also rises, perhaps more than proportionately. Although support for this model is by no means unanimous (see, eg., Tuck, 1980) it has some significant policy implications, the most obvious being that if the overall level of alcohol consumption can be lowered, it is thought that the health problems and possibly some of the other adverse consequences of heavy drinking will decline.

There are many ways the state could intervene to bring about reductions in the overall consumption of alcohol, including changing the spatial pattern of availability by closing or preventing the opening of certain outlets such as bars and liquor stores, changing the price of alcoholic beverages by manipulating the tax system, reducing the hours of sale and raising the minimum age for purchase, and regulating the quantity and content of alcohol advertising. The major area of controversy has been the debate between the proponents of supply-side tactics such as these, and others who argue that the only feasible strategy is to reduce the demand for alcohol through education about "responsible drinking" (Moore & Gerstein, 1981). It appears that the responsible drinking theme has so far dominated public policies toward alcohol control in the United States, in spite of a symbolic recognition of the potential benefits of attempts to stabilize or reduce overall alcohol consumption (Parker, 1984).

One of the major criticisms of the distribution of consumption model has been along theoretical lines. There is no convincing argument to explain why an increase in the mean level of alcohol consumption should necessarily be followed by an increase in the proportion of heavy and at-risk drinkers (Jessor & Jessor, 1980; Pittman, 1983). The closest researchers have come to a theoretical explanation involves a process of contagion, in which heavier drinking spreads through the population as a result of social interaction processes and the increased availability of alcohol (Skog, 1980, 1981). In the search for an adequate theory, a useful starting point is to expand on the definition of availability beyond the traditional notions of physical and economic availability (Rabow & Watts, 1983).

Subjective Availability

The concept of subjective availability has not been considered widely in the literature, mainly because of the difficulties involved in measurement. Smart (1980) suggested that individuals tend to drink according to how they perceive the subjective costs and benefits of drinking. In a recent study Rabow and Watts (1982) attempted to assess the extent to which individuals were willing to exert energy and expend resources in the conduct of their drinking. In a theoretical context, Gaines (1981) has argued that it is impossible or inadvisable to try to predict drinking levels and outcomes using either environmental or personality variables on their own (see also Braucht, 1983). As an alternative Gaines suggests that drinking should be viewed as an intentional act that serves to produce congruence between the drinker's current subjective state and his or her desired state. Obviously this process is to some extent situation dependent. For example, an individual who finds that his or her current disposition and environment are providing too much isolation might choose to drink to become more outgoing. This would be a short-term solution to his or her problem, one that does not require any major personal or environmental changes.

An important aspect of Gaines' "self-awareness" theory is that the context in which drinking occurs is critical, because some situations may require an individual to drink more heavily to achieve a desired state. In a crowded and anonymous setting such as a cocktail party or a bar, it may be difficult to fulfill one's expectations with subtle or minor changes in behavior. The assumption here is than an individual drinker is a rational plan-maker. He or she has to assess the situation, evaluate the options, and then draw up a plan of action in much the same way a criminal does in approaching a potential target. Clearly an individual's chosen strategy will also be to some extent "state dependent." As Gaines observed:

> When alcoholics had feelings of dependency, depression, anger, or anxiety, they said that they saw their bartender, drank alcohol, smoked and/or took pills. If they felt "on top of the world", they ate, drank milk, and withdrew. When they were relaxed, they kept busy or went to bed. (p. 146)

At this time we have only the vaguest idea about the sort of drinking environments that are likely to result in heavy and damaging drinking (Harford & Gaines, 1981), but as noted in the previous section, some pioneering efforts have already been conducted. In a recent study, Russell and Bond (1980) attempted to assess the mutual interaction of self and environmental evaluations on the subsequent selection of both the location of a place to drink and the style of drinking. The research demonstrated that both alcoholics and nonalcoholics who drank while they were in a pleasant emotional state were likely to want to drink in a pleasant setting. Others who hoped that their drinking would be able to put them in a more pleasant state of mind reported that they did not mind drinking in an unpleasant setting. It appears, therefore, that the physical characteristics of the setting are less important to drinkers who expect their drinking (rather than their environment) to produce some major changes in their affective state.

Social Availability

The relationship between the overall level of alcohol consumption and the prevalence of problem drinking is mediated by social factors. One component of this is the role of social norms or expectations in determining not only what an individual drinks, but also what he or she serves to others in the social group (Rabow & Watts, 1983). Much remains unknown in this area, although again Rabow and Watts (1982) have made a start by defining "social availability" in terms of the individual's obligation or perceived obligation to serve alcohol in the home, partly as a way of being sociable and partly to reciprocate for drinks received from others.

Social variables play a key role in determining the quantity of alcohol consumed (Skog, 1981). Among groups the amount that is drunk appears to be determined primarily by the consumption level of the heaviest drinkers and the size of the group. In larger groups, where individual differences in the rates of drinking are likely to be greater than in smaller groups, the mean consumption level will rise. Although it is possible that small groups have significantly different reasons for drinking than larger groups, and that heavier drinkers may actually self-select larger groups, Skog believes that group size is the major determinant of both the duration of the drinking episodes and the amount that is drunk. The reasoning here is that, other things being equal, larger groups are likely to have greater variations between the slowest (lightest) and fastest (heaviest) drinkers. In behavioral terms it has been suggested that the faster/heavier drinkers are more likely than slower/lighter drinkers to be able to influence the drinking of others because they provide "more behavior to model" (Skog, 1981, p. 127), and also because fast drinkers have a repertoire of strategies to speed up the drinking of slower drinkers. This theory fits well with some of the empirical observations of drinking behavior. In Scotland, for example, Dight (1976) reported that 90% of all drinking occasions are group events, and that heavier drinkers who also drink in groups report that more of their drinking occurs in large groups than is the case for moderate drinkers.

At the aggregate level much has been learned by observing drinking norms among different groups, including those in different age categories, occupations, and particularly ethnic groups. In some cultural or ethnic subgroups the prevalence of problem drinking is surprisingly low. Investigations of these groups show that a variety of informal social controls are in use to help prevent individuals from entering the vicious circle of heavy drinking and other forms of substance abuse (Maloff, Becker, Fonaroff, & Rodin, 1979). These controls appear to be traditions that are maintained through a combination of historical inertia and local circumstances. In this regard research on the drinking practices of American Jews is enlightening (Flasher & Maisto, 1984; Glassner & Berg, 1984). Numerous studies have demonstrated that as a proportion of the number of Jews who drink alcoholic beverages the prevalence of alcohol-related problems is extremely low (Greeley, McCready, & Thiesen, 1980; Snyder, 1978).

In a study conducted in Syracuse, Glassner and Berg (1980) reported that fewer than 1% of adult Jews are alcoholics or have serious drinking problems. The traditional explanation for such low rates of drinking and problem drinking is that informal social controls prevent many Jews from drinking excessively. Specifically, the culture of Orthodox Judaism prescribes drinking, but requires that it be integrated into religious practices within the family. Many observers predicted that the decline of Orthodoxy in the last few decades would erode the social controls on excessive drinking, but as yet there is little hard evidence that alcohol abuse among Jews has increased significantly (Blume, Dropkin, & Sokolow, 1980).

From their survey data Glassner and Berg (1980) identified four protective social processes that help to explain these low prevalence rates. In the first place, heavy alcohol consumption is perceived by most Jews to be a non-Jewish characteristic. Alcoholism is an "outgroup" trait, and moderate drinking is the norm. It appears that many Jews associate themselves with sobriety (Snyder, 1978). A second protective mechanism is the integration of moderate drinking norms during childhood by means of religious and secular rituals. Even though religious orthodoxy is now less pervasive, Jewish drinking habits that were originally dictated by religious prescription have been extended to secular domains. In other words, the tradition of moderate drinking has been handed down to present-day Jews, even though the religious practices that originally defined drinking behavior are significantly less evident. The third social control mechanism is the continual reiteration of moderate drinking by restricting primary relationships to other moderate drinkers. There is substantial evidence that an individual's drinking habits, particularly the quantity and frequency of drinking, are largely determined by the habits of his or her peers (Skog, 1980). Most Jews appear to prefer the company of others who are moderate drinkers, and in fact among the survey respondents, most said they did not know anyone who was a heavy drinker (Glassner & Berg, 1980). The fourth mechanism includes a repertoire of techniques designed to prevent an individual from drinking more than he or she wants to, even in the face of social pressure to drink more.

The example of Jewish drinking is often used to illustrate what is meant by socially integrated drinking, and it is recommended that other groups try to drink in a similarly responsible fashion. It is obvious, however, that to change attitudes and behaviors among groups who drink more heavily than the Jews would be a formidable task, one that could only be attempted a little at a time. To date, little evidence exists to demonstrate that educational programs and media campaigns focusing on the "responsible drinking" theme have been able to change drinking practices significantly (Dorn, 1983; Whitehead, 1979; Wittman, 1982). It is surprising to find that education still dominates the field of prevention and official public policy in the field of alcohol abuse (Parker, 1984), especially since legislative and fiscal strategies offer at least a viable alternative for making substantial inroads into heavy drinking behaviors (Bruun, 1975; Moore & Gerstein, 1981, Room, 1984).

PART THREE

SERVICE DELIVERY AND
THE MANAGEMENT OF PUBLIC PROBLEMS

5

Deinstitutionalization of the Mentally Ill

INTRODUCTION

A historical view of the strategies adopted to manage public problems during the last 2 to 3 centuries reveals a number of major shifts in emphasis. In the last few decades we have witnessed a strong push toward community-based solutions in an effort to reverse what had been a long-standing reliance on institutions (M. Katz, 1978).[1]

It comes as something of a surprise to learn that in spite of their pervasiveness the establishment of specialized institutions to meet the needs of unique populations is a relatively recent innovation. In the United States the only institutions in existence before the 19th century were generic ones; the almshouse was a refuge for all of society's marginal groups: the sick, the insane, and the poor. The major criterion for entry was the absence of a family or a community willing to provide care. Eighteenth-century institutions were the place of last resort, but during most of the 19th century they were the place of first resort. With the return to community care in the 20th century, the cycle has been completed. The irony of the timing involved here is difficult to escape. In the first place, the arguments made by the proponents of community care are essentially similar to those made by the supporters of institutions in the 19th century (Rothman, 1971). Secondly, the call for a return to the community became overwhelming just as academics, mainly sociologists, had convinced everyone that the old supportive *(''gemeinschaft'')* communities no longer existed.

To illustrate what was involved in the final phase of the cycle of care, this chapter explores the treatment of mental illness and the trend toward deinstitutionalization that began in the 1950s. The next chapter investigates the provision of services for alcoholics and public inebriates as an alternative to criminal processing; and Chapter 7 focuses on the diversion of youthful offenders away from the criminal justice system. In all of these areas a strong public sentiment against institutional treatment was reinforced by legislation in the 1960s and early 1970s, and the service responses to that legislation would dramatically alter the landscape of public problems.

This section begins by considering the modern developments in their historical context, opening with a brief review of the origins of the institutional state, and the gradual shift in emphasis toward the community. The idea of providing public support for people in need but who were not institutionalized ("outdoor relief") began to catch on in the early part of the 20th century. By the 1950s and 1960s outdoor relief would be the dominant welfare response to public problems.

THE SHIFT FROM INDOOR TO OUTDOOR RELIEF

The profusion of institutions in the first decades of the 19th century was not entirely the result of state activity. Many institutions began as private concerns, and it was only in the later decades that these would be added to and eventually replaced by institutions built and administered by the state. Instead of being run by enlightened and public-spirited citizens, the new institutions were administered by civil servants, which was a shift from paternalistic and corporate voluntarism to what M. Katz (1978) called "incipient bureaucracy." Another major change was a movement away from generic to specialized institutions. New places were built not only for the poor and the deviant, but also for the mentally ill, the disabled, and the retarded.

The institutions themselves were not new, but they did have some novel aspects, for example: (1) their role as the central feature of the state's policy toward deviant and dependent individuals; (2) their emphasis on reform and character building; and (3) the increasing level of specialization, not only between the deviant (criminal) elements and the dependent groups, but also between different categories of dependents. Institutions were built with a specific purpose in mind, and they were staffed by specialists who claimed scientific knowledge in their respective areas (Cohen, 1979). The unipurpose buildings and the careful guarding of unique professional territory would help to explain why these institutions persisted even long after they had outlived their usefulness (Scull, 1977).

In their attempts to piece together the development of institutions in the United States, social historians have provided a number of partially overlapping accounts. One is the "fear of disorder" in the post-Revolutionary society (Rothman, 1971), another was the humanitarian impulse of social reformers (Grob, 1966, 1973), and a third was the inability of the growing cities to provide for their deviants and dependents in the same way the villages had done (Scull, 1979). The functional and reformist accounts of social control have recently come under fire from a variety of "revisionist" sociologists and social historians. In the specific context of institutions, for example, Katz (1978) offers a number of criticisms:

1. They are unable to provide a link between the institutions created for deviants and other institutions created for dependents and children such as mental hospitals, public schools, and poorhouses;

2. The concept of disorder that resulted from urbanization is a loose one; what it was specially about cities that created social disorder was not specified;

3. There is an assumption that institutions emerged out of a general consensus but it is clear that some groups were more in favor and had more to gain from institutions than others;

4. There is no consideration of the essential role played by class interests in the development of institutions; to many it seems naive to suggest that the promoters of institutions were simply acting in what they perceived to be the best interests of the poor, the criminals, and the mentally ill;

5. No attempt is made to challenge the definitions of social problems that existed in the 19th century, many of which appear to have been based largely on ethnic and racial stereotyping, and an unquestioning faith in the official statistics of the time. (There was an assumption, for example, that immigrants were not only poor, but were also likely to be drunkards, criminals, and mentally ill. Some groups, especially the Irish and blacks, were thought to be inherently degraded, and these beliefs often went unquestioned.)

As an alternative account, Katz suggests that the origin and growth of institutions can only be fully understood as a response to economic and social change, specifically the three-stage shift from the mercantile/peasant economy to one dominated by commerce, and finally to one dominated by industrial capitalism. Accompanying these transitions were a number of processes that would establish the need for institutions. One of these was the growth of new types of dependents (in addition to the sick, the poor, and the criminal) as a result of the structural unemployment that is typical in capitalist societies, and the physical and mental strains associated with factory life. Another contributing process was the gradual breakdown of family and community life, which had provided some traditional ways for coping with poverty.

The major organizational principle of industrial capitalism was the division of labor; according to Katz, this principle was adopted wholeheartedly by the new institutions:

> The unproductive became more than a nuisance; they became unworthy. In an attempt to raise their usefulness, the unproductive were swept into massive brick structures that looked distressingly like factories and there taught those lessons in social and economic behavior which, it was hoped, would facilitate their re-entry into real work places. (p. 19)

This argument is based on a combination of the various themes outlined by other accounts of the rise of institutions. It involves a relatively optimistic view of human nature and a strong commitment to the idea of a spiritual millenium (P. Johnson, 1978). Some historians have argued that institution builders were in the business of shaping and saving souls (Grob, 1973), but for Katz the shaping was done with a clear prototype in mind. The institution was intended to help restore the spiritually wounded and to instill in them some of the required traits for the capitalist mode of production. The most important of these were sensual restraint, hard work, dependability, willingness to save, acquiescence to the existing social order, and acceptance of one's place within it. These traits were seen as not only useful, but essential for the reproduction of capitalist social relations.

Accounts such as this do not necessarily deny that the reformers were initially well-meaning, but it is clear that positive motives were drowned in the push toward the less admirable goals of establishing control, and spreading conformity to middle-class values. As the history of institutional care has demonstrated, over time the control and coercive aspects of institutions would come to dominate institutions, and in the 20th century, in the face of well-publicized abuses, a new humanitarianism began to lead the way toward much-needed reforms (Scull, 1977). The first attempts involved efforts to improve the quality of life in institutions. After some early progress in this direction in the 1950s, there was what K. Jones (1982) refers to as a "strategic retreat from objectives." According to Jones, the humanitarian objectives were beginning to have some effect and had resulted in the establishment of national standards and the collective sense of responsibility for the reform of institutions. What frequently happened, however, was that with deinstitutionalization came a dispersal of authority. Although there was national legislation to guide the provision of treatment for dependent groups like the mentally ill, alcoholics, and delinquents, the legislation did not set definitive standards for service. Recommendations were made and some funds were made available for new facilities, but decision making was decentralized and individual states and localities were allowed to determine their own level of provision. The result was an enormous variation in both the quantity and quality of services, and in only a few places has adequate and humane care been made available in the community (Smith & Hanham, 1981a).

Wildly optimistic hopes were established for community care. In the field of mental health, for example:

> community care promised more than just a resolution of institutional problems, more than just an alternative setting. It was itself to be a treatment modality. Care in the community would keep patients in touch with the significant others in their lives, with the jobs and routines they relied upon for order, with the social skills they need for independence. The companionship, activity, warmth and non-stigmatizing nature of the community was to act as its own therapeutic agent, and it was this promise more than any other that has made community care the dominant ideology for more than a decade. (Baron & Rutman, 1979, p. 5)

Many communities were either unwilling or unprepared to forge this sort of ideology into a reality. In recent years a familiar argument has been the suggestion that the humanitarian concern was by no means the only and perhaps not even the most important reason for the dismantling of institutions. As

M. Levine (1981) has observed, deinstitutionalization only became possible after the shift from indoor to outdoor relief began to provide even a minimum level of services to individuals living in the community. In other words, deinstitutionalization was a pragmatic strategy—it was what had become possible. The extreme form of this argument also implies that the individual states had something to gain financially from deinstitutionalization (Rose, 1979). The growth of federally funded programs like Medicare, Medicaid, and Supplemental Security Income (SSI), together with the loosening of eligibility rules for other welfare programs, allowed individuals to survive in the community at the expense of the federal government. This was a fiscal advantage for the individual states, who were no longer required to dip into their own pockets to support their dependent populations. To use Scull's (1981) terminology, the mentally ill had become a "commodity" and concern for them was largely financial rather than humanitarian:

> [the] modern welfare state . . . provides a state guarantee to the indigent and impotent of at least minimum levels of subsistence. But once programs of this sort are in place, the chronic mental patient, whose fate previously was to be consigned to the neglect of the back wards of the state hospital, now acquires [the] new attractiveness of a transactionable commodity, a source of income. (p. 744)

There have been numerous other attempts to account for the widespread popularity of dispersal and deinstitutionalization strategies. The civil rights issue, pushed both by concerned lawyers and self-help patient groups, was one important factor (P. Brown, 1981). The use of chemotherapy also made it possible for disturbed patients to live reasonably normal lives in the community. Whatever the explanation of deinstitutionalization, it seems more useful in the 1980s to evaluate its implications (Brown, 1985).

As we shall see in this chapter, community care for the mentally ill has resulted in more rather than less intervention. What Cohen (1979) refers to as the "dispersal of social control" has actually reproduced many aspects of the complex systems of classification and surveillance of the 19th-century institutions, although in different forms and under the guise of liberal reforms. In Cohen's words, "The overwhelming impression is one of bustling, almost frenzied activity, all these wonderful new things are being done to the same old group of troublemakers" (p. 358). These "wonderful new things"—such as newly created categories of deviance, new human service specialities, increased surveillance, and escalating state intervention into private lives—are in fact, as Cohen points out, not new at all, but are simply a continuation of existing patterns that began over a century ago.

The most furious dispersal activity began in the 1950s, but the precedent for it was established in the 1930s with the passage of the Social Security Act in 1935. The Act prohibited elderly residents of the poorhouse from receiving federal Old Age Assistance benefits, which in turn helped to reduce the populations in many state institutions. What happened then was similar to what would happen in the 1960s and 1970s. Individuals were released from the institutions if the daily cost of keeping them exceeded what the states would have to pay in matching funds to provide them with outdoor relief (M. Levine, 1981). The net effect was that the local poorhouse became the repository for those who were too ill or disabled to be placed in the community. In spite of strong criticisms there was often local opposition to closing down the poorhouses. The alternatives, however, were not enviable. The exodus from institutions encouraged the growth of substandard boarding homes and private nursing homes for the elderly. As Levine observed, "The 1935 . . . Act had created conditions that were later to influence the deinstitutionalization process" (p. 74).

As this example illustrates, the dispersal process was by no means a revolutionary shift in social policy; it was in fact a trend that had its origins in an earlier era. The failure to anticipate some of the most damaging outcomes of deinstitutionalization perhaps attests to the failure to learn a lesson from history. On the other hand the magnitude of the changes that came about in the 1960s could not have been predicted. The dispersal of social control was launched with missionary-like zeal and overinflated expectations. It was hardly surprising that within 2 decades there would be widespread calls for new social programs.

DEINSTITUTIONALIZATION: MOVING THE MENTALLY ILL ONTO THE STREETS

The Community Mental Health Centers (CMHC) Act of 1963 was an innovation in mental health policy in the United States. At that time it was described as a bold new approach to the problem, the first national campaign to fight mental illness; but less than 20 years later the Act was repealed by the Reagan administration and its funding was consolidated into block grants for the whole field of mental health, alcoholism, and drug abuse. The funds now go to the states first rather than directly to the the centers, and although it is unlikely that all of the centers will disappear, the future of the community mental health (CMH) movement is uncertain, and the era of innovation has come to an end (Biegel, 1982; C. J. Smith, 1983; Winslow, 1982).

The CMH program was widely criticized (Bloom, 1977; P. Brown, 1985; Chu & Trotter, 1974; Kenig, 1981), and the criticisms can be broadly grouped under four headings: (1) the services have been poorly administered; (2) they have been too costly; (3) the centers have not really involved "the community"; and (4) they have not been able to lower the prevalence of mental illness. It is important to point out that these criticisms should be considered in light of the considerable achievements of the movement. Since the early 1960s, for example, mental hospital populations have been reduced to an all-time low in many states; over 700 new centers started to provide mental health services; mental health care is now offered to three times as many people; and public attitudes toward the mentally ill are more positive than ever before (Dear & Taylor, 1982; C. J. Smith & Hanham, 1981b). Before considering the impacts of the movement, therefore, it is important to put the CMH innovation into its political and historical context, by reviewing the development of the American welfare state in the 1960s.

The CMHC legislation has been described as just one part of a widespread shift in the way the federal government was beginning to tackle social problems in the early 1960s (Bloom, 1977). The sharp growth in social welfare spending at that time could have been predicted from what had already occurred in many other capitalist countries, particularly in Europe. During the 19th century and the first part of the 20th century, the American welfare system was geared mainly toward indoor relief, which as we have noted helps to explain why social services were dominated for so long by institutional forms. With the passage of the Social Security Act in 1935 came the first real commitment to outdoor relief payments, which were made either in cash or kind in an attempt to redistribute wealth to individuals while they continued to live in their own communities (Lerman, 1982).

It is difficult to explain why the expansion of the American welfare state occurred when it did, especially in light of the observations made from both the Left and the Right that such growth was contrary to the goal of capital accumulation (Doyal, 1979; Navarro, 1977, 1981). There is a feeling that such a development can only occur in special circumstances, such as when the state has some degree of autonomy from the direct representatives of the capitalist class (Gough, 1979). This might occur when one branch of the state, a "class conscious political directorate," to use O'Connor's (1973) term, steps forward to argue for an accelerated program of welfare. According to Piven and Cloward (1971), this function was performed by the executive branch during the Kennedy and Johnson Presidencies, and it served to placate and "pay off" the deprived urban groups, especially blacks, for their electoral support of the Democratic Party.

Looking back, the gains made by the deprived urban groups in the 1960s were superficial and temporary. One possible explanation for this is that the gains were achieved in the absence of either a militant labor movement or any mass support from the white majority (J. T. Patterson, 1981). In more general terms, problems for the welfare state are inevitable, because efforts to enhance the lot of the poor will always sooner or later be defined as counter to the interests of capitalist accumulation.

It is preferable, therefore, to interpret what happened in the 1960s as a temporary alliance of opposing forces that converged on the same policy. This argument was used by Friedland (1976) to explain the "political accommodation" between the major corporations and the labor unions that paved the way for some of the Great Society programs. Similarly, the CMHC legislation represented an unusual alliance between groups with radical views about how to solve social problems and others with the elitist, traditional views associated with professional medicine and psychiatry. Although this was a unique and inherently unstable coalition, the program was able to withstand substantial opposition for a number of years (Foley & Sharfstein, 1983).

As this brief summary of the CMH movement illustrates, the expansion of social welfare programs can be interpreted in different ways. In one sense, it can be viewed as an extension of social control that was designed to make the working classes responsive to or at least passive about the interests of ruling elites (an issue taken up in more detail in Chapter 10). In another sense the expansion of social programs like community mental health can be considered a victory for the deprived groups and a partial solution to their endemic poverty and lack of opportunity.

These divergent interpretations are possible because the creation of the welfare state itself reflects some of the antagonisms between the major functions of the state: capital accumulation on the one hand and social legitimation on the other (Corrigan & Leonard, 1978). It is inevitable that problems will result, especially as administrations change and different interests are represented in the government. On the legitimation side, in spite of the distributional gains made by the recipients of social welfare, at best such programs can only preserve the status quo because the continuation of subservient relationships is essential for the existing economic system (Lee, 1979). On the accumulation side, as we have seen in the 1980s, the social welfare programs came under attack and many were dismantled because they threatened the imperatives of the capitalist system (Gilbert, 1984; Jirovec, 1984; Stoesz, 1981; Wolfe, 1981).

To put the CMH movement into its theoretical context, it is important to begin by considering the functions of the larger welfare state of which it is but a small part. One function of the welfare state is to help in the reproduction of labor power, both in quantitative and qualitative terms (Gordon, 1978); another is to maintain nonworking populations at a satisfactory level (Gough, 1979). Although the case is not as clear-cut as it is with other welfare programs such as health care and income maintenance, the provision of mental health services can contribute to both functions. Quantitative contributions to the reproduction of labor power include such items as taxes and benefits to redistribute wealth, state subsidies to change the "use values" of consumption goods such as housing and transportation, and the direct provision of use values in the form of low-cost or free social services. In this last category CMHCs were intended to offer a variety of services to poor and deprived populations, although there has always been some doubt about how accessible these services actually were.

Qualitative aids to reproduction include mechanisms that are intended to maintain and reinforce beliefs in the existing system (Harvey, 1981). In the mental health context this might include such services as education and consultation with community groups, attempts to solidify and encourage stable family life, and the promotion of socially acceptable behavior. Although these were not always the specific functions of the CMHCs, the spread of mental health ideology that the CMH movement made possible meant that values such as these were widely disseminated.

With the help of federal grants, the new CMHCs were able to offer services to the public that had previously only been available at the opposite ends of the private–public continuum. The centers were mandated to provide individual services, and if appropriate, psychotropic drugs were made available to people who presented themselves for treatment. The implicit goal of such services is to help clients return to "normal" functioning in the community, and although it is difficult to generalize about normality, it is safe to assume that one of the major evaluation standards is an individual's ability to be self-supporting in the community—in other words to be an effective and productive worker (Ralph, 1983; C. J. Smith, 1985c). This standard is consistent with the medical model of health care that still dominated the CMH movement. According to such criteria, ill health is defined primarily as a system dysfunction, and the required treatment involves surgical, chemical, and/or psychological intervention to restore the human machine to working order (Doyal, 1979). The CMH movement was based largely on this functional model, both in its dealings with individual pathology and in relation to community-wide problems.

The provision of mental health services in CMHCs also contributed to the other major function of the welfare state, which is to transfer part of the social product from the direct producers of wealth to the nonworking and disabled poor. A large and expanding proportion of this latter group have been disabled by the rigors of the workplace, others have been systematically excluded as a result of their age or their lack of education, and still others have been made redundant by capital migration or structural changes in the economy (Bluestone & Harrison, 1982). It is hoped that the provision of mental health services to individuals in this unfortunate position can help to ease the transition into the world outside the workplace (Ralph, 1983), and in some cases to facilitate the long process of re-entry (Buss & Redburn, 1987).

Another goal of the CMH movement was to help the chronically mentally ill to lead a normal life in the community (Goldman, Adams, & Taube, 1983). Again the standards for normality tend to be defined largely in terms of being independent and, if possible, economically self-supporting. This goal has rarely been accomplished, largely because of the lack of development and coordination between services in the community. An additional problem is the increasing level of chronicity among the patients who have remained in inpatient care, many of whom are young men who have become known as the—"new chronics" (Pepper *et al.,* 1981). Many of the individuals who were deinstitutionalized as a result of CMH initiatives proved to be poorly suited to the world of work. For them the best the mental health system can offer is partial compensation, a sort of consolation prize of weekly consultation and regular medication (Goldenberg, 1982).

The services provided by CMHCs can be roughly assigned to the categories of state expenditures outlined by O'Connor (1973)—namely social investments, social consumption expenditures, and social expenses. Social investments are intended to socialize the costs of production and accumulation by providing goods and services that can be used to improve productivity, increase surplus value, and speed up the circulation of capital. Social consumption expenditures are intended to lower the costs and increase the rate at which labor is reproduced; and social expenses are required to help maintain social harmony. Although there are overlaps in this categorization (Moseley, 1979), it is useful for analyzing the impacts of social welfare spending, which in turn helps to predict the fortunes of such programs. In most cases social expenditures (those in the investment and reproduction categories) are directly productive in that they contribute to capital accumulation, but in the mental health field it is impossible to calculate the extent to which CMH services have performed this function. On the other hand, there is little doubt that federal subsidies have helped to swell the market for mental health care by building up the psychiatric workforce (staffing and training grants), creating new institutions (construction and remodeling grants), and supporting a new academic infrastructure (research grants). Mental health has become a giant industry, and one that helps to circulate capital throughout the community (Foley & Sharfstein, 1983; M. L. Gross, 1978; M. Levine, 1981). It is much more difficult to determine the outcome of this investment. After millions of dollars have been spent, countless hours of therapy undergone, and billions of pills dispensed, there is no evidence that the population is mentally more healthy than it was before. Many individuals have improved the quality of their lives as a result of mental health care, but the incidence rate of new "cases" continues to grow in the absence of effective preventive mental health care.

The social expenses incurred by the government are generally perceived to be "necessary but unproductive" (Gough, 1979, p. 51). Most of the services provided by CMHCs, such as inpatient and outpatient care and emergency services, fall into this category. The majority of the clients at the centers are either working already or they are too disabled to work even after their treatment. In other words, it seems unlikely that mental health services per se will significantly expand or improve the labor force. In comparison to treatment services, the indirect services such as community consultation and education have, in most cases, been dealt with half-heartedly by CMHCs. In the original legislation it was hoped that indirect outreach programs would be a major item in the prevention of mental illness in factories, workplaces, schools, and communities (Naparstek *et al.*, 1982). With a few exceptions (Jeger & Slotnick, 1982), the long-run potential for creating "healthier" and more "productive" social entities has not been achieved, partly because so few people in the CMHCs had any really good ideas about how to prevent mental illness and partly because outreach services could not be reimbursed by insurance companies, a problem that would become crucial when the centers tried to become financially independent (C. J. Smith, 1983c).

The CMHC program was criticized for doing "too little, too late" to achieve its stated goals. One of these goals involved the redistribution of public benefits, to help reduce the debilitating impacts of inequality in American society. The CMH movement and many of the other Great Society programs were based on the assumption that public problems like mental illness were intimately related to such macrolevel concerns as poverty, social class, race, and a general lack of opportunity resulting from social and spatial inequality. This was not a new observation, it had in fact been noted as early as 1856 by Edward Jarvis in Massachusetts, who discovered that the "pauper class" was responsible for 64 times as many cases of insanity as the "independent class" (Monahan & Vaux, 1980). In more recent times, these observations have been repeated in the huge psychiatric epidemiology surveys (Hollingshead & Redlich, 1958; Langner & Michael, 1963). These surveys demonstrated that an individual's economic status and social class is: (1) negatively related to his or her chances of being diagnosed as psychologically disordered; (2) positively related to the chance of receiving treatment once diagnosed; and (3) positively related to the probability of receiving preferred treatment, if treatment is provided at all. In other words, not only are individuals of lower social status more likely to exhibit symptoms of mental disorder, they are also much less likely to receive care for their problems from individual psychotherapists. The net effect is that there is a "social selection" process working to ensure that disproportionate numbers of lower-class individuals have no other option but to seek treatment in public mental hospitals (Morrissey & Tessler, 1982).

In a book entitled *The Enduring Asylum,* Morrissey, Goldman, and Klerman (1980) argued that in spite of all the gains made by the CMH movement the state hospital was still the primary source of inpatient care, particularly for patients with more serious symptoms. A study conducted in New Haven, Connecticut demonstrated that the social selection mechanism responsible for this phenomenon is perhaps operating now more forcefully than ever before (Mollica & Redlich, 1980). The data show that in spite of the proliferation of outpatient services and inpatient services at CMHCs and other agencies, the vast majority of inpatient services for minorities, the elderly, and special populations such as alcoholics were still provided by state hospitals (95% for blacks, 100% for Hispanics, 91% for the elderly, and 95% for alcoholics). It is clear, therefore, that the "two-tiered" system of mental health care has not been significantly altered by the addition of CMHC services.

At the national level there is also some support for the New Haven findings. As the data in Table 5.1 show, in many states, the elderly (65 +) were institutionalized in 1982 at a greater rate than the nonelderly (18–65 years); but in all of the states for which data were available, the elderly were significantly less likely to receive outpatient mental health services than younger persons. For blacks the discrepancy in hospitalization rates was even more noticeable than for the elderly. In all states blacks were institutionalized at higher rates than whites, with the ratio varying from 2:1 to 4:1 in some states. Somewhat

Table 5.1. Patient Characteristics in Public Inpatient and Outpatient Mental Health Facilities—1982

| STATE | Age Characteristics[a] | | | | Racial/Ethnic Characteristics[b] | | | |
| | Inpatient[c] | | Outpatient | | Inpatient | | Outpatient | |
	65+ Years	18–64 Years	65+ Years	18–64 Years	White	Black	White	Black
Alabama	82.4	73.9	265.7	987.1	44.7	97.8	808.0	744.6
Alaska	—	—	—	—	—	—	—	—
Arizona	33.2	12.4	375.9	1154.0	11.4	33.8	926.8	1327.3
Arkansas	3.4	19.7	330.0	1053.8	7.8	35.4	826.3	1052.4
California	11.8	32.0	—	—	22.1	58.9	—	—
Colorado	17.8	30.6	678.8	855.9	22.4	61.9	708.2	1095.2
Connecticut	84.0	102.0	389.1	1079.1	68.0	162.7	713.9	1065.9
Delaware	291.8	103.6	384.0	1163.1	—	—	—	—
Florida	89.7	43.0	218.5	1028.3	—	—	800.6	1067.9
Georgia	166.7	116.7	443.5	774.5	89.0	125.3	580.5	739.2
Hawaii	3.5	15.8	414.1	775.9	15.9	11.8	740.2	476.5
Idaho	—	—	369.3	791.2	—	—	—	—
Illinois	29.4	42.5	484.4	1086.3	26.6	66.7	826.2	1280.4
Indiana	52.0	60.2	—	—	41.8	87.8	—	—
Iowa	18.5	34.4	—	—	26.9	39.0	—	—
Kansas	19.3	67.9	408.2	1529.8	47.7	150.8	1275.7	1136.5
Kentucky	14.8	30.8	—	—	18.0	50.0	—	—
Louisiana	20.0	65.8	814.4	1403.4	—	—	825.1	1723.4
Maine	—	—	—	—	—	—	—	—
Maryland	171.9	83.0	303.1	605.4	—	—	460.9	666.9
Massachusetts	101.1	47.1	—	—	—	—	—	—
Michigan	—	—	—	—	—	—	—	—

surprisingly, however, the use of outpatient mental health services by blacks tends to be higher than for whites in many states, which suggests that CMHC and other mental health services have become increasingly available to blacks, particularly in the inner-city areas (Smith, 1984).

One of the goals of publicly provided services is to establish a delivery system that is equitable. In spite of the overall increase in availability of mental health services, the evidence reviewed here has cast some doubt on the ability of catchmented services to meet the ambitious goals of the 1963 CMHC Act. The New Haven researchers observed that it is a common and often grievous error to equate equity with accessibility (Mollica & Redlich, 1980). Mental health services may be available for the elderly and for minorities, but if the services are perceived to be either inhumane or culturally biased toward the majority group, their mere existence does not guarantee equity.

One conclusion that can be drawn from this discussion is that although the philosophy behind the CMH movement essentially recognized the relationship between social status and mental disorder, the actual programs themselves only considered the problem in distributional terms. For this reason most mental

Minnesota	—	—	—	—	—	—	—	—
Mississippi	—	—	—	—	—	—	—	—
Missouri	67.7	59.1	189.3	561.1	41.5	107.0	342.5	959.6
Montana	41.1	50.4	—	—	37.2	100.0	—	—
Nebraska	22.2	47.3	210.4	896.2	31.2	116.3	706.8	587.8
Nevada	—	—	—	—	—	—	—	—
New Hampshire	30.3	49.0	—	—	—	—	—	—
New Jersey	151.1	79.3	257.9	566.7	66.4	114.0	456.8	699.7
New Mexico	—	—	—	—	—	—	—	—
New York	472.1	118.5	694.4	1536.7	140.5	183.8	1692.1	2699.4
North Dakota	109.4	60.8	618.1	1337.7	47.1	77.1	1052.0	1380.4
Ohio	44.4	64.1	—	—	40.8	111.8	—	—
Oklahoma	63.8	48.7	429.7	1208.8	36.5	71.1	800.9	1343.1
Oregon	26.8	49.7	133.8	515.7	34.2	129.7	417.5	732.4
Pennsylvania	247.7	74.4	1368.8	3313.9	80.0	103.4	—	—
Rhode Island	28.8	75.5	372.0	1093.9	—	—	851.8	1344.4
South Carolina	356.5	103.5	421.9	844.7	78.9	162.5	603.0	765.0
South Dakota	130.9	65.7	613.8	1472.7	49.4	100.0	1122.5	700.0
Tennessee	73.4	52.3	685.4	1267.4	42.1	75.5	980.3	1223.5
Texas	77.7	48.3	278.3	628.7	39.5	59.1	466.7	717.7
Utah	15.3	24.7	207.6	1285.5	17.6	88.9	912.0	1644.4
Vermont	76.7	65.1	713.3	1960.0	48.9	200.0	1692.9	3600.0
Virginia	329.4	62.0	—	—	62.0	141.1	—	—
Washington	—	—	—	—	—	—	—	—
West Virginia	—	—	—	—	—	—	—	—
Wisconsin	7.9	23.1	739.9	753.3	9.2	30.1	—	—
Wyoming	130.8	67.3	—	—	50.9	200.0	—	—

[a] Rates per 100,000 civilian population in age group.
[b] Rates per 100,000 civilian population in racial/ethnic category.
[c] Inpatients in state mental hospitals.

health planners had a highly restricted view of the problem. The solution they advocated was to rearrange resources in such a way that the existing inequities would be ameliorated. By providing mental health services in certain areas, it was hoped that CMHCs could help to redistribute wealth, if only in a small and indirect way, from the haves to the have-nots (D. M. Smith, 1977; R. Lee, 1979). Needs assessment studies conducted by the states for each catchment area would help to indicate which locations were most in need of additional mental health services. At the same time it was also hoped that other Great Society programs—those more specifically related to poverty, education, and racial equality—would provide access to services that in the long run would lower the demand for mental health services.

To evaluate the redistribution of resources that occurred as a result of the CMHC legislation, it is important to differentiate some of the areas of inequality or lack of access in the mental health system. Inequality may, for example, be location specific, that is, restricted to certain areas such as the multiply deprived central parts of the city. In other cases the inequality may be group or individual specific, limited to certain groups of the population who are rel-

Inequality occurs as a result of:	*Areas or Groups Involved*	
	Group (class) Specific	Location Specific
Faulty Allocation Mechanisms	1. Regional and State level inequality in *allocation* of CMHC funds	2. Inequality in *locational* pattern of comprehensive CMHC services
Poor Access	3. CMHC care unequally *available* to all population groups	4. Location of CMHCs fails to maximize *accessibility* to all special groups

Figure 5.1. Inequality in the distribution of community mental health services.

atively deprived as a result of their social class, gender, age, or racial characteristics (Kirby, 1982). Resources (in this case mental health services) may be unevenly distributed as a result of variations in allocation mechanisms, or as a result of geographical differences in accessibility (Figure 5.1). The CMHC legislation spelled out that the funds were intended to provide services in areas that for a variety of reasons were unable to provide adequate mental health services independently (Bloom, 1977). A formula was established for allocating the available funds in such a way that the states with the greatest inequality, measured in per capita incomes, would receive a disproportionate share of the wealth. An evaluation of the pattern of CMHC funding throughout the 1965–1980 period suggests that during the 1970s new services were slowly being introduced in areas where mental health needs were greatest (Smith, 1984). Unfortunately, it was just at this time that the CMHC Act was repealed, effectively bringing an end to a 2-decade era of innovation in mental health care service delivery.

It has been suggested that intervention by the federal government is the only way to guarantee that the best interests of the truly needy will be uppermost in determining the level of service provision. With the current policies of the Reagan administration, the major fear is that if the primary responsibility for social programs like mental health is returned to the state level, the geographical vicissitudes in philosophies and resources will result in a patchwork of services. In some areas the truly needy will be provided with the "safety net" they require, but in other areas no such guarantees will be made (C. J. Smith, 1986).

NOTE

1. As Katz observed:

We live in an institutional state. Our lives spin outwards from the hospitals where we are born, to the school systems that dominate our youth, through the bureaucracies for which we work, and back again to the hospitals in which we die. If we stray, falter, or lose our grip, we are led or coerced toward institutions of mental health, justice or public welfare . . . characteristically, we respond to a widespread problem through the creation of an institution, the training of specialists, and the certification of their monopoly over a part of our lives. (1978, p. 6)

6

Decriminalization of Public Drunkenness

INTRODUCTION

When a person appears in public in an inebriated state, the societal response may take two very different approaches. If an illness definition of alcohol abuse prevails, the public drunk will be "treated" by medical, psychiatric, or lay helpers; but if a deviance definition prevails, the criminal justice system will take over. Until the 1950s and 1960s drunkenness in public places in the United States was considered to be deviant and was cause for legal proceedings. Being drunk in public was interpreted as being unable or unwilling to perform the normally expected roles within society. The most common response was a sequence of arrest, incarceration, release, and recidivism—a cycle of recurring events that became known as the "revolving door" (Pittman & Gordon, 1958).

Skid-row drunks would usually be sentenced to a short stay in the local jail, where they would spend anywhere from 30 to 90 days. After drying out in their cells, they would return to the streets to start the process over again. It was like "serving a life sentence on the installment plan" (Goldfarb, 1970), but in spite of the obvious humanitarian concerns that arise in the face of this repeated phenomenon, the revolving door was functional. City planners and Chamber of Commerce civic boosters liked having the drunks off the streets, and some of the drunks themselves may have even appreciated the opportunity to take "time out" from their harsh lives on skid row. In jail, they had better food, shelter, medical care, and most importantly, a chance to dry out to prepare themselves for the next binge.

All through the 1960s this issue had been keenly debated at the state and federal levels, and in the early 1970s a federal initiative emerged that would bring about major changes in the way public drunks were handled (Gusfield, 1984). The Uniform Alcoholism and Intoxication Treatment Act of 1971 made a series of recommendations about how individual states ought to deal with public inebriates (Regier, 1977). Throughout the 1970s many states began to transform the Uniform Act's recommendations into laws and by 1981, 34 states (including Washington, DC) had adopted a version of the Act. Similar legislation existed or was pending in ten more states, leaving only Arkansas, Indiana,

Ohio, South Carolina, Tennessee, Texas, and West Virginia with no legislation.[1]

The intent of most of these laws was effectively to "decriminalize" public drunkenness, thereby putting an end to the "two million unnecessary arrests" (Nimmer, 1971). The most important provision of the Uniform Act was stated as follows:

> Alcoholics and intoxicated persons may not be subjected to criminal prosecution because of their consumption of alcoholic beverages but rather should be afforded . . . treatment in order that they may lead normal lives as productive members of society. (Fagan & Mauss, 1978, p. 233, quoting from the 1971 Act)

The roots of the decriminalization movement can be traced back to the 1950s. As with deinstitutionalization, a convergence of liberal reform views and fiscal conservatism provided the background for a lengthy debate about how to deal with the problem of public drunkenness (Room, 1976). Social scientists had contributed to the debate some important conclusions both about the disadvantages of treating drunks as criminals, and about the advantages of providing them with treatment. There was evidence that criminal action did not deter drunkenness; in fact the mixing of first time offenders with chronic skid-row drunks tended to produce higher levels of recidivism (Rodin, Pickup, Motton, & Keatinge, 1982). Processing drunks through the courts was a long and costly procedure, but it was clear that the use of criminal proceedings was obviously not directed at all sectors of the drinking population. The threat of incarceration was being used as a form of social control, specifically to "keep the peace" downtown, and to help keep skid-row drunks off the streets (Speiglman & Wittman, 1982).

The reformers considered that the solution to the problem of public inebriates was not to put them in jail but to provide them with a range of treatment options. Instead of the police "drunk tanks" public detoxication centers were to be provided. Under ideal circumstances, after they had dried out, the alcoholics would select a treatment option from within a "continuum of care." In this way it was hoped that public drunks would be able to leave behind the revolving door syndrome forever. The criminal label would be removed and the permanent stigma associated with inebriation would be reduced, opening a new set of doors toward rehabilitation and sobriety. The burden on the criminal justice system would be reduced, and the clients would benefit from more humane treatment. Most important of all, the new system provided medical back-up throughout the treatment period, and the optimism that medical care could successfully deal with the problem. From the range of treatment facilities within the continuum the client would be able to select the most appropriate as his or her condition changed. With improvement it would be possible to move into less restrictive and less medically oriented settings, until at the least restrictive end of the continuum (Bachrach, 1980), the client could return to a normal life in the community (see Figure 6.1).

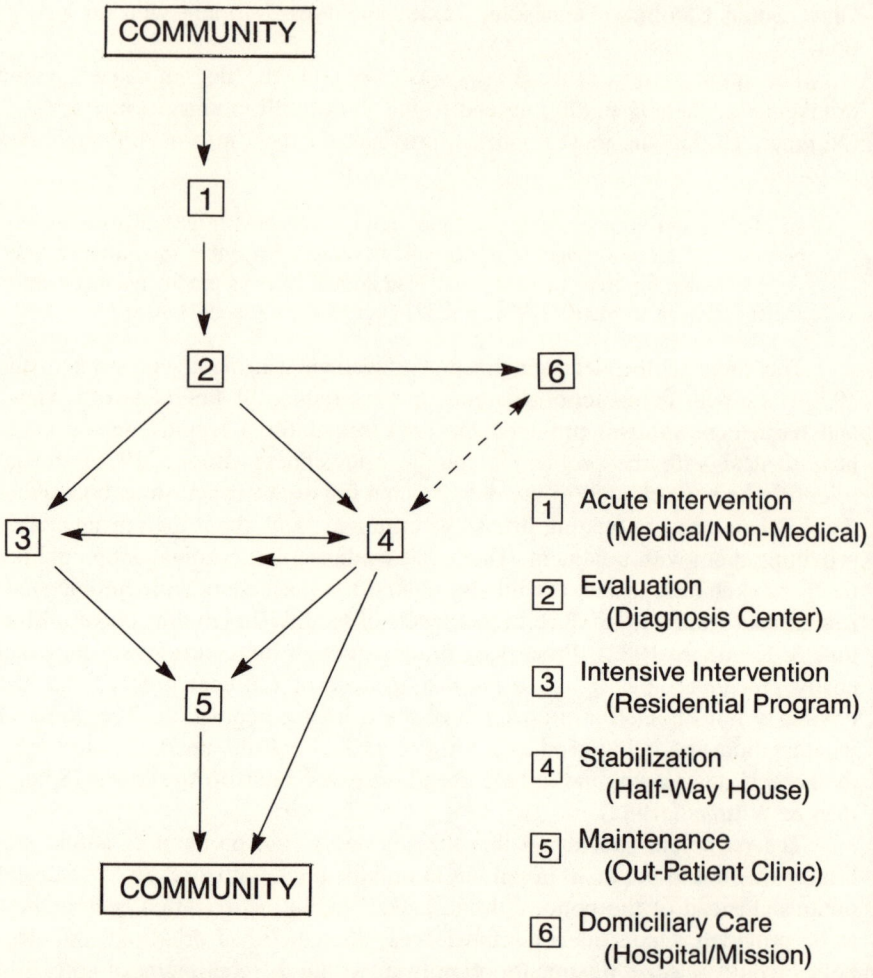

Figure 6.1. The components of an alcoholism treatment system.
Source. Smith (1983b, p. 371).

After more than a decade, the Act and its underlying philosophy have directly and indirectly stimulated an enormous growth of alcoholism treatment programs of all types, both publicly and privately supported. With the addition of CMHC mandated alcoholism programs after 1975, there was in every state an assortment of federal, state, local, and private alcoholism treatment facilities (Akins & Williams, 1982; R. G. Dunham & Janik, 1985).

There were a number of similarities between the program of the 1971 Act and the deinstitutionalization of the mentally ill. For example, the Act had recommended that alcoholics be treated rather than jailed, and the federal government made available funds (through the state alcoholism agencies and as direct grants) to help establish new treatment facilities. Transferring individuals from the criminal justice system to the arena of medical and human services also helps to reduce the financial burden on the individual states, because many of these services were initially federally supported (Room, 1972). Another interesting analogy with deinstitutionalization is the issue of motives. It is generally considered that detoxication centers and medical surveillance units are more humane than drunk tanks and jail cells, but arguably these were little more than cosmetic changes, made for political reasons and supported by "arena-building" agency initiatives (see Chapter 9). Long-term prevention was not a priority, and no attempts were made to improve the life conditions and opportunities for the residents of skid row. As with the alternatives to mental hospital care, it was argued that the new way of handling public inebriates was more humane than incarceration, because the Act assumes voluntary participation on behalf of the client. However, as Fagan and Mauss (1978) have pointed out, incapacitated drunks could still be placed in custody for up to 48 hours to protect themselves and others.

In the following sections an attempt is made to evaluate the progress that has been made in providing alcoholism services during the last 2 decades. The first part deals with the specific goals of the Uniform Act; in the second and third parts the focus is broadened to consider the geographical distribution of alcoholism services. Before beginning, however, it should be noted that the Uniform Act itself was not entirely responsible for the growth in treatment services for alcoholics in the 1970s. There were some services being offered earlier, but as the data in Table 6.1 illustrate, the most significant changes by the 1970s were the vast growth in the number of services provided and the contribution of federal funds. By the middle of the 1970s, for example, it was estimated that more than 1.7 million individuals were treated for alcoholism and alcohol abuse in private and public programs (Vischi, Jones, Shank, & Lima, 1980), with perhaps as many as 700,000 more enrolled in Alcoholics Anonymous groups (Diesenhaus, 1982).

Before the 1950s the majority of treatment for alcoholics was provided in state mental hospitals, but state and local funds were first used to support alcoholism programs in the 1950s and 1960s (Akins & Williams, 1982). In 1970 the Comprehensive Alcohol Abuse and Alcoholism Prevention Treatment and Rehabilitation Act was passed, and this had a significant impact on the development of state and local programs. The Act and its amendments, as well as the federal incentive grants made available to help states implement the 1971 Uniform Act, had the effect of solidifying the federal commitment to fighting alcohol abuse. The National Institute on Alcohol Abuse and Alcoholism (NIAAA) was created at this time as the conduit for direct project grants to individual states. One of the major stimulants to the states was a new program of formula grants, which formed the basis for the "rapid and systematic growth of state and local alcoholism programs. . . . These . . . funds enabled states to pro-

Table 6.1. Alcoholism Treatment Services in the United States: 1942 and 1976

Treatment Location	1942	1976
State and county mental hospitals	10,461	111,000
Private mental hospitals	4,754	11,000
Public and other general hospitals	22,147	476,000
Federally funded alcoholism programs (NIAAA funded)	—	260,000
VA hospitals	3,886	133,000
Special institutions for alcoholics	6,689	—
Community Mental Health Centers	—	113,000
Other federal programs (Department of Defense, Indian Health Services)	—	79,000
Drug abuse facilities	—	17,000
Drinking Driver programs	—	28,000
Private physicians	NA[a]	423,000
Outpatient psychiatric clinics		53,000
Halfway houses		36,000
Mental health facilities		260,000
Alcoholics Anonymous		671,000
Total	47,937	2,383,000
Total U.S. Population	133,000,000	214,000,000

[a] Data not available

Sources. Adapted from information in NIAAA (1981a, p. 139), and Diesenhaus (1982, p. 223).

vide a wide range of services to previously unserved persons'' (Akins & Williams, 1982, p. 329).

The National Institute also required each state to produce plans for the development of alcoholism programs, and to coordinate such programs with those provided in other social service agencies. It is interesting to note that the early dominance of the NIAAA in the provision of alcoholism treatment programs did not continue. By the end of the 1970s what had once seemed like a vast infusion of NIAAA funds was dwarfed by funds from other sources. In 1981, for example, the public funding for alcoholism programs in the United States amounted to almost $811 million, of which only 13% ($102 million) was from NIAAA (NIAAA, 1981b). Almost 50% ($392 million) was contributed by the states themselves, and 26% ($212 million) came from other federal agencies such as the National Institute of Mental Health, the Veterans Administration system, and the Department of Transportation.

EVALUATING THE IMPACT OF THE UNIFORM INTOXICATION ACT

In recent years there have been many attempts to define exactly what components are needed to provide a fully comprehensive continuum of care (Costello,

1973a, 1973b). Pattison (1979) for example, has observed that the necessary components include information and referral centers to screen and channel clients into the most appropriate programs, general hospital programs, private physician outpatient care, mental hospitals, half-way houses, vocational rehabilitation clinics, outpatient clinics, skid-row agencies (including missions), industrial and military programs, and Alcoholics Anonymous-based self-help programs. Other studies have described similar sets of components (D. J. Anderson, 1979; Glaser, Greenberg, & Barrett, 1978), and with this literature as a guide it is possible to determine the extent to which a comprehensive alcohol service delivery system is available in a given state. In Pennsylvania Glaser and his colleagues classified alcohol programs according to the services they offered. The components were: (1) acute intervention facilities (detoxication centers); (2) evaluation centers (diagnostic and referral services); (3) intensive intervention (residential programs); (4) stabilization facilities (half-way houses); (5) maintenance programs (outpatient clinics); and (6) domiciliary care facilities (hospitals or missions) (see Figure 6.1). Although the labels for the components vary from place to place, Glaser argued that these six components constitute the functional requirements of a fully comprehensive service delivery system for alcoholics. In addition, each component has a logical relationship to the others, which under ideal circumstances allows clients to "flow" through and out of the system in one of a number of possible sequences, as shown in the illustration. The next section includes an evaluation of the extent to which such ideal arrangements are actually available for alcoholics. However, before dealing with this issue it is important to consider some of the human goals of decriminalization: Who would the clients be in the newly created facilities? How would they use what was made available? What impact, if any, would it have on them? What impact would they have on it? (Kurtz & Regier, 1975).

The evidence that quickly became available from the detoxication centers demonstrated that for the most part the clients entering the system were the same sort of people who had previously been arrested by the police. They had similar socioeconomic characteristics, and most of them came from the skid-row sections of town (Fagan & Mauss, 1978; Garber, Dolander, & Dexter, 1974; Keeley & Bell, 1976). In general, the length of stay in the detoxication centers was short, varying form 3.7 to 7 days (Rodin *et al.*, 1982). This was not a good sign because the length of time spent in these facilities is thought to be a good indicator of the use of other treatment services, it also meant that in comparison to earlier times, inebriates were now spending less time being sober and off the streets. It was felt that this could have serious impacts on their health, without the enforced period of sobriety that came with incarceration.

One expectation of the Uniform Act was that police intervention in the process would diminish, thereby "softening" what many critics had viewed as the more odious social control elements involved with public drunkenness processing. With inebriation now officially treated as an illness, it was hoped that most admissions would be voluntary, and the major institutional contacts would be with social service personnel. In Seattle, for example, Fagan and Mauss (1978) showed that an Emergency Service Patrol (a corps of civilians) brought most of the clients to the detoxication programs. However, their data also demonstrated that although the police were less involved, the overall level of "social control activity" did not diminish (Finn, 1985). As Cohen (1979) observed, the "machine" of social control may have become "softer" in recent times, but it has certainly not become smaller. Fagan and Mauss (1978) suggest that there may be a "constancy dictum" at work, a minimum threshold level of deviance or crime in a community, that has to be dealt with by official actions. When the police were no longer involved with arresting public drunks, they were free to deal with the other "crimes" and public problems that are prevalent on skid row. As a result, the combined activity of the police and the detoxication centers after decriminalization would be approximately equal to the volume of police activity before decriminalization, and the evidence from Seattle seemed to substantiate this. Whether public drunkenness is treated as a crime or as an illness, the overall amount of social control activity remained constant, averaging between 10,000 to 11,000 persons per year between 1970 and 1976.

Perhaps the most optimistic and probably the most unrealistic expectation following the Uniform Act was the hope that by treating public inebriates as sick people in the detoxication facilities, they would assimilate the sick role and start presenting themselves regularly for treatment in other parts of the delivery system. Consistent with this expectation was the hope that readmissions through the revolving door would decline, as the overall prevalence of public drunkenness became lower. From most empirical accounts it appears that this has not been the case; in fact in many instances the level of recidivism is now anywhere from two to six times higher than it was before decriminalization (Annis & Smart, 1978; Fagan & Mauss, 1978; Finn, 1985; Hamilton, 1979).

In-depth studies of the recidivists conducted by Rodin and her colleagues (1982) show that the clients involved are generally those with the worst prognosis for rehabilitation, so that the expectation that the overall prevalence of public inebriation would be reduced is not being met. It appears in fact that public inebriates are using the detoxication facilities, but not the other treatment programs that are available. In this sense, the detoxication program has become just another institution on skid row, albeit a more humane and less stigmatized one than the drunk tanks and the jails. To use Fagan and Mauss' (1978) term, this has not closed but merely "padded" the revolving door. Rodin *et al.'s* (1982) conclusion on this issue was that "chronic inebriates incorporate detox into pre-existing patterns of resource exploitation" (p 24). The new system simplifies skid row for the drunkard. Even before the passage of the Uniform Act, J. P. Wiseman (1970) had used the analogy with a transit system to describe skid row, with individuals shuffling drunkenly from one "station" to another—from the court to the jail, to the mission, and so on. After the Act, skid row decriminalized had fewer "stations," but because the facilities were better, people wanted to visit them more frequently.

It is also possible that the attempts to incorporate chronic alcoholics into treatment programs has had a profoundly negative effect on the providers of care. The chronic inebriate fundamentally challenges the medical model of alcoholism treatment, in which the cycle of detoxication followed by treatment and accompanied by enforced abstinence is seen as the only route to rehabilitation. Instead, it appears that the inebriates use the detoxication facility as a place to stop for awhile before returning to the street. In other words, for them drinking has become a way of life, perhaps an adaptation to the stress of poverty and deprivation, and the medical model of individual treatment simply does not offer a viable alternative. The presence of even a small number of chronic street alcoholics in the treatment system challenges the unitary paradigm of treatment, and their failure to assimilate the goals of treatment contributes to staff demoralization and burnout, which reinforces the already prevalent view of alcoholism as a difficult problem to deal with (Rodin *et al.*, 1982).

In light of the empirical evidence available so far, there is no reason to believe that the encroachment of the medical treatment philosophy into the realm of public drunkenness has had any positive effects (Conrad & Schneider, 1980). In human terms, little has changed on skid row, and the new facilities made possible by the Uniform Act may simply be allowing skid-row residents to perpetuate their lifestyles: "There is nothing to stop the chronic inebriate from self-referral to the detox center . . . two or three times in a given week. A few days of drunkenness can be interspersed with a few days in detox, and this round of life can continue indefinitely, at public expense . . ." (Fagan & Mauss, 1978, p. 244).

Equity and Efficiency in the Provision of Alcoholism Services

At the end of an exhaustive investigation of the alcoholism treatment programs in Pennsylvania, Glaser and his colleagues (1978) concluded that the pattern of treatment was essentially the same from one program to the next, and from one area to the next. They also observed that the clients tended toward unformity. A typical profile was of an older white male with working-class origins and a history of chronic alcoholism, dotted with multiple readmissions to a range of different programs. Most of the available facilities were for these chronic alcoholics, the individuals who were "far gone into an alcoholic lifestyle long before the intervention was begun" (Glaser *et al.*, 1978, p. 61).

The authors added that the client homogeneity they had observed in Pennsylvania was probably a result of the shortage of funds and the difficulty of providing effective treatment for chronic inebriates. After a review of similar studies in other American states and Canadian provinces, they concluded that the Pennsylvania situation was fairly typical of the late 1970s. Innovative programs do exist in many states, but in general they are outweighed by the mass of uniformity of the type found in Pennsylvania.

In a fully comprehensive service delivery system as envisioned by the Uniform Act, a client would have access to all six of the components identified earlier (see Figure 6.1). However, as Glaser *et al.* observed in Pennsylvania, 57 (71%) of the 80 programs they looked at had only one component, and another 13 (16%) had only two components. None of the programs contained all of the six components, although residents of Allegheny County (Pittsburgh) had access to all six. Furthermore, the majority of clients who used treatment facilities used outpatient clinics. Glaser's team concluded that alcohol treatment in Pennsylvania consisted of a large number of small programs operating virtually in isolation. There was almost no evidence of any comprehensive system of services, and presumably no underlying philosophy behind the delivery of services. The dominance of outpatient treatment is typical of most states, and probably reflects both the ease of establishing such programs and a resigned acceptance that the best that can be done for alcoholics is to maintain them at an impaired level of functioning.

To look further into the pattern of delivery of services for alcoholics, the distribution of different programs in the state of Oklahoma was investigated, in an attempt to assess the extent to which residents in different parts of the state had access to a comprehensive range of facilities (C. J. Smith, 1983b). As a result of the Uniform Act there were many different alcoholism programs across the state, but as of 1980, 33 (43%) of Oklahoma's 77 counties provided no alcohol services at all, another 15 (19%) had only one satellite facility, and 10 (13%) had only one independent outpatient facility. In only 19 (25%) of Oklahoma's counties were alcoholism services provided in more than one of the three basic categories and only 7 had fully comprehensive services. Three of these counties are the state's most urbanized areas, and three others are the locations of the state's oldest established community mental health centers, all of which offer alcoholism services. The three counties in the second comprehensiveness category are the sites of Oklahoma's public mental hospitals. In most states public mental hospitals have continued to dominate the alcoholism service delivery system even after the Uniform Act; in Oklahoma almost a third (31.5%) of all hospital admissions in 1980 were patients with alcohol-related diagnoses.

In one sense the spatial pattern of alcoholism programs indicates an uneven distribution of facilities across the state. In spite of obvious attempts to decentralize the programs to reach rural and "special" populations (Native Americans and women), there are many counties that still had at best only one outpatient facility, and in some cases this was only a satellite clinic of a community mental health center. This suggests that the service delivery in Oklahoma is similar to that in Pennsylvania (Glaser *et al.*, 1978) in that it is dominated by outpatient programs, with fully comprehensive services available in only a few locations.

On the other hand, the map of comprehensiveness at the county level (Figure 6.2), shows that the seven counties with comprehensive services are fairly evenly spread throughout the state. Taking the distribution of population into account, it appears that the 1980 pattern is a relatively efficient way to distribute alcoholism services. In these seven counties live almost half of the entire population of Oklahoma, and in general terms the level of comprehensiveness is positively related to the degree of urbanism, which means that the remote and rural parts of Oklahoma are largely unserved. There are 33 counties with no alcoholism services at all, but in only 5 of these are there towns with populations above 10,000. In strictly economic and geographical terms, Oklahoma's alcoholism service delivery system can be evaluated positively, because the lion's share of the services are provided where most of the people live.

When we consider the equity of the distribution of services, a somewhat different picture emerges. Equity refers to the degree of equality in the distributive system, and one way of evaluating the equity in a specific pattern is to consider the idea of territorial justice (Pinch, 1985). If a delivery system is socially and spatially just, we would expect to find that the availability of services in a particular locality is positively correlated with the demand for services across the locality (Pinch, 1979, 1980). If we assume that there are a number of possible indicators of the demand for services, we should expect to find that the level of need is highest in the counties with the most comprehensive services, and vice versa. In Oklahoma, using seven different indicators, there is only limited evidence that this is the case (C. J. Smith, 1983b). There is apparently little relationship between the distribution of alcoholism services and the need for such services.

Alcoholism Services at the Macrolevel: Some Empirical Observations

Extending this discussion of alcoholism treatment services to the national level, it is evident that the distribution of resources earmarked for alcoholism is only partly responsive to the need for service (C. J. Smith, 1986). In a nationwide study of the availability of alcoholism treatment services, R. G. Dunham and Janik (1985) discovered that the states that have adopted the Uniform Act or an equivalent have generally provided a greater range of services (Table 6.2). It is of course possible that the provision of services is only indirectly related to the new legislation, and that the most significant predictor of both service provision and adoption of the Act is a third, unaccounted-for variable, such as political "liberalness."

The Dunham and Janik study also demonstrated that the geographical pattern of alcoholism services is not particularly responsive to the pattern of needs. In a regression model the authors found that the indicators of need were poor predictors of the actual availability of alcoholism services in each state ($R = .13$ in metropolitan areas, and .11 in nonmetropolitan areas). When the adoption

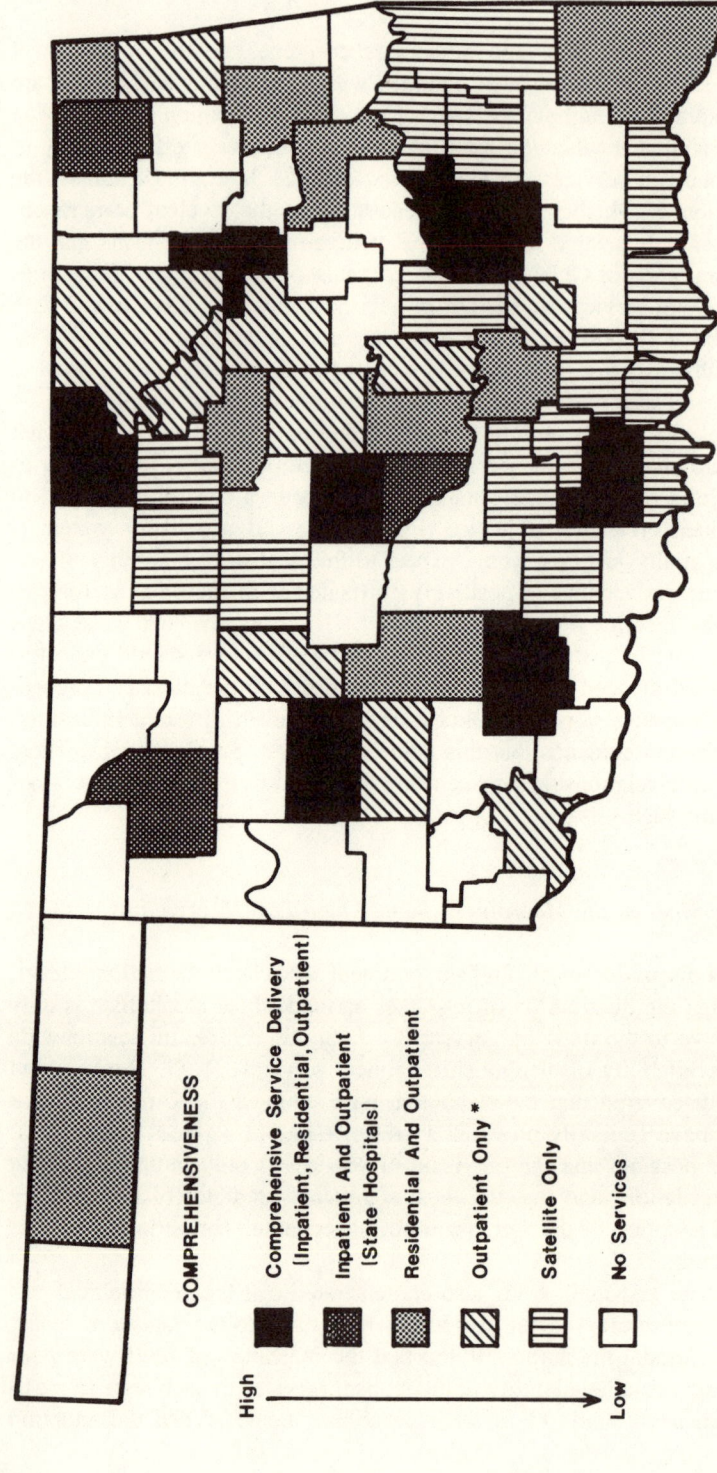

Figure 6.2. Alcoholism treatment comprehensiveness: 1980.
*Delaware and Washita Counties have one residential facility (halfway house) each, but no outpatient facility.
Source. Smith (1983b, p. 375).

Table 6.2. Availability of Alcoholism Treatment Programs and Adoption of the Uniform Alcoholism Act (by Region and Census Divisions)

Region and Division	Number of Programs per million population	Percent of States Adopting the Uniform Act
Northeast	30	44
New England	38	50
Middle Atlantic	14	33
North Central	32	75
East North Central	24	60
West North Central	38	86
South	21	29
South Atlantic	21	56
East South Central	21	0
West South Central	23	0
West	43	85
Mountain	44	88
Pacific	41	80

Source. Adapted from Dunham and Janik (1985, p. 513).

of the Uniform Act was entered into the models, the predictions increased considerably, to .30 and .26 respectively. It appears that by adopting the Act states were indicating a willingness to increase the provision of alcoholism treatment services, but it is equally clear that variables other than need played a major part in determining the actual level of program activity in each state.

A look at the allocation to states of federal funds for alcoholism treatment programs by NIAAA shows that in 1981 this amounted to almost $102 million. In an attempt to predict which states would receive proportionately more than their "share" of these federal funds, per capita NIAAA allocations are regressed against a range of potential indicators of the needs for alcoholism services (C. J. Smith, 1986). Most of the variance was accounted for by two variables: spirits consumption per capita, and the percentage of Native Americans in the population. Although this is a controversial issue, there is significant evidence that rates of alcohol-related problems are higher among Native Americans than among the population as a whole (Cahalan, Cisin, & Crossley, 1969). The empirical evidence demonstrates that a significant portion of the treatment resources are allocated by NIAAA on a "formula" basis, according to variations in the level of need. It is fairly well known from the alcoholism epidemiology literature that problem drinking is at least in part a function of the overall alcohol consumption level, which is particularly high in areas heavily populated by Native Americans (C. J. Smith & Hanham, 1982).

Turning to the priorities given to alcoholism treatment in each of the states, using the per capita capacity of treatment programs as the dependent variable, it is again clear that service provision at the state level is reasonably responsive to the perceived level of demand. Again the percentage of Native Americans in the population is the first variable to enter the regression model, followed by education levels, and the supply of physicians (C. J. Smith, 1986). This suggests that treatment for alcoholism is more likely to be available in the more enlightened (or better educated) states, but the negative relationship with physician supply is more difficult to interpret, because it implies that alcoholism treatment is more available in the states that are not well endowed with physicians. In terms of equity and social justice, this is an optimistic finding, because it suggests that in some states the commitment to providing alcoholism services works to counter the existing inequities.

The empirical studies that have been conducted at a number of different geographical sites have produced some mixed results. In the wake of the Uniform Intoxication Act a wide range of alcoholism treatment facilities began to appear, and the net effect has been that, on average, individual access to alcoholism services has increased considerably. On the other hand, outside the nation's largest cities, potential clients rarely have access to a full continuum of alcoholism services, as the architects of the Uniform Act had hoped. With a few exceptions it appears that the location of alcoholism services is only marginally related to the need for such services. In this sense the legislation has done little to overturn the "inverse care law," which predicts that services are most likely to be located where they are least needed (C. J. Smith, 1986; Knox, 1982).

NOTES

1. In some states, California for example, decriminalization is a by-county option and in others like Arkansas, the Act has been passed without provisions for decriminalization.

7

Diversion of Youthful Offenders

INTRODUCTION: FINDING ALTERNATIVES
FOR YOUTHFUL OFFENDERS

In the last 15 years there have been significant changes in the operation of the juvenile justice system in the United States. This chapter focuses on the diversion of juveniles away from the criminal justice system.[1] Diversion can be defined generally as the process of substituting alternatives to further judicial processing for juvenile offenders (Bullington, Sprowls, Katkin, & Phillips, 1982; Palmer & Lewis, 1980a). In general, a more benign intervention is substituted for official processing through the courts. For example, the police may refer an arrested youth to an agency for employment counseling rather than on to probation, or the probation officer may refer a youth to a mental health clinic rather than petitioning the court (Binder & Geis, 1984). Although this definition seems to be straightforward, there has been some ambiguity about exactly what is meant by diversion. Some authors have used other terms to describe the process, including "judicious nonintervention" (Lemert, 1967; Schur, 1973) and "minimal penetration" (Lemert, 1981). Those who have used the term diversion point out that it has two major parts: diversion *out of* the criminal justice system without further action, and diversion *to* a variety of services in the community (Bullington *et al.*, 1978; Klein, 1979).

The concept of diversion is not new to the field of juvenile justice. One of the major goals of the reformers in the late 19th century was to provide some humane alternatives to the harshness of the existing system (Howlett, 1982). These reforms eventually paved the way for the establishment of the juvenile court system in 1906. As we saw in Chapter 5, the philanthropic motives of the 19th-century reformers have subsequently been challenged by revisionist social historians. Platt (1969), for example, has interpreted the juvenile court movement as an attempt by the middle classes to exercise further control over the new urban poor. This cycle of optimism and disillusionment with social reform policies has an interesting parallel in the current critical evaluation of the reforms that were launched in the 1960s and 1970s. As we shall see, there were great hopes for what diversion could achieve, but by the 1980s few if any of those hopes had materialized.

THE HISTORY OF JUVENILE DIVERSION

The juvenile justice reform movement was publicly initiated by the report of President Johnson's Commission on Law Enforcement and the Administration of Justice in 1967 (Blomberg, 1983). Long before this time, however, there had been extensive public debates about the need to reform the juvenile system. One of the outcomes of the juvenile court legislation of the early 20th century was the creation of additional categories of children who were to come under the jurisdiction of the courts. These categories included children whose status was "dependent" and "neglected," as well as those whose behavior was defined as "incorrigible," "immoral," "truant," or "runaway" (these children were collectively referred to as "status offenders" implying that their offenses resulted from their status as children). This extension of decision-making discretion was justified by the legal and social philosophy of *"parens patria,"* which asserted that the court would act in the best interests of the child, and could do this effectively only if it was unencumbered by formal rules and procedures (Rendleman, 1979).

One of the major goals of the recent diversion movement was to reduce the reach and discretion of the courts over children, especially those who had not committed a criminal act. The widespread use of self-report measures of delinquency in the 1960s also indicated that the jurisdiction of the court was spread too widely. The self-report data showed that a majority of youth admitted to minor delinquency and status offenses (Hindelang, Hirschi, & Weis, 1981). The fact that only a relatively small proportion of them went to court suggested that the entire process was arbitrary and discriminatory.

A second major argument for diversion was based on the evidence that court processing produced negative effects on youth. As a result of the broad reach of the juvenile justice system, many children were being institutionalized or placed under court jurisdiction in the name of rehabilitation. The studies conducted in juvenile institutions demonstrated that far from being rehabilitative, life inside was often coercive, restrictive, and punitive (Lerman, 1975; Palmer & Lewis, 1980a). A more influential argument was the one based on labeling theory. It was argued that the formal imposition of stigmatizing labels such as "delinquent" reinforced the development of a deviant identity and encouraged further law breaking (Palmer & Lewis, 1980a).

According to the labeling theorists, a delinquent career rarely follows an isolated act of deviance. The reaction of the individual to the discovery of his or her actions is critical in the development of "secondary deviance" (Lemert, 1981). The court ceremony of officially labeling an adolescent as delinquent for behavior that is typical of many of his or her peers tends to reinforce the likelihood of further deviant acts (Bullington *et al.*, 1982). This becomes even more likely when the individual is removed from the normalizing influence of family and school and placed in an institution with others in a similar situation.

At the extreme end of the argument we find the work of Schur (1965), who believed that the best approach to delinquency was to leave youth alone whenever possible. Although this proved too radical for most reformers, it is clear that labeling theorists of a milder persuasion have exerted a significant effect on the development of juvenile justice policy in recent years.

Another motivation for diversion was the evidence that alternatives to formal processing often had beneficial results. Even before the legislation introducing diversion in 1974, the provision of alternatives for youthful offenders had been occurring on an informal basis, mainly as a result of police initiatives (Bullington *et al.*, 1982). In many cases juveniles were steered away from the courts and were referred to whatever programs were available in the community. This alternative was usually disproportionately available to affluent and largely white middle-class youth, so the extension of the practice to a wider population was interpreted as the redistribution of services to populations in need. The major hope of the new legislation was that youth could be better served if the juvenile justice system was made "softer" and less coercive (Blomberg, 1979; Cohen, 1979).

As we have already seen in the case of deinstitutionalization and decriminalization, there were multiple goals for diversion. The most important of these was to reduce the number of youth processed in the courts and ultimately incarcerated. It was also hoped that diversion would help to reduce the worst effects of labeling and the stigmatizing experience of going to court. The provision of services in the community would offer some viable alternatives to troubled adolescents, in an attempt to keep them away from further formal contacts with the criminal justice system (Bohnstedt, 1978). Diversion would also help to lower the rate of recidivism, partly by reducing the amount of secondary deviance, and partly by providing alternative services. Another attraction of diversion was the possibility of a considerable cost saving, as a result of reducing the volume of court processing and lowering the rate of institutionalization (Palmer & Lewis, 1980a).

The report of the President's Commission in 1967 stated explicitly that diversion could not succeed without the provision of viable alternatives in the community. A primary function of diversion was to provide services that were independent of the formal court system. The Commission anticipated that a range of different services would be provided, including vocational assistance, after-school education and recreational programs, and family counseling (Blomberg, 1983). The Commission also suggested the creation of Youth Service Bureaus, which were to perform a coordinating and referral function within the network of community services (Tonry, 1976). In later years the widespread availability of funding through the Law Enforcement Assistance Administration (LEAA) would help some of these suggestions to materialize. Unlike the situation for former mental patients and alcoholics, in many areas there was no shortage of community services for diverted and deinstitutionalized youth.

In 1973 the report of the National Advisory Commission on Criminal Justice Standards and Goals reiterated the themes of diverting juveniles, reducing institutionalization, and decriminalizing status offenses. In comparison to earlier reports, there was more emphasis given at this time to due process procedures that would provide procedural safeguards to youth. The effect of this would be to narrow the jurisdiction of the juvenile court system (Lemert, 1981; Tonry, 1976).

In 1974 many of these reform ideas were embodied in new legislation by the passing of the Juvenile Justice and Delinquency Prevention Act. Status offenders were especially targeted for deinstitutionalization, and diversion programs were recommended as an alternative. A priority was also given to the early identification and prevention of deliquency. Throughout the 1970s diversion would become increasingly associated with these other reform policies. Because diversion programs had been relatively well funded, they were used by a variety of subgroups within the troubled youth population: Status offenders, young offenders who were outside the jurisdiction of the juvenile court, and predelinquent youth were now eligible for the new services that had been created under the auspices of diversion. Although the new programs were being asked to provide services for clients who were targeted by these other policy initiatives, the objectives of these other policies were not always compatible with those of diversion (Palmer & Lewis, 1980b).

EVALUATING DIVERSION

Diversion has been widely criticized in recent years, largely as a result of the inflated expectations that were generated (Blomberg, 1979, 1983; Bullington *et al.*, 1982; Dunford, Osgood, & Weichselbaum, 1982; M. Klein, 1979). Early attempts to evaluate the effects of diversion amounted to little more than a simple listing of the range of services that had been funded, but in later years federal funding was made available to support more rigorous evaluation attempts (Palmer & Lewis, 1980a). Before reviewing the findings of these studies, it is useful to point out some of the enormous difficulties encountered by the evaluation researchers. One of the major problems has been the conceptual ambiguity of the original concept of diversion (Rojek, 1982). It has proved almost impossible to compare programs whose goals were dramatically different. For example, some programs were based on a ''hands-off'' approach with no follow-up (Schur, 1973); but others involved much more direct involvement with troubled youth and referrals to community services (M. Klein, 1979). It has also been difficult to evaluate diversion programs because they have been serving clients who were not originally intended to be served by such programs. The major category of inappropriately placed clients in diversion programs are minor offenders who would probably not have entered the system at all before the new practices were implemented (Van Dusen, 1981). Although there have no doubt been some advantages to providing troubled juveniles with services, this was not the original mission of diversion.

Another obstacle to evaluation is the general lack of appropriate research designs. Many studies have failed to provide adequate experimental control groups whose outcomes could be compared with diverted groups (M. Klein, 1979). It has also been difficult to establish meaningful outcome measures, which are often limited to official rearrest records on the negative side, and vague indicators of school performance and truancy rates on the positive side (Dunford *et al.*, 1982). Unfortunate though it may be, negative findings that result from flawed research tend to discredit the policy research itself rather than the policy (Rausch & Logan, 1983). For this reason it is important that high-quality research continues to evaluate diversion programs, which have remained popular in spite of the lack of any clear evidence of their effectiveness.

Direct Outcomes

The original goals of diversion were (Palmer & Lewis, 1980a):

1. To avoid the stigma and negative consequences of labeling;
2. To reduce the overall amount of social control within the juvenile justice system;
3. To reduce the total volume of illegal behavior among youth;
4. To increase the quantity and quality of community-based services;
5. To reduce the overall costs of operating the juvenile justice system.

Self-report studies have been used to assess the extent to which individuals feel less stigmatized as a result of diversion efforts. According to one nationwide study, a diversion disposition proved to be no more effective in reducing the perception of stigma than either normal judicial processing or outright release (Dunford *et al.*, 1982). A further analysis of this data suggested that labeling experiences differed widely depending on the particular program under study (Osgood & Weichselbaum, 1984). The clients in diversion programs were generally not sensitive to the way others, particularly the service providers, perceived them, and their own perceptions of their stigmatization were more benign than those of the service providers.[2]

One of the problems involved in evaluating the ability of diversion programs to reduce the amount of illegal behavior is the difficulty of assessing whether the juveniles who were diverted would have progressed to other illegal behaviors had the programs not been available. M. Klein (1979) has argued that inappropriate clients were selected for diversion—many of those who were diverted would not have been processed formally in the criminal justice system. Similarly, Palmer and Lewis (1980b), who noted a 17% reduction in recidivism in a large diversion program, reported that almost a half of the clients would probably not have received any attention were it not for diversion. In these studies as well as in others, evidence of significantly lower rates of recidivism have been reported for diverted clients in comparison to petitioned offenders (Blomberg, 1983; Bohnstedt, 1978; Gibbons & Blake, 1976). On the other hand, one study suggested that diversion with no referrals was more successful than diversion with referrals (M. Klein, 1979) and another showed that diversion to community services was no more effective in reducing recidivism than outright release (Dunford *et al.*, 1982). Interestingly, however, this latter study found that the clients had been truly diverted, in that they would have been processed through the court system if diversion programs had not been available.

It was hoped that diversion would help to reduce the duration and degree of coercive sanctions on juveniles (the social control argument). As noted earlier in the chapters dealing with deinstitutionalization and decriminalization (Chs. 5 & 6), it is difficult to argue that this has in fact occurred, in spite of the humane objectives of the policy. There are indications that "at risk" juveniles are diverted from the court process; Bohnstedt (1978), for example, found that about one-half of the clients in 11 California diversion projects would have been processed further, and this finding has been replicated in other studies (Dunford *et al.*, 1982; Palmer, 1979). Some diversion programs have also resulted in a general decrease in status offense referrals to court, as well as status offender incarcerations (Decker, 1985; Krisberg & Schwartz, 1983). On the other hand, diversion has resulted in far more juveniles than ever before being placed under some form of social control (Austin & Krisberg, 1981; Nejelski, 1976; Van Dusen, 1981). Diverted clients do not vanish from the system altogether as some academics and policy makers had hoped or predicted (Schur, 1973). Instead they are referred to a variety of service programs where there is an explicit or implicit mandate to accept them as clients. One of the problems here is the question of interpretation. It is possible to argue that the greater level of involvement of juveniles in counseling and educational programs can only have beneficial effects, and that the provision of services to a larger number of clients meets rather than violates one of the goals of diversion (Binder & Geis, 1983). The other side to the argument is the fear that the state and its human service agencies are interfering unnecessarily in the lives of individuals with potentially negative consequences (Cohen, 1979).

The issue of cost saving is also difficult to evaluate at the present time. If as many as 50% of the clients in diversion programs would not have been processed under normal circumstances, it seems extremely unlikely that any cost savings would be possible (Blomberg, 1979; Bohnstedt, 1978). In an investigation of the costs involved in four diversion projects, Dunford and his colleagues (1982) found wildly divergent costs for services, ranging from a low figure of $429 per client enrolled, to a high of $4,136. Court costs on the other hand ranged from $298 to $652 per client. Data such as this raises some serious questions about diversion programs on the grounds of cost alone. In this study, which has been widely acclaimed for its sound research methodology, the evidence that diversion with services resulted in no measurable advantages over diversion without services strongly favors the cheaper alternative.

Indirect Outcomes

Two major types of indirect and largely unanticipated effects of diversion have been highlighted in the recent literature. The first is an increased level of social control exerted by the state over youth ("net widening"), and the second is the tendency to fit youth into the available programs by creating new categories of deviance ("relabeling").

Net widening has been used as a general label to describe what is in fact a very complex phenomenon (Binder & Geis, 1984). Some social scientists have been greatly concerned that surveillance and social sanctions have been extended to an entirely new subgroup of youth in the name of diversion (Cohen, 1979; Van Dusen, 1981). The original goal of diversion was to provide noncoercive alternatives to court processing for troubled youth, but in fact many youth along with their families have entered into some type of social control arrangement as a result of diversion. Some of the services to which individuals have been referred have themselves contracted a spoiled identity, and in many cases entry into such programs is not voluntary. Obviously such programs are not as coercive or as punitive as juvenile institutions, but they nevertheless are perceived in the community as stigmatized facilities (Blomberg, 1979; Bullington *et al.*, 1982; Austin & Krisberg, 1981). Youth who would formerly have been released without attention now enter into the official records, and in this way new cases of "delinquency" are created (Cohen, 1979; Lerman, 1975).

The role of the police has been crucial in this respect. Under the new guidelines the police have been able to extend their role as social control agents by focusing their activities on a broader group of the juvenile population (Lemert, 1981). Most of the contact between the police and juveniles is shielded from public view. In comparison to court hearings, diversion decisions have become increasingly nonreviewable and discretionary. The referral agents have become less accountable for their decisions, and to a large extent the entire procedure is insulated from due process safeguards (Bullington *et al.*, 1982).

The other side to this argument is that potentially troubled youth and their families have benefited from the exposure to a greater range of community-based services (Binder & Geis, 1984). The critical stance of many academics is based on the assumption that net-widening is a sinister and intrusive trend (Gusfield, 1984), but in fact this assumption has rarely been subjected to systematic study. In the relatively few studies that have been conducted, the results appear to be contradictory (Rausch & Logan, 1983; Saul & Davidson, 1982).

As noted earlier, the use of diversion programs for juveniles who do not need such services has resulted in part from the use of such programs to fulfill the goals of other policies, particularly deinstitutionalization (M. Klein, 1979; Lemert, 1981). It is also likely that the net-widening phenomenon is related to organizational goals and arena building (see Chapter 9). Individual diversion programs continually have to justify their existence by demonstrating a need for their services. One of the most effective ways to achieve this is to keep enrollments up and intakes high (Cohen, 1979; Rojek, 1982). With a well-developed network of community services, it is possible for providers to "beat the bushes" for referrals from schools and the police. As we have seen in many other branches of the human services, there are usually enough potential clients in the community who are experiencing some degree of trouble for which formal services are potentially appropriate.

The relabeling phenomenon refers to the deliberate alteration of a juvenile's status to justify some continuation of mandated service. This process commonly occurs for status offenders who can be relabeled as delinquents or dependents (Spergel, Reamer, & Lynch, 1981). A related process is the transfer of offenders from one system to another, a phenomenon that has been referred to as "transinstitutionalization" (C. A. B. Warren, 1981; Wolch, Nelson, & Rubalcuba, 1987). As we saw in the case of the mentally ill and chronic inebriates, the social service system often replaces the criminal justice system as the major service provider, but this in itself does not guarantee a more humane form of treatment. In the case of juveniles there is evidence that length of stay in diversion programs often matches and sometimes exceeds that in the juvenile justice facilities, and the experience is often equally stigmatizing (M. Klein, 1979; Rojek, 1982).

Diversion programs have proved extremely difficult to implement and even more difficult to evaluate. According to most observers the outcomes of diversion have been radically different from the goals that were proposed (Lemert, 1981). Others feel that diversion has never been implemented in its original form as a result of theoretical confusion and organizational obstacles. The net effect of this is that we do not really know whether diversion could have worked (M. Klein, 1979). Attempts to evaluate the existing programs have been inconclusive, and many of them have been flawed by methodological difficulties. An assessment of what has been done, however, indicates that there is little empirical support for the widespread continuation of diversion as a juvenile justice policy (Polk, 1984). As we have seen in the previous two chapters, the story of diversion is largely one of failure to achieve its stated goals, but in retrospect those goals were probably unrealistic. As a social policy diversion was initially a popular and humane effort to reform the juvenile justice system. Even in the absence of clear-cut evidence of its benefits, diversion has persisted, largely because it has generated a growing constituency of service providers and interest groups.

NOTES

1. Diversion should be differentiated from three other reform strategies that emerged in the treatment of juvenile offenders, namely deinstitutionalization, due process, and decriminalization. Deinstitutionalization involves the community placement of juveniles who have already been processed through the courts and are currently in institutions. Decriminalization is the change in legal status of an offense that is currently defined as illegal but that has subsequently been redefined as not illegal. Due process involves giving defendents greater adversarial procedural rights during the pretrial stage of the criminal justice process (Austin & Krisberg, 1981). Instead of a concern with swift case disposition and the presumption of guilt, this would emphasize formal procedural rules and the presumption of innocence.

2. These findings cast considerable doubt on the validity of labeling theory as a theoretical rationale for diversion (Osgood & Weichselbaum, 1984; Dunford *et al.*, 1982) and confirm criticisms of the theory itself (Blomberg 1978, 1979; Rausch & Logan, 1983). A study of the effect of diversion programs compared to juvenile court processing on subsequent rates of delinquency indicates that official labeling of offenders appears to make little difference (Rausch, 1983).

PART FOUR

THE POLITICAL CONTEXT
OF PUBLIC PROBLEMS

8

Structural Accounts of Public Problems

INTRODUCTION

Social scientists have produced some sophisticated theoretical explanations to account for the etiology of public problems, and although most of them have abandoned strictly positivist interpretations, for pragmatic reasons the provision of services still tends to be based on a positivist account of public problems. The provision of services for alcohol abusers, for example, is dominated by the medical model and the assumption that the problems associated with alcohol have a clear medical or psychological cause that is amenable to treatment (Peele, 1984). The sharp discrepancy between the research conducted by social scientists and the actual provision of services should not surprise us, but the impact on those who receive the services may be significant. The critics of the positivist accounts of public problems argue that until the political and economic underpinnings of such problems are addressed, any attempts to solve them will be inadequate.

THE POSITIVIST ACCOUNT OF PUBLIC PROBLEMS

The positivist view is based on the assumption that problems are real and are objectively experienced by the individual in question. The task of scientists of all persuasions is, therefore, to search for causal explanations. It is assumed that the source of the problem will be located within the individual rather than in his or her social and physical environment. There is good reason for the proponents of such a view to cling doggedly to their beliefs. In the field of alcohol abuse the struggle for scientific recognition was an arduous task, and it was not until the 1950s that alcoholism was officially recognized as a disease by the medical profession in the United States (Beauchamp, 1980). After such a struggle to have alcoholism defined as an individual problem, it is unlikely that other accounts of alcoholism will easily dislodge the medical model. For the defenders of the disease concept the alternatives are not only poor substitutes, they are anachronisms, because to accept that alcoholism is primarily a social or a cultural problem implies that the field is unscientific and therefore not respectable.

The positivist account assumes that there is a norm of functioning that has been defined over a long period of time. Against this norm the physiological and psychological symptoms of the individual can be compared and a set of propositions defining the condition can be established. In the alcoholism field the concept of a disease evolved slowly into a small number of beliefs that were generally agreed upon, even though they could not be supported by research findings (Watts, 1981):

1. Alcoholics have predisposing characteristics that are significantly different from nonalcoholics. The search for an "alcoholic personality" has failed to substantiate that alcoholics are significantly different from nonalcoholics; the only unequivocal fact is that alcoholics drink more than everyone else (Freed, 1979; Roebuck & Kessler, 1972).

2. Alcoholics develop an allergic reaction to drink, and they are unable to stop once they start drinking. The "loss of control" hypothesis obviously fits some alcoholics, but reviews of the literature show that this trait is nowhere near universal (Pattison, 1976; S. Shaw, Cartwright, Spratley, & Harwin, 1978).

3. Alcoholism is a progressive, chronic, and irreversible process that evolves inexorably toward death. This piece of crude social Darwinism simply does not fit the facts (Cahalan, 1970). Many individuals move backwards and forwards along the consumption curve, with a corresponding waxing and waning in the level of alcohol-related problems (Peele, 1984).

4. Alcoholism can only be treated if the individual abstains completely from drinking. Evidence accumulated in the last decade shows that some alcoholics are able to return to moderate drinking (Armor, Polich, & Stamboul, 1976), although this conclusion is hotly contested in the alcoholism treatment field, particularly in the United States (Heather & Robertson, 1981).

Critics of the disease model of alcoholism argue that its ascendance is an example of the "social construction" of reality. A concept, in this case the concept of disease, is borrowed from another field, and through time "the borrowed concept will determine what subjects or things or processes are to be considered for treatment . . . under the heading 'alcoholism' " (Watts, 1981, p. 98). Some of the implications of the disease model for the treatment of alcoholism are clear: It is assumed that alcoholics cannot stop themselves from drinking; they are sick and therefore they cannot be "blamed" for their situation, but they can be restored to health by the most appropriate form of treatment that is available.

The medical model is a humane response to alcoholism, especially in comparison to past alternatives, according to which alcoholics have been treated as degenerates, sinners, or criminals. On the other hand, treating alcoholism as a disease may preclude a search for other causes, and it may obscure the need for developing preventive strategies (P. M. Miller & Niremberg, 1984). The persistence of the disease concept of alcoholism in the face of compelling counterevidence from many branches of the social sciences attests to the strength of medical dominance in the area of human health and public problems (Room, 1984).

THE INTERACTIONIST ACCOUNT OF PUBLIC PROBLEMS

Partly as a result of the empirical inadequacies of the positivist view, many sociologists have argued that "deviance" is largely an ascribed status, one that is related only marginally to an individual's symptoms (Room, 1975). Being identified as a problem sufferer is a status conferred upon an individual. It is, in other words, an emergent outcome of social interaction, and it results from the contacts made between rule breakers and the social actors who define their behaviors as deviant. Once the label is assigned it tends to become fixed, with the result that some individuals gradually acquire a deviant self-image and drift into an increasingly deviant lifestyle. In one of the earliest studies of public inebriates, Pittman and Gordon (1958) described how certain individuals brush up against the agents of social control who create the categories of deviance and provide the facilities for processing drunks. At first the individuals may not be alcoholics, but they find that they can fit comfortably into the niches created for them. After making the rounds of all the available programs in the community, and passing through all the "revolving doors" many times, these individuals become firmly established as chronic drunkenness offenders. Before the widespread decriminalization of public drunkenness in the 1970s, it was estimated that arrests in this category represented up to one-third of all arrests in the United States (Morris & Hawkins, 1969). Even after decriminalization, in 1981, for example, drunkenness arrests were still the third largest single category, after "driving while intoxicated" and larceny/theft arrests (E. J. Brown *et al.,* 1984).

It is implicit in the interactionist perspective—and was made explicit by some of the major proponents—that the actions of social control agencies could "amplify" or reinforce the deviance, which would increase the prevalence rate of what became know as "secondary deviance" (Ditton, 1979; Wilkins, 1964). One example of this is the societal response to marijuana smokers in the late 1960s in Britain (Young, 1971). Public stereotypes about marijuana were vastly exaggerated by the police, who were virtually the only intermediaries between the community and the potential deviants. According to Young, the policeman, from his position of power, negotiated the evidence to fit his and society's preconceived ideas about marijuana users. After many interactions between smokers and the police, the former amplified their deviance to fit the stereotypes:

> When society defines a group of people as deviant it tends to react against them so as to isolate and alienate them from the company of "normal" people. . . . The group . . . tends to develop its own norms and values, which society per-

ceives as even more deviant than before. As a consequence of this increase in deviancy, social reaction increases even further, the group is even more isolated and alienated, it acts even more deviantly, society acts increasingly strongly against it, and a spiral of deviancy amplification occurs. (Young, 1971, p. 33)

In its simplest form the interactionist view assumed that a general consensus in society helped to define what would be a public problem. Some of its exponents, however, and in fact the most influential ones, argued that it was unrealistic to assume that the agents of social control merely carried out the majority wishes of society (H. S. Becker, 1963; Matza, 1969). They argued that designations of deviance would emerge from the interactions between a plurality of different groups within society, but they agreed that groups with the most power would usually be able to impose rules that reflected their own interests. In this way it is possible for some relatively minor problems to be stretched into major social responses, but in some cases for major problems to be ignored. The pluralist studies helped to silence one of the major criticisms of the simple form of interactionism, that is, its focus on individual transactions. The pluralists argued that groups interacted to forge collective definitions of deviance. Their studies also allowed a consideration of macroscopic forces, by showing how social or political trends in society at large could produce changes in the labels assigned to deviant behavior.

The term "moral entrepreneur" was first used by H. S. Becker (1963) to describe groups that have a vested interest in the social control of deviance. Under this heading we would usually find the rule creators, those who are outraged about a particular problem and are morally committed to bringing it under control, as well as the rule enforcers, those who carry out the controls on an everyday basis. Becker's study of the passage of the Marijuana Tax Act showed that until the 1930s there had been little public interest in controlling marijuana, but at that time an intense campaign was launched by the Bureau of Narcotics, led by Commissioner Henry J. Anslinger. In the absence of any organized opposition from marijuana smokers, and in the presence of a largely apathetic but impressionable public, the Act was passed in 1937, and the sale and use of marijuana became a deviant act. The moral outrage notion provided an acceptable explanation for launching what would eventually be a successful campaign, even though in this case the outrage was not initially a major public concern.

Some of the successful moral enterprise crusades were exclusively products of their time, and could probably never be replicated. One of the best examples of this is the passage of the Eighteenth Amendment in 1919, which prohibited the public sale and consumption of alcohol. The Prohibition movement has been interpreted as a moral crusade that was led by a group of individuals, including many women, who were mostly small-town, middle-class Protestants. (N. H. Clark, 1976). Drinking and drunkenness were certainly not problems among this group, so adequate explanations for the successes of the Women's Christian Temperance Movement (WCTU) and other Prohibitionist groups like the Anti-Saloon League (ASL) have to be sought in their historical context (C. J. Smith, 1985b). One such account is rooted in the changing demographic character of the United States during the first 2 decades of the 20th century. The country had been dominated by native-born Protestants who were closely tied to the land, but by the end of the 19th century the demographic balance of power was shifting toward foreign-born Catholics, most of whom were city dwellers who worked in factories. The former group could do little more than watch as its influence on the mainstream of American culture faded. Realizing that on the whole they were powerless to alter this trend, the Temperance forces focused on Prohibition as a symbol of their own cultural values, which they felt were rapidly being diluted in an ocean of intemperance. Gusfield (1963) argued that the Prohibition movement could be interpreted as an exercise in "status politics," in which one group attempted to force its moral standards on the entire country. The crusaders were not especially concerned with how the Prohibition legislation would be enforced, or with whether it could actually solve the many problems associated with alcohol abuse. They merely wanted to see the law passed, and they wanted everybody to know whose law it was.

As this example illustrates, the individuals and groups who define certain behaviors as problems may not be personally involved with or threatened by such behaviors. With the exception of the Washingtonians, who were a group of reformed drunkards, very few of the major personalities in the Prohibition and Temperance groups had experienced drunkenness personally or in their own families. It is also likely that few of them were really concerned about the suffering associated with alcoholism, and relatively little thought was given to how alcoholics should be treated (Tyrrell, 1979). They were obsessed mainly with the way the problem of alcoholism was defined, and their major goal was to persuade others that their definition and their solution were the only ones worth considering.

The success of the Prohibitionists implies that they were able to make demands or "claims" upon the existing institutions, and to have their definition of deviance legitimated (Spector & Kitsuse, 1977). In most cases such claims are made by groups who feel they have a valid grievance on a particular issue. There is also evidence that in many different problem areas the service agencies themselves operate as powerful interest groups. By defining both the problems and their own responses, they are able to ensure their continued existence (H. G. Levine, 1984; Wiener, 1981). In this sense public concerns about social problems are at least partly created at the agency or governmental level, and then sometime later they are legitimiated by public acceptance and recognition of the problem, as we shall see more fully in the next chapter.

Attempts to create a public consensus about the etiology and treatment of public problems have been moderately successful in the last few decades. Public attitudes toward mental illness, for example, have softened a little since the 1950s, and the improvement has occurred in five general areas (Segal, 1979):

1. Members of the public today accept a broader range of symptoms of mental illness than they did 20 years ago;

2. Attitudes, particularly negative attitudes, no longer appear to be determined primarily by the mere label of mental illness or the specific diagnosis, but are most closely related to the actual behaviors associated with mental illness;

3. People now tend to require less social distance between themselves and the mentally ill;

4. Little evidence exists to demonstrate a direct link between negative attitudes and overtly hostile behavior toward the mentally ill living in the community;

5. If the mentally ill are viewed in normal roles most community residents will eventually begin to evaluate them positively and accept their right to live in the community.

A similar trend can be detected from changes in public attitudes toward alcoholism (P. M. Miller & Niremberg, 1984; Mulford & Fitzgerald, 1983a, 1983b). The public is now much less likely to think of someone who is an alcoholic or mentally ill as dangerous. They are thought of as having problems that are serious, but for which help is easily available and generally effective. These are considerable achievements and they have contributed greatly to the public legitimation of mental health and alcoholism services in recent years.

CONFLICT ACCOUNTS OF PUBLIC PROBLEMS

The previous discussion illustrated some of the ways that policy responses to public problems have been interpreted from a pluralist perspective. Most of the studies conducted from this perspective view society as a mix of competing interest groups that are fighting for status. Some of the most sophisticated interactionist accounts take into consideration the plurality of interests, but it is still assumed that the solutions are reached by consensus between the actors who are involved. Critics of these accounts pointed out that the consensus model of society was unrealistic and could not be empirically validated. Marx, for example, had argued that conflict between social classes was the basis for society, and that the law, rather than representing the consensus viewpoint, reflected the interests of the dominant classes.

In 1958, Dahrendorf attacked the consensus model as a "utopian" view of society, and one that portrayed normal social change unrealistically as a process of organic growth. As he observed, "Societies . . . are held together not by consensus but by constraint, not by universal agreement but by coercion of some by others" (p. 127). Dahrendorf recommended that a conflict model supplement the consensus model to help explain how fundamental social changes come about. According to the consensus view such change could only occur as a result of extraordinary circumstances, but as Dahrendorf noted, these changes are in fact the norm in society. In other words, it is not the presence but the absence of conflict that is abnormal, "and we have good reason to be suspicious if we find a society . . . that displays no evidence of conflict" (p. 126).

In the same year Vold (1958) had outlined a theory of crime that was also based on conflict theory. As Vold wrote 20 years later, "whichever group interest can marshall the greatest number of votes will determine whether or not there is to be a new law to hamper and curb the interests of some opposition group" (Vold, 1979, p. 287). From this perspective Vold was able to explain most crimes, with the exception of those involving impulsive and irrational acts. In a work that was obviously based heavily on Vold's ideas, Quinney (1970) extended the conflict theory to include not just the opposition between organized interest groups, but also the conflicts between any "segments" of society that share similar values. Although there may be no overt political struggle, the behavior of one group is defined as "criminal" by others who have more power and are protecting their interests. Almost all groups define certain acts as criminal, but it is usually only the definitions made by the most powerful segments of society that are widely legitimated:

> The reality of crime that is constructed for all of us by those in a position of power is the reality we tend to accept as our own. By doing so, we grant those in power the authority to carry out the actions that best promote their interests. This is the politics of reality. The social reality of crime in politically organized society is constructed as a political act. (Quinney, 1970, p. 312)

In his later work Quinney (1977) extended this, arguing that the existing criminal justice system must be replaced by one based on more equitable power relationships between the different groups within society. Quinney rejects authoritarianism of any kind in his vision of a future society in which there will be no power and therefore no need to define certain behaviors as criminal. By this time Quinney had abandoned his earlier view about the different segments of society, and replaced it with a class-based theory. This also occurred in the "new criminology" school developed in Britain (Taylor, Walton, & Young, 1973). The new criminologists argued that interactionists and the early conflict theorists had simplified and misunderstood the nature of power in society:

> By characterizing society as a simple diversity of values, they [the pluralists] blinded themselves to the existence of a very real consensus—the hegemonic domination of bourgeois values. By pointing to power without analyzing its class basis and the nature of the state, they transformed the actions of the powerful into an arbitrary flexing of moral muscles. (Young, 1976, pp. 12–13)

There are some important differences between Marxist and non-Marxist conflict theories of crime. The earlier Quinney, for example, along with Vold (1958) and also Turk (1969), did not specifically argue that crimes were defined by ruling elites, nor did they suggest that crime is necessarily a result of the capitalist mode of production. Perhaps a more subtle difference, however, is the debate about whether or nor crime is interpreted as a pathological or a normal behavior. For the non-Marxist conflict theorists crimes are committed by normal people who have no power to control the processes by which crimes are defined. Marxist criminologists would be more likely to view people who commit crimes as "demoralized": They might argue that working class criminals have been systematically exploited and denied the opportunity to live full and meaningful lives, and that white-collar criminals have been led astray by the pointless pursuit of wealth for its own sake. In both cases, however, the crimes are defined by the dominant class as pathological and damaging to the capitalist mode of production.

To expand on the Marxist conflict account and to extend it to other public problems, it is useful to consider why such problems are likely to be excessively prevalent in capitalist societies. The most general explanation is that problems are a direct result of contradictions in the capitalist mode of production. The expanded accumulation of capital requires fit and healthy workers, but the process itself systematically debilitates many workers, making them unfit to offer their services in the marketplace. The sources of worker stress derive from both external and internal controls over the labor force (Eyer, 1977). The external controls include the division of labor, which has produced boring and alienating work (Braverman, 1974), and the requirement for labor to be increasingly mobile, which has consistently broken up families and communities and created stagnant pools of surplus labor in localities that were once thriving (Buss & Redburn, 1987). Eyer (1977) used the term "internal controls" to refer to the familiar patterns of socialization associated with capitalist production in which workers are rewarded for being competitive but not overly individualistic, and are encouraged to spend their rewards on the never-ending acquisition of material possessions.

These two sources of stress are endemic in the capitalist system, but they are unequally distributed among the classes. Workers, for example, experience more than their share of the costs involved, but they reap less than their share of the benefits. It is not surprising that the working classes are disproportionately represented in the prevalence data for such problems as mental disorder, drug and alcohol abuse, and crime, in addition to the high prevalence rates for a wide range of chronic and infectious diseases and accidental deaths (Doyal, 1979; Eyles & Woods, 1983).

The importance of the work environment in the etiology of stress-induced problems is evident in the mortality statistics. Only about a quarter of the mortality from heart disease, which is one of the leading causes of death in the

United States, can be explained by "individual" factors such as diet, exercise, medical care, and genetic inheritance (Renaud, 1978). The rest of the variance is unexplained, but a strong case can be made for the importance of social and environmental factors, including the nature of the work environment. As Renaud concluded, "the strongest predictor of longevity was work satisfaction . . . [and] the second . . . was overall 'happiness' " (p. 114). Conclusions like this tend to be overlooked by the medical profession because they fail to reflect the individualistic bias of the medical research establishment (Navarro, 1977). For the most part they are also ignored by the owners of capital, because it is not in their best interests to provide anything other than the most basic work environment.

Another of the contraditions inherent in capitalism involves the production of a surplus population or a "reserve army." Most members of this population are either too powerless or too demoralized to care what happens to them, but some are considered to be dangerous, either because they make too many demands on the welfare state, or because they become increasingly resentful of the ruling classes. As a vulnerable group the surplus population can be exploited in the interests of accumulation. Until high unemployment became the norm in the 1980s, for example, temporary pockets of unemployment could exert a downward force on wages and inflation, which helped to maintain profits (Piven & Cloward, 1982). With the knowledge that workers in the surplus population can replace them, existing workers are likely to accept lower wages, reduce their workplace demands, and work more productively.

There are, however, some considerable costs associated with the maintenance of a "reserve army." People not working have to be provided for, and this implies a substantial social expense that eats away at the process of capital accumulation. The costs of providing welfare services presents an increasing fiscal strain on the state, and many employers believe that the level of worker security provided by income maintenance programs and other welfare entitlements will lower worker productivity (Piven & Cloward, 1982). From this perspective the actions of the welfare state conflict with the interests of the capitalist class (Gough, 1979), which helps to explain the substantial cuts in entitlement programs made by the current administrations in both the United States and the United Kingdom. Unfortunately this is probably the worst time of all to be lowering welfare benefits, because of the additional stresses that result from high unemployment, low morale among workers and nonworkers, and high inflation rates (Katznelson & Kesselman, 1979; C. J. Smith, 1983a). As we shall see later in this chapter, the impact in the United States of the federal cuts on some of the truly needy groups in the population has been significant.

A more indirect explanation for the high prevalence of public problems in capitalist economies is related to disturbances in the system of class rule (Spitzer, 1975). Some of the attempts made by the state to provide an infrastructure of services that could benefit the interests of the owners of capital have backfired, and have brought about further challenges to the elite groups in society. In Britain, for example, the creation of the National Health Service has been interpreted as an attempt to "deradicalize" the working classes by reducing the class inequality in health care. After more than 30 years, however, it is evident that such inequality still persists (Doyal, 1979; Eyles & Woods, 1983; Townsend & Davidson, 1982). The conflict between the owners of capital and the working classes continues, and to close the gap between the classes there are ever increasing demands made by the workers to raise the level of "social wages" (Navarro, 1977).

The development of mass education has had a similar contradictory effect (Spitzer, 1975). It is clearly in the interests of capital to train and prepare the future labor force in the educational system. On the other hand, education has allowed many people to appreciate more fully the extent of their alienation, and to realize how badly they lag behind the more privileged classes. One response is to become more radical and challenge the status quo, another is to drop out of the system altogether, either becoming dependent on the welfare state or a "free spirit" on the open road. In this sense the provision of a service such as education makes it necessary for the state to spend increasing amounts on other services.

It is also important to note that as a result of the greater organizational and geographical concentration of capital that has occurred in recent years, the proportion of the population that is "stagnant,"—that is, permanently redundant—continues to rise (Bluestone & Harrison, 1982). Most of the people involved can not be coopted back into the system by employment, so they must become dependent on the state, often for the rest of their lives. In this way the state's "social expenses" continue to grow (see Chapter 5). As O'Connor (1973) showed, this process has also been accompanied by the need to "socialize" more and more of the costs of production through the investment of state funds on such programs as road building and utility construction. Although this is public money, most of the profits accrue to individuals and corporations. The net effect is that the state continues to experience a deficit in transactions between itself and other sectors of society. In O'Connor's (1979) words, "The state budget grows because it grows," in other words, social capital financing requires more social expenses to mop up the casualties of capital accumulation. As the "structural gap" between expenditures and receipts widens, social problems may be exacerbated, partly because fewer resources are available to provide the human services that are needed.

The rate at which individuals who experience social problems are converted into "proper objects for social control," (Spitzer, 1975) is determined by three general sets of factors: the ability of public and private services to keep down the overall rate of prevalence; the current political and economic circumstances; and the characteristics of the problem population.

Keeping Down Prevalence Rates

Expenditures by the state on welfare services and income maintenance programs can be interpreted as attempts to serve and if necessary to control the working classes (Gough, 1979). However humane these trends may be, the Marxists argue that the capitalist mode of production will continue to "create" physical and psychological casualities at a faster rate than welfare state services can cater to their needs (Ralph, 1983). The perennial prevalence of most of the problems discussed in this book, which have occurred in spite of ever increasing expenditures and service provision, gives testimony to this depressing fact (Gusfield, 1982, 1984)

From this perspective the welfare state faces an impossible task because it can never hope to reduce significantly the prevalence of the problems it encounters. As Katznelson (1976) has argued, human service programs are not required and cannot be expected to "solve" social problems, only to "manage" them. In the state of New York, for example, current programs for alcoholics are filled to capacity, but they provide services for only 8% of the population in need (New York State Division of Alcohol Abuse and Alcoholism, 1985), the goal for the end of the 20th century being to serve 20%. The Marxist interpretation of this apparently hopeless dilemma is that the provision of at least a perfunctory level of services helps to convince the lower status groups that something is being done on their behalf, and that it is not in their interests to challenge the status quo. In the case of medical services, for example, Navarro (1977 has described the benefits of even the most inept delivery system:

> To the degree that the majority of people believe and accept the proposition that what are actually politically caused conditions can be individually solved by medical intervention, . . . from the point of view of the capitalist system, this is the actual utility of medicine, it contributes to the legitimation of capitalism. (p. 69)

In addition to the provision of formal services, informal methods of social control are often able to curb the excesses of certain individuals and sometimes entire subgroups of the population (Maloff *et al.,* 1979). The extent to which informal controls are effective will help to determine how many individuals need to make use of the formal services that are available. It is also possible that informal social support networks can be useful in preventing entry into formal programs, as has been demonstrated in the case of the elderly and the mentally ill (C. J. Smith, 1978). Another partial solution lies in the operation of self-help groups that are organized by individuals who share certain problems, such as alcoholics, child abusers, and the mentally ill. In recent years the proliferation of these groups has been remarkable, but it has been suggested that self-helping has become so popular only because the state is unwilling to tackle the root causes for societal ills and has essentially given up in the effort to prevent social pathology. In this sense many self-help groups have been effectively coopted by the state, and their claims that self-helping is more effective than official agency intervention actually reinforces this process. As long as self-help groups are actively publicizing their successes there is little pressure on formal service providers to improve their operations.

Current Political and Economic Circumstances

Attempts to cut back income maintenance programs during periods of high unemployment are likely to exacerbate the stresses among the poor and the working classes (P. Ehrenreich, 1982). In addition, budget cuts in the human services are often responsible for a subsequent reduction in services (Burt & Pittman, 1984). This may result in clients being dropped from caseloads, as a result, for example, of the stricter eligibility requirements for Supplemental Security Income (SSI) payments. In other cases clients are transferred into the hands of greedy and uncaring private care operators in nursing homes, room and board hostels, and hotels (P. Brown, 1985; Rose, 1979).

One of the major concerns about the current economic situation is that cuts in the human services have occurred at precisely the time when such programs need to be expanded. As a result of earlier retirements, higher levels of unemployment, and greater levels of insecurity among the workforce, the prevalence of health and social problems is likely to increase. The problem is that even though the demand for services is increasing, the state can not afford to expand services because all spare capital is needed for surplus-producing activities. The current "slash and burn" approach to social welfare programs (Stoesz, 1981) is based on the neoconservative view that the war on poverty has already been successful, and that it is now time to hand over a larger share of the existing welfare programs to the private sector (Weisner & Room, 1984). Such a strategy may be able to reduce overhead costs, increase efficiency and accountability, and reduce the role of "big government" in the delivery of services, but many questions remain about the motives of private care providers and their ability to provide decent and humane services for the needy (C. Becker & Stanley 1985; Gilbert, 1984).

It is also important to remember that the provision of welfare services represents the state's attempt to be neutral or "classless" in the conflict between labor and capital, by providing a buffer to some of the stresses inflicted on the workforce in the process of capital accumulation. The current administrations in both the United States and Britain appear to have suspended even the pretense of being classless. It is still difficult to assess the impact of these policies on the provision of services for the truly needy in the population, but some evidence collected by Burt and Pittman (1984) provides a warning. They considered three groups who have to rely largely on the state for services: abused and neglected children, the chronically mentally ill, and the low-income elderly. In case studies conducted in four U.S. cities, they compared budget changes for the three populations, and caseload changes between 1981 and 1983 (Table 8.1). The four cities experienced a decrease in federal funding for all types of services, although in some cases these funds were at least partly replaced by state or local revenues. The figures in the fourth column of Table 8.1 show that in most categories the services in question experienced absolute decreases in funding (after adjusting for inflation).

One typical response from the fiscal conservatives to such evidence is a suggestion that the funding cuts resulted from reduced need, but as the data in the fifth column indicates, in a total of 13 of 17 instances, the agencies found themselves in 1983 with increased ratios of people served per dollar available. Burt and Pittman use this data to argue that "budget reductions happened despite continued or increased need for services, not because demand slackened" (p. 262). Another response from conservatives—or rather a hope—is that the welfare agencies became more efficient at providing services, and in fact Burt and Pittman report from their fieldwork that in two cases there was some evi-

Table 8.1. Budget Changes (After Inflation) and Caseload Changes for Three Needy Populations, 1981 to 1983

Cities and Programs	Budget Changes (%)				Caseload Changes (%)
	Federal	State	Local	Total	
San Diego (CA)					
Adult Social Services	−6	10	−44	−24	−13
Area Agency on Aging	−11	174	−48	1	21
Child Intake Services	−12	—[a]	−21	−16	29
Placement and Supervision	8	—[a]	−30	−17	−5
Mental Health	—[a]	−26	45	−13	6
Detroit (MI)					
Adult Social Services	−36	43	—[a]	8	8
Area Agency on Aging	−4	34	−69	−1	−3
Children's Services	—[b]	—[b]	—[b]	—[b]	60
Mental Health	−29	10	9	4	32
Richmond (VA)					
Adult Social Services	−32	−38	−38	−34	−15
Area Agency on Aging	—[b]	—[b]	—[b]	−14	10
Foster Care	−11	—[a]	−18	−14	−2
Protective Services	−64	—[a]	−70	−65	167
Mental Health	—[a]	11	−19	−17	18
Boston (MA)					
Adult Social Services	−100	64	—[a]	7	7
Area Agency on Aging	−6	—[a]	−17	−8	112
Child Welfare	−22	30	—[a]	7	6
Mental Health	−7	−24	—[a]	−23	—[b]

[a] no funding from this source
[b] data not available
Source. Burt and Pittman (1984, p. 261).

dence for this. In most cases, however, the shrinking funding resulted in agencies cutting their caseloads and reducing the level of services to individual clients. The actual responses appeared to vary from city to city, and indeed from state to state, because it was the states that had to shoulder most of the burden of replacing the lost federal dollars.

The impact on the level of service provision for the truly needy depends largely on two factors: the states' resources, and their long-term commitment to the provision of welfare services. In Michigan, for example, a state that was hit extremely hard by economic decline, a traditionally strong liberal outlook resulted in serious efforts to find the needed resources. In California and Massachusetts the situation was different. Both states had encountered taxpayer revolts, but both are traditionally supporters of social welfare programs. The actual outcomes in these two states were determined by state and local relationships. In Massachusetts it was possible to protect two of the three needy populations (only funding for the mentally ill was reduced), but in California, where local jurisdictions are allowed much more control over social programs, no such guarantees were possible. The result was that in conservative San Diego, an area that had not suffered seriously from either the recession or unemployment, welfare services were cut back sharply.

One of the most publicized consequences of the current fiscal crisis has been the impact of unemployment on the prevalence of public problems. Within the last decade some impressive evidence has been gathered to demonstrate a significant and positive relationship between unemployment and a range of medical, psychological, and social problems: including mental hospital admissions (Brenner, 1973), suicides (S. Stack, 1981), child abuse (Dooley, Catalano, Jackson, & Brownell, 1981), and alcoholism (Brenner, 1975). This work— particularly the pioneering studies conducted by Brenner (1973)—has been influential in both Britain and the United States. The relatively sophisticated time-series studies have impressed policy makers, even though they were demonstrating a relationship that was already well accepted at an intuitive level. On the other hand, few if any specific economic policies have been based on the results of such studies, because it has proven impossible to manipulate employment rates in the desired direction.

In recent years the presence of a simple relationship between unemployment and social pathology has been questioned. Perhaps the most important criticism is the argument that Brenner and his followers have overemphasized the importance of economic downturns, so the policy implications only go as far as suggesting that attempts be made to smooth out the business cycle. In other words, Brenner is not critical of the capitalist economic system as a whole, only of unemployment. It is possible that the boom phase of the business cycle is equally if not more pathogenic, and that economic growth under capitalism is the major stress-producing phenomenon of our time (Eyer, 1976; Linsky *et al.*, 1985).

The Characteristics of the Problem Population

As the prevalence of a specific problem rises, it becomes increasingly likely that official agencies will be required to intervene by offering formal services. The current level of unemployment in both the United States and Britain, for example, might eventually create a greater demand for health, mental health, and other human services. If the resources to fund such new services are not forthcoming, it is possible that we may encounter some new form of "social control entrepreneurship," in addition to the entry of private care providers in the field of human service delivery (Weisner & Room, 1984). One possibility is the creation of new deviance categories, the process discussed in Chapter 7 that has been referred to as "relabeling." This may occur at the client level; for example, an individual may adopt a criminal, suicidal, or drug strategy to ensure his or her entry into a facility. It is more likely, however, to occur at the program level. Individuals tend to be processed according to whatever services currently have vacancies, rather than according to their particular needs. It is clear from studies such as the one conducted by Melick, Steadman, and Cocozza (1979) in New York State, that a substantial number of individuals with criminal records have been admitted to mental health facilities. In California a similar trend has occurred among referrals to alcohol treatment programs (Weisner, 1983).

Another type of movement between problem categories occurs when a specific problem, for whatever reason, suddenly becomes excessively prevalent, causing some reshuffling of service priorities. This has happened recently in the alcoholism treatment field, where the sharp increase of clients referred from the courts for driving-while-intoxicated (DWI) offenses has "pushed out" other clients whose problems are not DWI related. The short-term result is long waiting lists, but the potential exists for individuals with untreated drinking problems to drift into other problem categories such as child or spouse abuse, crime, mental disorder, and serious ill health.

Another important factor influencing the rate at which individuals become problem "cases," is the relative power of a particular group in the political arena (Schur, 1980). The elderly, for example, represent an increasingly visible and vocal political force, and they have been able to defend themselves against some attacks on the level of service provision. In recent years the mentally ill have also been able to influence social policies with some success. The level of service provision is also to some extent a function of the "utility" of the specific problem population. As we shall see in Chapter 9 the "war on drugs" and the association of drugs with street crime has often played an important role in electoral politics. In another context, state mental hospitals and prisons are so important in economic terms to their local communities, that attempts to cut back or eliminate services are usually fiercely contested in the local political arena (G. A. Moore, 1981).

As these examples have illustrated, the processes that could, in theory, work to reduce the prevalence of problems are often unable to do so. Although it is apparent that many problems are strongly influenced by economic, social, and political forces, in the majority of cases, service responses are based on explanations that are individual and medical in character. In the case of alcoholism, for example, in spite of the recognition that people drink excessively for many reasons, the major service response is the provision of treatment according to the medical model (Nathan, 1983; Peele, 1984). This guarantees that the predominant goal underlying service provision is an attempt to "cure" the individual patient by responding to his or her symptoms. From the Marxist perspective this response is to be expected, because it supports the prevailing economic and social organization of society. The interactionists and social constructionists, on the other hand, might argue that the provision of services is primarily a result of such agency-level concerns as institution building, professional self-preservation, and economic survival. From either perspective the provision of direct services is interpreted as a diversion away from the more important task of uncovering the deep-rooted causes of social pathology. Most of the services that are provided are clearly needed, but it seems that the best they can do is chip away slowly at the existing prevalence rates. With the incidence of new cases and the reentry of the "failures" and the repeat offenders, the overall prevalence rates continue to grow, and the service providers find themselves continually falling behind in their attempts to cater to the people in need.

The following sections include a more detailed look at the service dilemmas in two problem areas: mental health and alcoholism services. We shall consider the arguments made by Marxist scholars that public problems are primarily a function of the organization of production in capitalist society and that service responses can be interpreted as attempts to control those problems in order to aid the smooth functioning of capital accumulation.

MENTAL DISORDERS

One of the most frequent complaints leveled at the welfare state in recent years has been its role in the deepening fiscal crisis of the state. The argument is that as the welfare roles expand, the cost of providing human services increases exponentially (Stevenson, 1976). In the last decade the demand for services has expanded as a direct and indirect result of economic hardships, and this has placed an ever-increasing drain on the state's reserves.

Many accounts of the deinstitutionalization of the mentally ill have included an economic interpretation of attempts to empty state hospitals, working from the assumption that individual states were trying to save money by "federalizing" the costs of hospitalization, and at the same time transferring responsibility to a different level of government (Brown, 1985). Once they were living in the community, former mental patients were financially supported by federal welfare payments, which provided some relief for the individual states. Because many of the expenses involved in social welfare programs are not directly productive, the state finds itself in a dilemma. Although some level of social expense is required to grease the wheels of capital accumulation and reproduction, inexorable growth in this category of expenses—especially for clients whose problems are long-term in nature—threatens to draw much needed reserves away from the goal of accumulation (O'Connor, 1973). The choices are unenviable:

> [T]he legitimacy of the state . . . rests on its capacity to provide a range of services to the population. . . . At the same time . . . the state is required to provide services to capital to aid the accumulation process. When the state finds itself unable to finance these different undertakings with available revenues, its managers are on the horns of a dilemma. On the one hand they can risk a reduction in legitimacy by cutting back services to the population or by raising taxes . . . [or] . . . they can undermine the accumulation process by reducing services needed by capital or by raising additional revenues in an inflationary manner. (Block, 1981, p. 2)

Variations on this basic theme have been heard in the last decade from both the left and the right (Bacon & Eltis, 1976; Garfinkel & Haveman, 1977; Gilder, 1980), but this argument ignores the "return flow" of the state's welfare benefits and services that eventually find their way back into the "marketed" sectors of the economy (Hirschorn, 1978). For example, welfare payments made to former mental patients who are now living in the community as a result of deinstitutionalization policies will be used to buy goods and services, and to rent accommodations. The individual states that deinstitutionalized large numbers of mental patients also hoped to save scarce resources by reducing the costs of inpatient care. An additional economic spin-off occurred as a result of the "commodification" of the mentally ill as a result of deinstitutionalization (Scull, 1981). A new class of profiteering home and hostel operators were waiting eagerly to feed upon what Scull called "the new trade in lunacy." Another economic benefit that resulted from the deinstitutionalization of the mentally ill and other service dependent groups occurred as a result of the location of new residential and treatment facilities in otherwise crumbling inner-city neighborhoods. Although it was only a drop in the ocean, these new programs brought some much-needed economic relief after decades of residential and commercial abandonment (Dear, 1980).

As these examples illustrate, the economic side of deinstitutionalization is not an entirely unidirectional flow. The extent to which the states' social spending puts a burden on the economy depends on how resources are allocated between the reproductive (social consumption) sector and the nonreproductive (social expenses) sector (O'Connor, 1973). If the state has to raise revenues merely to maintain social welfare spending at its present rate, it may be necessary to increase taxation on capital, households, or consumption. In the United States, the Reagan administration has fought against raising taxes, and in fact taxes on the capital-owning class were reduced. The only viable solution was to "rationalize" social services and make a series of cuts in the program. Obviously, none of the available choices were popular, but the actual mechanism selected was determined partly by the level of class conflict within the society, and partly by current economic circumstances. The Reagan administration and that of Margaret Thatcher in Britain, made clear decisions on this dilemma, and the results have been referred to as the "New Class War" (Piven & Cloward, 1982).

To its critics, the growth of the welfare state has had some odious consequences. Not only does it contribute to a sky-rocketing of state expenditures, it also jeopardizes the accumulation process and requires the state to make difficult policy decisions about either raising taxes or cutting services. As Gough (1979) solemnly observes, the welfare state "exacerbates the conflict between capital and labor in the economic, political and ideological spheres" (p. 127).

In recent years some alternative interpretations of the welfare state have questioned the wisdom of rationalizing welfare services, even on purely economic grounds. Hirschorn (1978, 1979), for example, has argued that social service spending involves the creation of surplus value in addition to the simple transfers of real income (redistributing surplus value). From this perspective cutting social services hinders the long-term development of the economy in several different ways. Rising social disorder, which in recent years has been exacerbated by unprecedented increases in unemployment, could cause social expenses to escalate in spite of attempts at rationalization. In the absence of new job opportunities and viable job training programs, the cost of controlling an increasingly alienated group of the unemployed and unemployable will rise. In addition there is the current situation of the "service paradox" that was described earlier, in which the demand for social services increases while, and partly because, existing services are unable to ameliorate community distress (Catalano & Dooley, 1981; C. J. Smith, 1983a). In other words, cuts in one set of programs might result in spending increases for other measures of social control (Cohen, 1979; Gough, 1979).

Social service cuts may also result in reduced demand for industrial output, a phenomenon that has occurred dramatically in Britain, particularly in the construction industry. In this case it is evident that the realization of surplus value depends on the ability of producers to sell their output in the marketplace (Hirschorn, 1978). Education, health, and welfare services are in one sense costs to the economy, but they may also contribute, directly and indirectly, to the maintenance and reproduction of the labor force. Thus, for example, if some individuals are able to learn new tasks and adapt to changes in the workplace, then the overall outcome will benefit the economy. From this perspective, rationalizations could threaten to make the labor force less able to meet the changing demands of modern industry, which is a particular fear in those states that are trying to retool for high-technology-oriented growth (Castells, 1985).

In the mental health field it is difficult to determine unequivocally whether the expansion of state spending and the wider provision of services has contributed directly to the fiscal crisis of the state. One of the few avenues for empirical investigation is to analyze the costs of providing community-based as opposed to hospital-based services. It has been suggested that one of the forces underlying deinstitutionalization was the desire to lower the costs of providing mental health treatment (Rose, 1979; Scull, 1977). It is unlikely, however, that any real savings would be made, because so few of the discharged patients have been able to live (or return to) economically productive lives. What normally happens is that the former patients become a burden to their families and communities (see Chapter 3). There is also evidence that providing high-quality care in the community can be as, if not more, expensive than providing hospital care. Savings are possible only if substandard services are provided, but in this case the savings would be made at too high a cost in the long run.

In one of the few studies comparing the costs of a high-quality community support program to the costs of a hospital program, Weisbrod, Test, and Stein (1980) showed that although the former was more expensive by almost $800 per patient per year, the community programs created greater long-term benefits by allowing former clients to return to work. By emphasizing a return to work, the community support program more than pays back its higher initial costs. In the study conducted by Weisbrod and his colleagues it was estimated that the annual earning power of patients in the community-based program was almost double that of the patients who were treated in a traditional hospital-based program ($2,364 as opposed to $1,168).

The major problems associated with such cost and benefit studies is that the program being evaluated may not be representative of those that are generally available in the community. The support program studied by Weisbrod and his colleagues in Madison, Wisconsin is recognized as one of the best of its kind (Stein & Test, 1980; Test & Stein, 1980). Clients in other communities will probably not benefit as much from their own treatment programs. Poorly developed and weakly coordinated programs, the type that seem to be the norm in most communities, may end up deeply on the deficit side, because patients are deinstitutionalized without adequate supports to help them adjust to life in the community. In addition, the patients who remain in hospitals are increasingly likely to be long-term "new chronic" patients (Bachrach, 1980a), many of whom are still relatively young and will probably require a lifetime of close supervision and costly care (Pepper *et al.,* 1981). The changing demographic structure of public mental hospitals will drive up service costs even further as their overall populations fall (C. J. Smith, 1988). The elderly are now far more likely to be housed in community residences than in mental hospitals (Estes & Harrington, 1981; C. J. Smith, 1982), and this deprives the state of federal reimbursements through Medicaid. Most of the younger chronic patients still in the hospital are ineligible for Medicaid, but if they are too disturbed to be discharged, the per patient costs to the state will rise even further (New York State Office of Mental Health, 1981).

On balance it appears that if the community mental health movement had been able to complement the deinstitutionalization movement by providing comprehensive services for former patients in the community, the benefits to the patients and their communities may well have outweighted the costs. Unfortunately, what actually occurred in most communities fell far short of such a goal (Kirk & Therrien, 1976, M. Levine, 1981; Rose, 1979).

The question about what will happen to the chronically mentally ill now that the federal government has begun to back out of the provision of welfare services is still difficult to answer. One of the few attempts to assess this issue has concluded that the direct effects thus far have been relatively insignificant (Burt & Pittman, 1984). In 1980, for example, the Reagan administration began to accelerate the process of cutting back on the federal share toward mental health programs. The Burt and Pittman study suggests that the federal cuts have had less of an influence than cuts made at the state and local levels. In California and Massachusetts, government philosophies that have been less generous toward welfare services than in the past and referenda constraining public revenue activities (eg., Proposition 13 in California, $2\frac{1}{2}$ in Massachusetts, and J in San Diego) have resulted in severe budget cuts. In states like Michigan, unemployment and recession generated higher needs for services at exactly the time when less revenue was available to fund such services.

The major impact of the fiscally conservative Reagan administration was indirect, resulting from subtle but potentially devastating changes in the eligibility requirements for disability benefits. The major component of this is SSI, which is an entitlement program that acts as an income supplement to different groups of disabled individuals. It is estimated that about 25% (approximately 375,000 clients) of the chronically mentally ill receive SSI payments. This represents a huge federal outlay, in fact it is one of the largest federal components in the mental health field, amounting to about $360 million in 1980— much greater than the annual amount allocated to community mental health centers. SSI is a cash payment that is made directly to the individual, and because the cash can be used to purchase the necessities of life such as food, clothing, and housing, SSI is more directly useful than most of the traditional mental health services. An additional benefit is the SSI recipients are categorically eligible for Medicaid, which is a vital support to many former mental patients living in the community.

Changes in the procedures used to determine eligibility for SSI meant that the Social Security Administration began to review all recipients to determine if they were truly disabled. These reviews used more rigid criteria than had previously been the case, and as a result many people living in the community at the edge of poverty lost their benefits. In the state of New York, for example, it was estimated that 5,500 individuals, most of them from New York City, became ineligible in 1982 alone (New York City, Office of the City Council President, 1982). A study of 451 clients who had been terminated showed the typical portrait to be a single male in his 40s, with no other source of income and few prospects of employment. The decisions can be appealed, and the appeals are often successful, but for clients who do not have caseworkers to help them the task of appealing is a monumental one. Losing SSI benefits is devastating to a client's well-being, and it generally forces people into the public assistance programs, or onto the city streets with the other legions of the lost and homeless (Bassuk, 1984).

ALCOHOLISM AND PROBLEM DRINKING

The United States government launched a serious attempt to deal with the "alcohol problem" in the early 1970s. The creation of the National Institute of Alcohol Abuse and Alcoholism (NIAAA) in 1970 placed the official response to alcoholism within the realm of the welfare state. At approximately the same time the Uniform Intoxication Act (1971), a version of which has since been passed in about three quarters of the states, began the move toward decriminalizing public drunkenness (Regier, 1977). As was noted in Chapter 6 these steps were the culmination of a long process throughout the 20th century in which the "alcohol problem" was being redefined as a medical rather than a criminal or a moral problem (Beauchamp, 1980; Gusfield, 1982c).

Consistent with this trend most state alcohol agencies drew up plans for a "continuum" of alcoholism programs based in the community (Dunham & Janik, 1985). Wherever possible the responsibility for dealing with alcoholism was being dispersed into the community, with a minimal emphasis on institutional care. It is apparent, however, that in many states mental hospitals continued to provide the bulk of the services for alcoholics, and that this will probably be the case for the foreseeable future. This suggests that the response to alcoholism was similar in more ways than one to the treatment of mental illness. In both situations there was a shift toward community care, but the class and racially biased system of provision remained in evidence. Down-and-out alcoholics continued to be treated, if they were treated at all, in city jails, detoxication units, and state mental hospitals; while middle- and upper-middle-class problem drinkers had the luxury of private and confidential treatment.

Another similarity was that the bulk of the alcoholism programs funded under the new guidelines have consistently been directed toward treatment programs, with only a secondary focus on public education and prevention (Glaser *et al.*, 1978; Wittman, 1982). Although many states and the NIAAA are now making a determined effort to shift this emphasis (New York State Division of Alcohol Abuse and Alcoholism, 1985; NIAAA, 1982), the task will be a daunting one. In fiscal year 1981, for example, there were 6,290 alcoholism treatment units in the United States receiving at least some federal support. The total outlay for treatment units amounted to more than $940 million, well over half of which came from government sources at the federal, state, and local levels. By comparison fewer than 2,000 programs had a major focus on prevention issues (NIAAA, 1982). This orientation strongly reflects the continued dominance of the medical model, in which alcoholism is defined primarily as an individual problem that only affects a small proportion of the drinking population (Peele, 1984). Other models of alcoholism are discussed frequently in the literature, but at the present time their influence on policy and service provision remains peripheral (Siegler, Osmond, & Newell, 1968; Whitehead, 1979).

It is ironic that just when the federal role in combatting alcohol abuse was being formalized, "the de facto policy of Congress . . . [was] . . . to promote consumption of alcoholic beverages through lower taxes" (Cook & Tauchen, 1981). Between 1960 and 1980, for example, alcohol became cheaper: The real price of liquor fell by 48%, beer by 27%, and wine 20% (Cook, 1981). Throughout this period federal taxes remained at the 1951 level of $10.50 per proof gallon of alcohol. If this tax had been tied to the Consumer Price Index it would have risen to $28.00 per gallon by 1980, a level that may have significantly reduced the rate of alcohol consumption (Cook, 1984).

Federal alcohol policy in the United States has thus far shown little evidence of any interest in supply-side controls, with the exception of the recent changes in the drinking-age laws. This apathy has been matched at the state level, where Alcoholic Beverage Control (ABC) administrators have been loathe to try anything other than a policy of "regulated maximum availability" (Medicine in the Public Interest, 1979). Current alcohol policies simply attempt to maximize revenues and control the market, with public health goals rarely even on the agenda (Bunce, Morgan, Mosher, Wallack, & Wittner, 1979). The alcoholic beverage industry is obviously not going to regulate itself in the direction of reduced availability, so it is hardly surprising that the industry actively supports the medical model of alcoholism. Their argument, and that of the medical model proponents, is that because relatively few individuals consistently abuse alcohol, it is unfair to penalize the millions who enjoy drinking without any harmful effects. On balance the apathetic or ambivalent public is also happy with the status quo. Most people can get a drink at a low price pretty much whenever and wherever they want, but to satisfy local groups of neoprohibitionists there are "dry" options and other limits on alcohol sales in many areas.

From the conflict perspective the treatment of alcoholism can be interpreted as another way to reproduce labor power (P. Morgan, 1980). The notion of a sober and hard-working labor force is consistent with the dominant ideology of capitalism, so to provide services to alcohol abusers will contribute to the reproduction of values that help to maintain the status quo (Doyal, 1979). The perceived value of alcoholism treatment programs to the owners of capital is reflected in their widespread adoption of industrial alcoholism programs, which are clearly as much in the interests of the employers as of the workers (Ralph, 1983).

The state has been required to find a workable solution to the dilemma it faces over the alcohol problem. Clearly the production and distribution of alcohol and the revenues generated by consumption contribute enormously to the accumulation process in capitalist economies. On the other hand, government is the last line of responsibility for those people who suffer from the effects of excessive drinking. This means that the state has to keep the wheels of accumulation turning, while at the same time mopping up the casualties and if possible putting them back to work. In the United States this has been achieved with some success by separating the responsibilities for control and prevention: leaving one in the hands of the local ABC boards and the other in the hands of federal and state agencies of alcohol abuse and alcoholism. This separation has allowed "control policies to develop relatively unfettered by old moralistic or temperance arguments against greater availability, lower taxes, and state supported production policies (P. Morgan, 1980, p. 135).

Another side to the conflict perspective on alcoholism involves the role of economic interests in the production, distribution, and consumption of alcohol. Alcohol is a multi-million-dollar industry, and in this respect there is a clearer link between economic processes and the "creation" of alcoholism than is the case for most other public problems. In their search for profits, the corporations who make and sell alcohol obviously share a major part of the responsibility for the prevalence of problem drinking. The corporations themselves tend to dispute this by arguing that as the providers of alcohol they are not responsible for the obvious fact that some people are simply addicted to alcohol and are unable to drink responsibly.

The role of economic interests in the creation of the alcoholism problem can be illustrated from a historical perspective. A number of historians have suggested that the domestic production of rum and bourbon resulted in a higher level of alcohol consumption and drunkenness in 19th-century America than had been the case in colonial times (Lender & Martin, 1982). The early settlers drank plenty of alcohol, but they concentrated on beer and cider, as had their British forefathers. In later years the consumption of "ardent spirits" increased greatly, and as Lender and Martin observed, corn whiskey and particularly bourbon earned the honor of becoming the national drink. It was indigenous, and to drink it was almost a symbol of what it meant to be an American (Carson, 1984).

In Britain during the 18th and 19th centuries, the spread of industrial capitalism, both in general and in the production of alcohol, created an entirely new set of pressures to drink among the working classes (Park, 1983). The capitalist mode of production vastly expanded the array of goods reaching the market, but the unique feature of capitalism was that the working classes were required not only to produce the goods but also to consume them, thereby speeding up the circulation of capital (Singer, 1986). Commercial brewing was one of the earliest forms of manufacturing to be organized along the principles of capitalist production, and the expanding supply of alcohol reaching the market had to be made easily available to the masses of thirsty workers. The alcohol producers went to considerable lengths to make sure drink was available to the workers, for example, through the mechanism of the "tied house," which was a tavern under contract to sell only the beer of the controlling brewery. "With the commercialization of taverns under capitalism . . . drinking places increasingly became hangouts . . . for the laborers, and under the relentless pressure of the drink suppliers, their drinking reached heights never reached before, or perhaps since" (Park, 1983, p. 69).

The mechanism of production under capitalism results in almost limitless market expansion. This occurs because goods like alcohol are produced not for their utility, or use value, but to be bought and sold in the marketplace, for their exchange value. The logic of capital accumulation required that consumers be encouraged to drink, and that new distribution outlets be provided to market the products of the ever-expanding industries (Sulkunen, 1983).

At various times national markets become oversaturated as a result of the relentless drive toward accumulation. It is at such times that capitalism encounters one of its major contradicitons, that of overproduction (Harvey, 1981). When this occurs, capitalists, acting as individual corporations but usually supported by the state, have to seek new outlets to keep up the level of consumption. One of the most popular outlets for alcohol producers has been overseas. The story of how the colonial Europeans introduced the "natives" to alcohol is a sad but familiar one (Pan, 1975). From the colonist's perspective alcohol played a number of important roles. In the first place, it is well accepted that one of the most important reasons European governments initially acquired territory in Africa was to boost their exports, and liquor occupied a major place in the interests of the trading companies that were involved.

Once colonial governments had been established, another major function of alcohol was to generate revenues for their upkeep. Liquor revenues were essential in the African colonies for a number of reasons: (1) there was a strong push for the colonies to support themselves, with minimal grants-in-aid from the mother country; (2) direct taxation was extremely unpopular and difficult to administer as a source of revenue; and, (3) most of the profits made in the colonies by colonial investments were repatriated, so alcohol duties were crucial for financial solvency. In French West Africa, for example, revenues from alcohol amounted to 60 to 75% of total revenues during the years from 1908 to 1913 (Pan, 1975, p. 16). The German colony of Togo was known as a "model" colony because it was entirely self-supporting. The budget was balanced by the revenues from import duties, almost half of which in the 1890s came from liquor imports (Gifford & Louis, 1967).

In many African colonies, the desire to limit the financial drain on foreign exchange led to the strategy of "import substitution" (Jacobs, 1984), which often began in consumer goods industries, and particularly in brewing and distilling. As Lloyd (1971) noted, breweries have often provided the first signpost on the road to industrialization. It has also been argued that the local production and consumption of alcohol helped the colonists in their imperialist mission by effectively narcotizing the local population. Doyal (1979) has suggested that the traditional ways of producing and consuming alcohol had acted to constrain and control the level of drinking, but these were eroded in the colonial era:

> In most African societies, the brewing of beer had been carried out within "traditional" modes of production. . . . Beer drinking was literally a celebration of the economic surplus, . . . [but] from the colonial period onwards . . . the social character of drinking began to change. Among migrant laborers the reasons for taking a drink turned on the alleviation of personal suffering and alienation . . . their consumption of alcohol had become totally divorced from the kind of production in which they now engaged. (p. 114)

In other words the local population now drank for different reasons than they had earlier, but the activity was still in the best interests of the colonials:

> The availability of alcohol provided an outlet for boredom and frustration which might otherwise have exploded in more coherent forms . . . and . . . the presence of local brewing . . . [was] a useful mechanism for stabilizing the workforce. (p. 115)

In recent times alcohol has continued to play a significant role in the relationships between developed and less developed countries. As Park (1983) has argued, "Alcohol caught up in the unending spiral of profit making in the capitalist economy leads to high levels of consumption both within the producing countries and the world system of nations . . . this is what explains the world-wide rising tide of alcohol consumption observed during the past decades" (p. 60). This process has been particularly evident in the 1970s, as alcohol producers in developed countries found their domestic markets were leveling off. They were forced to seek markets elsewhere around the globe, and particularly in developing countries. This coincided with the rapid strides that had been made in transportation and telecommunications, facilitating the "globalization" of marketing and managerial decision making. Contributing to these push factors have been a number of pull factors in the developing countries themselves: rapid urbanization, which produced higher levels of demand; the spread of westernized consumption patterns among the growing high-income elite groups; and the desire to substitute imports. All of these have contributed to the expansion of domestic production capacity in developing nations. But as Edwards (1983) has noted, they also provided a golden opportunity for the European and American corporate giants to extend their beer and liquor operations overseas:

> Among the pioneers in the transnationalization of the beer sector were the quasi-monopolies Heineken (Netherlands), United Breweries (Denmark), and Guinness (UK/Ireland), each controlling over three-fifths of their national markets by the

1960's. Overseas penetration by distilled spirit firms was spearheaded by the highly oligopolistic whisky sectors in the UK and North America, and the giant cognac houses of France. (p. 9)

Through the sale of their products, the export of capital, and the sale of licenses, it has been possible for these transnational corporations to increase the availability of alcohol in developing countries, and this has contributed to significant changes in consumption patterns. In the 46 countries where beer output grew by more than half between 1975 and 1980, 42 were developing countries; by 1977, 36 developing countries depended on transnationals for more than one fifth of their spirits consumption (Edwards, 1983). From 1960 to 1980 there has been a clear shift in the world pattern of alcohol production and consumption. The beer industry, for example, has grown spectacularly: Latin American, Asian, and African output rose by over 400%, and by 1980 the developing countries had captured 18.3% of the global output.

The history of temperance and prohibition movements around the world illustrates that nations have responded differently to the alcohol problems that have been aided and abetted by capitalism (Davies & Walsh, 1983; Makela, Room, Single, Sulkunen, & Walsh, 1981). In the United States the attempt to prohibit the production and sale of alcohol in the early part of the 20th century was successful. In the second half of the 20th century a much more subtle approach to the problem has evolved, in which only symbolic attempts have been made to control the supply of alcohol. The "problem" of alcoholism had by this time been brought under the umbrella of the welfare state during an era of liberal expansionary views about public problems and the way they should be tackled (Levine & Levine, 1970). In the relatively prosperous 1960s and the early 1970s, the expansion of welfare state activities to cover an increasing range of social problems could be interpreted as serving the best interests of capital accumulation. It provided services for the casualties, which it was hoped would help to prevent a large scale repudiation of the existing system. In the alcohol field the increasing role of the state was not interpreted as being counter to the interests of the capitalist class because, as noted earlier, it did not significantly interfere with the production, distribution, and consumption of alcohol.

The state has thus been able to act successfully as a mediator between the various groups that have been competing with each other to gain control of the alcohol problem (P. Morgan, 1980). A solution in which prevention and control were completely separated from issues of treatment, and in which treatment was based on the medical model, was acceptable to most of the parties involved. It could be clearly dissociated from Prohibition moralism; it allowed the market to operate freely and consumption to increase gradually; and it was scientifically "respectable," unlike the public health model of alcoholism (Room, 1984). Most importantly, particularly in the 1970s and 1980s, it was an approach to a social problem that preserved individual rights. It allowed adults to choose for themselves when, where, and how much they should drink, without imposing on them the unnecessary burdens of further state interventions.

In reaching this compromise the state's solution to the alcohol problem has practically guaranteed that it will fail, because to make significant inroads into the problem it is essential that the incidence rate be sharply reduced by preventing moderate drinkers from becoming heavier drinkers (Celluci, 1984; Miller & Niremberg, 1984). It has been estimated that the incidence rate of serious alcohol-related problems is in the range of 500,000 new cases per year (Keller, 1975). Treatment programs for existing alcoholics will slowly reduce the overall prevalence rates, and mortality will account for a further reduction, but the extent of the problem remains overwhelming. It seems likely that the alcoholism treatment movement as it is currently operating has little chance of seriously attacking the issue with which it has been charged.

In the middle of this gloom there are some signs that the situation is changing and that the prevalence of the medical model is being reduced somewhat. By the middle of 1985 it appeared that the entire issue of alcohol control policy had become more prominent in public debates and the media. This was partly a result of the fervent campaigns waged by citizen groups such as Remove Intoxicated Drivers, Mothers Against Drunk Driving, and Students Against Drunk Driving to establish stricter DWI laws and to tackle the growing problem of drunk driving. The campaign has reached other fronts: For example, in the summer of 1985, there was a petition launched to demand "equal time" in the media to point out the hazards of alcohol abuse. The campaign was not successful, but it appeared at a time when the public was becoming more aware of the alcohol issue. Many state alcoholism agencies were starting to launch all-out campaigns in the direction of prevention (see, e.g., NYSDAAA, 1985). In the dramatic phrasing of a popular weekly magazine, these trends have been referred to as "The New Prohibition," which has been accompanied by or has resulted in a small but significant reduction in the level of alcohol consumption in many parts of the United States. A new "dry" trend appears to be sweeping across college campuses, many of which have taken steps to ban fraternity and dormitory parties, and some have even banned alcohol from the campus entirely. It remains to be seen whether these efforts will in the near future become organized and coordinated to launch a new all-out crusade for tighter controls over the supply of alcohol.

The current situation is complicated by some recent research that suggests that it may not be necessary to have any further controls on the supply of alcohol. In the first place there is evidence that even when alcohol availability increases, the level of drinking does not increase as significantly as many observers feared. In Scotland, for example, drinking levels have not risen significantly as a result of the recent changes in licensing laws that increased the availability of alcohol. There is also some reason to believe that even in times of rising levels of alcohol consumption, the prevalence of problem drinking will not necessarily increase. This conclusion was reached in a series of studies conducted in Iowa by Mulford and Fitzgerald (1983a, 1983b). They observed that during the 1960s and 1970s, Iowans were "drinking more alcohol more frequently and at an earlier age" (1983b, p. 685), which was a result of the liberalization of the liquor-control laws. In spite of this there was no increase in the prevalence of problem drinking in Iowa. Mulford and Fitzgerald suggest that between the consumption of alcohol and the prevalence of problems, some set of intervening variables is at work. Their research leads them to the conclusion that these variables include a change in the "climate" of attitudes toward alcohol use. Specifically, they observed an increase in tolerance of social drinking, and the relaxation of emotionally charged attitudes toward alcohol, combined with a continued disapproval of intoxication. This combination has enabled Iowans to integrate alcohol into their way of life without seriously adverse consequences:

> The evolution of a climate of attitudes and legal controls that allow people to drink openly without guilt, together with a widespread disapproval of excessive drinking, constitute a set of conditions consistent with, if not conducive to, the alcohol-integration process. (1983b, p. 686).

Still a third trend that has recently become apparent is the decline in alcohol consumption in many Western and industrialized countries (Davies & Walsh, 1983; Makela *et al.*, 1981). In the United Kingdom this trend has been observed since 1979, after which alcohol consumption fell by between 3 and 4% each year (Brewers Society, 1984). During this period there has also been a drop in some of the major indicators of alcoholism: (1) first admissions for alcohol dependence fell by 19% between 1979 and 1982; (2) drunkenness convictions fell by 16%; (3) drinking and driving convictions fell by 7%; (4) liver cirrhosis mortality rates fell by 4% (Kendell, 1984).

Not all of these decreases should be attributed to the decline in alcohol consumption in the United Kingdom, but the evidence strongly points to the sort of phenomenon that Mulford and Fitzgerald (1983b) have observed in the United States. The major danger of course is that the transnational alcohol corporations will simply use this new market information to step up their production and sales efforts in third-world countries, a process that could have far-ranging adverse health and social consequences.

CONCLUSION

As the two case studies have illustrated, the essential Marxian insight is that surplus value arises out of the domination of labor by the capitalist class that must, if it is to reproduce itself and its domination, continually expand its profit-making abilities (Harvey, 1981). In other words, production occurs for its own sake, and it follows that one of the most serious problems for capitalism is nonreproduction. The most damaging situation would be the total loss of the labor force through annihilation. Less serious but more likely would be the physical and psychological deterioration of the workforce (Ralph, 1983), and equally if not more damaging would be the ideological impasse that would occur if significant numbers of workers decided it was no longer in their interests to accept the status quo. Each of these situations would in different ways damage the subservient relationship of labor to capital that is essential for continued accumulation.

The problems dealt with this book and the many others that appear to be endemic in an advanced capitalist society are considered to be serious not because they involve individual suffering but because they threaten the structure and survival of the entire social system. In other words, as R. Lee (1979) has argued, "social problems become significant only insofar as they threaten reproduction" (p. 57).

9

Arena Building and the Social Construction of Public Problems

INTRODUCTION

History demonstrates that the way problems are perceived and acted upon differs significantly over time. Some of the changes represent drastic turnabouts, which suggests that problems are socially "constructed" at various times and for different reasons. Some issues are elevated to the status of major public problems, but others remain dormant. It appears that the outcome has less to do with the "facts" of the situation than with the processes involved in defining and interpreting the facts.

Sociologists and historians have devoted a great deal of thought to the process involved in a public issue becoming a public problem. One obvious line of research was to explain the process as a logical outcome of pluralism in society. The assumption is that a variety of interest groups and institutions compete with each other continually to make sure their particular concern receives its due consideration. As noted earlier, the groups that constituted the Temperance movement in 19th-century America were concerned to make sure that it was their definition of "moral" behavior that dominated (Gusfield, 1963). Competing with them were groups who argued that Temperance views about drinking were a denial of the individual's rights either to drink or to make a profit from the drinking of others. All of these groups attempt to legitimate their own designation of what is "deviant" by a variety of "claims-making" activities in the public arena (Spector & Kitsuse, 1977). Under normal circumstances the group with the best organization or the most resources will win the battle, firstly by changing public opinions and then ultimately by forcing through legislation.

Traditionally the groups that have been most successful in their claims making have been professionals attempting to consolidate and expand their "turf." Other groups active in this endeavor include individuals who have encountered or in some way experienced the ill effects of the problems in question. Their actions demand a response from existing institutions, either to change a particular law or to bring about improved circumstances. In the last 2 to 3 decades

174

the changes in care for the mentally disabled have demonstrated the role of such groups. Mental patients, acting both as individuals and in groups, have achieved some success in making claims on policy makers and service providers to bring about much needed changes in the delivery of care (P. Brown, 1985; Naparstek *et al.*, 1982).

This example illustrates that the eventual outcome is not a simple matter of a demand for better conditions on behalf of the problem sufferers. In the first place, it is evident that not all of the claims makers are directly involved with the problem in question. Some are involved for purely professional and economic reasons, such as the lawyers who supported the mental patients rights groups (P. Brown & C. J. Smith, 1987). Others are involved for moral or religious reasons, as was the case for many of the leading figures in the Temperance movement. It is also naive to assume that the official agencies are purely passive reactors in the process. The agencies providing the services are in fact a powerful interest group in themselves (N. J. Davis & Anderson, 1983), and they manipulate definitions of the problems and change their policies in ways that are most consistent with their continued existence.

To return to the earlier example of mental disorder, patient demands for more humane care were successful only because they happened to coincide with the official policy of deinstitutionalization as a means of lowering state hospital budgets (P. Brown, 1981). It follows that to some extent the goals of releasing patients from hospitals and emphasizing community care were based on considerations that were largely independent of concerns for the well-being of the patients themselves. However, to legitimate such policies it was also necessary for the service providers to attempt to change public opinions about mental illness, as a way to ensure that the public would be supportive of the new emphasis on community-based care. Although this has proved to be a difficult task, there is some evidence of improvements in public attitudes toward the mentally ill over the last 20 years (Dear & Taylor, 1982; C. J. Smith & Hanham, 1981a).

THE "FACTS" ABOUT PUBLIC PROBLEMS

Even a casual observation shows that many more problems are officially recognized by public agencies today than ever before. As noted in Chapter 1, for many of these problems the available evidence suggests an almost inevitable tendency for the prevalence rates to rise. It is of course notoriously difficult to measure changing prevalence rates with any degree of certainty; and it is equally difficult to determine the implications of a sharp increase (or decrease) in prevalence rates. Epidemiological evidence of a major increase in prevalence is a necessary but by no means sufficient condition for a particular issue to be defined as a major public problem. To take a contemporary issue for illustrative purposes: There is no doubt that the "facts" about the sexual abuse of children indicate a level of seriousness that requires prompt official action. The actual evidence, however, should be closely scrutinized to determine whether the new level of prevalence is indeed significantly higher than it was earlier. All too often an issue becomes a major public concern because it receives more media attention, which leads people to assume that the prevalence has risen sharply, when in actuality the numbers themselves do not necessarily support such a conclusion.

Official data describing the prevalence of a particular problem can be used flexibly, sometimes even to support contradictory goals. Police forces, for example, have been accused of manipulating their data to show that certain crime rates are rising, which is one way of arguing for new and higher levels of funding. At other times,using the same data but making comparisons with the past, they are able to show how effective they have been at controlling the problem in question.

Even if we can be reasonably sure that the data is reliable, it is still difficult to determine with any certainty whether a higher rate of prevalence implies that the problem in question is increasing. Apparent increases are often the result of "uncovering" processes, in which a higher proportion of the total pool of problem sufferers are counted as "cases" (Catalano & Dooley, 1981). This might occur as a result of new methods of data collection; higher levels of public awareness, which make it more likely that individuals will identify themselves as problem sufferers; or even as a result of the increased availability of services. In recent years there has been some concern that there are now more women alcoholics and problem drinkers than ever before, but bearing in mind the uncovering argument, this may simply mean that more women are defining their problems as alcohol-related, and are coming forward for treatment (Wilsnack, 1982; Wilsnack, Wilsnack, & Klassen, 1985).

A more controversial issue, and one that also involves women, is the use of official statistics to demonstrate a sharp increase in crime among women in recent years. The female crime wave is thought to be, in some unspecified way, a result of the women's movement. This argument suggests that women have been "liberated" to such an extent that they have begun to compete with men in many problem areas, including crime (N. J. Davis & Anderson, 1983). Detailed analyses of crime statistics provide some support for this view, but it appears that crime among women is only increasing in certain categories (Table 9.1; Simon, 1975). There is no evidence of an increase in "violent" crimes during the last decade but there has been a slight increase in "property" crimes (which include burglary, larceny, theft, and motor vehicle theft). Overall crime rates for women are still far below those for men, but the greater prevalence of arrests for property crimes in part reflects the traditional role of women as consumers (Leonard, 1982; Steffensmeier, 1980), and perhaps also the increasing burdens that have resulted from the so-called "feminization of poverty" (B. Ehrenreich, 1983). Women are also overrepresented in some of the victimless crimes such as prostitution and runaways. In 1981 the Uniform Crime

Table 9.1. Total Arrests by Sex, and Arrest Trends For Women, 1975–1979

Offense Charged	Total Number (1979)	% Men	% Women	% Change for Women 1975–1979
Murder and Nonnegligent manslaughter	18,264	86.3	13.7	−19.1
Forcible Rape	29,164	99.2	0.8	−10.2
Robbery	130,753	92.6	7.4	−8.6
Aggravated Assault	256,597	87.6	12.7	4.3
Burglary	468,085	93.7	6.3	4.6
Larceny-Theft	1,098,398	69.7	30.3	−1.2
Motor Vehicle Theft	143,654	91.7	8.9	30.7
Arson	18,387	88.7	11.3	8.8
Total "Violent Crime"[a]	434,778	89.8	10.2	−0.4
Total "Property" Crime[b]	1,728,529	78.2	21.8	0.1
TOTAL Index Crimes	2,163,302	80.5	19.5	

[a] murder, forcible rape, robbery, aggravated assault
[b] burglary, larceny/theft, motor vehicle theft, arson
Source. National Institute of Justice (1979, Tables 29, 31, 34).

Reports showed that 73.4% and 53.7% of those arrested in these two categories were women.

A further analysis of the official crime statistics also shows that race and social class are more likely than sex to determine arrest rates. This suggests that it is not all women who are appearing more frequently in the crime statistics, but specifically poor black women. Black women are 2½ times more likely than white women to be arrested for larceny, forgery, and vagrancy; and 5 times more likely to be arrested for prostitution (N. J. Davis & Anderson, 1983). Overall, black women account for more than half of all women arrested. The issue of female crime has, according to Davis and Anderson, been vastly overstated. Much of this involves using the criminal justice system as a "fall-back structure" that constructs crimes for women and uses them as "symbolic offenses for validating conventional female roles and punishing deviations from traditional role assignments" (p. 108).

In addition to the problems associated with the collection of the facts, there is the problem of how these facts are to be interpreted. Even if the prevalence rates for a particular problem have increased significantly, it is possible that the public and official reactions to the problem have been blown out of proportion. This may well be the case if we compare life in the 19th-century American city with life in the contemporary city. In many ways modern society is considerably less violent, less crime-ridden, and more wholesome (Boyer, 1978). In this sense it is difficult to understand why we are so morbidly preoccupied with deviance and disorder, and so fearful of its effects on our lives, when in fact most city dwellers (particularly suburbanites) are far less likely to be personally involved with the problems than they would have been 100 years ago. It is possible that the recent trends toward decentralization and deinstitutionalization have increased the public's exposure to the range of public problems. In addition, the media have no doubt played a major role in forcing such issues into public consciousness on a daily basis (N. Corwin, 1984). Deviance has become a major spectator sport, not only at the make-believe level of the soap opera and the crime and violence shows but also in real life on the daily network news.

It is also possible to interpret our morbid fascination with public problems and the desire to do something about them as a healthy escape valve in a world of excess. As one of the world's richest nations, we in the United States have more resources and more energy to devote to solutions for these perennial problems that make us feel guilty about having so much. Another plausible explanation is related to the ever-increasing divergence between our private and public worlds (Fischer, 1981). As life becomes increasingly private and homogeneous in the suburbs, what we witness in the disordered and public city appears to contrast more and more starkly (Alexander, 1967). The insulation of suburban everyday life from the real world may help to escalate the desire to help put things right, or at least to be concerned that solutions are found. An even deeper source for our current fascination with problems and deviance has been suggested by N. J. Davis and Anderson (1983). They argue that the gap is growing between what we have come to expect from the state and its welfare institutions, and what they are actually able to achieve. As the gap widens, it fuels the belief that the whole country is "going to the dogs," and that "nothing works." Having tried all sorts of Great Society solutions and watched them fail, we conclude that we have unrealistic expectations about how life and society ought to be.

Our current concern about specific public problems is a function of how likely we think it is that we ourselves will experience such problems in our own lifetime. This would obviously be a function of the overall prevalence of the problem and the individual's risk of contracting or suffering from it. Concern for the elderly is clearly at one end of the spectrum in this respect. Growing old is nobody's fault, and of course it is the one minority group that everyone will eventually enter, assuming they live long enough. At the other end of the spectrum is a problem like Acquired Immune Deficiency Syndrome (AIDS). Because this is still a relatively rare problem and one that is considered by many to be partly a result of one's lifestyle, it was not until fairly recently able to command a wide base of public sympathy (D. Altman, 1987). Somewhere between these two extremes fall the other problems discussed in this book, such as mental disability, alcoholism, and crime. Not everyone will encounter these problems, but almost everyone knows someone in their family or social network who is or has been somehow involved with at least one of them.

The history of the Temperance movement in the 19th century illustrates this issue in an interesting way. The movement was dominated in the middle and late decades of the century by middle-class women. Very few of these women had directly experienced the problem of drunkenness, either themselves or via their families (B. L. Epstein, 1981). We must assume, therefore, that a concern about this issue was based on a personal blueprint for the way things ought to be in society, and perhaps this blueprint was shaped by a realistic opinion of how easily one's own situation could change for the worse. The middle-class housewife probably did not have to fear that her husband would abuse her and her children and drink away all the family's savings, but the evidence of even a few such cases reminded her of the vulnerability of being a woman in a male-dominated world. The worst-case scenario was being played out on a daily basis in working-class ethnic households. The Temperance women must have realized that the dividing line was thin between such families and their own, and they had convinced themselves that the major determinant of who steps over that line was drinking (H. G. Levine, 1980). This realization emphasized to them the inherently tenuous nature of possessions and wealth, and the status that accompanied them.

THE MECHANISMS FOR CONSTRUCTING PUBLIC PROBLEMS

In any area of social life there are different groups with their own ideas about what is good and bad, and what should be done to transform the bad into the good. These groups have to struggle continuously to compete with others who hold opposing views. To survive, they need to be flexible; they must decide to make alliances or to strike out on their own if they see fit. In most cases this activity begins a long time before the issue comes clearly into the public spotlight, and as time passes some groups will perish in the struggle, while others will flourish.

The process involved can be illustrated by the development of alcohol-control policies. There are many different groups that have an interest in this issue, including agency bureaucrats at all levels of government, treatment providers, volunteer groups, researchers, law enforcement officers, the beverage industries, the temperance crusaders, and perhaps most importantly alcoholics and problem drinkers themselves. All of these groups have had to define their own position in the ongoing debates about the use and abuse of alcohol (Beauchamp, 1980). In selecting its position, each group has had to steer a reasonable course between two treacherous extremes. Those groups favoring the development of alcohol control policies have had to put some distance between themselves and the old morality of the Prohibitionists, whereas the others have had to argue that even though drinking to excess can be dangerous, the majority of drinkers are able to drink without obvious harm.

Because of the nature of most of the issues that become public problems, it is necessary for the state to act as the guarantor that services will be provided. Until quite recently the state had a virtual monopoly in many problem areas, both in the provision of direct services, and also indirectly through its financing of welfare benefits such as SSI, Medicaid, and Medicare. With the growing emphasis on community-based services as an alternative to institutions, the delivery of care gradually passed into the hands of "nonpervasive" professional service organizations, such as social welfare agencies, mental health centers, and family service agencies (N. J. Davis & Anderson, 1983). These agencies are expected to provide treatment for those in need, in addition to offering preventive services where they are appropriate. Although many of these agencies are large bureaucracies staffed by professionals, in most cases the personnel are not high-status professionals like doctors and lawyers.

Social service agencies tend to have rigid hierarchies, close supervision, limits on the time spent with clients, and invariably, serious budget constraints—all of which tend to foster cynicism and a rapid rate of job "burnout." Many of the workers in these agencies find they are the first line of contact with people experiencing hard-core persistent problems such as alcoholism, habitual delinquency, and child abuse. There are no instant solutions and the agencies offer little hope to the clients over and above keeping a lid on their problems.

Some social service agencies act as resource mobilizers to help clients develop a collective voice in the public realm, and, if necessary, begin to make claims on legislatures and other decision-making bodies. In this way workers in the welfare agencies combine with the clients to build up an "arena" around their specific problem. They do this in many different ways: by protesting and continually drawing media attention to the issue in question, fund raising, lobbying, and creating alliances with other organizations. As the arena develops, the public and their elected representatives may begin to recognize the seriousness of the problem and the need for action. In this sense public problems are political constructions because the protagonists have had to fight in a resource-scarce environment to "renew their mandate." The ultimate goal of each group is to ensure that it survives, and ultimately, if the group is successful, that the problem is legitimated. The best evidence that this has occurred is when the state, acting through one of its agencies, adds the problem in question to its own agenda.

Relative newcomers in the problem landscape will be more easily legitimated if they can be incorporated into already established institutional and ideological categories, the best example of which is obviously medicine. Cigarette smoking and drug and alcohol abuse could be fitted into a model that explained the addictive process in medical or psychological terms, and that suggested specific courses of treatment. Other problems such as marital disharmony, homosexuality, and hyperactivity among children have also been able to borrow some of the legitimacy and prestige of medicine in their struggle to build arenas (Conrad & Schneider, 1980).

Another group of highly prestigious institutions that has been successfully pulled into service in the business of arena building is the universities. Major educational campaigns have been launched to convince the public that a specific behavior is hazardous, or to improve public attitudes toward a specific issue such as mental disorder. In a society that craves information and is obsessed with the prestige of education, it is not surprising that scholarly research into public problems has multiplied. Once a problem begins to receive significant funding, assuming the research is being conducted at some of the major centers of learning, the process of legitimation is further advanced. In this sense education lends its prestige to the issues involved. The knowledge that some of the nation's greatest brains are at work on a particular problem helps to bolster the belief that some type of solution is eventually possible, or that an effective course of action will be drawn up.

Many of the processes described here have been at work in the arena that has grown up around the problem of alcohol use and abuse in the last 2 decades. Wiener (1981) has identified three stages in the recognition of any issue as a social problem:

1. "Animating" the problem: establishing territorial rights, developing constitutencies, funneling advice, and importing skills and information;
2. "Legitimizing" the problem: borrowing expertise and prestige, redefining its scope, building up respectability, and establishing and maintaining a separate identity;
3. "Demonstrating" the problem: competing for attention, combining with other groups for extra strength, selecting and publishing supportive data, persuading potential opponents, and enlarging the bounds of responsibility.

In the case of the alcoholism arena, Wiener provides summaries of the three stages, and examples of each of the subprocesses (see Table 9.2). As we shall see in the following case studies, some of the stages and processes in Wiener's model can be identified, although the actual sequence of events varies from one problem to another.

PROBLEM DRINKING AND THE DESIGNATION OF SPECIAL POPULATIONS

The federal agency that was given the responsibility in 1970 for dealing with the "alcohol problem" within the larger umbrella of Health, Education, and Welfare, was the National Institute of Alcohol Abuse and Alcoholism (NIAAA). Although the creation of a separate agency suggests that the problem has been officially recognized, it certainly does not automatically follow that members of the public and their elected representatives agreed that alcoholism was a problem for which public monies should be allocated. The per capita allocation of federal funds for the establishment of alcoholism programs varies signifi-

Table 9.2. The Establishment of An Arena Around the Problem of Alcohol Use: Major Processes Involved, Subprocesses, and Examples

Animating the Problem

Establishing turf rights:

The growth of associations, the burgeoning of the resource world and the relationship to the macrosociological conditions of the history of the arena and federal, state, and county programming.

Developing constituencies:

The growth of "citizen participation" through advisory boards, special minority boards and commissions, and the awarding of grants and contracts.

Funneling advice and imparting skills and information:

The relationship of the National Center on Alcohol Education to the growth of area education and training, and the growth of a training constituency.

Legitimizing the Problem

Borrowing prestige and expertise:

The history of the area's eclecticism. Roots of that eclecticism in closely protected turf rights, the intellectual isolation of the early "alcohologists," and the disinterest and inability of other professional worlds to take on the problem of alcohol use.

Redefining the scope:

The shift from a moral to a medical/psychological model of alcoholism, the conditions leading to a disease concept, the conditions undermining a disease concept. The next stage in the redefining process: social setting detoxication and the social model of recovery.

Building respectability:

Strategy for attaining respectability: the enhanced status lent to the problem of alcohol use by prominent recovered alcoholics, by interested legislators, by the existence of a national institute, by softening the labeling to "alcoholic persons." Consequences of the drive for respectability: the establishing of a clearinghouse for information, an epidemiology division and research centers.

Maintaining a separate identity:

The rationale behind maintaining a separation from mental health and drug problems.

Demonstrating the Problem

Competing for attention; combining for strength:

Competing for jurisdiction, funding, eminence, and the attention of the public eye. A consequence of the competing process: intersecting of worlds around the issue of the public inebriate; the relationship of this issue to the macrosociological condition of urban redevelopment and to the redefining process.

Selecting supportive data:

Problems avoided and encountered by the need for accountability. Relationship to the macrosociological condition of cost-benefit thrust in government. Intersection of the bureaucratic world and the alcoholic beverage industries world over the issue of "responsible drinking."

Convincing opposing ideologists:

The contra-ideologies behind the "controlled drinking" issues. Relationship to organizational turf carving and to turf rights of the research world.

Enlarging the bounds of respectability:

The expanded "ownership of the problem" in terms of careers, prevention approaches and pressure on the alcoholic beverage industries world. New turf broken by the co-alcoholic. Relationship of career growth and prevention stance to the "professional reform" movement. Contrast in turf strength of the alcoholic beverage industries world and the temperance world. Relationship of prevention activities to insurance and legal worlds.

Source. Wiener (1981, pp. 20–22).

cantly from state to state. In some states spending is more than 20 times higher than in others; for example, per capita funding in Minnesota is $6.92 and in Connecticut it is $5.06, compared to $.13 in North Dakota and $.25 in Arkansas (NIAAA, 1981b). The proportion of the state's total budget that is spent on alcoholism programs also varies significantly, from 0.79% in Nebraska and 0.74% in Montana, to as low as 0.03% in Arkansas, Hawaii, and North Dakota (NIAAA, 1981b).

In recent years NIAAA has identified a series of "special populations" that have been earmarked for preferential treatment, which usually involves high-priority funding for treatment programs and greater availability of research funds (NIAAA, 1982). In general it is reasonable to expect that the prevalence of alcoholism or problem drinking is a particular concern within these subgroups of the population, or that for one reason or another individual members of the group do not have access to adequate services in times of need. Whether or not this is the case is a question that can be answered empirically. There are a number of epidemiological studies based on nationwide household surveys, that break down the prevalence data by the major social, economic, racial, and demographic categories. (For an example of this, see Table 9.3, which shows the 1979 percentage of drinking problems by sex and age.)

Women have been designated by NIAAA as one of the special populations, but the empirical evidence thus far suggests that this designation is based more on the need to provide special services for women than the obvious fact of a significant increase in the prevalence of problem drinking. In spite of some recent increases, women still drink far less heavily than men, and they are much less likely to experience alcohol-related problems (Wilsnack *et al.*, 1985), although some studies have shown evidence of slight increases in both categories in recent years (S. Shaw, 1980). Based on the data collected in a 1981 survey, Wilsnack *et al.* (1985) have shown that there has been a modest increase in alcohol consumption during the 1970s, particularly among middle-aged women. Although the survey data did not show any evidence of an "epidemic" of problem drinking among women, a number of subgroups appear to be at particular risk for alcohol abuse, particularly younger women, never-married women, and unemployed women. Unfortunately we have no way of knowing from this data alone whether the increasing prevalence rates are a result of an "uncovering" process, in which more women than ever before are either being treated or apprehended for drinking problems. This could occur as a result of greater public tolerance toward women with drinking problems, or it may simply be that there are more facilities offering services for women alcoholics (Beckman & Amara, 1985). In either case it is quite possible that the higher prevalence rates do not imply that the "true" prevalence of alcohol problems among women has increased.

For another of the special populations, the elderly, the survey data have clearly shown that problem drinking is relatively less prevalent than it is among younger persons. As people get older they tend to drink less alcohol and they

Table 9.3. Drinking Patterns and Drinking Problems in the United States Adult
Population (in Percentages)

Age Group		Drinking Categories[a]					
	Abstainers	1–60 drinks a month	60+ drinks a month	Social Consequences	Loss of Control	Loss of Control (% based on drinkers only)	N
Men							
18–20	5	79	17	15	35	37	37
21–25	10	54	36	13	25	28	82
26–30	20	50	29	10	25	32	87
31–40	25	55	19	8	16	21	154
41–50	27	52	21	2	8	11	107
51–60	32	51	17	3	5	8	130
61–70	38	53	8	5	6	11	91
70+	41	45	13	4	2	4	72
Women							
18–20	31	64	5	5	16	24	52
21–25	15	78	6	6	13	16	130
26–30	30	65	5	3	7	10	125
31–40	27	65	9	5	8	12	208
41–50	43	46	10	4	5	9	137
51–60	50	46	4	1	4	8	143
61–70	61	38	1	0	0	0	102
70+	61	39	0	0	0	0	103
Total Sample	33	54	13	5	10	15	1,772
Men	25	54	21	7	15	20	762
Women	40	54	5	3	6	10	1,010

[a] All percentages, except where indicated, are percentage of the total population.
Source. Clark and Midanik (1982, p. 29).

experience fewer alcohol-related problems. This observation has not prevented
the growth of research investigating drinking habits among the elderly (Gomberg, 1982; NIAAA, 1984). It is important to point out here, however, that
clear-cut statistical evidence is not and should not be the sole determinant of
the level of priority assigned to a particular issue. In the case of drinking among
the elderly, there are a number of reasons to expect that the magnitude of the
problem is not adequately reflected in the available data. In the first place, there
is evidence that even though they drink less than younger people, elderly drinkers may experience relatively higher rates of alcohol-related problems, particularly in the health area (Baker, 1982; Sherouse, 1982). This may be because
of a lower tolerance for alcohol, the compounding effect of alcohol-related
problems with other problems related to the aging process, or the effect of
interactions between alcohol and other prescription drugs that elderly persons

are likely to be taking (M. Williams, 1984). It is also possible that the relatively low prevalence of problem drinking among the elderly is a consequence of the "self-limiting" effect of alcoholism. After many years of heavy drinking, people who would have entered the problem statistics have already died from alcohol-related illnesses (Drew, 1968).

A second possible source of underestimation occurs in the methods used to estimate the prevalence of alcohol-related problems among elderly drinkers. The scales used in self-report surveys are not age specific enough to capture accurately the scope of the problems encountered by older drinkers. Some of the problem events included in these scales are simply not appropriate for many elderly persons. This is particularly the case for problems experienced at work, problems with spouse and family, and difficulties associated with driving a car.

A third source of potential error is in the data collected about elderly persons who seek treatment for their alcohol-related problems. For a number of reasons, the official statistics from treatment programs may seriously underestimate the "true" prevalence rates. The drinking problems of many elderly persons are either misdiagnosed or are undetected and not treated (Crook & Cohen, 1984). This may occur as a result of confusion with other symptoms, or, what is more likely, because the drinkers or their families deny that drinking has become a problem for them. Again the different lifestyles of the elderly may be important, in that individuals who do no go out to work or who do not have families are less likely to have their behavior scrutinized for potential problems. A final possibility is that elderly persons may simply not know where to go for treatment, or if they do know they may be limited by their lack of mobility (Hinrichsen, 1984). It has also been suggested that some service providers may deliberately or inadvertently discourage utilization by elderly drinkers, who then find themselves in a predicament: They feel they can neither receive services in general programs because of their drinking problems nor enter specialized alcoholism programs because of their age. Whatever the reasons, the elderly are clearly underrepresented in traditional treatment programs. This is evident in the state of New York, for example, where a "point prevalence" study indicated that of almost 14,000 clients receiving treatment in 1983, only 568 (4.1%) were older than 60 (NYSDAAA, 1985).

Another special population on which considerable public attention has been focused is teenagers. More teenagers drink today then ever before, but there is no unequivocal proof that this drinking has resulted in a significantly higher prevalence of alcohol-related problems (Rachal *et al.,* 1982). In spite of this, there is a general consensus on the need to provide information about teenage drinking, in part because this will allow policy makers to identify potential targets for intervention programs. In other words, dealing with the youthful end of the drinking spectrum is consistent with the recent move in the direction of prevention programs as a complement to treatment programs. The net effect of this concern is that the topic of teenage drinking has become a growth industry within the alcoholism field. In 1977 a 5-year $83 million National Teenage

Alcohol Education Program was launched and since then a vast literature has emerged (Braucht, 1982).

A review of the literature, however, fails to provide unequivocal evidence of growing problems among teenagers who drink (Blane & Hewitt, 1977; Hubbard, Cavanaugh, Rachal, Schlenger, & Ginzburg, 1983). Among the data that has recently become available, the results of the Research Triangle Institute's 1978 National Survey indicated that teenage alcohol use had peaked at a fairly high level, but had not risen during the 1970s (Rachal *et al.*, 1982). According to Chauncey (1980), the FBI Uniform Crime Reports show an actual decline in arrests for juvenile drunkenness during the 1970s, and membership in teen-based Alcoholics Anonymous (AA) groups has been short-lived. Although the interpretation of this evidence is controversial, a case can be made for the existence of arena-building motives in the growth of the teenage drinking issue. The extreme form of this argument has been stated by Chauncey (1980):

> This manipulation of teenage drinking as a public and political issue by the NIAAA offers self-preservation as a dominant motive behind the campaign. This is not to demean the agency or its employees, but merely to emphasize the entrepreneurial aspect of welfare organizations. (p. 51).

To begin to explain why an agency like NIAAA felt it necessary to push the teenage drinking issue, it is important to consider its status vis-à-vis other agencies, particularly those within the parent organization. NIAAA is the smallest agency within the Department of Health and Human Services, so as a response to the threat of being subsumed within the more general "substance abuse" umbrella, NIAAA bureaucrats may have been particularly concerned to carve out their own territory within the teenage drug field. The alcohol treatment industry has also faced the problem of continual public apathy bordering on opposition. This apathy is in part an outcome of widespread cultural ambivalence toward alcohol. Many people like to drink, and most of them do so without problems, so that to overcome this ambivalence it may have been necessary to overstate certain parts of the "alcohol problem". In the case of teenage drinking this was not difficult to achieve, because once the agency set the ball rolling, the media took over, and the result was that teenage drinking problems were depicted as reaching near-epidemic proportions (Dorn, 1983).

The evidence suggests that the problem of teenage drinking was to some extent "created," but a question remains as to whether the problem has subsequently been validated and legitimated by society. In other words, do members of the public agree that the problem exists, and are they willing to support the newly created programs? As Chauncey (1980) has noted, "the legitimacy of an officially created social problem . . . is established by the arousal of public controversy or discussion coupled with the popular participation in some ameliorative program" (p. 53).

The evidence for such a legitimation is slim, and what does exist is contradictory. Public attitudes toward alcoholism in general have improved to the extent that most people agree with a disease definition of alcoholism (Mulford & Fitzgerald, 1983b; C. J. Smith & Hanham, 1982). On the other hand, the majority still think of self-help groups like AA as the solution to alcohol problems, rather than formal treatment programs, which implies that treatment of alcoholism has only been partly legitimated and that many people still think of alcoholism not as a true form of illness but as a "folk illness" (Rodin, 1981). Public behavior toward the alcohol problem, especially for teenagers, seems to reflect this ambivalence. Referrals have been slow, and new programs are often running at less than full capacity (Chauncey, 1980). We are tempted to ask: Where are all the teenage problem drinkers? Are they much less prevalent than has been reported, are they being siphoned off by other agencies such as drug clinics and diversion programs, or are they simply being absorbed in the community as a result of informal coping mechanisms? It is possible that by defining its own territory as being "alcohol only," NIAAA may have actually carved out too minute a territory for itself.

On the positive side, it is likely that relatively few people are hurt when agencies construct their own reality of social problems by providing more services than are really needed. The service programs help those people who enter them, jobs are created, and an aura of prevention and education—in this case in the schools—is created. The special population thrust has also helped the alcoholism arena to expand its constituencies by demonstrating the importance of the alcohol issue to groups whose primary interests have not traditionally involved alcohol. This is particularly the case among women's groups and those representing the interests of the elderly. Another advantage is that the potential sources of funding for alcoholism research have expanded to include agencies that deal specifically with the subpopulations in question (e.g., the National Institute on Aging provides funding for research projects dealing with drinking habits and problems among the elderly).

On the negative side, unnecessary program expansion tends to drain federal and state resources, and it may have inadvertantly contributed to the growth of an increasingly avaricious class of private service providers (Weisner & Room, 1984). Perhaps the most serious outcome is the erosion of public confidence in social programs of all types. In the case of alcoholism programs, designating so many "special populations" has allowed cynical observers the opportunity to raise the issue of reverse discrimination. It has been suggested, for example, that the only nonspecial population group is white males—which happens to be the population with the highest prevalence rates of problem drinking. Although there is some validity to this argument, it is imporant to remember that treatment services are most easily available and accessible to white men. One of the major goals of the "special population" designation was to reverse the inequity in the existing pattern of service provision. The establishment of special populations can also be interpreted as a proactive measure of the type that is rarely seen in the delivery of social services. Although the designated groups do not have higher prevalence rates [at the present time], it is highly likely that they will some time in the near future. In this sense the establishment of special populations can be interpreted as an uncharacteristicly prescient action.

THE WAR ON HEROIN

Until the beginning of the 20th century, opiate use was fairly common in the United States among all social, racial, and demographic segments of the population. Although some doctors were aware that heroin could be addictive and physically harmful, legal sanction was unknown and social disapproval was rare. This rather tranquil picture was dramatically altered in 1914 by the legislation that made the use of heroin a criminal offense (Duster, 1970; Lindesmith, 1956; Musto, 1973). From this time on, almost all members of the medical profession ceased treating heroin addicts, and for 40 years the heroin problem became synonymous with a wide range of social problems in the inner city. By making heroin illegal without developing any specific services for addicts, a criminal heroin subculture emerged. Addicts became criminals to support their addiction, and the world of heroin users was the world of street crime.

In the 1960s the long period of treating addicts as criminals was coming to an end. Heroin addicts in large numbers started to receive professional treatment, at least partly the result of an attempt to break the tie between drug use and street crime. Treatment was offered in addition or sometimes as an alternative to criminal proceedings. The general evaluation of this shift is that it represented a more humane, scientific, and medical view of heroin use. Addicts were thought of as people who were ill and in need of professional care rather than as criminals who had to be punished (Schur, 1965).

In the late 1960s the trend toward medical care of heroin addiction was boosted dramatically by two developments, one that was largely political and the other largely medical or technological. The increases in drug addiction reported in the media were closely linked to the rising crime rates in American cities. There was an urgent call to do something about the drugs–crime connection, and as usual, politicians responded to the call with the introduction of sweeping changes. At about the same time some medical practitioners had demonstrated that heroin addicts could be successfully maintained on methadone, a substance that relieves the addict's craving for narcotics and also blocks the euphoric effects of an average dose of heroin (Conrad & Schneider, 1980). As we shall see, the actual turn of events was neither as simple nor as humane as this conclusion indicates. Neither is it correct to assume that what happened was a triumphant return of the medical profession to the treatment of addiction. In fact, "Medical interest . . . was limited, since most physicians did not regularly come into contact with opiate addicts . . . [and] on a theoretical level, no well-developed disease concept of opiate addiction was generated to justify medical intervention." (Conrad & Schneider, 1980, p. 142)

In the late 1960s, the newly elected President, Richard Nixon, announced his now famous "war" against heroin. Nixon's campaign would usher in a series of major legislative, organizational, and programmatic changes in the field of drug abuse. One of the key issues in the 1968 election had been the escalating problem of street crime. The new President felt the need to produce some results quickly, and was convinced by his advisors of the clear link between crime and heroin addiction.

As usual in such circumstances, there was some fact and some fiction involved. There was evidence that the prevalence of heroin addiction had been rising to almost epidemic proportions throughout the 1960s, and also that it was diffusing through the population to new cohorts, especially the young (DuPont, 1971; Hunt, 1974). On the other hand, the available data was used to make a number of questionable claims about the evils of heroin abuse, to support the President's portrait of a "national emergency" (Bellis, 1981). The first of these was the assertion of a simple and inexorable causal link between heroin addiction and crime, which was used to explain the increases in crime rates that had been reported nationwide in the late 1960s (Wilson, 1975). The second claim was that heroin addiction was spreading geographically and socially—to new parts of the city and to new sectors of the population—notably white middle-class youths in the suburbs. The third claim was that heroin abuse spread like an infectious disease, which is clearly not the case (Sheppard, Smith, & Gay, 1972); and the fourth was the questionable assumption that another heroin epidemic would be brought back from Southeast Asia by young American servicemen returning from the Vietnam war. Sooner or later, it was argued, the new epidemic would reach these shores and exacerbate an already dire situation (Stanton, 1976).

It was with this subtle mixture of fact and fantasy that the Nixon administration was able to bring about a dramatic change in the approach to drug abuse. As the data in Table 9.4 indicate, the federal government was able to make its presence felt in two basic areas: (1) by continued and upgraded attempts to control the supply of drugs through law enforcement; and (2) by attempting to reduce the demand for drugs through a mix of treatment, rehabilitation, prevention, and education.

The supply issue was first addressed in 1970 by a change in the constitutional basis of drug law enforcement. The Comprehensive Drug Abuse Prevention and Control Act of that year transferred the responsibility for enforcement away from the Treasury Department. Since the days of Henry Anslinger, drug abuse had been dealt with by the Federal Bureau of Narcotics (H. S. Becker, 1963), but in 1970 it became a Justice Department concern, under the auspices of the newly formed Bureau of Narcotics and Dangerous Drugs (BNDD). This allowed the federal government to become more directly involved in suppressing the illegal trafficking of drugs. The expansion in federal power was possible because the 1970 Act gave the Justice Department (led by the Attorney General) rather than the Treasury Department full control over the possession and traffic of illegal drugs.

Table 9.4. Federal Government Drug Budget by Function, Fiscal Years 1970–1978 (in Millions of Dollars)

Year	Treatment and Rehabilitation	Education, Prevention and Training	Research	Planning	Law Enforcement	TOTAL
1970	33.5	8.5	17.1	—	42.8	101.9
1971	86.8	38.2	21.5	—	65.9	212.4
1972	196.1	50.4	42.2	—	125.8	414.5
1973	350.3	45.7	64.3	23.9	200.0	684.2
1974	329.4	58.6	52.1	21.7	292.1	753.9
1975	309.9	65.5	48.3	23.0	320.8	767.6
1976	321.9	55.6	46.4	28.5	370.8	823.2
1977	367.6	47.1	43.8	25.3	381.5	865.3
1978	366.0	48.2	43.8	25.5	400.6	884.1
TOTAL[a]	2,442.0	431.8	391.1	155.0	2,293.0	5,712.9

[a]Yearly totals do not sum because of the transition quarter between Fiscal Years 1976 and 1977.

Source. Goldberg (1980, p. 57).

Accompanying this change was a direct and largely successful attempt by the Nixon administration in 1971 to streamline the chaotic and fragmented machinery involved in the demand side of the heroin problem. This was achieved by the creation of a Special Action Office for Drug Abuse Prevention (SAODAP) within the Executive Office of the White House. This office would coordinate the functions that had previously been shared by 16 separate federal agencies, all of whom had some responsibilities in the areas of treatment, rehabilitation, education, prevention, or training. The director of SAODAP was immediately accountable to and hand-picked by the President. Although such an administrative arrangement was highly irregular, centralization at the White House level was, it was argued, justified by the seriousness of the drug problem. There was also considerable ill feeling between the administration and the NIMH about the best way to attack the drug problem (Goldberg, 1980). Nixon and his advisors wanted to speed up the methadone programs, which they saw as a quick "technological fix" to bring about some rapid results in the war against crime on the streets (Nelkin, 1973). The psychiatrically oriented bureaucrats at NIMH were naturally more cautious and less convinced that methadone could achieve all that it appeared to promise.

The trend toward methadone maintenance also signified a pharmacological solution to a problem with which organized psychiatry had clearly been unable to cope (E. J. Epstein, 1977). The new office in the White House was therefore a way for the administration to bypass the slow-moving and potentially obstructive Health, Education, and Welfare (HEW) bureaucracy and thus guarantee swift action. This was of course a high-risk/high-gain strategy. If the war on heroin could be won—at least by the next election in 1972—the administration could take full political credit, whereas obvious failure after so much rhetoric would be an acute embarrassment.

What subsequently occurred can best be described as a frenzy of activity. In one year (1970–1971) the federal budget for the treatment and rehabilitation of drug abusers rose from $33.5 million to $86.8 million, surpassing (if only temporarily) even the expenditures on drug law enforcement. Probably the most controversial aspect of the administration's new policy was the wholehearted support for methadone maintenance as the major way of dealing with heroin addiction. Methadone appeared to be a relatively simple and certainly far cheaper way to deal with addiction than committing users to mental hospitals, imprisoning them, or treating them with traditional psychotherapy (Nelkin, 1973). From a scattering of clinics in 1970, there were as many as 80,000 addicts in treatment by 1974, which was about a quarter of all estimated heroin addicts in the country (D. Klein, 1983).

This was by no means a universally popular strategy. Critics argued that the push toward methadone maintenance was little more than an arm of law enforcement disguised in medical clothing. By reducing the supply of heroin, so the argument went, the administration guaranteed that the price would rise and the quality diminish, which in turn would lead to more rather than less crime, and more rather than fewer addicts (E. J. Epstein, 1977). These new addicts would populate the new methadone clinics, and their successful treatment could be used as hard evidence of the success of the new policies.

In 1972 the executive maneuver that had been so successful earlier was used again. This time it was to allow the Nixon administration, now in its second term, to lay the groundwork for the inevitable shift back to criminalization after its brief encounter with the world of treatment. The major drug law enforcement agency, BNDD, was not compliant enough and was accused of heel dragging. President Nixon's solution was a new and soon-to-be notorious Office of Drug Abuse Law Enforcement (ODALE). Law enforcement "strike forces" were dispatched into cities all across the country in an attempt to make good on the President's promise "to drive drug traffickers and pushers off the streets of America . . . [and] . . . to assist state and local agencies in detecting, arresting, and convicting those who would profit from the misery of others" (cited in Bellis, 1981, p. 30)

Nixon and his advisors could demonstrate that in addition to treating addicts, they were willing to respond to the public's demand for stronger actions to reduce the prevalence of heroin-related crime. They had taken some bold steps and made extravagant claims about what could be achieved. The new policies were an amalgam of medical and criminal strategies, which demonstrated to a doubting public that an all-encompassing drive on drugs had been launched that could satisfy both the liberals and the conservatives.

Perhaps the most startling aspect was he speed with which visible "progress" was made. The public could not fail to see that the administration was doing something about drug abuse:

> By creating a separate agency to co-ordinate drug policy, some entrenched resistance could be circumvented and the Administration's war against heroin could be fought with double barrels: the BNDD continuing its law enforcement approach, with SAODAP becoming a proponent for methadone maintenance. (Conrad & Schneider, 1980, p. 139)

The administration changed its drug policies rapidly as soon as the political winds began to change. In his now famous "turning the corner" speech, President Nixon announced that the war against drugs had been won, and the administration was withdrawing from the battle. This was only 18 months after the 1972 Act had been passed, but Nixon was skillfully taking advantage of some apparent evidence that the heroin "epidemic" had peaked. Heroin was in short supply on the East Coast, and its price had risen. There had been some well-publicized drug seizures and some positive statistics had reached the media. Heroin-related crimes appeared to be lower, and there were fewer new users, presumably as a result of the greater emphasis on treatment, education, and prevention. However, as was noted earlier, this sort of evidence needs to be evaluated with great caution, because what looked like the end of the heroin epidemic was in part simply the hierarchical diffusion of heroin addiction to smaller cities (Hunt & Chambers, 1976). The heroin problem had moved elsewhere and had slipped out of the public spotlight.

Whatever the statistics meant, or however they were interpreted, the Nixon administration had some reason to believe that they had achieved much of what they had set out to do. They could point to a new comprehensive and streamlined approach to drug treatment, and they had some key examples to focus on. In Washington, DC, for example, a city always in the spotlight, there was a significant drop in major crimes in 1971, for the first time in many years. This was in part attributable to the city's new methadone programs, under the supervision of Robert L. Dupont, who would later head the new federal drug agency. For the hardliners the administration could now offer ample evidence of highly visible efforts to reduce the distribution of narcotics. Drug raids and border blockades such as Operation Intercept demonstrated the administration's apparent commitment to solving the heroin problem on all fronts. On the other hand, by 1973 the election had already been won, and both the administration and the public had begun to lose interest in drug abuse as a political issue. The anticipated flood of heroin-addicted Vietnam veterans had not materialized, and some of the new strategies like the "no-knock" entries and searches of ODALE had backfired, producing a wave of negative publicity.

The administration felt it was time to announce yet another new direction for drug policy. Part of this was to turn over the burden of responsibility to the individual states, in one of the earliest examples of the "new federalism." The federal war on heroin dropped down to a lower key; it was less publicized and eventually the funding boom ended. In 1973 the management of drug treatment and rehabilitation policies was handed over to the welfare state bureaucracy, in the form of a new agency within the Bureau of Health, Education, & Welfare (HEW), which was called the National Institute of Drug Abuse (NIDA). It was intended that NIDA would succeed SAODAP in the battle over the demand side of the drug issue. However, although NIDA was given most of the responsibilities for drug treatment, it would never have the considerable coordinating powers that SAODAP had enjoyed.

In just a few years there had been more activity in the area of drug policy than there had been in the 5 decades before. There are two ways to interpret what had taken place. There had been a major shift in public attitudes toward drug addiction, which was increasingly seen as an illness rather than a crime and thus as treatable rather than punishible. On the other hand, it was only the programs that had been changing and not the actual drug policies. The law enforcement perspective had been temporarily upstaged in the public arena. Some addicts were treated, but many more were punished, because the Nixon administration believed that the public demanded a hard line on drugs (Goldberg, 1980).

It is also evident that the medicalization of drug addiction was not necessarily a ''softer'' or ''more liberal'' response to drugs than the crime and punishment approach. Although methadone maintenance was strongly supported by significant members of the medical, legal, and social science communities, and was well regarded by the liberal press (Bellis, 1981, Ch. 4), it was arguably little more than a pharmacological form of social control—a chemical approach to urban pacification that had strong racial undertones. The clients in methadone programs were drawn disproportionately from the black inner-city populations (D. Klein, 1983). For example, a federal study conducted by NIDA in 1973 showed that of 35,000 clients in federally funded facilities, 73% were men, 48% were white, 40% were black, 67% were under 25 years old, and 67% were unemployed (D. Klein, 1983). This argument provides a different slant on the Piven and Cloward (1971) critique of the role of welfare agencies in diffusing dissent among the potentially disruptive poor. It was outlined in its most extreme form at a 1971 Conference on Methadone Maintenance Treatment. According to Bellis (1981) the following statements were made to support the argument:

1. The white power structure encourages methadone maintenance because it weakens the will of those likely to resist the dominant order;
2. Because methadone is highly addictive, the state will be able to maintain lifelong supervision and surveillance of clients, which is a useful strategy during times of insurgency;
3. With heroin addicts off the streets, the middle classes can hold more safely onto their property, wealth, and possessions because methadone addicts will no longer need to steal to feed their habit. (It is evident from

this that property values have effectively replaced human values as the driving force behind the selection of treatment programs for drug addiction.)

These statements represent, albeit in rather extreme form, what has been described as a social control interpretation of the methadone program. The following statements spell out some aspects of this perspective. The demand for continued law enforcement activity against drug users was effectively "accommodated" by medical technology. The choice of this technology continued the focus of drug problems at the individual level. Drug users were defined as people with specific medical or psychological problems that could be treated on a case-by-case basis. Treatment provided in community-based methadone clinics was also consistent with the existing ideas about how best to deal with public problems such as mental illness and delinquency. It was hoped that such treatment would not only be more effective than institutionalization, but also that it would ultimately reduce the financial burden on the state.

From this perspective, the medical treatment of heroin addicts added another layer to the states' repertoire for ordering and reshaping the lives of deviants. Although the new strategy was scientific, medical, and humane, the line between the medical and the criminal approaches had been blurred even further. The methadone clinics offered a new way to police addicts by adding an additional phase of treatment and providing a new source of access to the private lives of addicted individuals. This situation was similar to the provision of detoxication facilities on skid row, which were provided as part of the new movement to decriminalize public drunkenness (see Chapter 6). The detoxication clinics, like the methadone clinics, provided a new outpost on skid row, another station at which the "lost" members of society could linger before shuffling along into oblivion (Rodin *et al.*, 1982). The extreme versions of this argument imply that the drug scene had hardly been altered, the only difference now being that for many addicts the state had become the supplier, with the methadone clinic effectively replacing the street pusher:

> Heroin was seen as illegitimate not just because it was illegal and disreputable, but because it was outside the prescriptive fold and the laboratory-developed pharmacopeia around which medicine revolved. (D. Klein, 1983, p. 45)

The demarcation between the medical and legal approaches to drug addiction was blurred even further as a result of the rapid growth of methadone clinics. To stay in operation, many of the clinics increasingly came to rely on court referrals and diversions from the criminal justice system—in fact, going to a methadone clinic became the chosen alternative for many addicts who faced potential imprisonment. Ironically, the symbiosis between the clinics and the courts would also operate in the reverse direction. The increasing supply of treatment facilities made it possible for the courts to impose tougher legal sanctions on drug users, who could no longer argue that their addiction was excusable because no treatment was available (D. Klein, 1983).

What was achieved as a result of all this furious activity? The new strategies offered the best of both worlds: They could promise reform and humane treatment, but at the same time would extend the pervasiveness of social control. In retrospect, however, it appears that even a well-planned and technologically sophisticated approach still failed to make a significant dent in the illegal drug market or the pattern of street crime (Goldbert, 1980). In some ways this failure was absolute, because medicine and technology had been given a chance, and even the new "wonder drug" had been unable to deal with the problem. On the other side, the law enforcement strategy had failed equally comprehensively:

> More than six decades of effort to eliminate the drug . . . through strong law enforcement measures have not caused the number of users to drop below levels observed at the beginning of this century. (Meyers, 1980, p. 243)

On a more positive level, the medical treatment of addiction attracted many new constituencies that would continue to play an important role in helping to shape future drug policies. In theory this could help to infuse fresh blood into the policy debates, although in actuality the strength of the medically oriented constituencies has worked to inhibit the serious discussion of alternatives such as decriminalization (Meyers, 1980). The new constituencies have managed to weather the storm of decreasing the federal involvement in drug-abuse policy that was so instrumental in their formation. Now they have a life of their own, and an agenda far removed from the presumed goal of eradicating drug abuse. The giant pharmaceutical corporations manufacturing the new legal drugs, the medical companies providing the compulsory urine tests, the research consultants looking for contracts, and the vast empire of drug treatment and rehabilitation agencies have all helped to build up the drug abuse arena into a vastly profitable "drug-abuse industrial complex" that now dominates and dictates the direction of drug policies.

COMMUNITY MENTAL HEALTH: THE "BOLD NEW APPROACH"

The growth of activity in the areas of alcohol and drug abuse during the expansionary era of the late 1960s and early 1970s was maintained at least partly by the self-interest of powerful new constituencies. The growth process had begun even earlier in the traditionally low-status and unglamorous field of mental disorder. The rapid growth of the NIMH and the elevation of mental health issues into public policy debates in the Great Society era provide powerful examples of successful arena building. As has been mentioned in Chapter 5, the major component of the developing mental health arena was the CMH movement, which was catapulted into public view in 1963 by the passage of the Community Mental Health Centers Act.

The story of the Act and its history has been told many times (Bloom, 1977; Foley, 1975; M. Levine, 1981), but one of its most remarkable achievements was the survival capabilities of the CMH movement in the face of scathing criticism and an almost total failure to achieve its stated goals. The CMH movement was able to strengthen its base and legitimate itself so effectively that by the middle to late 1970s, when the "liberal expansionist" era was over and the United States was in the grip of a debilitating fiscal crisis, it was able to weather the storm. Although this period was not one of growth in terms of dollars and programs, CMH had burrowed itself into the public and legislative consciousness to such an extent that it would survive a series of hostile administrations and would survive until the 1980s.

In the 1950s and 1960s a new era was emerging in the treatment of mental illness. The emphasis was gradually shifting toward attempts to prevent mental disorder and promote mental health, in addition to providing treatment for those who were already ill. The other major emphasis in this new era was the desire to treat mental disorder "in the community" rather than in institutions. It is difficult to pinpoint specific causes for this major shift in emphasis, but it was the result of a mixture of both pragmatism and ideology (P. Brown, 1985). The shift toward deinstitutionalization had already begun, although in a small way; and a number of relatively new theories were emerging that could provide ideological support for the continued emphasis on community care. The "facts" of the situation were quite clear: Mental hospitals had started to reduce their populations in the 1950s (Scull, 1977; C. J. Smith & Hanham, 1981a) and an increasing number of former patients were able to live in the community as long as they were maintained on medication. It made sense to continue both of these trends because they appeared to be "working," and it was possible that far more individuals had been hospitalized than was necessary.

The ideological shifts that accompanied these trends are obviously not as clear-cut, nor is it possible to assign any obvious causality, or to say which of them was most significant. The critique of mental hospital treatment that had been popularized by Goffman (1961) was being extended into a more comprehensive attack on the role of psychiatry in treating mental illness (P. Brown, 1984; Sedgwick, 1982). The traditional medical model view of mental illness was being sharply criticized, not only by labeling theory sociologists, but also by many different social scientists who were arguing that mental health problems were associated in some complex ways with the social, ecological, and demographic characteristics of neighborhoods and residential communities (Jeger & Slotnick, 1982; Naparstek *et al.,* 1982). The concern that individuals not only would receive more effective care in community settings but also had a right to such care played an additional key role in supporting the trend toward deinstitutionalization (P. Brown, 1981).

These ideological forces had different intellectual roots, but for a brief period there was a convergence of apparently opposing forces on the same general set of policies. Civil rights liberals found themselves agreeing with fiscal conservatives that mental illness could be treated in the community. The CMH movement also represented an unusual alliance between groups with radical views about how to solve social problems, and others with the elite traditional views of professional psychiatry and medicine. The unique aspect of CMH was that it had grassroots support and federal funding, which was historically a rare combination, albeit an obviously unstable one (Kenig, 1981).

Prior to World War II, most of the publicly provided mental health care was the responsibility of individual states and localities. The system of care, such as it was, consisted of two basic tiers: private psychiatric services, both outpatient and inpatient, for the rich; and public mental health hospitals for the poor. Studies conducted by psychiatric epidemiologists had demonstrated that within the population a sizeable minority suffered serious mental health problems, in addition to those who were hospitalized. The success of psychiatrists in both identifying and treating mental disorders during and after World War II had shown that this problem was one that could and should become a viable issue of public policy.

Ten years after the war, Congress passed the Mental Health Study Act (1955), which set up a Joint Commission on Mental Illness and Health to make some recommendations about how best to combat mental disorder. The landmark report of the Commission, which was called Action for Mental Health, suggested that the federal government (specifically NIMH, which had been created in 1946), should establish and fund some new mental health programs. It was recognized that human problems like mental disorder were at least partly the result of adverse living conditions such as poverty and a lack of education. The Commission felt that in addition to providing actual services, mental health programs should also provide consultation and education in community settings to help individuals and community leaders recognize the mental health implications of their everyday activities. In physical terms the Commission recommended that the state hospitals be reduced in size, and that facilities for acute care, after-care, and rehabilitative services should be expanded in community settings.

Action for Mental Health paved the way for the 1963 legislation that would provide funding for a new type of mental health facility, the community mental health center. Ideally there were to be about 1500 of these centers, each of them located within a catchment area serving about 100,000 people. To receive federal funding the center had to provide 5 "essential" services, but later this was increased to 12: inpatient, outpatient, emergency, screening, follow-up of discharged patients, consultation and education, partial hospitalization, children's services, elderly services, transitional halfway houses, alcohol abuse services, and drug abuse services (Jeger & Slotnick, 1982).

This represented the first significant attempt to establish a federal mental health policy in the United States. The centers were intended to provide access to mental health services for all Americans, regardless of social class, race, and ability to pay (M. Levine, 1981). The initial legislation and its various amendments were completely new, not only in the type of mental health care that was to be offered, but also in the arrangements of funding and the implications this had for federal–state–local relationships. The basic principles of community mental health care were completely different from those of traditional psychiatric practices (Bloom, 1977). The community rather than the institution was the locus of care, and the catchment area, rather than the individual patient was the target for service provision. There were to be preventive services such as consultation and education to complement treatment programs, and a comprehensive system of services for the mentally ill in the community. Clinical innovations such as brief psychotherapy and crisis intervention were emphasized over traditional long-term therapy. A deliberate effort was made to identify the environmental and social causes of mental illness, in addition to the traditional search for "intrapsychic" causes. Nonprofessional workers were to be incorporated into service delivery and community residents were to have a major role in establishing service priorities, evaluating programs, and administering the centers.

What was different about the funding arrangements of the CMHC legislation was the specific attempt made by the federal government to bypass the states and the cities and provide funds to individual communities. The ostensible reason for this was to make sure that the federal funds were used directly to serve local needs for mental health care. Another explanation is provided by Piven and Cloward (1971), who suggest that this method of funding for CMHCs was chosen by the Democratic administration for specifically political reasons. In the first place, many northern cities were dominated by Republicans, who it was felt could probably not be trusted to disburse mental health funds equitably. The states in the South, although still largely Democratic at that time, were also not considered reliable enough to distribute funds that would provide services mainly intended for blacks.

Depending on the local population geography, the community in question could be a part of a city, a collection of rural counties, or a small city and its surroundings suburbs. The grants were categorical in nature; the community had to write a proposal to demonstrate the need for services, and specify a plan for delivering those services. Some of the centers would be newly constructed, others would take over existing buildings, and still others would be affiliated with and housed in existing institutions like hospitals.

Community mental health and some other Great Society programs shared a number of features that were a sign of the liberal expansionary times:

1. They represented a different perception of social responsibility, one that involved entitlements and civil rights for all citizens;
2. They were part of a geopolitical "revolution," in which local com-

munities rather than cities and states were to be given the responsibility for planning and coordinating services;

3. They were part of a comprehensive restructuring of solution finding for public problems that was to be more coordinated and centralized;

4. They were to involve citizens as true participants in the process involved in planning, coordinating, and executing the delivery of services;

5. They were to herald a shift toward preventive strategies and a search for root causes, and a move away from the mere treatment of symptoms.

During its lifespan, the CMH movement has been roundly criticized on a number of counts (Chu & Trotter, 1974), to such an extent that an impartial observer could be forgiven for concluding that none of the changes in emphasis listed earlier have been realized. Most serious have been the criticisms that CMHCs have not catered to the chronically mentally ill; that continuity of care and comprehensive services have not been provided in most communities; that CMHCs have continued to be dominated by medical and psychiatric philosophies and practices; that citizens have not been effectively brought into the picture; and that too little emphasis has been placed on the provision of indirect services such as consultation and education. (For summaries of the major criticisms of CMHCs, see Bloom, 1977; P. Brown, 1985; Foley & Sharfstein, 1983; M. Levine, 1981; C. J. Smith, 1983c).

It is remarkable that the CMHC program was able to survive these enduring criticisms for so long. In the late 1970s it was publicly acknowledged by the National Institute of Mental Health (NIMH) that the centers had failed to respond to the needs of the chronically mentally ill, and an entirely new program was announced (the CSP initiative which is described in Chapter 3). The CMHC program was attacked repeatedly and its appropriations were cut continuously, which contributed even further to the overall perception of failure. Each year the program received less funding and fewer new centers were opened, and by 1980 only about half of the nation's catchment areas had centers operating. Perhaps the most surprising fact, however, is that the CMHC concept remains strong, in spite of opposition from an administration that is diametrically opposed to a federal categorical program such as CMH, and to federal involvement in such problems as mental health. Admittedly the CMHC Act itself was repealed in 1981, but no existing CMHCs have been dismantled and most states have assumed the financial burden for them (Burt & Pittman, 1984). In other words, only the funding patterns have changed. The program itself has survived even though it is in a no-growth or slow-growth state (Table 9.5).

To account for this impressive achievement it is possible to suggest at least three factors. In the first place, the CMH movement has been extremely successful at building up constituencies that would be willing to go out on a limb for the program, either because they truly believed in it, or because its continuation was clearly in their best interests (M. Levine, 1981). The 1975 amendments to the CMHC Act (Table 9.5), which were passed in spite of strong

Table 9.5. Comprehensive Community Mental Health Programs—1964–1980

Fiscal Year	Public Law	Major Legislation Significance	Obligations (in $M)		Number of CMHCs—Cumulative			% U.S. Population Covered	No. of Patients Treated
			In Year	Cumulative	Funded	Operational	Tot. Term.		
1964	88-164	CMHC Act—construction only	0	0	0	0	0	0	0
1965	89-105	Staffing support (51 mos.) CMHC Amendment	0	0	0	0	0	0	(unknown)
1966			55	55	130	104	0	7	156,000 (est)
1969	90-574	Alcohol and Addiction support— CMHC Amendments	75	294	376	175	0	11	318,500
1970	91-211	Staffing extended to 8 years; CMHC poverty rates introduced; Part F MH Children added	72	365	420	245	0	27	497,350
1975	94-63 enacted	Title III, Health Revenue Sharing and Health Services Act	223	1,228	603	507	0	41	1,618,746
1976	94-63	From 5 to 12 req. services operations fund base, CMHC. From 3 to 6 grant programs	251	1,478	650	547	30	43	1,877,676
1978	95-83	1 year renewal, CMHC. PCMH report	268	1,978	726	625	90	47	2,361,250
1979	95-622	CMHC 2-year renewal, with minor technical changes, anticipating major revision. Carter Message and S 1177-HR 4156 introduced.	310	2,288	763	701	167	50	2,639,996
1980	96-32		290	2,578	796	740	203	52 (115M)	3,082,100
1981	96-398	Mental Health Systems Act	323	2,901	796 Develop. 26	758 26	306	(119M) 54	3,314,734 39,000

Source. Foley and Sharfstein (1983, p. 263).

opposition from the administration, "signalled the arrival of some powerful constituency support for CMHCs and the federal role" (Foley & Sharfstein, 1983, p. 89). This support came from such organizations as the National Mental Health Association (NMHA), a lobby group composed of professionals and citizens with charters in all states and many cities.

The CMHC program always had some important champions in Congress, but presidential support varied from the strong support of Kennedy and Johnson to the consistent opposition of Nixon, Ford, and Reagan. The program's supporters in Congress had to work diligently with the CMHC lobbyists and NIMH bureaucrats to defend against the "new federalism" all through the 1970s. Another important constituency supporting the continuation of the CMHC program was the intergovernmental lobby composed of governors, mayors, county supervisors, and city managers. These groups perceived that the federal CMHC funds being used in their jurisdictions were useful to them and their constituents, and they lobbied strongly for their continuation (Foley & Sharfstein, 1983).

The availability of NIMH funds to train mental health professionals would also increase both the number and the diversity of interest groups lobbying for the continuation of federal support for CMHCs. Although psychiatrists would still play an important role in the centers' programs, they were complemented by a growing number of psychologists, social workers, and nurses—all of whom had professional organizations who lobbied members of Congress about mental health services. Another powerful group was the so-called "third-party" payers—the insurance companies who had contracted with businesses and unions to provide expanded coverage for mental health services (P. Brown, 1985).

In addition to the political broadening that occurred, the CMH concept was also spread across the country successfully. Although the original goal of providing centers in all of the catchment areas was not achieved by 1980 and probably will never be, the evidence suggests that, overall, many centers began operating in places where they were needed (Longest, Konan, & Tweed, 1976).

It is also evident that during the program's lifetime, CMHC funding was spread around the country in an equitable fashion. In the early years of the program there was a tendency for the funds to be allocated disproportionately to the largest cities, but in later years this trend was reversed (C. J. Smith, 1984). Although the evidence is by no means overwhelming, it appears that the geographic pattern of funding was inherently redistributive. Most of the available federal funds were allocated to states and regions where mental health needs tended to be greatest: in the southern states; in states where social welfare spending, including mental health, was traditionally low; and in areas where there were significant minority populations. The pattern of CMHC funding was socially and spatially just, even if the level of funding and the number of centers remained hopelessly under target.

A final explanation for the persistence of the CMHC program in the face of its opposition was a phenomenon that should rightly be considered a mixed blessing, namely the "psychiatrization" of society (Conrad & Schneider, 1980; Dear, 1980). Throughout its relatively brief history the CMH movement had helped to boost the importance of psychiatry and spread the acceptance of the psychiatric doctrine to such an extent that attempts to dismantle the program were not only impractical but unthinkable. It is ironic of course that the CMHCs should have had this effect, because the movement's underlying philosophies were in many ways committed to replacing the dominance of the psychiatric/ medical model of mental disorder with a model that was much more social and environmental in essence. However, as many of the program's critics have pointed out, most CMHCs never really managed to relinquish the medical model (M. Levine, 1981). The dominant activity at CMHCs, was and still is the provision of treatment of individuals who are already experiencing mental health problems. Many centers are still dominated by psychiatrists or by psychiatrically inclined psychologists and social workers, and some are actually still physically located in mental hospitals and general hospitals. As a result, CMHCs have expanded the medical model and extended the jurisdiction of psychiatry into the community and into a broad range of problem areas that were not previously considered to be within the psychiatric domain. This has occurred in part because the successive amendments to the original CMHC Act required the centers to provide services to the elderly, to children, alcoholics, drug abusers, rape victims, and adolescents. It was assumed that the psychiatric model could contribute significantly to the solution of these problems.

In this way CMHCs had successfully widened the definition of mental disorder to include not just the traditional psychoses and neuroses, but also a vast range of problems associated with being young, growing old, losing a job, experiencing marital problems, abusing family members, being delinquent, and abusing substances. In other words community psychiatry had become much more pervasive than ever before. It appears to have abandoned the custodial care of the chronically mentally ill, and adopted the new role of treating the "behavioral problems" of people who were not previously receiving any psychiatric care. The net effect is that psychiatry since World War II bears little resemblance to its earlier counterpart; in fact, "It treats an entirely different population, for different symptoms, with different methods, using different personnel" (Ralph, 1983, p.13).

To some extent the expansion of psychiatry into these other problem situations was welcomed. It had been demonstrated in community-based surveys, for example, that a significant proportion of the population experienced at least some mental health problems, and that anywhere from 15 to 30% may be in need of psychiatric services (Srole & Fischer, 1978). Thus for some individuals the new availability of services at CMHCs offered an acceptable solution. They could now go for treatment for otherwise intractable problems and may be able to increase the quality of their lives. The promise offered by psychiatric treatment was perhaps overpackaged, and helped to produce unrealistically high expectations, but bearing in mind the hard-core nature of many of these problems and the fact that their prevalence continued to rise, perhaps it was not unrealistic to expect psychiatry to offer some solutions.

On the other hand, the pervasiveness of psychiatry throughout the world of public problems has a sinister side, involving the increasing amount of social control exerted by the welfare state. The CMH movement was actually intended to offer a new type of mental health care that was to be less restrictive, less sinister, and less violent than the care provided in institutions. It was hoped that providing such services would become much more of a community responsibility, and would therefore be far less segregative and exclusive than had been the case in the past. The evidence shows that the locus of care has indeed been decentralized as a result of the CMH movement and deinstitutionalization policies. Mental illness is now much more likely to be treated on a noninstitutional basis. An example of this is the fact that in 1955, 77% of all mental health care was for inpatients, but in 1975, 72% was for outpatients (C. J. Smith & Hanham, 1981a). In spite of this, the type of care provided at the new centers was actually no different from what had always been provided, in that it was still largely individual treatment provided and administered by psychiatrically trained mental health workers (P. Brown, 1984; Chu & Trotter, 1974).

There is also a question about whether the new system is actually less restrictive than the old one. More people are receiving mental health care today than ever before. New institutions and agencies have appeared like mushrooms, offering both treatment and residential services, so that the mental health system is certainly bigger and more visible than before, but there is little evidence that it is any more humane. Institutional policies in the new settings may differ from the old "lockups," but many still use exclusionary practicers such as locks, physical restraints, seclusion, and curfews (Lerman, 1982). Moreover, an unprecedented number of clients are now maintained on psychotropic drugs (Koumjian, 1981; Kovel, 1980). The new mental health landscape presents something of a paradox, in that the traditional publicly controlled institutions have been reduced in number and size, while a wide range of new and private institutional forms have developed (Bassuk & Gerson, 1978; Estes & Harrington, 1981; Scull, 1981). This represents still another mutation in the evolution of social control. The responsibility for problem sufferers is now being passed increasingly from the state to a growing class of private sector interests that are not directly supervised by the welfare state but are supported by federal funds (Gilbert, 1984).

Some groups in the population are now more likely than ever before to be institutionalized, even though the institutions are smaller and are at least nominally in the community (e.g., nursing homes for the elderly, residential care facilities for teenagers). To fill these institutions it has often been necessary to raid other programs for clients or to create new categories of problems (Van Dusen, 1981). To the cynical observers of this scene, very little has changed other than the location and appearance of the institutions (Cohen, 1979). In many ways, the mentally ill of the mid-1980s are as excluded from the mainstream of society as they were before 1963. Some progress has been made in the area of community inclusion (Dear & Taylor, 1982), but being chronically mentally ill in the community is still an intolerable deviation from normative standards for social behavior.

CONCLUSION

The case studies discussed in this chapter illustrate some of the processes that have been involved in the spectacular expansion of services intended to deal with public problems in the United States. To help people cope with their problems, whatever they are, a wide array of community-based programs has come into existence since the 1960s. To help account for this growth it is illuminating to compare the populations receiving services in the community with those still being treated in the institutions. One of the major differences between the two groups is their ability to be effective and productive members of the labor force. This observation supports a "labor theory" that was proposed by Ralph (1983) to explain the emergence of community psychiatry, but which can also be used to interpret the expansion of drug and alcoholism services. Ralph suggested that psychiatric programs provided in the community are mainly intended to serve the interests of industry in capitalist societies. There are two sides to this argument. Firstly, treatment is made available to displaced and underutilized workers such as housewives, adolescents, and minorities, not necessarily to make them employable but to render them passive and to help them adjust to the prospect of permanent unemployment. Secondly, services are offered to those people who are currently working, to help them and their families cope with the symptoms of an increasingly pressured and alienating work situation (Braverman, 1974).

In support of this theory Ralph argued that the major innovations of community-based treatment have been motivated by the fear of labor militancy and the debilitating effects of stress in the workplace. It was considerations such as these rather than concerns about the welfare of people experiencing specific problems, that have directed the search for new treatment strategies in recent decades. According to Ralph the roots of these new strategies can be found in industrial psychology, a field that has "consistently focused on increasing worker productivity by eliminating . . . lack of cooperation, apathy, and worker–management conflict" (p. 46).

As Ralph's theory implies, the major motivation behind the expansion of community-based programs has been the desire to exercise greater control over the labor force. This type of control can be interpreted in part as a cooptation of the labor force, because most of what was achieved took place nonviolently; in fact, most care givers would argue that clients have been able to improve the quality of their lives as a result of the services made available. As we shall see in the next chapter, it is important to distinguish between the different possible types of social control and their different target populations.

10

The Social Control of Public Problems

INTRODUCTION

In recent years the term "social control" has been used loosely to describe the coercion of one group in society by another. It implies a set of mechanisms by which "society secures adherence to social norms, . . . specifically how it minimizes, eliminates, or normalizes deviant behavior" (Conrad & Schneider, 1980, p.7). This usage of the term social control implies either repression by the state or attempts to "manage" the problems of modern urban life with no real attempt to tackle their root causes (Katznelson, 1976). An example of this view of social control was provided in the discussion in Chapter 9 of the increasing pervasiveness of psychiatry in the area of public problems.

This definition of social control is a sharp contrast to the original way the term was used in academic sociology. In the writings of Mead and Ross, for example, social control implied harmony and cohesiveness within society (Meier, 1982). To achieve social control was simply to help society attain or return to its natural order, which was not a situation of perpetual conflict, but one of cooperation and goodwill (Rothman, 1983). In this sense the historians and sociologists talking about social control were inherently conservative. From their perspective the Progressive era at the start of this century and the Great Society programs of the 1960s would be interpreted as "reform" movements that were responding to acute public problems.

From the conflict perspective on social control, social scientists studying the Progressive and Great Society eras have offered some sharply divergent or "revisionist" interpretations (Foucault, 1977; Ignatieff, 1978; Rothman, 1971). These accounts suggest that the reform views are too simple-minded and are based on a naively optimistic model of human behavior. The building of institutions to house criminals or the mentally ill should not be interpreted simply as a result of demands for more humane treatment. As Ignatieff (1983) has observed, "the motives and programme of reform were more complicated than a simple revulsion at cruelty or impatience with administrative incompetence" (p.77). As an alternative Ignatieff suggested that "This strategy of power could not be understood unless the history of the prison was incorporated into a his-

tory of the philosophy of authority and the exercise of class power in general."
(p.77).

The revisionist accounts have investigated the social, political, and historical circumstances in which new forms of social control emerged. Many of
them followed Ignatieff's strategy and produced structural or Marxist interpretations of the events that took place during the periods in question (see, e.g.,
Piven & Cloward, 1971, on the New Deal and Great Society eras). Recently
these revisionist works have themselves come under critical fire. It has been
pointed out, for example, that structural accounts of social situations are in
many cases as functionalist as the accounts they were attempting to replace
(Steadman-Jones, 1983).

The earlier functionalist view of social control described a variety of strategies that were used to hold together a potentially disintegrating social structure. In this sense social control was being thought of as an independent variable, something that is intended to bring about a better future (e.g., a "Great
Society"). The actions taken are interpreted as attempts to establish equilibrium
in the society, and for the most part this desirable state is reached through
social consensus (Meier, 1982).

An alternative was to view social control as a dependent variable (Meier,
1982), as an end in itself. From this perspective a criminal justice system,
rather than being viewed as a way to bring about a more harmonious society,
is seen as a set of institutions that are designed partly to punish (or rehabilitate)
criminals, and partly to help perpetuate a set of official correctional agencies
and their staffs. This type of social control is not always benevolent, neither
does it necessarily result from a consensus about the direction in which society
should be moving. What needs to be explained here are the social control actions themselves—how they come about, and what their consequences are. Most
of the studies conducted from this perspective reach the conclusion that social
control efforts are motivated by the vested interests of certain groups and their
attempts to dominate other groups that are less powerful.

THE GREAT SOCIETY: A CASE STUDY IN SOCIAL CONTROL

Within this general framework, a number of social scientists have attempted to
account for the explosion of the American welfare state during the 1960s,
(Friedland, 1976; Katznelson, 1976; Perry & Watkins, 1977; Piven & Cloward,
1971, 1982). Although there have been several different interpretations of this
phenomenon, they can be broadly characterized by Albritton's (1979) phrase
"social amelioration through mass insurgency." The categorical aid programs
of the Great Society have been interpreted as either bribes or rewards made by
the ruling elite to the urban and largely black poor (Piven & Cloward, 1971).

According to this view, the programs designed to combat poverty, unemployment, delinquency, drug abuse, and mental illness are interpreted as ways

of dealing with urban problems that were perceived to be a threat to the existing economic and political system, rather than attempts to really do something to prevent such problems from occurring. Most of the new programs laid out two broad avenues for this strategy: One was to provide services and create opportunities to help ease the deprivation among the poor, the other to allow representatives of the poor to enter the world of politics through the mechanism of citizen participation.

With hindsight it appears that the first strategy amounted to little more than a symbolic gesture. A few million dollars trickled through to the cities, but no real attempts were made to address the root causes of deprivation (Friedland, 1976). The anti-poverty programs are a good example of this, because although the attack on poverty was initially successful, the problem itself would not go away. In 1960, 39.9 million individuals were living in poverty (22.2% of the population), and although by the late 1970's this number had been reduced to 24.5 million (11.5%) as a result of the redistributive programs, the numbers and percentages had since crept back up to 35.3 million by 1983, or 15.2% of the population (Levitan, 1985).

The second strategy was intended to incorporate some of the politically unstable groups into the new bureaucratic structures that were providing the new services. The attempt to give some "power to the people" has been sharply criticized as cooptation in an attempt to forestall a more militant repudiation of the existing power structure. The new service programs did not have a mandate to solve the problems of the cities, nor could they realistically offer more than a ray of hope. Unfortunately the rhetoric of the times may have oversold the new programs and given the people in need false hopes for the future.

From this perspective the movement discussed in the previous chapter can be re-evaluated. It is hardly surprising that the movement did not bring about more change than it did in mental health practices, because from the social control perspective all that was really required was the legitimation of the status quo and the provision of some additional services. New structures were built and many new programs began, some of them in places that would probably never have been reached under normal circumstances, but there was no radical change in the way things were done. It was a case of "innovation without change" rather than the "bold new approach" President Kennedy had promised when he launched the program (Chu & Trotter, 1974).

The CMH movement was essentially conservative, or at best, redistributive. It did not, and in fact it could not, begin to tackle the community-wide problems that were damaging to mental health. There was some citizen participation in the CMH movement, but it is difficult to find evidence of strong local control of the movement. In spite of the volunteers who answered the phones and the citizens on the CMHC boards, the professionals kept a tight rein on the operation of the centers, and any real attempts to take control by community members were quickly squashed (P. Brown, 1979; Foley & Sharfstein, 1983).

The new welfare programs of the Great Society can be interpreted as the modern equivalents of the old-style political parties. The "machines" had always been able to control both the corridors to power (the inputs), and the distribution of benefits (the outputs). The new service agencies of the 1960s had similar functions but they could never hope to perform them so well. They could only regulate inputs indirectly through the vehicle of community participation, and their hold over outputs diminished with the shrinking size of the overall welfare budget in the 1970s. In addition, the bureaucratic, inhuman face they presented to the public often served to annoy and alienate what the politicians had hoped would be a grateful clientele. This was a sharp contrast with the smiling ward-bosses bearing gifts and offering patronage.

When a critical backlash occurred it is not surprising that it was directed at the change agents themselves, the welfare bureaucracies. Letting the agencies take the heat in this way possibly helped to deflect a real revolt at the community level about the causes of poverty and other related problems. With the Great Society programs in disarray the issue would become how best to replace the programs and policies that had failed with new ones that could do the job more effectively (Morrissey & Goldman, 1985). One era of innovation was over, another was just beginning, and so the cycle of failed reforms would continue.

MODELS OF SOCIAL CONTROL

The revisionist accounts of social control have captured the imagination of many social scientists in recent years. One development has been in the direction of "social science history" (Zunz, 1985), in which historical events have been reinterpreted from the perspective of the common people and their everyday lives.[1] Other critiques of the contemporary social control accounts of reform movements have focused more on the methods used than the politics of its adherents. Some have argued that they offer too simplistic an account of social phenomena that were highly complex. The most radical social control accounts probably assumed too much consensus among the individuals and groups that were involved. This is illustrated by the class conflict accounts of the Temperance and Prohibition crusades (Aaron & Musto, 1981; N. H. Clark, 1976). As the recent histories have shown there were long and often bitter conflicts between members of the middle classes about how best to go about their task (Dannenbaum, 1984; Kerr, 1985). It was never a simple matter of one class trying to impose its will on another.

To provide useful accounts of historical events the social control concept needs to be considerably refined. It is necessary, for example, to distinguish between different times and places, and to avoid simple generalizations (Mayer, 1983). On the other hand, the concept needs to be broadened to include not only the exertion from the "outside" of physical controls over deviants but also the attempts made by members of a group to regulate their own behaviors (Maloff *et al.*, 1979). A broader definition of social control would therefore include all of the efforts made by a group to regulate the behavior of its members, without recourse to forcible coercion (Janowitz, 1978). According to this definition, the bulk of social control is persuasive, in the sense that it offers rewards or provides noncoercive punishments in order to reach a required degree of consensus among the group members. Only when these self-regulation mechanisms break down is it necessary to turn to coercive methods of control.

From this broader definitional base, social control includes such activities as adult education and psychotherapy, where involvement is voluntary and the changes in behavior and attitudes are considered to be desirable. One way to characterize the different types of social control is to identify two major dimensions: firstly, an emphasis on internal (or moral) as opposed to external (or legal) sanctions, and secondly, the pervasiveness of the sanctions that are applied. By varying these two criteria, six categories of social control can be identified (N.J. Davis & Anderson, 1983):

1. Externalized Control/High Pervasiveness: structures that have a virtual monopoly on their participants (e.g., asylums and prisons);
2. Externalized Control/Low Pervasiveness: structures that demand compliance, but only in specific circumstances, such as work (e.g., bureaucracies and businesses);
3. Internalized Norms/High Pervasiveness: traditional quasi-religious and highly cohesive "communities" that stress the internalized consensus of norms, with a particular emphasis on moral or behavioral transformation (e.g., Alcoholics Anonymous, and Synanon);
4. Internalized Norms/Low Pervasiveness: similar to the third category, but no major transformation in values or lifestyle is required (e.g., self-help groups such as Weight Watchers and Parents Anonymous);
5. Externalized Control and Internalized Norms/High Pervasiveness: often the most effective types of social control, relying on both external and internal forces (e.g., traditional families and kin groups, and militant religious groups);
6. Externalized Control and Internalized Norms/Low Pervasiveness: professional structures such as law, medicine, and social work that encourage consensual views, but only in the world of employment.

The revisionist accounts of the evolution of institutions were correct in assuming that the "reform" interpretations were too simplistic, and they argued that social control efforts were related to the distribution of wealth and power (M. Katz, 1978; Platt, 1969; Scull, 1977). Although it seems reasonable to argue that the ability to keep order in society was essential to the functioning of the capitalist economy, it does not follow that social control can only be imposed through the exercise of power and the ability of one social group to make another subordinate to its interests. One of the revisionists has in fact, in a reinterpretation of his own work, argued that sanctions from the state and from the owners of capital were not necessary to keep the working classes working (Ignatieff, 1983). Scores of examples have been cited in which individuals continue to work compliantly, even in highly undesirable situations, without being forced to do so, (Dawley & Faler, 1976; Laurie, 1974). They did this for many reasons, including their own self-esteem, the satisfaction of working hard, or simply as a necessary social outlet.

The schema constructed by N.J. Davis and Anderson (1983) also illustrates that coercion is not required to impose social control, although there is some ambiguity in the definition of "coercion." Families and self-help groups do not usually have to rely on physical coercion, but they do require behavior that meets with group norms and expectations. Deviations from these norms may result in subtle forms of "punishment" such as exclusion and verbal reprimand.

Ignatieff (1983) also pointed out that the state and its social control agencies are only involved in a minority of the total volume of social transactions. The vast majority of conflicts and disputes are handled on an informal basis, in families, communities, and in the workplace. Thus the focus on institutions like prisons represents only one very specialized and (statistically) small-scale operation. According to Ignatieff, a vast uncharted area of social control is still waiting to be explored, an area he calls "the anthropology of dispute settlement" (1983, p. 103) at the local level.

At various points throughout this book, attempts have been made to explore some of the informal practices that both create problems and help to provide solutions. A discussion of the role of informal social supports in the maintenance of mental health was included in Chapter 3, but in this chapter some of the formal methods of providing social control will be investigated.

Therapeutic Social Control: High Status Clients

By the turn of the century in the United States, it was evident that a gradual shift had occurred in the way deviance was perceived. The traditional view of "natural" and irreversible deviance was being replaced by a new-found optimism. In spite of the apparent hopelessness of life in the cities, some people felt that social progress was possible by improving individual life circumstances through therapy and intensive casework. Throughout the 20th century there was a gradual shift away from punishment for deviant groups, and a move toward a more humane form of treatment. Although this process would continue through to the present day, the treatment provided would retain the notion of the welfare recipient as a second-class citizen. Eligibility laws are still largely based implicitly on the differences between the "deserving" and the "undeserving" poor (Estes, 1981; A. Walker, 1981, 1983).

When focusing on the treatment of mental disorders, it is evident that this gradual shift was occurring after institutional treatment had passed its peak, but before treatment in the community was in vogue. The asylum was essentially a single-purpose institution that was intended to exclude sufferers from the mainstream of society and provide them with some type of treatment (Grob, 1977; Rothman, 1971). Opinions vary about the reasons why such institutions came to dominate the treatment of mental disorders. On one side is Rothman's view that the asylum was a necessary response to the enormous social upheavals that occurred in post-Revolutionary America (the "fear of social disorder" hypothesis). Another view was more paternalistic and saw the asylum as the source of humane treatment required by individuals in a free society (Grob, 1973).

In the second half of the 20th century we have witnessed a major trend toward community treatment of mental disorders. The asylum has now become the "last resort' in the mental health system, something that is only considered necessary in extreme cases. Complementing the community theme was the realization that people less disturbed than the obviously psychotic could make a valid claim on the mental health system. This has been referred to as the "disappearance of madness" (Armstrong, 1980, p.295), and its progress can be charted by the gradual removal of such terms as "madness," "lunacy," and "insanity" from public usage by the middle of the 20th century. The change was partly a result of improvements in public attitudes toward the mentally ill, and partly a result of legislation. In the United Kingdom, for example, the Mental Treatment Act of 1930 replaced the word "lunatic" with the phrase "person of unsound mind," and in 1959 this was replaced by the term "mental disorder." According to Armstrong these changes would have a more lasting significance than simple shifts in public attitudes and official labels. They were signals for a "new era of liberalism and humanitarianism . . . [that] . . . would be marked by the disappearance of the asylum and the end of insanity as it had been understood" (p. 293). This movement, as Armstrong notes, was the shift away from the study of serious mental illness among the few, to the study of lesser disorders among the many. The new era was marked by a focus not just on mental illness but on how most people managed to stay relatively symptom free and mentally healthy.

To provide a theoretical underpinning for this trend, Armstrong draws an analogy with Foucault's (1977) description of the shift in the treatment of criminals from the 17th-century crudities of the scaffold and violent corporal punishment to the more disciplined control provided by Bentham's Panopticon. The "panoptic vision," according to Foucault, came to govern a whole society, to be the controlling element in its prisons, armies, schools, hospitals, and workplaces. It was

> an invisible power which monitored and controlled time and the movement of bodies, a discipline which differentiated, individualized, normalized and which finally . . . synthesized an efficient social organization. (p. 301)

In the inter-war years in Britain this panoptic vision began to be applied to the mind, but to the mind of the sane rather than the mentally ill. As Armstrong describes it, this was "A medicine which gazed into the smallest interstices of human lives" as a way of maintaining positive mental health and ultimately an orderly society. This would be achieved in a number of ways, including the continual surveillance of children by schools and doctors, the selling of the concepts of mental hygiene to the entire population, and the observation and classification of individuals by the use of epidemiological methods. By earlier definitions these methods were nonrepressive, even though they required the constant monitoring of individuals:

> From the teacher in the school and the psychiatric social worker in the community right up to the proposed expert in psychological medicine in the Cabinet Office, a vast mechanism was instituted to monitor the well-being of the community. (Armstrong, p. 304)

In this way it became possible for the medical and psychiatric community to exercise control over the health of the population. It also provided a vision of a new and healthier form of public life in the modern world, a vision that would be incorporated into the CMH movement and would generate a new level of optimism about what could be achieved. As noted in the previous chapter, one of the motivating forces for the spread of community-based psychiatry was the need to provide services to employed and potentially employable members of the work force, in an effort to increase worker productivity and neutralize alienation and discontent (Ralph, 1983).

The increasing pervasiveness of psychiatry and the rising concern with mental disorders in the general population was not a result of the work done by professionals who were already dealing with the institutionalized mentally ill. It was an extension of the medical professions into the new territory of the mind. The discovery of neurosis as a valid mental disorder produced some status differentiations within the domain of mental illness; the "insane" or the psychotic would probably always need to be excluded from society, but the neurotic could expect some improvement with the help of psychotherapy, if he or she were willing to undergo treatment.[2]

The symptoms of mental disorder may call forth a number of different types of social control. One of these is psychotherapy, which is among other things an attempt to provide order where there is considered to be chaos and unpredictability. The therapist tries to help the client to account for behaviors that seem meaningless to the larger community, providing a culturally relevant frame of reference for the client's distress. In contemporary times most therapy is provided on a one-to-one basis, usually in the comfort of the therapist's office; but by looking back just a few years, we can observe some significant changes in the type of social control that has been used. Twenty years ago, an individual experiencing serious mental disorder would probably have been institutionalized involuntarily, and treated either with medication or some vague attempts at "milieu therapy," which amounted to little more than a humane and nonthreatening environment within a mental hospital ward. Moving back even further, to before Freud's time, psychological ailments were treated, if they were treated at all, by medical doctors using a variety of blood curdling techniques.

As shown in Table 10.1, psychotherapy differs significantly from the other forms of social control, which are labeled adjudicatory, conciliatory, and indoctrinatory (Horwitz, 1982). What separates therapy from the other possible forms of social control is that it must involve and in fact depends on the willing participation of the client. He or she must believe the treatment will be effective, and be ready to enter into a relationship of trust with the therapist. This relationship is quite different from coercive forms of social control, which usually occur without the individual's consent. It is also different from medicine, which can proceed with the involuntary physical manipulation or technological invasion of the body. Nevertheless, the differentiation between voluntary and involuntary forms of social control is not one that is clear-cut. The stressed worker who receives therapy, for example, is partly helping to improve his or her quality of life, but such "quality" may be defined by social norms and such treatment mandated or at least strongly encouraged by an employer whose primary interest is reducing worker discontent or increasing productivity.

Another important difference between involuntary treatment and psychotherapy is that the latter requires the use of a specific language ("jargon," if you will) or some culturally accepted symbols as a means of communication between the two parties. It follows that the likelihood of two individuals entering into a therapeutic relationship is strongly determined by the social class and cultural differences between them. We would expect the social distance between them to be far smaller than the distance between two people who are entering into a coercive relationship. It is no surprise to find that the least powerful members of a society are the ones most likely to receive the coercive types of social control (in prisons or mental hospitals). If their problems are not serious enough to warrant such extreme treatment, their only recourse may be to find help from a lay network of friends and relatives (Friedson, 1970). Although in many cases this can provide an effective source of care, the need

Table 10.1. Different Styles of Social Control

Focus of Control Effort	Relationships between Parties	
	Coercive	Persuasive
Conduct	*Adjudicatory*	*Conciliatory*
Personality	*Indoctrinatory*	*Therapeutic*

Source. Horwitz (1982, p. 124).

for professional help in more serious cases may be delayed by a significant lack of access. Individuals in the higher status groups are far more likely than others to receive analytically or psychologically oriented types of therapy, while those in the lower status groups are more likely to receive the nonpersuasive or "organic" therapies, which include drugs, shock treatment, custodial care, and (in earlier times) lobotomies (Hollinghead & Redlich, 1958).

The decision to seek psychotherapy is a highly selective activity, to such an extent that those receiving the care closely resemble the providers. They are typically well-educated urban professionals, often with Jewish ancestry (Kadushin, 1969). A study conducted in the 1970s found that among the patients of psychiatrists there were 13 times as many lawyers as there were in the population at large, 12 times as many social workers, 6.5 times as many writers, artists, and entertainers, 2.7 times as many teachers; the greatest overrepresentation of all, 20 times, was for psychiatrists themselves (Marmor, 1975). Psychotherapy is generally the treatment of choice for individuals who are the most affluent and the least seriously disturbed. Thus we find that private practice psychiatrists, who generally see the least disturbed clients, account for 41% of all psychiatric hours, compared to 14% for psychiatrists who practice in mental hospitals (Horwitz, 1982). In addition, the therapists who work in mental hospitals and who see the most disturbed clients, tend to be less well trained: "[They] . . . have less experience, are graduates of less prestigious medical schools, and are (more often) foreign born" (p.139, parentheses added). This situation is a clear-cut case of the "inverse care law" in the distribution of psychiatric resources (Dengerink, Marks, Hammarlund, & Hammond 1981). The best minds are reserved for the least sick clients; in Horwitz's words, "The provision of psychotherapy is differentially distributed in social space depending on the social location of patient and therapist" (p. 143). It is important to point out here that this maldistribution is only partly the result of a deliberate selection bias on behalf of the client and the therapist. The importance of mutually understood symbols (usually language) in the development of the therapeutic relationship means that in the extreme cases of disorder, where language is often seriously impaired, the required therapeutic relationship cannot develop.

It has been suggested that the types of psychiatric social control most commonly practiced in a particular society tend to reflect that society's social structure (Horwitz, 1982). In communal settings where individuals are strongly interconnected, the dominant form of therapy will be consistent with this level of solidarity. Where the social structure is less cohesive, as it is in the West and most of the developed world, the forms of therapy tend to reflect this by emphasizing individuality and intrapsychic processes. In making this point, Horwitz draws on the work of Foucault (1976). The idea of mental illness as a problem rooted in individual personalities is a relative recent development, one that can be dated back to the latter part of the 18th century in Europe. At this time, according to Foucault, madness became inscribed within the dimensions of interiority; and by that fact, for the first time in the modern world, madness was to receive psychological status, structure and significance. (1976, p.72)

The quintessential form of individualistic psychotherapy is Freudian psychoanalysis, which is arguably a reflection of the urban, cosmopolitan culture of Vienna at the turn of the 19th century. By comparing psychoanalytical therapy with the sort of therapy that might be practiced in more traditional and cohesive societies, Horwitz (1982) suggests that Westerners have become quite removed from their communal ties.[3]

This argument helps to explain why individually oriented psychotherapy, and particularly psychoanalysis, is most likely to flourish in cosmopolitan cities, and is most popular among artistic and intellectual circles, where individuals tend to be less strongly tied to the bonds of traditional culture and communal relationships (Hale, 1971). It should be no great surprise that psychoanalysis attained its greatest following and exerted its strongest influence in the United States, where people tend to have a heightened sense of self, but only weakly developed community ties.[4]

Rehabilitative Social Control: Low Status Clients

The focus in this section is on a very different subgroup of the population, one that can not afford the luxury of individual therapy. For this group social control is not voluntary; it is not something that will help to make an already comfortable life more pleasing. It is a way of life, in many cases a life from which there is no possible reprieve. These are the vagrants, the homeless, the ''down-and-outs''—the legions of unfortunates who populate the marginal territory known as ''skid row.''

The popular view that skid row is home only to chronic alcoholics is far from the truth. Only about one quarter of skid row's residents are alcoholics and fewer than 5% of all alcoholics live on skid row (Archaud, 1979). The others are poor people down on their luck. Many of them are homeless, a phenomenon that in recent years appears to have increased as a result of the ''dumping'' policies associated with deinstitutionalization from nursing homes and mental hospitals (Baxter & Hooper, 1982; Lamb, 1984; Walsh, 1985). Others who have never been institutionalized may have drifted down to skid row involuntarily, as a result of unemployment or disability. Still others have ended up there voluntarily. Large numbers of disaffiliated young people began to appear in the 1960s on the streets of cities like San Francisco and in the smaller college towns all around the country. A survey of ''street people'' who were clients at Berkeley's Emergency Food Project showed that there were significantly more women than would normally be found on skid row (19%), and most of them (64%) were under 20 years old (Baumohl & Miller, 1974). Not surprisingly, the people on the Berkeley streets were relatively well educated, in fact many had parents whose educational levels were higher than their own, which indicates downward social mobility. The new residents of skid row did share one characteristic with their older brethren: They were highly mobile, in fact nearly 70% of those interviewed said they had never stayed in one place for any length of time.

There is little agreement about the social and geographical territory that should be defined as skid row. Traditional definitions describe skid row in at least four different ways: (1) a geographically concentrated area, usually located close to the downtown area of large cities; (2) a cluster of socioeconomic characteristics that are shared by its occupants; (3) a culture or a way of life; and (4) a set of institutions and agencies that exert a form of special control over a specific population.

Although skid row often has an identifiable spatial extent, it is more appropriate to think of it as a psychological and sociological territory (Blumberg, Shipley, & Barsky, 1978). Skid row is also associated with a familiar mix of institutions and agencies, usually including police cells, soup kitchens, missions, mental hospitals, rehabilitation hostels, prisons, bars, cheap cafés, parks and open spaces, derelict buildings, and railroad stations. Because some of these institutions are located in different parts of the city, a major feature of life on skid row is a perpetual movement between the institutions. This phenomenon encouraged J. P. Wiseman (1970) to draw an analogy between skid row and a transportation system made up of various "stations." Most of the stations are familiar to the residents, but none of them provides a permanent home.

Throughout the 20th century there have been some changes in the way skid row has been perceived. In general the legal and moralistic views of skid row have given way to more therapeutically oriented views. Being on skid row today is more likely to be interpreted as a sickness that can be treated rather than as a moral failing that should be eradicated. To reflect this diversity Archaud (1979) has identified the dominant images of skid row and its institutions as salvation, correction, treatment, and rehabilitation (Table 10.2). In most cities we see evidence of all four images at the same time, in addition to which some of the skid row institutions are likely to embody more than one approach (Rooney, 1980). Perhaps the most notable change on skid row in recent years has been the shift from the punitive toward the treatment perspective, which is part of the overall softening of social control strategies that is discussed elsewhere in this book (see Chapters 5, 6, & 7). Under the auspices of the welfare state, attempts have been made to provide a continuum of services for skid-row residents. What is involved here is an effort to "humanize" skid row, and to build a network of care similar to the community support programs that were discussed in Chapter 3. The net effect of these changes is that skid row has been flooded with new services, which, it has been hoped, would improve the quality of life in the inner city.

Several blueprints for the transformation of skid row have appeared in the

Table 10.2. Different Views of and Strategies toward Skid Row

Dominant Ideological Base	Dominant View of Skid Row Alcoholics	Main Strategy for Recovery	Institutions
Moral	Spiritually Weak	Salvation	Missions
Penal	Offender	Correction	Police Cells, Courts, Prisons
Medical	Diseased	Treatment	Alcoholism Treatment and Detoxication Centers
Social	Socially Inadequate	Rehabilitation	Halfway houses, Outpatient clinics

Source. Archaud (1979, p. 14).

literature (Bogue, 1963; Nimmer, 1971). Under ideal circumstances treatment facilities located on skid row should be able to provide a comprehensive set of services for alcoholics, homeless people, and other truly needy persons. These would typically include screening services, hospital and outpatient care, short-term free shelter and cheap lodging places, daytime shelters and recreational facilities, rehabilitation camps and semicustodial facilities, psychological and social programs, vocational training and placement, and protective settings like half-way houses. Most of these facilities would be provided by the state, but an increasing number of for-profit operations have started to appear in recent years (Gilbert, 1984). Since the decriminalization of public drunkenness in many American states, many of these services are already in existence, although a fully comprehensive network of services is available in very few places (see Chapter 6).

It is probably unrealistic to expect that the legal/coercive aspects of skid row can be completely eliminated. An intermediate strategy therefore is to ensure that the services that cater to the needy are in place. In the case of the skid-row chronic alcoholic, this would translate into a range of facilities that would be available to help the individual at any stage of his or her affliction. Numerous models for a fully comprehensive system of alcoholism services have been described in the literature (Archaud, 1979; Glaser *et al.,* 1978). Most of them assume that alcoholics will enter at the street level for screening, from where they will be referred to the most appropriate and "least restrictive" setting available. In many cases the professionals who work with skid-row alcoholics are resigned to the fact that many of their clients are not willing to succumb to such an orderly progression of steps to sobriety. Most of them have, in Archaud's (1979) words, "a long-standing attachment to life on skid row" (p. 118), and a marked reluctance to enter into consistent therapeutic relationships with service providers.

While attempts were being made to humanize skid row, another strategy emerged, that of physically removing its institutions. Opposition to skid row is not a new phenomenon, in fact a number of different groups, including city planners, moral entrepreneurs, and chamber of commerce boosters, have traditionally tried to rid their cities of skid row and its inhabitants. The natural decline of skid row was confirmed in a study conducted by Bahr (1967), who interviewed officials in 24 cities. In all but one city the officials reported that their skid row was decreasing, either in size or in terms of population.[5] One contribution to this process was the demolition of low-rent housing in neighborhoods adjacent to the city center, using urban renewal funds. In many cases the housing units were replaced by office buildings or luxury apartments, which had the effect of displacing the former residents (N. Smith, 1985). The Federal Housing Act of 1949 that created urban renewal was in part the result of a temporary coalition of two groups that would not normally see eye to eye. Civic-minded business interests and social welfare supporters both saw urban renewal as an opportunity to build a better future, although the marriage between the two groups would prove to be one largely of convenience (Room, 1976). In later years the effect of urban renewal on skid row would be complemented by more broadly based programs of urban revitalization, much of which has been the result of private initiatives, with some support from state and federal funds (Holcomb & Beauregard, 1981).

Skid row emerged as a result of both "natural" and premediated forces in the city, and it appears that its decline has been a response to the same processes operating in reverse. Urban ecologists have argued that skid rows will appear in all cities of a certain size, because they serve the needs of individuals who can not be dealt with by the traditional urban institutions (Bogue, 1963). It is also possible to predict roughly where skid row will be located within a given city. According to the ecologists, skid rows will be found in the "zone of transition" between the central business district and the blue-collar residential areas (Johnston, 1985; Knox, 1982). It is realistic to modify this simple deterministic account of skid row by adding a "managerial" interpretation (Pahl, 1977). From this perspective skid row exists where it does because of the decisions made (or not made) by city planners and politicians, who direct skidrow land uses to specific locations by denying them entry to other areas. This process occurs largely through the mechanism of zoning and other less formal methods of social exclusion (Wittman, 1982), which ensure that typical skidrow institutions are progressively squeezed into one or more inner-city neighborhoods (Pinch, 1985). The locational conflicts that occur over the siting of bars, liquor stores, rescue missions, blood banks, pawn shops, pool halls, and shelters for the homeless are settled in a way that, over time, produces a familiar pattern of land use in the inner city (Blumberg *et al.,* 1978; Burnett & Moon, 1983; Mair, 1986).

In the last 2 to 3 decades some major changes have occurred in the social geography of skid row. The fear among the street people is that skid row is slowly being demolished. As one street poet put it:

The bulldozer's rollin' through my part of town.
The iron ball swings and knocks it all down.
You knocked down the flophouse, knocked down the bars,
And blacktopped it over to park all your cars . . .

Now, where will I go and where can I stay
When you've knocked down the Skid Row and hauled it away?
I'll flag a fast rattler and ride it on down, boys.
They're runnin' the bums out of town.

> (Bruce (Utah) Phillips; quoted in R. J. Miller, 1982, p. 1)

Actual evidence for the demolition of skid row is mixed. In some cities skid row has been dispersed. In other cities the physical extent of skid row has stayed the same, but some demographic changes have occurred; for example, there are more young residents (Besser, 1975; Segal & Baumohl, 1980) and more former mental patients (Lamb, 1984). In still other cities there is evidence that skid row has been physically shrinking, for example, in Seattle (R. J. Miller, 1982) and Philadelphia (Blumberg *et al.*, 1978). Between 1958 and 1970 there was a marked decline in the prevalence of public drunkenness, vagrancy, and disorderly conduct in the traditional skid row areas of philadelphia (Blumberg *et al.*, 1978). The rate of decline varied geographically, with some areas actually recording an increase. This raises the possibility that spatial variations in the arrest data may tell us more about differences in the level of police activity than about the prevalence of alcoholism and problem drinking on skid row (Finn, 1985; Hakim & Rengert, 1981). Part of the reduction in the arrest rates throughout the 1970s could also be attributed to the new laws decriminalizing public drunkenness.

In spite of these reservations, the overwhelming impression is that in geographical terms skid row is shrinking. The most important issue arrising from this is the fate of the remaining residents on skid row. As R. J. Miller (1982) has asked, ''When the open asylum of skid row is sharply reduced in ability to accommodate, where do the regulars and the recruits go?'' (p. 27). To answer this question, Blumberg and his colleagues (1978) and R. J. Miller (1982) searched the literature for models that could predict the location of new skidrow areas and then looked in specific cities for empirical evidence. In Philadelphia, Blumberg's team suggested four possibilities: (1) a totally new skid row may emerge; (2) a number of smaller skid-row areas may develop; (3) skid row may be totally eliminated and its residents dispersed into the general population; or (4) skid row may be replaced by a custom-built residential facility, similar to the one planned in Chicago (Vanderkooi, 1973). In the Philadelphia study, Blumberg tried to identify the ''potential and incipient skid rows'' (p. 80) by locating some of the necessary conditions for skid-row development. To do this the team examined trends in some of the key indicators, such as the existence of bottle gangs, the prevalence of skid-row-type offenses, and evidence that housing quality and rental prices were in sharp decline.

After an intensive search they concluded that although they could identify areas where both commercial and residential deterioration were occurring, they could not predict exactly which areas would become skid rows. They observed that for a place to become a part of skid row, it requires the presence of skid-row-like people, skid-row institutions, and most importantly, a public stereotype of the area as skid row. Some parts of Philadelphia have the first two characteristics but not the third. This suggests that for a neighborhood to become part of skid row it has to be labeled as such by the media, the general public, and by other groups such as planners, politicians, businessmen, and realtors.

In his study of Seattle's skid-row neighborhoods, R. J. Miller (1982) also made some predictions about the future geography of skid row, adding to Blumberg's list the possibility of a gradual erosion of skid row without replacement. To test his predictions, Miller used the traditional sources of data: police arrest rates in various neighborhoods, census data to show changes in social and economic characteristics, statistics from detoxification and other alcoholism treatment facilities, and interviews with skid-row residents. The data suggested that skid-row-type offenses dropped significantly in the 1970s, from 12,566 in 1973 to 2,308 in 1978. This trend is mainly a result of the discriminalization law (M. C. Regier, 1977), which also helps to account for the increase during the same period in the use of alcoholism treatment services (R. G. Dunham & Janik, 1985; Finn, 1985).

R. J. Miller (1982) also devised a scale to measure "skid-rowness" in the field. In eight different parts of Seattle this instrument was used to assess the extent of the most typical skid-row institutions and behaviors. Using this scale Miller could clearly identify Seattle's skid-row areas during a 7-year period. Over time skid-rowness appeared to be in decline in Seattle, but there was no consistent evidence of new skid-row areas emerging. In 1978 the total score for all neighborhoods was 1,315, compared to 1,613 in 1972, a decline that was consistent over time, with the exception of the last year. The decline was most noticeable for the "institutions" found on skid row, the score for which fell from 418 to 257 in the 7-year period; and for "derelicts," which fell from 385 to 162. During the same period some increases were noted, for example, in "loiterers" and discarded bottles (see Table 10.3).

The decline of skid-row institutions was greater than the decline in the "transitory" items (all other characteristics except institutions). This suggests that skid-row land uses are disappearing faster than skid-row behaviors, which tend to be persistent over time. In spite of this, Miller's data shows that neither skid-row residents nor their institutions are as prevalent in what used to be their core "turf." This is most evident in the Pioneer Square neighborhood, Seattle's most celebrated skid-row area, and almost a tourist attraction in its own right. Miller argues that this area is no longer so clearly dominated by the highly visual symbols of skid row. The old missions and the cheap hotels are gradually being closed and replaced with higher rent land uses.

The battle for skid row is being won by the wealthy, and by those who

Table 10.3. Changes in Skid-Row Items by Year and Area, Showing 1978 Totals and Percentage of 1972 Totals

Area	Institutions		Transitory		Derelicts		Loiterers		Discarded Bottles	
	1978	1972	1978	1972	1978	1972	1978	1972	1976	1972
International District (26 Blocks)	43	0.79	129	0.96	15	0.39	74	1.57	22	2.75
Pioneer Square (54 Blocks)	62	0.70	546	0.95	100	0.58	230	1.64	53	0.71
First Avenue (37 Blocks)	37	0.54	63	0.54	11	0.28	35	1.21	5	0−.50
Belltown (51 Blocks)	70	0.65	263	1.18	25	0.30	53	1.29	116	10.55
Pike Street (4 Blocks)	12	0.92	2	0.08	1	0.10	0	—	0	0
Fremont (4 Blocks)	9[a]	[a]	10[a]	[b]	1[a]	[b]	3[a]	[b]	5[a]	[b]
Ballard (4 Blocks)	19[a]	0.73	10[a]	0.24	3[a]	0.33	3[a]	[b]	1	[b]
Tacoma (4 Blocks)	42	0.68	55	0.71	10	0.32	17	1.31	15	[b]
TOTALS	257	0.61	1,058	0.88	162	0.42	409	1.42	211	1.92

[a] 1977 data only.
[b] 1972 baseline too small for meaningful comparison.
Source. Adapted from Miller (1982, pp. 63–77).

want the postindustrial city to be cleansed of both production activities and poverty (Mair, 1986; N. Smith, 1982). Skid row is shrinking without evidence that it is reappearing in other parts of the city. In Denver, for example, Larimer Square has been transformed from a skid-row area into a nucleus of high-priced stores and offices. A former resident complains that this is really nothing more than the contemporary version of the old war between the classes:

> Well, you ran out the hookers who worked on the street
> And you built a big club where the playboys can meet.
> My bookie joint closed when your cops pulled a raid
> But you built a new hall for the stock market trade.
>
> These little storekeepers just don't stand a chance
> With the big uptown bankers a callin' the dance.
> With their suit-and-tie restaurants that're all owned
>   by Greeks,
> And the counterfeit hippies and their plastic boutiques.
> Now I'm finding out there's just one kind of war,
> The one going on 'tween the rich and the poor.
> I don't know a lot about what you'd call class,
> But the upper and middle can all kiss my ass.
>
> (Bruce (Utah) Phillips; quoted in R. J. Miller, 1982, p. 1)

At the beginning of his research Miller thought of skid row primarily as a geographical entity, one that had identifiable geographic boundaries, but by the end of the 1970s this was no longer so clearly the case. The view that skid row is more a human condition than a place implies that even if all skid rows were demolished, their inhabitants will continue to exist. By the late 1980s this still appears to be the case. Skid-row people can be found wherever there is poverty and in all the places people usually go to for help. The implications of this are substantial. In the first place, it means that skid-rowness is probably much more prevalent than even Miller's data indicates, because it can exist in small pockets even in non-skid-row areas. A second concern is that the gradual dispersal of obvious skid-row areas may result in reduced efforts to do something about the human conditions associated with skid row. If a whole area of the city is "cleaned up" and purged of its skid row individuals and institutions, the city politicians and planners can argue that a major barrier to economic and social development has been removed (Room, 1976). The plight of the poor and the homeless may be pushed into the background, and the demand for social reforms may take a back seat to the more glamorous push toward economic revitalization.

CONCLUSION

The two types of social control discussed in this chapter, therapeutic and rehabilitative, illustrate the different ends of a continuum. There are a number of important differences between them: Therapeutic social control occurs on an individual basis, usually in a private setting, and it is voluntary. By comparison, the term "rehabilitative social control" describes situations in which attempts are made to provide basic services to groups of individuals, often without their consent. The most significant differences between the recipients involves their class differences and their perceived "utility" in the labor force. As we have seen here, these differences predict sharply different futures for the two groups. Those in therapy have been expanding their ranks, and an initially skeptical public is becoming increasingly amenable to the addition of mental health care to the normal repertoire of health behaviors. The other group has also been expanding in recent years, although with far less public acceptance, and it is to this group that we now turn in the last chapter.

NOTES

1. This has been referred to as the "new history," in contrast to the "old history," which studied politics and constitutional events. Not surprisingly the new history has met with some harsh treatment. According to Himmelfarb (1984) this trend toward

critical reinterpretations of historical events causes historians to lose sight of the "big picture":

> Where the old history concerned itself with regimes and administrations, legislation and politics, diplomacy and foreign policy, wars and revolutions, the new [history] focuses on social groups and social problems, factories and farms, cities and villages, work and play, family and sex, birth and death, childhood and old age, crime and insanity. While the old featured kings, presidents, politicians, and distinguished individuals, the new takes as its subjects classes and masses, the anonymous many rather than the identifiable few. (p. 85)

Clearly Himmelfarb is objecting to what she perceives to be a breath of radical air in her discipline. She admits that the new approach to history is not totally wrongheaded. What she objects to is its creeping pervasiveness throughout the field, and the belief among its proponents that it is the only form of history, in fact, "a higher form of history, more real and significant, more elemental and essential, than the old history" (p. 89).

2. An alternative account of the acceptance of therapy has been pointed out by Phil Brown (personal communication, 1986). The rising affluence and greater amounts of leisure time experienced by the middle classes after World War II helped to foster a new level of narcissism, and what some authors have referred to as a "commodification" of the emotions.

3. As Horwitz (1982) observes,

> "Symbols drawn from self-experience, not ritualized and communal symbols that do not correspond to a personal state of mind, are used to interpret personality problems. Cure occurs through self-exploration and consequent self-awareness, not through conformity to the normative order of the group. The individual personality is not denigrated by the therapeutic process, as in communal therapy, but becomes of paramount concern. . . . Finally, the therapeutic process itself becomes a private relationship between the patient and the therapist that is an oasis from the social world, rather than a communal affair mobilizing the energies of the community. (p. 170)

4. The migration of many psychoanalytic practitioners to the United States was also accompanied by a marked deemphasis in their political involvement. Many of the early European Freudians were politically active, mostly identifying themselves with the extreme left (Jacoby, 1983). Many Jewish psychoanalysts were forced to move to the United States during the 1930s and 1940s, and from that time onward, psychoanalysis in this country became politically neutral. One explanation for this was the realistic fear of being associated with Marxism in the United States in the middle decades of the twentieth century. As Jacoby notes, the hostility had a clearly nativist tone, and "forced radicals, especially radical refugees, to clean out their bookshelves and censor their pasts" (p. 341). Another explanation for the depoliticization of psychoanalysis was the immensity of the cultural gap between Vienna and Berlin in the 1920s and Chicago and Topeka in the 1940s and 1950s. In the vast American institutes "psychoanalysis fattened into a quiet trade; the intellectual fervor, reforming zeal and theoretical boldness of classical psychoanalysis were history" (pp. 341–3422).

As it was Americanized, psychoanalysis was also affected by two other forces, professionalization and medicalization. From the earliest years in America, most practitioners agreed that only medical doctors should be psychoanalysts. It was felt that in this way alone could the fledgling field receive any prestige and be associated with the respectability of science. A medical training was also considered necessary to enable the doctor to discriminate between somatic and psychosomatic disorders. Most importantly, the professional requirement would seriously restrict the total number of practitioners, thereby ensuring those who were medically trained a lucrative practice. Freud himself detested the idea of turning psychoanalysis into a branch of medicine, arguing that the only hope for it in the future was the extensive development of lay psychoanalysis (Jacoby, 1983).

The exclusion of lay analysis effectively delivered psychoanalysis into the hands of the medical profession. It became just another part of the medical school curriculum. The requirement of a medical training strongly preselected the students who could consider psychoanalysis as a profession. The net effect was that American psychoanalysis became increasingly pragmatic and conservative. Dissenters, intellectuals, and most notably women were excluded. A generation of newly arrived psychoanalytic refugees learned to be more circumspect and cautious in their thinking. This helped them to survive, but in the long run it also insured their demise as a uniquely free-spirited group of social thinkers (Jacoby, 1983).

5. The visual and economic blight of skid row offered an exciting challenge to many city planners, and to other civic interest groups, who longed for extensive urban renewal. In the 1950s and 1960s federal funds became available to help transform these dreams into reality. One of the most comprehensive plans was Bogue's (1963) proposal to eliminate Chicago's skid row in 6 years. Bogue noted that the external effects of skid row poisoned economic development in an extensive part of the inner city. There was some evidence that skid row was already shrinking, so it was possible to argue that the plans would only be speeding up a process the market had begun. For example, urban economic growth in the 1950s provided increasing employment opportunities for skid-row residents and welfare benefits had helped to raise their living standards. In addition, changes in industrial hiring policies had reduced the amount of casual day-work that had long been a staple on skid row.

11

Home and Homelessness in
the Postindustrial City

INTRODUCTION

In the 1980s we have witnessed a dramatic increase in concern for the poor, inspired partly by the rising level of income inequality in the United States. In 1984 the major issue in the Presidential election was an economic one, in spite of the looming threat of global conflict. In answer to the question "Are you better off now than you were in 1980?" most Americans could answer in the affirmative, but at the same time there were almost daily reports of people sleeping on park benches and on top of warm air vents in public places. Not since the Great Depression had so many poor people taken to the streets of American cities.

The homeless have usually experienced at least some of the problems that have been discussed in this book, so that a focus on them in the last chapter makes for an appropriate ending. This is not to suggest that homelessness is the worst or the ultimate urban problem, or that the public has lost interest in the other issues. The selection of homelessness as the theme on which to close the book is appropriate because it can best be understood as a problem that is the result of a mix of the forces that have been considered throughout. In the first place, homelessness exhibits many of the characteristics of an epidemic. The problem appears to have mushroomed within a short time period, and this invites attempts to identify the key etiological forces that have been at work. As we shall see, however, it has been extremely difficult to measure the prevalence of homelessness in the city, and the lack of consensus on this issue has further complicated the search for etiological clues. A second consideration is that the homelessness phenomenon is at least partly a result of earlier social policies that were intended to solve other public problems. As we have noted many times in this book, some policies have not only failed to ameliorate a specific problem but have actually helped to make an already bad situation worse. The third reason why homelessness is an appropriate topic for the conclusion of this book is that it has been able to generate some powerful constituencies that have helped to build a successful arena around the problem. The homelessness phenomenon of the 1980s provides examples of all of the major building blocks on which this book has been organized.

THE HOMELESSNESS PHENOMENON

Attempts to assess the prevalence of homelessness in American cities have produced some wildly diverging statistics (Bassuk, 1984; Baxter & Hopper, 1982; Lamb, 1984). The National Coalition for the Homeless estimated that there were 2.5 million homeless people in 1983, an estimate that was 500,000 greater than the one made a year earlier (Arce & Vergare, 1984; Hombs & Snyder, 1982). More conservative figures were circulated by the National Governor's Association Task Force on the Homeless, which estimated some 60,000 homeless persons in New York City, 30,000 in Los Angeles, and 20,000–25,000 in Chicago. Clearly the actual numbers themselves are not particularly important. No matter how many homeless people are counted, the evidence that people can not meet the most basic needs for food and shelter on a daily basis in one of the world's wealthiest nations is deeply disturbing. In a country where the very concept of having a home has acted as a benchmark for status, the evidence that so many are unable to find even the most humble home is a serious challenge to the legitimacy of the existing economic and social system.

In this final chapter two interrelated questions about homelessness will be raised. The first one is the issue of etiology. Whatever difficulties are encountered in making accurate estimates, there is a general consensus that the incidence of the problem is growing at a rapid rate. We shall consider some of the alternative explanations that have been put forward to account for these increases. The second question asks how and why the issue of homelessness has been able to capture the attention of the media and the imagination of the public with such dramatic force. This question is not intended to underestimate the seriousness of the problem, but simply to ask why this specific issue has become so prominent in the mid-1980s.

Homelessness as an Epidemic

It is relatively easy to generate a number of factors that are likely to have contributed to the excess prevalence of homelessness in the 1980s. It is much more difficult, however, to estimate the relative importance of these different factors with any certainty and to assess the exact nature of the relationships involved. One of the most publicized causal factors in the etiology of many public problems has been the performance of the economy. For nearly 2 decades we have been provided with evidence of a quantitative relationship between economic decline, usually measured in terms of unemployment, and such problems as mental illness, alcoholism, suicide, crime rates, and even child abuse (Brenner, 1973; Brenner & Mooney, 1983; Greenberg, 1977). It is reasonable to expect that the state of the economy is a contributor to homelessness as well, although the causal sequence may well be an indirect one. For example, the loss of a job may exacerbate a individual's drinking problems, and the subsequent depletion of personal resources may end with him or her being evicted and forced onto the streets.

The media are rather partial to sad stories that make such causal sequences seem plausible, but as a macrolevel explanation, the economic loss hypothesis is far from convincing. There is equal theoretical and empirical support for the alternative hypothesis, namely, that economic growth is more likely than economic decline to generate community and individual stresses that can result in public problems (Eyer, 1977; Linsky *et al.,* 1985). There is also evidence that the overall relationship between unemployment and problem prevalence rates breaks down when the data is disaggregated. The effect on admission rates to mental hospitals, for example, varies significantly from one county to the next. This suggests that other variables such as the location and capacity of mental health facilities play an important role.

This reservation is not intended to question the existence of a relationship between unemployment and personal and family hardships, it simply suggests that we ought not to overstate this relationship. There is evidence that many families are able to cope reasonably well with such adversity, and the resulting stresses are often short-lived (Buss & Redburn, 1983). It seems unlikely that a single experience of unemployment will disturb an individual to such an extent that he or she loses everything and ends up living on the street. When this does happen, it is likely that a number of contributing circumstances are not reported, or that this is the latest in a long string of stress-inducing and impoverishing events (Ball & Havassy, 1984).

At various times the media provide extensive coverage of individuals and families that have experienced a rapid fall in status following the loss of a job. A couple in Chicago were evicted from their home when the man lost his job, and they ended up living in their car. On a particularly cold night both of them died of carbon monoxide poisoning, having left the car running in an attempt to keep warm (New York Times, February 3, 1983). Although the story is deeply disturbing, it is unlikely that this sequence of events is commonplace.

A popular explanation for the dramatic increase in homelessness in the 1980s has been the effect of the fiscally conservative policies of the Reagan administration. The shift of resources away from welfare programs into what are considered to be more "productive" sectors of the economy and the decentralization of fiscal responsibility from the federal government to local and state sources of funding must surely have contributed to the increased number of marginal individuals who are pushed out onto the streets. Again it is extremely difficult to draw any firm conclusions between the funding cutbacks and specific cases in which individuals have drifted down the social hierarchy into homelessness. As was noted in Chapter 5, a more direct effect of the new austerity came as a result of the changes in the eligibility requirements for SSI payments made to individuals with disabilities (Burt & Pittman, 1984). For a short time it was feared that many of the people who lost their SSI money would be forced onto public welfare, and ultimately onto the streets. Although this no doubt happened in some cases, the process of reviewing eligibility was terminated in 1984 as a result of the public outcry it generated. It seems safest to suggest that the fiscal stringency at all levels of government has exacerbated a situation that was already deteriorating.

The rising prevalence of homelessness has also been associated with changes in the housing market in many American cities. As a result of urban revitalization and "gentrification" there has been a marked shortage of cheap housing. Although it is unlikely that many of the individuals who are displaced by gentrifiers immediately join the ranks of the homeless, it is plausible that the rising house prices that result from such phenomena have a reverse filtering effect (Ley, 1983). As house prices rise rapidly, families in a particular income category are forced to settle for a smaller and cheaper house than they would have preferred. At the bottom of the market this may result in an entire group being unable to afford any kind of housing at all. There is some circumstantial evidence to support such a hypothesis. Although there was a significant drop in the number of families living below the poverty level ($7,000) in the 1970s, the number of cheap rental units (those below $175 per month) fell from 17.9 million in 1970 to 6.4 million in 1970 (Bassuk, 1984). Obviously, the extent to which the housing shortage is felt by the poor depends on the nature of the specific housing market in question, and in terms of the availability of cheap rental housing, some markets are much worse off than others (Scott & Scott, 1980; C. J. Smith, 1980c).

Another possible contributor to the growing problem of homelessness has been the competition for space in the old and crumbling neighborhoods that had once provided a home for many of the city's skid-row and homeless. As we saw in Chapter 10, the "demolition" of skid row in many cities may have forced countless numbers of residents to take to the streets in search of cheaper and even less desirable places to live. The attempts by planners and politicians to revitalize and "beautify" many downtown areas by adding new residential, retail, and commercial areas has also contributed to this phenomenon (C. J. Smith, 1987). It has been estimated, for example, that in New York City between 1970 and 1982 more than 80% of the single-room occupancy (SRO) buildings, which have long been the domain of low-income elderly and the mentally ill, were either demolished or converted to more profitable uses (Walsh, 1985). It has proved extremely difficult to study the worst effects of such displacement, because it is virtually impossible to trace individuals once they become undomiciled. It appears that many of the displaced families who are able to find a new home manage to cope reasonably well (Schill & Nathan, 1983), but almost by definition we would expect that the transients experience more hardships.

Probably the most publicized contributor to the problem of homelessness in recent years has been the deinstitutionalization of the mentally ill. As Goldman and Morrissey (1985) noted, "Community mental health brought mental patients 'home'; deinstitutionalization left them homeless" (p. 729). Within a fairly short time period this argument has become so popular that it is rarely questioned (Baxter & Hopper, 1982; Lamb, 1984). There is little doubt that some of the new homeless are on the street as a result of changes in mental health policy, but it would be wrong to suggest that there are no problems with this interpretation of homelessness. In the first place, although many of the people living in shelters for the homeless are or appear to be mentally ill, the majority of the homeless are not mentally ill, so presumably deinstitutionalization has not been a factor for them (Morrissey & Gounis, 1987).

There is also a problem of timing associated with this argument. Deinstitutionalization of the mentally ill began in the mid-1960s, and it has continued until the present time (P. Brown, 1985). If deinstitutionalization were as significant a factor as suggested in the literature (Bachrach, 1984), its effect should have resulted in an increased incidence of homelessness in the early 1970s. But in fact homelessness did not reach epidemic proportions until the 1980s, by which time many states had made significant efforts to slow down their deinstitutionalization policies (C. J. Smith & Hanham, 1981a). From the late 1970s onwards there have also been some significant efforts made in several states to provide more effective long-term community support services for the chronically mentally ill (Tessler & Goldman, 1982). The fact that homelessness began to be noted as a major problem at approximately the same time suggests that other forces were making an equal and perhaps a greater contribution than deinstitutionalization.

In addition to changes in the policies affecting the release of patients from institutions, an equal and perhaps greater component of the new mental health policies was a change in admission procedures. In almost all states it became more difficult to gain entry to a hospital for symptoms of mental illness. At a facility in downtown Chicago the number of admissions fell from 23,000 in 1971 to 10,000 in 1980 (Appleby & Desai, 1985). This means that a significant proportion of individuals who experienced some type of mental disorder were not being institutionalized at all. It is generally believed that being homeless increases one's chances of being admitted to a mental hospital, and the evidence from Chicago supports this, because the proportion of admissions who were homeless more than doubled during the 1970s. A further analysis of the data showed, however, that the factor most closely related to admission was not homelessness but the referral source (Table 11.1). Most of the clients who are brought to the hospital by the police or a relative or referred by a community hospital were admitted. Self-referrals on the other hand were much less likely to be admitted; in fact fewer than half of the self-referred applicants were admitted, regardless of whether or not they had a home (Appleby & Desai, 1985).

Table 11.1. Applications and Inpatient Admissions to an Urban Chicago Mental
Health Facility

| | HOMELESS CLIENTS | | | |
| | Applications | | Admissions | |
Source of Referral	*n*	% of total	*n*	% of total
Self	27	25%	127	46%
Police	558	49%	431	77%
Private Hospital	212	19%	202	95%
Family	25	2%	19	76%
	DOMICILED CLIENTS			
Self	1034	17%	494	48%
Police	1870	31%	1501	80%
Private Hospital	1615	27%	1470	91%
Family	895	15%	631	71%

Source. Appleby and Desai (1985, p. 735).

Homelessness as an Artifact

An alternative to the epidemic account of homelessness is the possibility that
in some way the rising rate of prevalence is an artifact rather than the result of
some objective etiological forces. It has been suggested, mainly by supporters
of the Reagan administration's policies, that homelessness and other types of
dependency are somehow the result of the debilitating effects of the welfare
state. As we saw in Chapters 5, 6, and 7, the policies that were intended to
solve the problems of mental disorder, public inebriation, and delinquency have
not only failed to achieve their stated goals, but they were at least partly responsible for drawing an ever-increasing number of individuals under the umbrella of state-supported human services.

Many of the clients in the newly created programs had not previously been
receiving services, and the provision of new services may have had the effect
of creating additional demands. It is plausible that this process is initiated by
the clients themselves, in an attempt to sample the new range of services and
hopefully improve the quality of their lives, but it is more likely to result from
the zealous "recruiting" activities by service providers in an attempt to maintain and expand the arenas around their particular concerns (Wiener, 1981).
The 1960s and 1970s were a time of furious activity in the area of human
services (Cohen, 1979), but in spite of all the efforts to redistribute resources,
little was done to tackle the root causes of the problems in question. As a result
of rising expectations, a larger population than ever before came to rely on
publicly provided services as a way of solving their problems. It is reasonable
to suggest that from this expanded pool of dependent persons has come the

new homeless in the 1980s—people whose hopes have been raised and dashed many times by the prospect of new programs, and who have now depleted their energies and meager resources.

As we saw in Chapter 9, in some circumstances the prevalence of a specific problem increases only because the problem is "uncovered"—implying that the use of services increases without a corresponding increase in symptoms (Catalano & Dooley, 1977). Thus, for example, if additional services are provided they will most likely attract new clients who had not previously received any services. In this case it is apparent that the "true" prevalence of the symptoms involved has stayed about the same, but the treated prevalence has increased. It seems likely that such a phenomenon has occurred in the case of mental disorder and alcoholism, where it appears there has been an almost inexhaustibly elastic demand for services. It is possible that the expansion of shelters and other services catering to the homeless may have had a similar effect.

Although it would most often be argued that the supply of services is a response to the level of the need or perceived need, it also seems likely that this relationship could be reversed. In this sense at least part of the excess prevalence of homelessness may be an artifact of the provision of services for the homeless. If this were the case, part of the "epidemic" of homelessness could be attributed to increases in the rate at which homeless persons have come forward to seek support.

Further uncovering of the homelessness problem might occur as a response to the increasing public awareness of the problem that has resulted from extensive coverage in the popular media. This effect could work in at least two ways. The greater awareness of the problem helps professionals and politicans to make a more persuasive case for additional resources for the homeless. This in turn further expands the availability of services, which could result in more homeless cases being uncovered. Another effect of the wider media coverage is the greater sensitivity on behalf of members of the public and human service providers to the problems encountered by homeless persons. This could result in earlier referrals to community-based programs, which would also boost the prevalence statistics.

It is important to note that public exposure on its own could not have "created" the problem of homelessness. There is no doubt that many people are homeless in the 1980s, and there is every reason to believe that the numbers have risen in recent years. The suggestion here is simply that at some stage during the recent past, homelessness became a major media event, at both the national and the local level. The pivotal year appears to have been 1982, when stories about the homeless were carried in the March issues of Newsweek, U.S. News and World Report, and the Wall Street Journal. In that year there were only a handful of stories about homelessness in the New York Times, but in 1983 there was an explosion of coverage, with an average of nearly two stories each week. At this time the problem remained a seasonal one, in that there were only 13 stories in the 5 summer months from May to the end of September. In 1984 and 1985 the coverage in the New York Times increased to an average of more than three stories a week, and the seasonal bias had almost disappeared. Homelessness had become a fully fledged media event all the year round.

Although newspaper coverage is not a perfect indicator of the relative seriousness of a public problem, the sharp increase in the rate of reporting in 1983 suggests that homelessness had become something of a "moral panic" (Dorn, 1983). In the 1960s there were panics about the "crime wave" and juvenile delinquency, in the 1970s and early 1980s the panic was about drinking and driving, but in the mid-1980s the panic centered on the homelessness issue.

The level of interest in homelessness suggests that it has captured the imagination of the American public more strongly than any of the earlier epidemics such as mental illness, alcoholism, drug abuse, and crime. Disregarding the other problems experienced by the homeless, the simple fact of being without a home has resonated deeply within the consciousness of middle-class America, and this issue has been able to generate more awareness and a higher level of emotion than most other issues in recent memory.[1]

Homelessness and the Building of Arenas

The strong feelings that have developed around the issue of homelessness have not always been favorable to the individuals who are without homes. Many of the newspaper stories about homelessness describe the conflicts that occur between groups who have radically different views about how certain land uses should evolve. The proposal to open a new shelter for the homeless or the day-to-day operation of such a shelter has been a rallying point for a number of different groups. Neighborhood residents band together to oppose a shelter, and in this way opposition to the homeless becomes an issue around which a sense of community is built. On the Lower East Side of New York City, for example, Assemblyman Sheldon Silver presented 2,000 signatures of local residents to Mayor Koch, in opposition to the opening of a shelter for the homeless (New York Times, July 23, 1983). The argument they used was one that been used successfully many times, namely that a neighborhood was saturated with human service programs (Dear & Taylor, 1982; Wolpert and Wolpert, 1976). In other situations groups of local business interests have come together to oppose shelters, on the grounds that the presence of skid-row individuals and land uses are not conducive to local economic development (Mair, 1984, 1986). In Brooklyn, local opposition to the selection of a number of sites for new shelters was based on the argument that the areas in question were on the brink of economic redevelopment (New York Times, December 14, 1983). As these examples illustrate, homelessness is an issue that has been able to serve as a powerful symbol in the building of local solidarity. The homelessness issue brings out strong feelings of repulsion that help to fuse the collective voice of a community (Dear & Long, 1978). Once the initial ties have been made among the residents, the locality is better prepared to act decisively on subsequent conflict issues.

The political function of homelessness is even more decisive for constituencies who are in favor of rather than opposed to dealing constructively with the issue of homelessness. As we saw in Chapter 9 a major role in the growth of the arenas around the human services has been played by the many different groups whose interests are at stake. In addition to the benefits that might accrue to individual homeless persons, support of this issue and its prominent place in the public's consciousness serves a useful purpose for many constituencies.

One of the most obvious examples is the role of homelessness as a symbol around which liberals were able to rally in their opposition to the Reagan administration (Bassuk & Lauriat, 1984). Faced with an immensely popular President, the liberal opposition has called attention to the growing army of homeless as one of the most poignant reminders of the administration's lack of concern for the poor. Statistics on unemployment and inflation, and even the staggering size of the budget deficit, have not been nearly as effective in combatting the conservative trend as the continued publicity about the homeless. The President himself is reported to have little sympathy for the homeless, preferring to believe that being homeless is a matter of choice (Baxter & Hopper, 1982).

The evidence suggests, however, that even the powerful image of the homelessness problem did not seriously reduce the popularity of the Reagan administration. It has, on the other hand, served an extremely useful purpose for city officials to extract additional funds from higher levels of government. Their argument is that homelessness, like other forms of dependency, has resulted from society-wide economic forces. They thus contend that though the cities themselves have not caused these problems, they are nevertheless responsible for dealing with them. In the 1960s this sort of argument was successful in winning federal funding through the Great Society categorical grant programs, but by the 1980s this type of funding had fallen very much out of favor. It would take an emotional issue like homelessness to help squeeze out scarce funds from such an unwilling source as the federal government. In 1983 the United States Conference of Mayors asked the federal government for its help in dealing with the problem of homelessness, including assistance with food supplies by the United States Department of Agriculture and $500 million from Congress for an economic assistance program that would create public service jobs, provide shelters and soup kitchens for the homeless, and avert foreclosures of mortgages on houses and farms (New York Times, January 29, 1983; February 2, 1983).

Clearly homelessness has become an issue on which a number of individuals and groups have been able to strengthen their own claims-making activities (Gusfield, 1984; Spector & Kitsuse, 1977). From the social constructivist point of view, studying the problem of homelessness as an objective set of conditions is but a small part of the overall endeavor. Much more important is the study of the processes of interpretation by which a particular phenomenon comes to be defined as a problem, and the activities of the persons who perceive it as a problem. From this perspective the definition of homelessness as a public problem is clearly a political activity. In their attempts to overcome the opposition of numerous other claims-making groups in the community, each constituency tries to stay alive in an often hostile and usually resource-poor environment. Their success and their long-term survival will ultimately be measured by their ability to convince others that theirs is the only viable stance on the issue.

Another advantage of the homelessness issue is that in comparison to such long-term problems as mental illness and crime, an obvious short-term solution is to provide more funds to create temporary homes for the homeless. The political value of taking such a highly visible stand is obvious, especially if it is successful. To support such an effort demonstrates compassion and a willingness to put community social issues before all others. Unfortunately, the simplistic solutions can act only as stop-gap measures that have to be continually reappropriated in the absence of any long-term solutions.

The problem of homelessness has also supported a whole new tier of social service providers: the people who operate and administer shelters. In many instances the shelter operators, which include a wide range of religious and voluntary organizations, have fiercely defended and jealously guarded their own turf. Some have actively rejected government intervention and the invasion of research teams, preferring to maintain an "us" versus "them" aloofness. One group of researchers has even gone so far as to suggest that some shelter operators have been hostile to long-term social welfare/public health solutions to the problem, preferring instead to continue offering places in shelters as a way of defending their empires (Bassuk & Lauriat, 1984).

The homelessness issue has helped to reverse or at least slow down the long-term trend toward the "medicalization" and "psychiatrization" of the public problems industries (Conrad & Schneider, 1980). Homelessness is seen as a long-term chronic problem, for which it is extremely unlikely that a medical or psychiatric solution can be effective. It is clear that professionals in these fields have publicly accepted their failure to solve such long-term problems as chronic mental illness and alcoholism (Finn, 1985; Goldman & Morrissey, 1985). In an unlikely turn of events, therefore, homelessness offers a new set of possibilities for overworked, underpaid, and seriously burnt-out social service workers. For more than 2 decades these people have had to stand by as the more glamorous professions associated with medicine and psychiatry took over an increasing share of the treatment for mental illness, alcoholism, drug addiction, and even crime. The evidence that very little has been achieved by such treatment helps to win back some status and a greater feeling of parity for the generalist providers.

As this discussion has suggested, the problem of homelessness has served a useful purpose to a wide variety of constituents, including politicians, city officials, service providers, and community groups. Like most of the other public problems around which significant arenas have been built, homelessness generates strong emotions. Few people are neutral about the issue of homelessness. It produces violent reaction and passionate sympathies, depending on the extent to which an individual or group is likely to be affected—practically, politically, or ideologically—by the problem. As we have seen with other public problems, the location of homelessness is a crucial factor. Once the homeless impinge on the middle-class businessman's turf or the middle-class family's neighborhood, they are likely to spark a violent reaction, even though in private the opponents may sympathize with the horror of being without a home.

Homelessness is an issue about which much has been written, but on which few unequivocal facts are available. We can only guess at the causes and we grope in the dark for reliable estimates of prevalence. The only safe position is to argue that homelessness has many contributing factors, and no matter how large or small the numbers are, to be without the most basic amenity in such an affluent society is intolerable. At the present time the emotion generated by the homelessness issue has produced a groundswell of popular support for decisive actions. The short-term result is that something is being done about the problem, and that "something" may help to ameliorate the most obvious deprivations associated with being homeless.

On the other hand, unless the root causes of the problem can be corrected, we face the prospect of extending such temporary solutions far into the future. The problem is that we still have only a blurred vision of the root causes of homelessness, which makes it difficult to suggest long-term solutions. In the meantime, a likely scenario is that the fickle public and their even more fickle representatives will grow bored with the homelessness phenomenon and start to look elsewhere. If that happens, and history suggests that it will, the homeless will be left without even their current minimal level of support.

CONCLUSION: HOME AND HOMELESSNESS IN HISTORICAL CONTEXT

To understand why homelessness has been able to capture the imagination of the American public, it helps to think about the issue from a historical perspective. Homelessness in America is the almost unthinkable opposite to the concept of "home." Throughout recent history the notion of domesticity and the benefits of having a home of one's own have been of crucial importance to the middle classes in America; in fact if has been argued that achieving the goal of a single-family home has to a large extent defined the middle classes in capitalist societies (R. A. Walker, 1981).

Before the 19th century the concept of home did not necessarily denote a private dwelling to Americans, even those with jobs and decent incomes. One's home would often be shared with a variety of other people, including members of one's extended family, servants, apprentices, and even laborers (Johnson, 1978). By the first few decades of the 19th century it was obvious that many middle-income families sought a quiet, peaceful, and independent life, one that would most often be in the newly emerging suburbs (Binford, 1985; Jackson, 1985). The single-family home was the place to which people aspired. Once they had such a home it was the place to which they longed to escape after the rigors of the workplace. The home was also the place where their middle-class values would be reproduced. The purpose of the home in the suburbs has been described by R. A. Walker (1981) as being

> to send father back into the fray rejuvenated, to optimize the life-chances of children, to avoid falling back into the working-class, and to reproduce a mode of life. . . . What is involved here is more than a refreshed worker and a well-tutored child, but a whole constellation of mutually supporting values, experiences, and social resources which go into the construction of human beings.(p. 392)

In the middle-class home children would be taught the values of family solidarity, hard work, saving, and most importantly, being able to look forward to having homes of their own in the future (Blumin, 1985). As historian Mary Ryan (1981) has noted in her book *The Cradle of the Middle Class,* "The American middle class moulded its distinctive identity around domestic values and family practices" (p. 15). The home allowed families to create a stable environment, within which they could instill in their children such values as prudence, restraint, and the need for a good education.

The middle-class home and the values that were taught within the home were seriously threatened by the social disorder that accompanied life in the rapidly growing industrial cities of the late 19th century (Boyer, 1978). The violence, poverty, disability, and degeneracy associated with the city illustrated to the middle classes exactly what they might have to encounter if they were to slip back down the social ladder and let go of their homes.

One of the pastimes among the inner-city poor that most seriously threatened to tear apart the middle-class home was the popularity of drinking in public places. Drinking in the saloon provided an attractive alternative for working-class men to spending time at home with their families. Presumably, middle-class men, if they were allowed to drink in saloons, might also succumb to these temptations. It is not at all surprising, therefore, to find that middle-class women were continually active and often influential in the long drawn-out struggle for Prohibition in America (B. L. Epstein, 1981; H. G. Levine, 1980). Such women knew what they might have to face if their spouse took up drinking seriously.

In the late 19th century the fragility of family life was threatened on all sides, but alcohol provided one of the most pervasive threats. The drinking place and the very act of drinking with friends offered recreation and companionship. The public drinking place was an alternative to the home; in fact, "The saloon and the substance it sold supplanted the most precious functions of domesticity" (Aaron & Musto, 1981, p. 144). The warm glow from the alcohol helped the drinking man to feel at home even when he was away from home. For some men the saloon provided the ambience of home and an alternative to the maternal support they longed for but could not get from their wives.

Obviously women, particularly middle-class women, had much to lose if their men chose the noisy saloon over the tranquility of the home. The middle-class dwelling was often not far removed from the working-class neighborhoods in geographical terms, but in social terms they were miles apart (Johnson, 1978).

Modern men were drawn to drinking places by an impetus perhaps analogous to that which spurred primitive men to gather around the fire at the mouth of the cave (London, 1913, pp. 6–7). In the saloon they could be part of a community, albeit one in which individual inhibitions were eroded by the chemical and psychological effects of alcohol. This sense of belonging to a larger community of men, was alien to the values of the middle classes, where the primary form of togetherness had always looked inward toward the family unit itself. Temperance activists argued that the man who drank heavily would lose interest in his family, would probably lose his job, his savings would be diminished, and eventually the family home would be lost.

Working-class men were faced with the drinking dilemma on a daily basis, although some had seen the benefits of sobriety and had embraced the temperance movement from its beginnings (Dawley & Faler, 1976). Considerably later than the middle classes, the working classes would also begin to aspire to the single-family home. For the factory worker whose life was spent in a world of noise and darkness, the home would become a "haven in a heartless world" (Cox, 1984). Although the turmoil of the city surrounded them, in their homes the working classes could find some degree of autonomy and privacy. In the home the working-class family could nurture and reproduce itself, thereby serving the goals of capital accumulation most effectively.

As this brief historical overview suggests, the idea of home has clearly meant much more than simply having an address and a place to seek shelter. It has also become an extension of one's self and one's values and has been something that people have been willing to go to very great lengths in order to have and to hold. For the individual who felt unable or unwilling to live independently and establish a home, in the 19th century the state began to provide some alternatives. Such people could find the sense of community and all the security they needed in institutions of many different types.

In the 1980s there are considerably fewer opportunities for such individuals to find a home in these institutions, as a result of the ever-expanding focus on the provision of services in the community. It is also apparent that the families wanting to establish their own homes are finding it much more difficult to do so in the 1980s, as a result of the structural changes in the economy. In other words, whatever one's concept of home may be, it has become increasingly likely that a satisfactory solution cannot be found. The community seekers and the autonomy seekers have found themselves together on the streets and in the city shelters (Segal & Baumohl, 1987; Segal, Baumohl, & Johnson, 1977).

The prospect of being without a home or a place to call home is terrifying to both those who have and have not experienced it. Unlike being mentally ill (or a drug addict, or a chronic alcoholic), being homeless is imaginable, but at the same time it is unthinkable. For this reason it has been relatively easy for politicians to use the media to generate a considerable amount of emotion about the issue of homelessness, emotion that can be chaneled into public support for immediate political action. Because of the intensity of public feeling about having and not having a home, it has been possible to win public support to provide services for individuals whose other problems (such as mental illness and alcoholism) generally tend to repulse the public. In this sense homelessness has provided a new label for the problem of chronic and multiple disability in the American city. In a relatively short period of time the homelessness issue became the nation's number-one social problem, where it stayed until dislodged by the AIDS epidemic in the middle of the 1980s. At this time the fear of being homeless was superseded by the fear of death. It remains to be seen whether the short-term intensity of the homelessness issue in the media can be translated into the long-term commitment needed to generate viable solutions to the problem.

NOTE

1. The one major exception to this would be the issue of drinking and driving, which has generated a level of emotion sufficient to persuade members of the public and politicians to support some major changes in alcohol control policies. For a fuller discussion of this issue see Smith (1985b).

Bibliography

Aaron, P. & Musto, D. (1981). Temperance and prohibition in America: A historical overview. In M. H. Moore & D. R. Gerstein (Eds.), *Alcohol and public policy: Beyond the shadow of prohibition* (pp. 127–181). Washington, DC: National Academy Press.

Adams, J. S., & Gilder, K. (1976). Household location and intra–urban migration. In D. T. Herbert & R. J. Johnston (Eds.), *Social areas in cities: Vol. 1. Spatial processes and form* (pp. 159–193). Chichester, England: Wiley.

Akins, C., & Williams, D. (1982). State and local programs on alcoholism. In *Prevention, intervention and treatment: Concerns and models* (Alcohol and Health Monograph No. 3, pp. 325–354). Rockville, MD: National Institute on Alcohol Abuse and Alcoholism (NIAAA).

Alba, R. D., & Batutis, M. J. (1984). The impact of migration on New York State. Albany, NY: The Public Policy Institute.

Albritton, R. D. (1979). Social amelioration through mass insurgency? A re-examination of the Piven and Cloward thesis. *The American Political Science Review, 73*, 1002–1011.

Alexander, C. (1967). The city as a mechanism for sustaining human contact. In W. R. Eward Jr. (Ed.), *Environment for man: The next fifty years* (pp. 60–102). Bloomington: Indiana University Press.

Altman, D. (1987). *AIDS in the mind of America: The social, political, and psychological impact of a new epidemic*. Garden City, NY: Anchor.

Altman, I. (1975). *The environment and social behavior*. Monterey, CA: Brooks-Cole.

Anderson, D. J. (1979). Delivery of essential services to alcoholics through the continuum of care. *Cancer Research, 39*, 2855–2858.

Andrews, H. F. (1985). The ecology of risk and the geography of intervention: From research to practice for the health and well-being of urban children. *Annals of the Association of American Geographers. 75*, 370–382.

Angrist, S. (1974). Dimensions of well-being in public housing families. *Environment and Behavior, 6*, 495–516.

Annis, H. M., & Smart, R. G. (1979). Arrests, readmissions and treatment following release from detoxification centers. *Journal of Studies on Alcohol, 39*, 1276–1283.

Appleby, L., & Desai, P. N. (1985). Documenting the relationship between homelessness and psychiatric hospitalization. *Hospital and Community Psychiatry, 36*, 732–737.

Arce, A. A., & Vergare, M. J. (1984). Identifying and characterizing the mentally ill among the homeless. In H. R. Lamb (Ed.), *The homeless mentally ill* (pp. 75–90). Washington, DC: American Psychiatric Association.

Archaud, P. (1979). *Vagrancy, alcoholism and social control*. London: MacMillan.

Armor, D. J., Polich, M. J., & Stamboul, H. B. (1976). *Alcoholism and treatment*. Santa Monica, CA: Rand Corporation.

Armstrong, D. (1980). Madness and coping. *Sociology of Health and Illness, 2*, 293–316.

Ashbaugh, J. W., Leaf, P. J., Manderscheid, R. W., & Eaton, W. (1983). Estimates of the size and selected characteristics of the adult chronically mentally ill population living in U.S.

households. In J. R. Greenley (Ed.), *Research in community and mental health* (Vol. 3, pp. 3–26). Greenwich, CT: JAI Press.

Ashbaugh, J. W., & Manderscheid, R. W. (1985). A method for estimating the chronic mentally ill population in state and local areas. *Hospital and Community Psychiatry, 36,* 389–393.

Austin, J., & Krisberg, B. (1981). Wider, stronger and different nets. *Journal of Research on Crime and Delinquency, 18,* 165–196.

Bachrach, L. L. (1976). *Deinstitutionalization: An analytical review and sociological perspective* (Monograph Series D, No. 4). Rockville, MD: National Institute of Mental Health.

Bachrach, L. L. (1980a). Is the least restrictive environment always the best? Sociological and semantic implications. *Hospital and Community Psychiatry, 31,* 97–103.

Bachrach, L. L. (1980b). Overview: Model programs for chronic mental patients. *American Journal of Psychiatry, 137,* 1023–1931.

Bachrach, L. L. (1984). Interpreting research on the homeless mentally ill. *Hospital and Community Psychiatry, 35,* 914–917.

Bacon, R., & Eltis, W. (1976). *Britain's economic problem: Too few producers.* London: MacMillan.

Bahr, H. M. (1967). The gradual disappearance of skid row. *Social Problems, 15,* 41–45.

Baker, S. L. (1982). *Substance abuse disorders in aging veterans.* Paper presented at the Sixth Annual Conference on Addiction Research and Treatment: Drugs, Alcohol and Aging, Coatsville, PA.

Ball, F. L. J., & Havassy, B. E. (1984). A survey of the problems and needs of homeless consumers of acute psychiatric services. *Hospital and Community Psychiatry, 35,* 917–921.

Barker, R. G. (1968). *Ecological psychology: Concepts and methods for studying the environment of human behavior.* Stanford, CA: Stanford University Press.

Barnes, J. A. (1954). Class and communities in a Norwegian island parish. *Human Relations, 7,* 39–48.

Baron, R. C., & Rutman, I. D. (1979). *These people: A citizen education project examining public response to community care for the mentally disabled.* Philadelphia, PA: Horizon House Institute for Research and Development.

Bassuk, E. L. (1984). The homeless problem. *Scientific American, 251,* 40–45.

Bassuk, E. L., & Gerson, S. (1978). Deinstitutionalization and mental health services. *Scientific American, 128,* 46–53.

Bassuk, E. L. & Lauriat, A. S. (1984). The Politics of Homelessness, In H. R. Lamb (Ed.), *The homeless mentally ill* (pp. 301–313). Washington, DC: American Psychiatric Association.

Baumohl, J., & Miller, H. (1974). *Down and out in Berkeley.* Berkeley, CA: City of Berkeley and University of California Community Affairs Committee.

Baxter, E., & Hopper, K. (1982). The new mendicancy: Homeless in New York City. *American Journal of Orthopsychiatry, 52,* 393–408.

Beauchamp, D. E. (1980). *Beyond alcoholism: Alcohol and public health policy.* Philadelphia: Temple University Press.

Becker, C., & Stanley, A. D. (1985). The downside of private prisons. *The Nation, 240* (23), 728–730.

Becker, H. S. (1963). *Outsiders.* New York: Free Press.

Beckman, L. J., & Amara, H. (1985). Patterns of women's use of treatment agencies. *Alcohol Health and Research World, 9,* 15–25.

Bellis, D. J. (1981). *Heroin and politicians: The failure of public policy to control addiction in America.* Westport, CT: Greenwood Press.

Berkman, L. F., & Syme, S. L. (1979). Social networks, host resistance, and mortality: A nine-year follow-up study of Alameda County residents. *American Journal of Epidemiology, 109,* 186–204.

Besser, J. D. (1975). The skid row explosion. *The Progressive, 39,* 51–53.

Betts, J., Moore, S. L., & Reynolds, P. (1981). A checklist for selecting board and care homes for chronic patients. *Hospital and Community Psychiatry, 32,* 498–499.

Biegel, A. (1982). Community mental health centers: A look ahead. *Hospital and Community Psychiatry, 33,* 741–746.

Binder, A., & Geis, G. (1984). Ad populum argumentation in criminology: Juvenile diversion as rhetoric. *Crime and Delinquency, 30,* 309–333.

Binford, H. C. (1985). *The first suburbs: Residential communities on the Boston periphery, 1815–1860.* Chicago: University of Chicago Press.

Blane, H. T., & Hewitt, L. E. (1977). *Alcohol and youth: An analysis of the literature 1960–1975* (Contract No. (ADM) 281-75-0026). Washington, DC: NIAAA.

Block, F. (1981). The fiscal crisis of the capitalist state. *Annual Review of Sociology, 7,* 1–27.

Blomberg, T. G. (1978). *Social control and the proliferation of juvenile court services.* San Francisco: R. & E. Research Associates.

Blomberg, T. G. (1979). Diversion from juvenile court: A review of the evidence. In F. L. Faust & P. L. Brantingham (Eds.), *Juvenile justice philosophy* (pp. 415–429). St. Paul, MN: West Publishing.

Blomberg, T. G. (1983). Diversion's disparate results: An integrated evaluation perspective. *Journal of Research in Crime and Delinquency, 20,* 24–38.

Bloom, B. L. (1977). *Community mental health: A general introduction.* Monterey, CA: Brooks/Cole.

Bluestone, B., & Harrison, B. (1982). *Capital versus community: The deindustrialization of America.* New York: Basic Books.

Blumberg, L. U., Shipley, T. F., Jr., & Barsky, S. F. (1978). *Liquor and poverty: Skid row as a human condition.* New Brunswick, NJ: Rutgers Center of Alcohol Studies.

Blume, S., Dropkin, D., & Sokolow, L. (1980). The Jewish alcoholic: A descriptive study. *Alcohol, Health and Research World, 4,* 21–26.

Blumin, S. M. (1985). The hypothesis of middle-class formation in nineteenth century America: A critique and some proposals. *The American Historical Review, 90,* 299–338.

Bogue, D. J. (1963). *Skid row in American cities.* Chicago: University of Chicago, Community and Family Study Center.

Bohland, J. R., & Davis, L. (1978). Sources of residential satisfaction amongst the elderly: An age comparison analysis. In S. Golant (Ed.), *Location and environment of the elderly population* (pp. 95–110). Chicago: V. H. Winston & Sons.

Bohland, J. R., & Treps, L. (1982). County patterns of elderly migration in the United States. In A. M. Warnes (Ed.), *Geographical perspectives on the elderly* (pp. 139–158). Chichester, England: Wiley.

Bohnstedt, M. (1978). Answers to three questions about diversion. *Journal of Research in Crime and Delinquency, 15,* 109–123.

Boissevain, J. (1974). *Friends of Friends.* Oxford: Basil Blackwell.

Borman, L. D. (1976). *Explorations in self-help and mutual aid.* Evanston, IL: Northwestern University, Center for Urban Affairs.

Bott, E. (1957). *Family and social network.* London: Tavistock.

Bourne, L. S. (1976). Housing supply and housing market behavior in residential development. In D. T. Herbert & R. J. Johnston (Eds.), *Social areas in cities: Vol. I. Spatial processes and form* (pp. 111–158). Chichester, England: Wiley.

Boyd, J. L., McGill, C. W., & Falloon, I. R. H. (1981). Family participation in the community rehabilitation of schizophrenics. *Hospital and Community Psychiatry, 32,* 624–632.

Boyer, P. (1978). *Urban masses and moral order in America, 1870–1920.* Cambridge, MA: Harvard University Press.

Braucht, G. N. (1982). Problem drinking among adolescents: A review and analysis of psychosocial research. In *Special population issues* (Alcohol and Health Monograph No. 4, pp. 143–166). Rockville, MD: NIAAA.

Braucht, G. N. (1983). How environments and persons combine to influence problem drinking. In M. Galanter (Ed.), *Recent developments in alcoholism* (Vol. 2, pp. 79–103). New York: Plenum.

Braverman, H. (1974). *Labor and monopoly capital: The degradation of work in the twentieth century.* New York: Monthly Review Press.

Brenner, M. H. (1973). *Mental illness and the economy.* Cambridge, MA: Harvard University Press.

Brenner, M. H. (1975). Trends in alcohol consumption and associated illness. *American Journal of Public Health, 65,* 1279–1292.

Brenner, M. H., & Mooney, A. (1983). Unemployment and health in the context of economic change. *Social Science and Medicine, 17,* 1125–1138.

Brewer's Society. (1984). *UK statistical handbook, 1983.* London: Brewing Publications.

Brown, E. J., Flanagan, T. J., & McCleod, M. (Eds.), *Sourcebook of criminal justice statistics— 1983.* Washington, DC: U.S. Government Printing Office.

Brown, P. (1979). The transfer of care: U.S. mental health policy since World War II. *International Journal of Health Services, 9,* 645–662.

Brown, P. (1981). The mental patients' rights movement and mental health institutional change. *International Journal of Health Services, 2,* 523–540.

Brown, P. (1984). Marxism, social psychology, and the sociology of mental health. *International Journal of Health Services, 14,* 237–264.

Brown, P. (1985). *The transfer of care: Psychiatric deinstitutionalization and its aftermath.* Boston: Routledge & Kegan Paul.

Brown, P., & Smith, C. J. (1987). Mental patients rights: An empirical study of variation across the United States. *International Journal of Law and Psychiatry.*

Brownlea, A. (1981). From public health to political epidemiology. *Social Science and Medicine, 2,* 57–67.

Bruun, K., Edwards, G., Lumio, M., Makela, K., Pan, L., Popham, R. E., Room, R., Schmidt, W., Skog, O. J., Sulkuner, P., & Osterberg, E. (1975). *Alcohol control policies in public health perspective* (Publication 25). Helsinki: Finnish Foundation for Alcohol Studies.

Bullington, B., Sprowls, J., Katkin, D., & Phillips, M. (1982). A critique of diversionary juvenile justice. In D. G. Rojek & G. F. Jensen (Eds.), *Readings in juvenile delinquency* (pp. 311–315). Lexington, MA: Heath.

Bunce, R. P., Morgan, P., Mosher, J., Wallack, L., & Wittner, F. (1979). *The structure of the alcohol market: A conceptual framework.* Unpublished Manuscript, University of California. Social Research Group, School of Public Health, Berkeley.

Burnett, A., & Moon, G. (1983). Community opposition to hostels for homeless men. *Area, 15,* 161–166.

Burt, M. R., & Pittman, K. J. (1984). *Helping the helpless: The impact of changes in support programs during the Reagan administration.* Discussion Paper, The Urban Institute, Washington, DC.

Buss, T. F., & Redburn, F. S. (1983). *Mass unemployment: Plant closings and community mental health.* Beverly Hills, CA: Sage.

Buss, T. F., & Redburn, F. S. (1987). Psychological well-being of workers in distressed communities. In C. J. Smith & J. A. Giggs (Eds.), *Location and stigma: Emerging themes in mental health and mental illness.* London: George Allen & Unwin.

Cahalan, D. (1970). *Problem drinkers: A national survey.* San Francisco: Jossey-Bass.

Cahalan, D., Cisin, I. H., & Crossley, H. M. (1969). *American drinking practices: A national study of drinking behavior and attitudes* (Monograph G). New Brunswick, NJ: Rutgers University, Rutgers Center of Alcohol Studies.

Cahalan, D., & Room, R. (1974). *Problem drinking among American men* (Monograph #7). New Brunswick, NJ: Rutgers University, Rutgers Center of Alcohol Studies.

Campbell, A., Converse, P., & Rodgers, W. (1976). *The quality of American life.* New York: Russell Sage Foundation.

Caplan, G., & Killilea, M. (1976). *Support systems and mutual help: Multidisciplinary explanations.* New York: Grune & Stratton.

Carp, F. M. (1977). Impact of improved living environment on health and life expectancy. *Gerontologist, 17,* 242–249.

Carson, G. (1984). *The social history of bourbon: An unhurried account of our star-spangled American drink.* Lexington: University of Kentucky Press.

Cassel, J. (1970). Physical illness in response to stress. In S. Levine & N. A. Scotch (Eds.), *Social stress* (pp. 189–209). Chicago: Aldine.

Castells, M. (Ed.). (1985). *High technology, space, and society.* Beverly Hills, CA: Sage.

Catalano, R., & Dooley, D. (1977). Economic predictors of depressed mood and stressful life events in a metropolitan community. *Journal of Health and Social Behavior, 18,* 292–307.

Catalano, R., & Dooley, D. (1981). The behavioral costs of economic instability. *Policy Studies Journal, 10,* 338–349.

Cavan, S. (1966). *Liquor license: An ethnography of bar behavior.* Chicago: Aldine.

Celluci, T. (1984). The prevention of alcohol problems: Conceptual and methodological issues. In P. M. Miller & T. D. Niremberg (Eds.), *Prevention of alcohol abuse* (pp. 15–54). New York: Plenum.

Chauncey, R. L. (1980). New careers for moral entrepreneurs: Teenage drinking. *Journal of Drug Issues, 10,* 45–70.

Chu, F., & Trotter, S. (1974). *The madness establishment.* New York: Grossman.

Clark, N. H. (1976). *Deliver us from evil: An interpretation of American prohibition.* New York: Norton.

Clark, W. A. V. (1981). Residential mobility and behavioral geography: Parallelism or independence? In K. R. Cox & R. G. Golledge (Eds.), *Behavioral problems in geography revisited* (pp. 182–208). New York: Methuen.

Clark, W. B. (1981). Public drinking contexts: Bars and taverns. In T. C. Harford & L. A. Gaines (Eds.), *Social drinking contexts* (NIAAA Research Monograph No. 7, pp. 8–23). Rockville, MD: NIAAA.

Clark, W. B., & Midanik, L. (1982). Alcohol use and alcohol problems among U.S. adults: Results of the 1979 national survey. In *Alcohol consumption and related problems* (Alcohol and Health Monograph No. 1, pp. 3–54). Rockville, MD: NIAAA.

Cohen, S. (1979). The punitive city: Notes on the dispersal of social control. *Contemporary Crises, 3,* 339–363.

Collins, A. H., & Pancoast, D. L. (1976). *Natural helping networks: A strategy for prevention.* Washington, DC: National Association of Social Workers.

Conklin, J. E. (1976). Robbery, the elderly, and fear: An urban problem in search of solution. In J. Goldsmith & S. Goldsmith (Eds.), *Crime and the elderly* (pp. 99–110). Lexington, MA: Heath.

Conrad, P., & Schneider, J. W. (1980). *Deviance and medicalization: From badness to sickness.* St. Louis, MO: C. Mosby.

Cook, P. J. (1981). The effect of liquor taxes on drinking, cirrhosis and auto fatalities. In M. H. Moore & D. Gerstein (Eds.), *Alcohol and public policy* (pp. 255–285). Washington, DC: National Academy Press.

Cook, P. J. (1984). Increasing the federal alcohol excise tax. In D. R. Gerstein (Ed.), *Toward the prevention of alcohol problems: Government, business, and community* (pp. 24–38). Washington, DC: National Academy Press.

Cook, P. J., & Tauchen, G. (1981). *The effect of liquor taxes on alcoholism.* Unpublished manuscript, Duke University, Center for Demographic Studies, Durham, NC.

Corrigan, P., & Leonard, P. (1978). *Social work practice under capitalism: A Marxist approach.* London: Macmillan.

Corwin, N. (1984). *Trivializing America.* Secaucus, NJ: Lyle Stuart.

Costello, R. M. (1973a). Alcoholism treatment and evaluation: In search of methods, I. *International Journal of Addictions, 10,* 251–275.

Costello, R. M. (1973b). Alcoholism treatment and evaluation: In search of methods, II. *International Journal of Addictions. 10,* 857–867.

Cox, K. (1984). Social change, turf politics, and concepts of turf politics. In A. Kirby, P. Knox, & S. Pinch (Eds.), *Public service provision and urban development* (pp. 283–315). New York: St. Martins Press.

Craik, K. H. (1973). Environmental psychology. *Annual Review of Psychology, 24,* 403–422.

Craik, K. H. (1976). The personality research paradigm in environmental psychology. In S. Wapner, S. B. Cohen, & B. Kaplan (Eds.), *Experiencing the environment* (pp. 55–79). New York: Plenum.

Creer, C., & Wing, J. K. (1974). *Schizophrenia at home.* London: National Schizophrenia Fellowship.

Crook, T., & Cohen, G. (1984). Future directions for research on alcohol and the elderly. *Alcohol Health and Research World, 8,* 24–30.

Cutler, R. E., & Storm, T. (1975). Observational study of alcohol consumption in natral settings: The Vancouver beer parlor. *Journal of Studies on Alcohol, 36,* 1173–1183.

Cutter, S. L. (1985). *Rating places: A geographers view on quality of life.* Washington, DC: Association of American Geographers, Resource Publication Series.

Dahrendorf, R. (1958). Out of Utopia: Toward a reorientation of sociological analysis. *American Journal of Sociology, 64,* 115–127.

Daiches, S. (1981). *People in distress: A geographical perspective on psychological well-being,* (Research Paper No. 197). Chicago: University of Chicago, Department of Geography.

Dannenbaum, J. (1984). *Drink and disorder: Temperance reform in Cincinnati from the Washington revival to the WCTU.* Urbana: University of Illinois Press.

Davies, P., & Walsh, D. (1983). *Alcohol problems and alcohol control in Europe.* London: Croom-Helm.

Davis, J. A., Spaeth, J. L., & Huson, C. (1961). A technique for analyzing the effects of group compensation. *American Sociological Review, 26,* 215–225.

Davis, N. J., & Anderson, B. (1983). *Social control: The production of deviance in the modern state.* New York: Irvington.

Dawley, A., & Faler, P. (1976). Working class culture and politics in the industrial revolution: Sources of loyalism and rebellion. *Journal of Social History, 9,* 466–480.

Dean, A., & Lin, N. (1977). The stress buffering role of social support. *The Journal of Nervous and Mental Disease 165,* 403–417.

Dear, M. (1976). Abandoned housing. In J. S. Adams (Ed.), *Urban policymaking and metropolitan dynamics: A comparative geographical analysis* (pp. 59–99). Cambridge, MA: Ballinger.

Dear, M. (1977). Psychiatric patients and the inner city. *Annals of the Association of American Geographers, 67,* 588–594.

Dear, M. (1980). The public city. In W. A. V. Clark & E. G. Moore (Eds.), *Residential mobility and public policy* (pp. 219–241). Beverly Hills, CA: Sage.

Dear, M., & Long, J. (1978). Community strategies in locational conflict. In K. R. Cox (Ed.), *Urbanization and conflict in market societies* (pp. 113–128). Chicago: Maarovfa Press.

Dear, M., & Taylor, S. M. (1982). *Not on our street.* London: Pion.

Decker, S. H. (1985). A systematic analysis of diversion: Net widening and beyond. *Journal of Criminal Justice, 13,* 207–216.

DeLannoy, W. (1975). Residential segregation of foreigners in Brussels. *Bulletin Societé Belge d'Études Géographiques, 44,* 215–238.

Dengerink, H. A., Marks, D. A., Hammarlund, M. R., & Hammond, B. E. M. (1981). The decision of psychologists to practice in urban or rural areas. *Journal of Rural Community Psychology, 2* (2), 1–11.

Dennis, R. (1984). *English industrial cities of the nineteenth century: A social geography.* Cambridge, England: Cambridge University Press.

Dicken, P., & Lloyd, P. E. (1981). *Modern Western society: A geographical perspective on work, home and well-being.* New York: Harper & Row.

Diesenhaus, H. (1982). Current trends in treatment programming for problem drinkers and alcoholics. In *Prevention, intervention and treatment: Concerns and models* (Alcohol and Health Monograph No. 3, pp. 219–292). Rockville, MD: NIAAA.

Dight, S. (1976). *Scottish drinking habits: A survey of Scottish drinking habits and attitudes towards alcohol carried out in 1972 for the Scottish Home and Health Department.* London: Her Majesty's Stationery Office.

Ditton, J. (1979). *Controlology: Beyond the new criminology.* London: Macmillan.

Dohrenwend, B. P., & Chin-Shong, E. (1969). Social status and attitudes toward behavioral disorder: The problem of tolerance of deviance. In L. C. Kolb et al. (Eds.), *Urban challenges to psychiatry* (pp. 91–118). Boston: Little, Brown.

Dohrenwend, B. P., Dohrenwend, B. S., Schwartz-Gould, M., Link, B., Neugebauer, R., & Wunsch-Hitzig, R. (1980). *Mental illness in the United States: Epidemiological estimates.* New York: Praeger.

Doll, W. (1976). Family coping and the mentally ill: An unanticipated problem of deinstitutionalization. *Hospital and Community Psychiatry, 27,* 183–185.

Doll, W. (1980). *The burden of coping: The family and the former mental patient in an era of deinstitutionalization* (NIMH Grant 5R01-NH-16927). Rockville, MD: NIMH.

Dooley, D., Catalano, R. J., & Brownell, A. (1981). Economic, life, and symptom changes in a non-metropolitan community. *Journal of Health and Social Behavior, 22,* 144–154.

Dorn, N. (1983). *Alcohol, youth and the state.* London: Croom-Helm.

Downs, R. M. (1981). Cognitive mapping: A thematic analysis. In K. R. Cox & R. G. Golledge (Eds.), *Behavioral Problems in Geography Revisited* (pp. 45–122). New York: Methuen.

Downs, R. M., & Stea, D. (1973). *Image and environment.* Chicago: Aldine.

Doyal, L. (1979). *The political economy of health.* London: Pluto Press.

Drew, L. R. H. (1968). Alcoholism as a self-limiting disease. *Journal of Studies on Alcohol, 29,* 956–967.

Duis, P. R. (1983). *The saloon: Public drinking in Chicago and Boston, 1880–1920.* Urbana: University of Illinois Press.

Dunford, F. W., Osgood, D. W., & Weichselbaum, H. F. (1982). *National evaluation of diversion projects: Executive summary.* Washington, DC: U.S. Government Printing Office.

Dunham, R. G., & Janik, S. W. (1985). Adoption of the Uniform Alcoholism Act and the availability of alcoholism treatment programs. *International Journal of the Addictions, 26,* 503–518.

DuPont, R. L. (1971). Profile of a heroin-addiction epidemic. *New England Journal of Medicine, 285,* 320–324.

Durand, R., & Eckart, D. R. (1973). Social rank, residential effects and community satisfaction. *Social Forces, 52,* 74–85.

Duster, T. (1970). *The legislation of morality: Law, drugs, and moral judgement.* New York: Free Press.

Edwards, G. (1983 December). Preface for "Alcoholic Beverages: Dimensions of Corporate Power." *The Globe, 4,* 3–43.

Ehrenreich, B. (1983). *The hearts of men: American dreams and the flight from commitment.* Garden City, NY: Anchor Press/Doubleday.

Ehrenreich, P. (1982). Entitlements—for whom? Where the health dollar really goes. *The Nation, 234,* 586–588.

Engels, F. (1958). *The condition of the working class in England* (W. Henderson & W. K. Chalomer, Trans.). Oxford: Blackwell.

Epstein, E. J. (1977). *Agency of fear.* New York: Putnam.

Epstein, B. L. (1981). *The politics of domesticity: Women, evangelism, and temperance in nineteenth century America.* Middletown CN: Wesleyan University Press.

Estes, C. L. (1981). *The aging enterprise.* San Francisco, CA: Jossey-Bass.

Estes, C. L., & Harrington, C. A. (1981). Fiscal crisis, deinstitutionalization, and the elderly. *American Behavioral Scientist, 24,* 811–826.

Etzioni, A. (1976). *Social problems.* Englewood Cliffs, NJ: Prentice-Hall.

Evans, R. L., & Northwood, L. K. (1979). The utility of natural help relationships. *Social Science and Medicine, 13A*, 789–795.

Eyer, J. (1976). Review of mental illness and the economy. *International Journal of Health Services, 6*, 139–148.

Eyer, J. (1977). Prosperity as a cause of death. *International Journal of Health Services, 7*, 125–150.

Eyles, J., & Woods, K. J. (1983). *The social geography of medicine and health.* New York: St. Martin's Press.

Fagan, R. W., & Mauss, A. L. (1978). Padding the revolving door: An initial assessment of the Uniform Alcoholism and Intoxication Treatment Act in practice. *Social Problems, 26*, 232–247.

Faris, R. E., & Dunham, H. W. (1939). *Mental disorders in urban areas.* Chicago: University of Chicago Press.

Federal Bureau of Invesigation. (1982). *Crime in the United States, 1981.* Washington, DC: U.S. Government Printing Office.

Finn, P. (1985). Decriminalization of public drunkenness: Response of the health care system. *Journal of Studies on Alcohol, 46*, 7–23.

Fischer, C. S. (1975). Toward a sub-cultural theory of urbanism. *American Journal of Sociology, 80*. 1319–1341.

Fischer, C. S. (1976). *The urban experience.* New York: Harcourt, Brace & Jovanovich.

Fischer, C. S. (1978). *Networks and places: Social relations in the urban setting.* New York: Free Press.

Fischer, C. S. (1981). The public and private worlds of city life. *American Sociological Review, 46*, 306–316.

Fischer, C. S. (1982). *To dwell among friends.* Chicago: University of Chicago Press.

Fisher, J. C. (1981). Psychosocial correlates of tavern use: A national probability sample study. In T. C. Harford & L. S. Gaines (Eds.), *Social drinking contexts* (Research Monograph No. 7, pp. 34–53). Rockville, MD: NIAAA.

Flasher, L. V., & Maisto, S. A. (1984). A review of theory and research on drinking patterns among Jews. *The Journal of Nervous and Mental Disease, 172*, 596–603.

Foley, H. A. (1975). *Community Mental Health legislation.* Lexington, MA: Heath.

Foley, H. A., & Sharfstein, S. S. (1983). *Madness and government: Who cares for the mentally ill?* Washington, DC: American Psychiatric Press.

Foucault, M. (1976). *Madness and civilization: A history of insanity in the Age of Reason.* New York: Vintage.

Foucault, M. (1977). *Discipline and punish: The birth of the prison.* New York: Pantheon.

Freed, E. X. (1979). *The alcoholic personality.* New York: Charles B. Slack.

Freeman, H. L. (1978). Mental Health and the Environment. *British Journal of Psychiatry, 132*, 113–124.

Friedland, R. (1976). Class, power and social control: The war on poverty. *Politics and Society, 6*, 459–489.

Friedson, E. (1970). *Profession of medicine.* New York: Harper & Row.

Froland, C., Pancoast, D. L., Chapman, N. J., & Kimboko, P. J. (1981). *Helping networks and human services.* Beverly Hills, CA: Sage.

Gaines, L. S. (1981). Cognition and the environment: Implications for a self-awareness theory of drinking. In T. C. Harford & L. S. Gaines (Eds.), *Social drinking contexts* (Research Monograph No. 7, pp. 138–154). Rockville, MD: NIAAA.

Galle, O. R., Gove, W. R., & McPherson, J. M., (1972). Population density and pathology: What are the relations for man? *Science, 176*, 23–30.

Garber, J. J., Dolander, E. V., & Dexter, J. D. (1974 February). Alcoholic detoxification: A one year experience. *Minnesota Medicine*, 143–145.

Garfinkel, I., & Haveman, R. H. (1977). *Earnings capacity, poverty and inequality.* New York: Academic Press.

Gerstein, D. R. (Ed.), (1984). *Toward the prevention of alcohol problems: Government, business, and community*. Washington, DC: National Academy Press.

Gibbons, D., & Blake, G. (1976). Evaluating the impact of juvenile diversion programs. *Journal of Crime and Delinquency, 22*, 411–420.

Gibbs, J. P. (1981). *Norms, deviance, and social control*. New York: Elsevier.

Gifford, P., & Louis, W. R. (Eds.), (1967). *Britain and Germany in Africa*. New Haven, CT: Yale University Press.

Giggs, J. A. (1979). Human health problems in urban areas. In D. T. Herbert & D. M. Smith (Eds.), *Social problems and the city: Geographical perspectives* (pp. 84–116). Oxford: Oxford University Press.

Gilbert, N. E. (1984). Welfare for profit: Moral, empirical, and theoretical perspectives. *Journal of Social Policy, 13*, 63–74.

Gilder, G. F. (1980). *Wealth and poverty*. New York: Basic Books.

Glaser, F. B., Greenberg, S. W., & Barrett, M. (1978). *A systems approach to alcohol treatment*. Toronto: Addiction Research Foundation.

Glassner, B., & Berg, B. (1980). How Jews avoid alcohol problems. *American Sociological Review, 45*, 647–664.

Glassner, B., & Berg, B. (1984). Social locations and interpretations: How Jews define alcoholism. *Journal of Studies on Alcohol, 45*, 16–25.

Goffman, E. (1961). *Asylums: Essays on the social situation of mental patients and other inmates*. New York: Anchor Books.

Golant, S. M. (1980). Locational-environmental perspectives on old-age segregated residential areas in the United States. In D. T. Herbert & R. J. Johnston (Eds.), *Geography and the urban environment* (Vol. 3, pp. 257–294). Chichester, England: Wiley.

Golant, S. M. (1982). Individual differences underlying the dwelling satisfaction of the elderly. *Journal of Social Issues, 38*, 121–133.

Golant, S. M. (1984). The effects of residential and activity behaviors on old peoples' environmental experiences. In I. Altman, M. P. Lawton, & J. Wohlwill (Eds.), *Elderly people and the environment* (pp. 239–278). New York: Plenum.

Goldberg, P. (1980). The federal government's response to illicit drugs, 1969–1978. In *The Drug Abuse Council: The facts about "drug abuse"* (pp. 20–62). New York: Free Press.

Goldenberg, I. (1982). On the creation of the new social settings. In T. R. Vallance & R. M. Sabre (Eds.), *Mental health services in transition: A policy sourcebook* (pp. 83–96). New York: Human Sciences Press.

Goldfarb, C. (1970). Patients nobody wants: Skid row alcoholics. *Disease of the Nervous System, 31*, 274–281.

Goldman, H. H. (1980). The post-hospital mental patient and family therapy: Prospects and populations. *Journal of Marriage and Family Therapy, 6*, 447–452.

Goldman, H. H. (1982). Mental illness and the family burden: A public health perspective. *Hospital and Community Psychiatry, 33*, 557–560.

Goldman, H. H., Adams, N. H., & Taube, C. A. (1983). Deinstitutionalization: The data demythologized. *Hospital and Community Psychology, 34*, 129–134.

Goldman, H. H., Regier, D. A., Taube, C. A., Redick, R. W., & Bass, R. D. (1980). Community mental health centers and the treatment of severe mental disorder. *American Journal of Psychiatry, 137*, 83–86.

Gomberg, E. (1982). Alcohol use and problems among the elderly. In *Special population issues* (Alcohol and Health Monograph No. 4, pp. 203–292). Rockville, MD: NIAAA.

Gordon, D. M. (1977). Class struggle and the stages of American urban development. In D. D. Perry & A. J. Watkins (Eds.), *The rise of the Sunbelt cities* (pp. 55–82). Beverly Hills, CA: Sage.

Gordon, D. M. (1978). Capitalist development and the history of American cities. In W. K. Tabb & L. Sawyers (Eds.), *Marxism and the metropolis* (pp. 25–63). New York: Oxford University Press.

Gough, I. (1979). *The political economy of the welfare state*. London: Macmillan.

Gove, W. R., & Hughes, M. (1983). *Overcrowding in the household: An analysis of determinants and effects*. New York: Academic Press.

Grad, J., & Sainsbury, P. (1966). Evaluating the community psychiatric service in Chichester: Results. *Milbank Memorial Fund Quarterly, 44:* 246–277.

Graff, T. O., & Wiseman, R. F. (1978). Changing concentrations of older Americans. *The Geographical Review, 68,* 379–393.

Graham, K., La Rocque, L., Yefman, R., Ross, T. J., & Guistra, E. (1980). Aggression and barroom environments. *Journal of Studies on Alcohol, 41,* 277–292.

Granovetter, M. (1973). The strength of weak ties. *American Journal of Sociology, 78,* 1360–1380.

Granovetter, M. (1976). Network sampling: Some first steps. *American Sociological Review, 81,* 1287–1303.

Greeley, A. M., McCready, W. C., & Thiesen, G. (1980). *Ethnic drinking subcultures*. New York: Praeger.

Greenberg, D. F. (1977). Socio-economic status and criminal sentences: Is there an association? *American Sociological Review, 42,* 174–175.

Grob, G. N. (1966). *The state and the mentally ill*. Chapel Hill: University of North Carolina Press.

Grob, G. N. (1973). *Mental institutions in America: Social policy to 1875*. New York: Free Press.

Grob, G. N. (1977). Rediscovering asylums: The unhistorical history of the mental hospital. *Hastings Center Report, 7,* 33–41.

Gross, M. L. (1978). *The psychological society*. New York: Simon & Schuster.

Gruenberg, E. M., Terns, D. M. & Pepper, B. (1976). The epidemiology of mental disorders. In A. Dean, A. M. Kraft, & B. Pepper (Eds.), *The social setting of mental health* (pp. 274–295). New York: Basic Books.

Gusfield, J. R. (1963). *Symbolic crusade*. Urbana: University of Illinois Press.

Gusfield, J. R. (1981). Managing competence: An ethnographic study of drinking–driving and the context of bars. In T. C. Harford & L. S. Gaines (Eds.), *Social drinking contexts* (Research Monograph No. 7, pp. 155–172). Rockville, MD: NIAAA.

Gusfield, J. R. (1982a). *The culture of public problems: Drinking–driving and the symbolic order*. Chicago: Univ. of Chicago Press.

Gusfield, J. R. (1982b). Deviance in the welfare state: The alcoholism profession and the entitlements of stigma. In M. Lewis (Ed.), *Research in social problems and public policy* (Vol. 2, pp. 1–20). Greenwich, CT: JAI Press.

Gusfield, J. R. (1982c). Prevention: Rise, decline and renaissance. In E. L. Gomberg, H. R. White, & J. A. Carpenter (Eds.), *Alcohol, science and society revisited* (pp. 402–425). Ann Arbor, MI: University of Michigan Press.

Gusfield, J. R. (1984). On the side: Practical action and social constructivism in social problems theory. In J. W. Schneider & J. I. Kitsuse (Eds.), *Studies in the sociology of social problems* (pp.31–51). Norwood, NJ: Albtex Publishing Corp.

Hakim, S., & Rengert, G. F. (Eds.). (1981). *Crime spillover*. Beverly Hills, CA: Sage.

Hale, N. G., Jr. (1971). *Freud and the Americans: The beginnings of psychoanalysis in the United States 1876–1917*. London: Oxford University Press.

Hamilton, J. R. (1979). Evaluation of a detoxification service for habitual drunken offenders. *British Journal of Psychiatry, 135,* 28–34.

Harford, T. C. (1979). Ecological factors in drinking. In H. T. Blane & M. E. Chafetz (Eds.), *Youth, alcohol, and social policy* (pp. 147–182). New York: Plenum.

Harford, T. C. (1984). Situational factors in drinking: A developmental perspective on drinking contexts. In P. M. Miller & T. D. Nirenberg (Eds.), *Prevention of alcohol abuse* (pp. 119–160). New York: Plenum.

Harford, T. C., & Gaines, L. S. (Eds.). (1981). *Social drinking contexts* (Research Monograph No. 7.) Rockville, MD: NIAAA.

Harford, T. C., Parker, D. A., Pautler, C., & Wolz, M. (1979). Relationships between the number of on-premise outlets and alcoholism. *Journal of Studies on Alcohol, 40,* 1053–1057.

Harford, T. C., & Spiegler, D. L. (1982). Environmental influences in adolescent drinking. In *Special Population Issues* (Alcohol and Health Monograph No. 4, pp. 167–193). Rockville, MD: NIAAA.

Harries, K. D. (1980). *Crime and the environment.* Springfield, IL: C. C. Thomas.

Harris, L. (1982, May 24). *The Harris Survey.* New York: The Chicago Tribune–New York Times Syndicate.

Harvey, D. (1981). The urban process under capitalism: A framework for analysis. In M. Dear & A. J. Scott (Eds.), *Urbanization and urban planning in capitalist society* (pp. 91–122. London: Methuen.

Hatfield, A. B. (1978). The psychological costs of schizophrenia to the family. *Social Work, 23,* 355–359.

Hatfield, A. B. (1979). The family as partner in the treatment of mental illness. *Hospital and Community Psychiatry, 30,* 32–34.

Heather, N., & Robertson, I. (1981). *Controlled drinking.* London: Methuen.

Heintz, K. M. (1976). *Retirement communities for adults only.* New Brunswick, NJ: Center for Urban Policy Research.

Helmer, J. (1975). *Drugs and minority oppression.* New York: The Seabury Press.

Herbert, D. T. (1982). *The geography of urban crime.* London: Longman.

Higham, J. (1978). *Strangers in the land: Patterns of American nativism, 1860–1925.* New York: Atheneum.

Himmelfarb, G. (1984). Denigrating the rule of reason: The "New History" goes bottom-up. *Harpers, 268,* 84–90.

Hindelang, M. J., Hirschi, T., & Weis, J. G. (1981). *Measuring delinquency.* Beverly Hills, CA: Sage.

Hinrichsen, J. J. (1984). Toward improving treatment services for alcoholics of advanced age. *Alcohol Health and Research World, 8,* 30–40.

Hinsie, L. E., & Campbell, R. J. (1970). Psychiatric dictionary, (4th ed.). New York: Oxford University Press.

Hirschorn, L. (1978). The political economy of social service rationalizations: A developmental view. *Contemporary Crises, 2,* 63–81.

Hirschorn, L. (1979). The theory of social services in disaccumulationist capitalism. *International Journal of Health Services, 9,* 295–311.

Hoenig, J., & Hamilton, M. W. (1969). *The desegregation of the mentally ill.* London: Routledge & Kegan Paul.

Holcomb, H. B., & Beauregard, R. A. (1981). *Revitalizing cities.* Washington DC: Association of American Geographers, Research Publications in Geography.

Hollingshead, A. B., & Redlich, F. C. (1958). *Social class and mental illness.* New York: Wiley.

Hombs, M. E., & Snyder, M. (1982). *Homeless in America: A forced march to nowhere.* Washington, DC: Community for Creative Non-Violence.

Horwitz, A. V. (1977). Social networks and pathways to psychiatric treatment. *Social Forces, 56,* 86–105.

Horwitz, A. V. (1982). *The social control of mental illness.* New York: Academic Press.

Howlett, F. W. (1982). Is the Youth Service Bureau all it's cracked up to be? In D. G. Rojek & G. F. Jensen (Eds.), *Readings in juvenile delinquency* (pp. 307–310). Lexington, MA: Heath.

Hubbard, R. L. Cavanaugh, E. R. Rachal, J. V., Schlenger, W. E., & Ginzburg, H. M. (1983). Alcohol use and problems among adolescent clients in drug treatment programs. *Alcohol Health and Research World, 7,* 10–18.

Huffine, C. L., & Craig, T. J. (1973). Catchment and community. *Archives of General Psychiatry, 28,* 438–488.

Hunt, L. G. (1974). *Recent spread of heroin use in the United States: Unanswered questions.* Washington, DC: Drug Abuse Council.

Hunt, L. G., & Chambers, C. D. (1976). *The heroin epidemics*. New York: Spectrum.

Ignatieff, M. (1978). *A just measure of pain: The penitentiary in the Industrial Revolution, 1750–1850*. New York: Columbia University Press.

Ignatieff, M. (1983). State, civil society and total institutions: A critique of recent social histories of punishment. In S. Cohen & A. Schull (Eds.), *Social control and the state: Historical and comparative essays* (pp. 75–105). Oxford: Martin Robertson.

Irving, H. W. (1977). Social networks in the modern city. *Social Forces, 55,* 867–879.

Ittelson, W. H., Rivlin, L. G., & Proshansky, H. M. (1970). The environmental psychology of the psychiatric ward. In H. M. Proshansky, W. H. Ittelson, & L. G. Rivlin (Eds.), *Environmental psychology: Man and his physical setting* (pp. 419–439). New York: Holt, Rinehart & Winston.

Jackson, K. T. (1985). *Crabgrass frontier: The suburbanization of the United States*. New York: Oxford University Press.

Jacobs, J. (1984). *Cities and the wealth of nations: Principles of economic life*. New York: Random House.

Jacoby, R. (1983). *The repression of psychoanalysis: Otto Fenichel and the political Freudians*. New York: Basic Books.

Janowitz, M. (1978). *The last half century*. Chicago: The University of Chicago Press.

Jeger, A. M., & Slotnick, R. S. (1982). *Community mental health and behavioral ecology: A handbook of theory, research and practice*. New York: Plenum.

Jessor, R., & Jessor, S. L. (1980). Toward a social-psychological perspective on the prevention of alcohol abuse. In T. C. Harford, Parker, D. A., & Light, L. (Eds.), *Normative approaches to the prevention of alcohol abuse and alcoholism* (Research Monograph No. 3, pp. 37–46). Rockville, MD: NIAAA.

Jirovec, R. L. (1984). Reaganomics and social welfare: An annotated bibliography. *Public Welfare, 42,* 23–27.

Johnson, P. (1978). *A shopkeeper's millenium: Society and revivals in Rochester, New York, 1815–1837*. New York: Hill & Wang.

Johnston, R. J. (1985). *City and society: An outline for urban geography*. London: Hutchinson.

Jones, K. (1982). Scull's dilemma. *British Journal of Psychiatry, 141,* 221–226.

Jones, P. N. (1979). Ethnic areas in British cities. In D. T. Herbert & D. M. Smith (Eds.), *Social problems and the city: Geographical perspectives* (pp. 158–185). Oxford: Oxford University Press.

Kadushin, C. (1969). *Why people go to psychiatrists*. New York: Atherton.

Kahn, R. L., & Antonucci, T. C. (1980). Convoys over the life course: Attachment, roles, and social support. In P. B. Baltes & O. G. Brim (Eds.), *Life-span development and behavior* (Vol. 3, pp. 253–286). New York: Academic Press.

Kaplan, R. (1977). Preference and everyday nature: Method and application. In D. Stokols (Ed.), *Perspectives on environment and behavior: Theory, research, and applications* (pp. 235–250). New York: Plenum.

Kaplan, S. (1972a). The challenge of environmental psychology: A proposal for a new functionalism. *American Psychologist, 27,* 140–143.

Kaplan, S. (1972b). *Knowing man: Towards a humane environment*. Unpublished Manuscript, University of Michigan, Department of Psychology, Ann Arbor, MI.

Kasl, S. V., & Cobb, S. (1966a). Health behavior, illness behavior and sick-role behavior: I. Health and illness behavior. *Archives of Environment Health, 12,* 246–266.

Kasl, S. V., & Harburg, E. (1975). Mental health and the urban environment: Some doubts and second thoughts. *Journal of Health and Social Behavior, 16,* 268–282.

Katz, A. H., & Bender, E. I. (1976). *The strength in us*. New York: New Viewpoints.

Katz, M. (1978, Winter). Origins of the institutional state. *Marxist Perspectives,* 6–22.

Katznelson, I. (1976). The crisis of the capitalist city: Urban politics and social control. In W. D. Hawley & M. Lipsky (Eds.), *Theoretical perspectives on urban politics* (pp. 214–229). Englewood Cliffs, NJ: Prentice-Hall.

Katznelson, I., & Kesselman, M. (1979). *The politics of power: A critical introduction to American government.* New York: Harcourt, Brace & Jovanovich.

Keeley, K. A., & Bell, R. A. (1976). Detoxification units and the prevention of alcoholism. *Annals of the New York Academy of Sciences, 272–273,* 395–402.

Keller, M. (1975). Problems of epidemiology in alcohol problems. *Journal of Studies on Alcohol, 36,* 1442–1452.

Kendell, R. E. (1984). The beneficial consequences of the United Kingdom's declining per capita consumption of alcohol in 1979–1982. *Alcohol and Alcoholism, 19,* 271–276.

Kenig, S. (1981). *Limits on theory: A cast study of the relationships of market and state to theory in the Community Mental Health movement.* Unpublished doctoral dissertation, University of Connecticut, Storrs.

Kennedy, J. M., & DeJong, G. F. (1977). Aged in cities: Residential segregation in ten USA central cities. *Journal of Gerontology, 32,* 97–102.

Kerr, K. A., (1985). *Organized for prohibition: A new history of the Anti-Saloon League.* New Haven, CT: Yale University Press.

Kirby, A. (1982). *The politics of location.* Andover, Hants, England: Methuen.

Kirk, S. A., & Therrien, M. E. (1976). Community mental health myths and the fate of former hospitalized patients. *Psychiatry, 38,* 209–217.

Klein, D. (1983). Ill and against the law: The social and medical control of heroin users. *Journal of Drug Issues, 13,* 31–55.

Klein, M. (1979). Deinstitutionalization and diversion of juvenile offenders: A litany of impediments. In N. Morris & M. Tonry (Eds.), *Crime and justice: An annual review of research.* (Vol. 1, pp. 145–201). Chicago: University of Chicago Press.

Knox, P. L. (1982). *Urban social geography.* New York: Longman.

Koumjian, K. (1981). The use of Valium as a form of social control. *Social Science and Medicine, 15E,* 245–249.

Kovel, J. (1980). The American mental health industry. In D. Ingleby (Ed.), *Critical psychiatry: The politics of mental health* (pp. 72–101). New York: Pantheon.

Kreisman, D., & Joy, V. (1974). Family response to the mental illness of a relative: A literature review. *Schizophrenia Bulletin, 10,* 34–57.

Krisberg, B., & Schwartz, J. (1983). Rethinking juvenile justice. *Crime and Delinquency, 29,* 333–364.

Kurtz, N. R., & Regier, M. (1975). The Uniform Alcoholism and Intoxication Treatment Act: The compromising process of social policy formation. *Journal of Studies on Alcohol, 36,* 1421–1441.

Lamb, H. R. (Ed.). (1984). *The homeless mentally ill: A task force report of the American Psychiatric Association.* Washington, DC: American Psychiatric Association.

Langner, T. S., & Michael, S. T. (1963). *Life stress and mental health: The Midtown Manhattan Study.* London: Collier-Macmillan.

Laurie, B. (1974). "Nothing on compulsion": Life styles of Philadephia artisans, 1820–1850. *Labor History, 15,* 337–366.

Law, C. M., & Warnes, A. M. (1980). The characteristics of retired migrants. In D. T. Herbert & R. J. Johnston (Eds.), *Geography and the urban environment* (Vol. III, pp. 175–222). Chichester, England: Wiley.

Law, C. M., & Warnes, A. M. (1982). The destination decision in retirement migration. In A. M. Warnes (Ed.), *Geographical perspectives on the elderly* (pp. 53–82). Chichester, England: Wiley.

Lawton, M. R. (1978). The housing problems of community-resident elderly. In R. Boynton (Ed.), *Occasional papers in housing and community affairs* (Vol. I, pp. 39–74). Washington, DC: Department of Housing and Urban Development.

Lee, R. (1979). The economic basis of social problems in the city. In D. T. Herbert & D. M. Smith (Eds.), *Social problems in the city* (pp. 47–62). New York: Oxford University Press.

Lee, T. R. (1976). *Psychology and the environment.* London: Methuen.

Lemert, E. M. (1967). The juvenile court—Quest and realities. In *The President's commission on law enforcement and administration of justice. Task force report: Juvenile delinquency and youth crime.* Washington, DC: U.S. Government Printing Office.

Lemert, E. M. (1981). Diversion in juvenile justice: What hath been wrought. *Journal of Research in Crime and Delinquency, 18,* 34–46.

Lender, M. E., & Martin, J. K. (1982). *Drinking in America: A history.* New York: Free Press.

Leonard, E. B. (1982). *Woman, crime and society: A critique of theoretical criminology.* New York: Longman.

Lerman, P. (1975). *Community treatment and social control: A critical analysis of juvenile correctional policy.* Chicago: University of Chicago Press.

Lerman, P. (1982). *Deinstitutionalization and the welfare state.* New Brunswick, NJ: Rutgers University Press.

Levine, H. G. (1980). Temperance and women in 19th century United States. In O. J. Kalant (Ed.), *Research advances in alcohol and drug problems: Vol. 5. Alcohol and drug problems in women* (pp. 25–67). New York: Plenum.

Levine, H. G. (1984). The alcohol problem in America: From temperance to alcoholism. *British Journal of Addiction, 79,* 109–119.

Levine, M. (1981). *The history and politics of community mental health.* New York: Oxford University Press.

Levine, M., & Levine, A. (1970). *A social history of helping services: Clinic, court, school and community.* New York: Appleton-Century-Crofts.

Levitan, S. A. (1985). *Programs in aid of the poor* (5th ed.). Baltimore: The Johns Hopkins University Press.

Levy, L., & Herzog, A. N. (1974). Effects of population density and crowding on health and social adaptation in the Netherlands. *Journal of Health and Social Behavior, 15,* 228–240.

Ley, D. (1983). *A social geography of the city.* New York: Harper & Row.

Lieberson, S. (1963). *Ethnic patterns in American cities.* Glencoe, IL: Free Press.

Lilienfeld, A. M., & Lilienfeld, D. E. (1980). *Foundations of epidemiology.* New York: Oxford University Press.

Lin, N., Ensel, W. M., Simeone, R. S., & Kuo, W. (1979). Social support, stressful life events, and illness: A model and an empirical test. *Journal of Health and Social Behavior, 20,* 108–119.

Lindesmith, A. R. (1956). Traffic in dope. *The Nation, 182:* 337.

Linsky, A. S., Straus, M. A., & Colby, J. P. (1985). Stressful events, stressful conditions and alcohol problems in the United States: A partial test of Bale's theory. *Journal of Studies on Alcohol, 46,* 72–80.

Liska, A. E. (1981). *Perspectives on deviance.* Englewood Cliffs, NJ: Prentice-Hall.

Lloyd, P. C. (1971). *Africa in social change.* Harmondsworth: Penguin.

London, J. (1913). *John Barleycorn.* New York: Century.

Longest, J., Konan, M., Tweed, D. (1976). *A study of deficiencies and differentials in the distribution of mental health resources* (Series B, No. 15). Rockville, MD: NIMH.

Loring, W. C. (1977). *The effect of the man-made environment on health and behavior.* Atlanta: Centers for Disease Control.

Lorrain, F., & White, A. C. (1977). Structural equivalence of individuals in social networks. *Journal of Mathematical Sociology, 1,* 49–80.

Mair, A. (1984). Locating shelters for the homeless. *Area, 16,* 338–340.

Mair, A. (1986). The homeless and the post-industrial city. *Political Geography Quarterly* Vol. 5, pp. 351–368.

Maizie, S. M., & Rawlings, S. (1973). Public attitudes towards population issues. In S. M. Maizie (Ed.), *Population distribution and policy* (pp. 599–630). Washington, DC: U.S. Government Printing Office.

Makela, K., Room. R., Single, E., Sulkunen, P., & Walsh, B. (Eds.). (1981). *Alcohol, society and the state: A comparative study of alcohol control.* Toronto: Addiction Research Foundation.

Maloff, D., Becker, H. S., Fonaroff, A., & Rodin, J. (1979). Informal social controls and their influence on substance abuse. *Journal of Drug Issues, 9,* 161–183.

Marans, R. W., & Rodgers, W. (1975). Toward an understanding of community satisfaction. In A. H. Hawley & V. P. Rock (Eds.), *Metropolitan America in contemporary research* (pp. 299–354) Beverly Hills: Sage.

Marin, P. (1975, October). The new narcissism. *Harpers,* 45–46.

Marmor, J. (1975). *Psychiatrists and their patients: A national study of private office practice.* Washington, DC: American Psychiatric Association.

Matza, D. (1969). *Becoming deviant.* Englewood Cliffs, NJ: Prentice-Hall.

Mayer, J. A. (1983). Notes towards a working definition of social control in historical analysis. In S. Cohen & A. Scull (Eds.), *Social control and the state: Historical and comparative essays* (pp. 17–38). Oxford, England: Martin Robertson.

McClintock, F. H., & Avison, N. H. (1968). *Crime in England and Wales.* London: Heinemann.

McKechnie, G. E. (1974). *Manual for the Environmental Response Inventory.* Palo Alto, CA: Consulting Psychology Press.

Medicine in the Public Interest. (1979). *The effects of alcohol beverage control laws.* Washington, DC: Medicine in the Public Interest, Inc.

Meier, R. F. (1982). Perspectives on the concept of social control. *Annual Review of Sociology, 8,* 24–55.

Melick, M. E., Steadman, H. J. & Cocozza, J. P. (1979). The medicalization of criminal behavior among mental patients. *Journal of Health and Social Behavior, 20,* 228–237.

Mercer, C. (1975). *Living in cities.* Harmondsworth, England: Penguin.

Meyers, E. J. (1980). American heroin policy: Some alternatives. In *The Drug Abuse Council, The facts about "drug abuse"* (pp. 190–247). New York: Free Press.

Miles, A. (1981). *The mentally ill in contemporary society.* Oxford, England: Martin Robertson.

Milgram, S. (1970). The experience of living in cities. *Science, 167.* 1461–1468.

Miller, P. M., & Niremberg, T. D. (Eds.). (1984). *Preventing alcohol abuse.* New York: Plenum.

Miller, R. J. (1982). *The demolition of skid row.* Lexington, MA: Heath.

Minkoff, K. (1979). A map of the chronic mental patient. In J. A. Talbott (Ed.), *The chronic mental patient* (pp. 11–37). Washington, DC: American Psychiatric Association.

Mishler, E. G. (1981). Critical perspectives on the biomedical model. In E. G. Mishler & L. R. Amarasingham (Eds.), *Social contexts of health, illness and patient care.* Cambridge: Cambridge University Press.

Mitchell, J. C. (1969). The concept and use of social networks. In J. C. Mitchell (Ed.), *Social networks in urban situations* (pp. 1–50). Manchester: University of Manchester Press.

Mitchell, R. E. (1971). Some social implications of high density housing. *American Sociological Review, 36,* 18–29.

Mollica, R. F., & Redlich, F. C. (1980). Equity and changing patient characteristics, 1950–1975. *Archives of General Psychiatry, 37,* 1257–1263.

Monahan, J., & Vaux, A. (1980). Task force report: The macroenvironment and community mental health. *Community Mental Health Journal, 16,* 14–26.

Moore, E. G. (1972). *Residential mobility in the city* (Resource Paper No. 13). Washington, DC: Association of Amercian Geographers.

Moore, G. A. (1981). Mental health deinstitutionalization and the regional economy: A model and case study. *Social Science and Medicine, 15c,* 174–189.

Moore, G. T., & Golledge, R. G. (1976). *Environmental knowing: Theories, research and methods.* Stroudsberg, PA.: Dowden, Hutchinson & Ross.

Moore, M. H., & D. R. Gerstein (Eds.). (1981). *Alcohol and public policy: Beyond the shadow of prohibition.* Washington, DC: National Academy Press.

Moos, R. H. (1973). Conceptualizations of human environments. *American Psychologist, 28,* 652–665.

Morgan, D. J. (1976). *Patterns of population distribution: A residential preference model and its dynamic*. Chicago: University of Chicago.

Morgan, P. (1980). The state as mediator: Alcohol problem management in the post-war period. *Contemporary Drug Problems, 9,* 107–140.

Moroney, R. (1976). *The family and the state: Consideration for social policy*. London: Longman.

Morris, N., & Hawkins, G. (1969). *The honest politician's guide to crime control*. Chicago: University of Chicago Press.

Morrissey, J. P. (1982). Assessing interorganizational linkages. In R. C. Tessler & H. H. Goldman (Eds.), *The chronically mentally ill: Assessing community support programs* (pp. 159–192). Cambridge, MA: Ballinger.

Morrissey, J. P., & Goldman, H. H. (1985). The alchemy of mental health policy: Homelessness and the fourth cycle of reform. *American Journal of Public Health, 75,* 727–731.

Morrissey, J. P., Goldman, H. H., & Klerman, L. V. (Eds.). (1980). *The enduring asylum: Cycles of institutional reform at Worcester State Hospital*. New York: Grune & Stratton.

Morrissey, J. P., & Gounis, K. (1987). Homelessness and mental illness in America: Emerging issues in the construction of a social problem. In C. J. Smith & J. A. Giggs (Eds.), *Location and stigma: Emerging themes in the study of mental health and mental illness*. London: George, Allen and Unwin.

Morrissey, J. P., & Tessler, R. C. (1982). Selection process in state mental hospitalization: Policy issues and research directions. In M. Lewis (Ed.), *Research in social problems and public policy* (pp. 35–80). Greenwich, CT: JAI Press.

Moseley, H. (1979). Monopoly capital and the state: Some critical reflections on O'Connor's "fiscal crisis of the state." *The Review of Radical Political Economy, 11,* 52–61.

Mulford, H. A., & Fitzgerald, J. L. (1983a). Changes in alcohol sales and drinking problems in Iowa, 1961–1979. *Journal of Studies on Alcohol, 44,* 138–161.

Mulford, H. A., & Fitzgerald, J. L. (1983b). Changes in the climate of attitudes toward drinking in Iowa, 1961–1979. *Journal of Studies in Alcohol, 44,* 675–687.

Mullins, N. C. (1973). *The Structuralists*. In N. C. Mullins (Ed.), *Theory and theory groups in contemporary American sociology* (pp. 250–269). New York: Harper & Row.

Musto, D. (1973). *The American disease*. New Haven: Yale University Press.

Naparstek, A. J., Biegel, D. E., & Spiro, H. R. (1982). *Neighborhood networks for humane mental health care*. New York: Plenum.

Nathan, P. E. (1983). Failures in prevention: Why we can't prevent the devastating effect of alcoholism and drug abuse. *American Psychologist, 38,* 459–467.

National Institute of Justice (Federal Bureau of Investigation). (1979). *Uniform crime reports, 1979*. Washington, DC: N. I. J.

National Institute on Alcohol Abuse and Alcoholism. (1981a). *Fourth special report to the U.S. Congress on alcohol and health*. Rockville, MD: NIAAA.

National Institute on Alcohol Abuse and Alcoholism. (1981b). *National status report: State Alcoholism Profile Information System (SAPIS)*. Rockville, MD: NIAAA.

National Institute on Alcohol Abuse and Alcoholism. (1982). *Prevention, intervention and treatment: Concerns and models* (Alcohol and Health Monograph No. 3). Rockville, MD: NIAAA.

National Institute on Alcohol Abuse and Alcoholism. (1984). *Nature and extent of alcohol problems among the elderly* (Research Monograph No. 4). Rockville, MD: NIAAA.

Navarro, V. (1977). The political economy of medical care: An explanation of the composition, nature, and functions of the present health sector of the United States. In V. Navarro (Ed.), *Health and medical care in the U.S.: A critical analysis* (pp. 85–112). Farmingdale, NY: Baywood.

Navarro, V. (1981). The economic and political determinants of human (including health) rights. In V. Navarro (Ed.), *Imperialism, health and medicine* (pp. 53–76). Farmingdale, NY: Baywood.

Nejelski, P. (1976). Diversion: Unleashing the hound of heaven. In M. K. Rosenheim (Ed.), *Pursuing justice for the child* (pp. 94–118). Chicago: University of Chicago Press.

Nelkin, D. (1973). *Methadone maintenance: A technological fix.* New York: George Braziller.

New York City, Office of the City Council President. (1982). *Passing the buck: Federal efforts to abandon the mentally disabled.* Unpublished report.

New York State Office of Mental Health. (1981). *The 1982–83 office of mental health program/ budget overview.* Albany: NYSOMH.

New York State Division of Alcohol Abuse and Alcoholism. (1985). *Five-year comprehensive plan for alcoholism services in New York State. 1984–1989.* Albany, NY: NYSDAAA.

Nimmer, R. T. (1971). *Two million unnecessary arrests.* Chicago: American Bar Foundation.

O'Connor, J. (1973). *The fiscal crisis of the state.* New York: St. Martins Press.

O'Connor, J. (1979). Some reflective criticisms on Mosely's "Critical reflections on the fiscal crisis of the state." *The Review of Radical Political Economy, 11,* 60–65.

Osgood, D. W., & Weichselbaum, H. F. (1984). Juvenile diversion: When practice matches theory. *Journal of Research in Crime and Delinquency, 21,* 33–56.

Pack, J. R. (1984). Urban spatial transformation: Philadelphia, 1850 to 1888, heterogeneity to homogeneity? *Social Science History, 8,* 425–454.

Pahl, R. E. (1977). Managers, technical experts and the state. In M. Hartoe (Ed.) *Captive cities* (pp. 50–60). London: Wiley.

Palmer, T. B. (1979). Juvenile diversion: When and for whom?" *California Youth Authority Quarterly, 32,* 14–20.

Palmer, T. B., & Lewis, R. V. (1980a). *An evaluation of juvenile diversion.* Cambridge, MA: Delgeschlager, Gunn & Han.

Palmer, T. B., & Lewis, R. V. (1980b). A differential approach to juvenile diversion. *Journal of Research in Crime and Delinquency, 17,* 209–229.

Pan, L. (1975). *Alcohol in colonial Africa.* Helsinki: Tae Finnish Foundation for Alcohol Studies, No. 22.

Park, P. (1983). Sketches toward a political economy of drink and drinking problems: The case of 18th and 19th century England. *Journal of Drug Issues, 13,* 57–75.

Parker, D. A. (1984). Alcohol control policy in the United States. In P. M. Miller & T. D. Niremberg (Eds.), *Prevention of alcohol abuse* (pp. 235–244). New York: Plenum.

Patterson, A. H. (1978). Territorial behavior and fear of crime in the elderly. *Environmental Psychology and Non-Verbal Behavior, 2,* 131–144.

Patterson, J. T. (1981). *America's struggle against poverty 1900–1980.* Cambridge, MA: Harvard University Press.

Pattison, E. M. (1975). A psychological kinship model for family therapy. *American Journal of Psychiatry, 132,* 1246–1251.

Pattison, E. M. (1976). Non-abstinent treatment goals in the treatment of drinking. In R. J. Gibbins (Ed.), *Research advances in alcohol and drug problems.* New York: Wiley.

Pattison, E. M. (1979). The selection of treatment modalities for the alcoholic patient. In J. H. Mendelson & N. K. Mello (Eds.), *The diagnosis and treatment of alcoholism* (pp. 125–228). New York: McGraw-Hill.

Peele, S. (1984). The cultural context of psychological approaches to alcoholism. Can we control the effects of alcohol? *American Psychologist, 39,* 1337–1351.

Pepper, B., Kirshner, M. C., & Ryglewicz, H. (1981). The young adult chronic patient: Overview of a population. *Hospital and Community Psychiatry, 32,* 463–469.

Perry, D. C., & Watkins, A. J. (Eds.). (1977). *The rise of the Sunbelt cities.* Beverly Hills, CA: Sage.

Perucci, R., & Targ, D. B. (1982). *Mental patients and social networks.* Boston: Auburn House.

Pilisuk, M., & Froland, C. (1978). Kinships, social networks, social support and health. *Social Science and Medicine, 12B,* 273–280.

Pinch, S. (1980). Local authority provision for the elderly: An overview and case study of London. In D. T. Herbert R. J. Johnston (Eds.), *Geography and the urban environment: Progress in research and applications* (Vol. 3, pp. 295–344). Chichester, England: Wiley.

Pinch, S. (1985). *Cities and services: The geography of collective consumption*. London: Routledge & Kegan Paul.

Pittman, D. J. (1983). An evaluation of the control of consumption policy. In M. Grant, M. A. Plant & A. Williams (Eds.), *Economics and alcohol* (pp. 159–172). London: Croom-Helm.

Pittman, D. J., & Gordon, C. W. (1958). *Revolving door*. Glencoe, IL: Free Press.

Pivar, D. J. (1973). *Purity crusade: Sexual morality and social control, 1868–1900*. Westport, CT: Greenwood.

Piven, F. F., & Cloward, R. A. (1971). *Regulating the poor*. New York: Pantheon.

Piven, F. F., & Cloward, R. A. (1982). *The new class war*. New York: Pantheon.

Platt, A. M. (1969). *The child savers: The invention of delinquency*. Chicago: University of Chicago Press.

Polk, K. (1984). Juvenile diversion: A look at the record. *Crime and Delinquency, 30,* 648–659.

Popham, R. E., Schmidt, W., & deLint, J. (1975). The prevention of alcoholism: Epidemiological studies of the effects of government control measures. *British Journal of Addictions, 70,* 125–144.

Quinney, R. (1970). *The social reality of crime*. Boston: Little, Brown.

Quinney, R. (1977). *Class, state, and crime: On the theory and practice of criminal justice*. New York: Longman.

Rabkin, J. G. (1979). Ethnic density and psychiatric hospitalization: Hazards of minority status. *American Journal of Psychiatry, 136,* 1562–1566.

Rabkin, J. G., & Struening, E. (1976). Life events, stress, and illness. *Science, 191,* 1013–1020.

Rabow, J., & Watts, R. K. (1982). Alcohol availability, alcohol beverage sales and alcohol-related problems. *Journal of Studies on Alcohol, 43,* 767–801.

Rabow, J., & Watts, R. K. (1983). The role of alcohol availability in alcohol consumption and alcohol problems. In M. Galanter (Ed.), *Recent developments in alcoholism* (Vol. 1, pp. 285–302). New York: Plenum.

Rachal, J. V., Maisto, S. A., Guess, L. L., & Hubbard, R. L. (1982). Alcohol use among youth. In *Alcohol consumption and related problems* (Alcohol and Health Monograph No. 1, pp. 55–95). Rockville, MD: NIAAA.

Ralph, D. (1983). *Work and madness: The rise of community psychiatry*. Montreal: Black Rose Press.

Rathbone-McCuan, E., & Hashimi, J. (1982). *Isolated elders: Health and social intervention*. Rockville, MD: Aspen Systems Corp.

Rausch, S. P., & Logan, C. H. (1983). Diversion from juvenile court: Panacea or Pandora's box? In J. R. Kleugel (Ed.), *Evaluating juvenile justice* (Sage Research Progress Series in Criminology, Vol. 20). Beverly Hills, CA: Sage.

Reckless, W. C. (1933). *Vice in Chicago*. Chicago: University of Chicago Press.

Regier, D. A., Goldberg, I. D., & Taube, C. (1978). The de facto U. S. mental health service system: A public health perspective. *Archives of General Psychiatry, 35,* 685–693.

Regier, M. C. (1977). *Social policy in action*. Lexington, MA: Heath.

Reinarman, C. (1979). Moral entrepreneurs and political economy: Historical and ethnographic notes on the construction of the cocaine menace. *Contemporary Crises, 3,* 225–254.

Relph, E. (1976). *Place and placelessness*. London: Pion.

Renaud, M. (1978). On the structural constraints to state intervention in health. In J. Ehrenreich (Ed.), *The cultural crisis of modern medicine* (pp. 101–122). New York: Monthly Review Press.

Rendleman, D. R. (1979). Parens patrie: From chancery to the juvenile court. In F. L. Faust & P. L. Brantingham (Eds.), *Juvenile justice philosophy* (pp. 58–96). St. Paul, MN: West Publishing Co.

Riger, S., & Lavrakas, P. J. (1981). Community ties: Patterns of attachment and social interaction in urban neighborhoods. *American Journal of Community Psychology, 9.* 55–66.

Rodin, M. B. (1981). Alcoholism as a folk disease: The paradox of beliefs and choice of therapy in an urban American community. *Journal of Studies on Alcohol, 42,* 822–836.

Rodin, M. B., Pickup, L., Motton, D. R., & Keatinge, C. (1982). *Gimme shelter: Ethnographic perspectives on skid row inebriates in detoxification centers.* University of Illinois–Chicago, School of Public Health.

Roebuck, J. R., & Kessler, R. G. (1972). *The etiology of alcoholism: Constitutional, psychological and sociological approaches.* Springfield, IL: C. C. Thomas.

Rojek, D. G. (1982). Juvenile diversion: A study of community cooptation. In D. G. Rojek & G. F. Jensen (Eds.), *Readings in juvenile delinquency* (pp. 316–321). Lexington, MA: Heath.

Room, R. (1972). Comments on "The alcohologists addiction." *Quarterly Journal of Studies on Alcohol, 33,* 1049–1059.

Room, R. (1975). Normative perspectives on alcohol use and problems. *Journal of Drug Issues, 5,* 359–368.

Room, R. (1976). Comment on the "Uniform Alcoholism and Intoxication Treatment Act." *Journal of Studies on Alcohol, 37,* 113–144.

Room, R. (1983). Region and urbanization as factors in drinking practices and problems. In B. Kissin & H. Begleiter (Eds.), *The pathogenesis of alcoholism: Psychological factors* (pp. 555–604). New York: Plenum.

Room, R. (1984). Alcohol control and public health. *Annual Review of Public Health, 5,* 293–318.

Rooney, J. F. (1980). Organizational success through program failure: Skid row rescue missions. *Social Forces, 58,* 904–924.

Rose, S. M. (1979). Deciphering deinstitutionalization: Complexities in policy and program analysis. *Milbank Memorial Fund Quarterly: Health and Society, 57,* 429–460.

Rosenzweig, R. (1983). *Eight hours for what we will: Workers and leisure in an industrial city, 1870–1920.* Cambridge, England: Cambridge University Press.

Ross, H. L. (1982). *Deterring the drinking driver: Legal policy and social control.* Lexington, MA: Heath.

Rothman, D. (1983). Social control: The uses and abuses of the concept in the history of incarceration. In S. Cohen & A. Scull (Eds.), *Social control and the state: Historical and comparative essays* (pp. 106–117). Oxford, England: Martin Robertson.

Rothman, D. J. (1971). *The discovery of the asylum: Social order and disorder in the new Republic.* Boston: Little, Brown.

Russell, J. A., & Bond, C. R. (1980). Individual differences in beliefs concerning emotions conducive to alcohol use. *Journal of Studies on Alcohol, 41,* 753–759.

Russell, J. A., & Ward, L. M. (1982). Environmental Psychology. *Annual Review of Psychology, 33,* 651–688.

Ryan, M. (1981). *Cradle of the middle class: The family in Oneida county, New York, 1790–1865.* Cambridge, England: Cambridge University Press.

Sarason, S. B., Carroll, C., Matton, K., Cohen, S., & Lorentz, E. (1977). *Human services and resource networks.* San Francisco: Jossey-Bass.

Satterwhite, B. (1978). Impact of chronic illness on child and family: An overview based on five surveys and implications for management. *International Journal of Rehabilitation Research, 1,* 7–17.

Saul, J. A., & Davidson, W. S. (1982). Implementation of juvenile diversion programs: Cast your net on the other side of the boat. In J. R. Kleugel (Ed.), *Evaluating juvenile justice* (pp. 31–46). Beverly Hills, CA: Sage.

Schill, M. H., & Nathan, R. P. (1983). *Revitalizing America's cities: Neighborhood reinvestment and displacement.* Albany: State University of New York Press.

Schur, E. M. (1965). *Crimes without victims: Deviant behavior and public policy.* Englewood Cliffs, NJ: Prentice-Hall.

Schur, E. M. (1973). *Radical non-intervention: Rethinking the delinquency problem.* Englewood Cliffs, NJ: Prentice-Hall.

Schur, E. M. (1980). *The politics of deviance: Stigma contests and the uses of power.* Englewood Cliffs, NJ: Prentice-Hall.

Schwab, J. J., & Schwab, M. E. (1978). *Sociocultural roots of mental illness: An epidemiologic survey.* New York: Plenum.

Scott, N., & Scott, R. A. (1980). The impact of housing markets on deinstitutionalization. *Administration in Mental Health, 7,* 210–222.

Scull, A. T. (1977). *Decarceration: Community treatment and the deviant—a radical view.* Englewood Cliffs, NJ: Prentice-Hall.

Scull, A. T. (1979). *Museums of madness: The social organization of insanity in 19th century England.* London: Allen Lane.

Scull, A. T. (1981). A new trade in lunacy: The recommodification of the mental patient. *American Behavioral Scientist, 24,* 741–754.

Searles, H. F. (1960). *The non-human environment in normal development and schizophrenia.* New York: International Universities Press.

Sedgwick, P. (1982). *Psycho politics.* London: Pluto.

Segal, S. P. (1979). Community care and deinstitutionalization: A review. *Social Work, 24,* 521–527.

Segal, S. P., & Baumohl, J. (1980). Engaging the disengaged. *Social Work, 25,* 358–366.

Segal, S. P., & Baumohl, J. (in press). No place like home: Reflections on sheltering a diverse population. In C. J. Smith & J. A. Giggs (Eds.), *Location and stigma: Emerging themes in the study of mental health and mental illness.* London: George Allen & Unwin.

Segal, S. P., Baumohl, J., & Johnson, E. (1977). Falling through the cracks: Mental disorder and social margin in a young vagrant population. *Social Problems, 24,* 387–400.

Shaw, C. R., McKay, H. D. (1969). *Juvenile delinquency and urban areas* (rev. ed.). Chicago: University of Chicago Press.

Shaw, S. (1980). The causes of increasing drinking problems amongst women. In *Women and alcohol* (pp. 1–40); Camberwell Council on Alcoholism. London: Tavistock.

Shaw, S., Cartwright, A., Spratley, T., & Harwin, J. (1978). *Responding to drinking problems.* Baltimore: University Park Press.

Sheehan, S. (1982). *Is there no place on earth for me?* Boston: Houghton Mifflin.

Sheppard, S. R., Smith, D. E., and Gay, G. R. (1972). The changing face of heroin addiction in the Haight-Ashbury. *International Journal of the Addictions, 7,* 109–122.

Sherman, S. R. (1971). The choice of retirement housing among the well-elderly. *Aging and Human Development, 2,* 111–138.

Sherouse, D. L. (1982). *Professionals' handbook on geriatric alcoholism.* Springfield, IL.

Shulman, N. (1976). Network analysis: A new addition to an old bag of tricks. *Acta Sociologica, 19,* 307–323.

Siegler, M. H., Osmond, H., & Newell, S. (1968). Models of alcoholism. *Quarterly Journal of Studies on Alcohol, 29,* 571–591.

Simon, R. (1975). *Women and crime.* Lexington, MA: Heath.

Singer, M. (1986). Toward a political economy of alcoholism: The missing link in the anthropology of drinking. *Social Science and Medicine, 23:* 113–130.

Skog, O. J. (1980). Social interaction and the distribution of consumption. *Journal of Drug Issues, 10,* 71–92.

Skog, O. J. (1981). Drinking behavior in small groups: The relationship between group size and consumption level. In T. C. Harford & L. S. Gaines (Eds.), *Social drinking contexts* (Research Monograph, No. 7, pp. 121–137). Rockville, MD: NIAAA.

Skogan, W. G., & Maxfield, M. G. (1981). *Coping with crime: Individual and neighborhood reactions.* Beverly Hills, CA: Sage.

Smart, R. G. (1980). Availability and the prevention of alcohol-related problems. In T. C. Harford (Ed.), *Normative approaches to the prevention of alcohol abuse and alcoholism.* (Monograph No. 3, pp. 123–146). Rockville, MD: NIAAA.

Smith, B. W., & Hiltner, J. (1975). Intra-urban location of the elderly. *Journal of Gerontology, 64,* 287–289.

Smith, C. A., & Smith, C. J. (1978). Locating natural neighbors in the urban community. *Area, 10,* 102–110.

Smith, C. J. (1976). Residential neighborhoods as humane environments. *Environment and Planning A, 8,* 311–326.

Smith, C. J. (1977). *Geography and mental health.* Resource Publication No. 76–4. Washington, DC: Association of American Geographers, Commision on College Geography.

Smith, C. J. (1978). Self-help and social networks in the urban community. *Ekistics, 45,* 106–115.

Smith, C. J. (1980a). Neighborhood effects on mental health. In D. T. Herbert & R. J. Johnston (Eds.), *Geography and the urban environment* (Vol. 3, pp. 363–415). Chichester, England: Wiley.

Smith, C. J. (1980b). Social networks as metaphors, models and methods. *Progress in Human Geography, 4,* 500–524.

Smith, C. J. (1980c). Residential needs of the deinstitutionalized mentally ill. In J. W. Frazier & B. J. Epstein (Eds.), *Applied geography conference* (Vol. 3, pp. 279–285). Kent, OH: Kent State University.

Smith, C. J. (1982). Home-based mental health care for the elderly. In A. M. Warnes (Ed.), *Geographical perspectives on the elderly* (pp. 375–398). Chichester, England: Wiley.

Smith, C. J. (1983a). The urban services paradox: Shrinking supply in times of rising demand. *Population Research and Policy Review, 2,* 149–160.

Smith, C. J. (1983b). Locating alcoholism treatment facilities. *Economic Geography, 59,* 368–385.

Smith, C. J. (1983c). Innovation in mental health policy: Community mental health in the United States of America, 1965–1980. *Environment and Planning D: Society and Space, 1,* 447–468.

Smith, C. J. (1984). Geographic patterns of funding for community mental health centers. *Hospital and Community Psychiatry, 35,* 1133–1140.

Smith C. J. (1985a, November). *The suburbanization of drinking behavior.* Paper presented at the Social Science History Association Meeting, Chicago.

Smith, C. J. (1985b). Mental health in an urban world. *Urban Geography, 6,* 88–99.

Smith, C. J. (1986). Equity in the distribution of health and welfare services: Can we rely on the state to reverse the "inverse care law"? *Social Science and Medicine, 23:* 1067–1078.

Smith, C. J. (1987). *Urban revitalization and social control: A case study in the management of public problems.* Unpublished manuscript, Department of Geography, SUNY at Albany.

Smith, C. J. (1988). The restructuring of mental health care in the United States. In J. Scarpaci (Ed.), *The privatization of health services: An international perspective.* Pittsburgh: University of Pittsburgh Press.

Smith, C. J., & Hanham, R. Q. (1981a). Deinstitutionalization of the mentally ill: A time path analysis of the American states, 1955–1975. *Social Science and Medicine, 15,* 361–378.

Smith, C. J., & Hanham, R. Q. (1981b). Proximity and the formation of public attitudes toward mental illness. *Environment and Planning, 13,* 147–165.

Smith, C. J., & Hanham, R. Q. (1982). *Alcohol abuse: Geographical perspectives* (Resource Publications in Geography). Washington, DC: Association of American Geographers.

Smith, C. J., & Hanham, R. Q. (1984). Regional change and problem drinking in the United States, 1970–1978. *Regional Studies, 19.2,* 149–162.

Smith, D. M. (1973). *The geography of social well-being in the United States: An introduction to social indicators.* New York: McGraw-Hill.

Smith, D. M. (1977). *Human geography: A welfare approach.* London: Arnold.

Smith, N. (1982). Gentrification and uneven development. *Economic Geography, 58,* 139–155.

Smith, N. (1983). Toward a theory of gentrification: A back to the city movement by capital, not people. In R. W. Lakde (Ed.), *Readings in urban analysis: Perspectives on urban form* (pp. 278–2198). New Brunswick, NJ: Center for Urban Policy Research.

Smith, N. (1985). Gentrification, the frontier and the restructuring of urban space. In N. Smith & P. Williams (Eds.), *Gentrification of the city* (pp. 15–34). London: George Allen & Unwin.

Snow, R. W. (1984). *The drinking locations of Mississippi DUI offenders: A preliminary exami-*

nation. Mississippi Alcohol Safety Education Program, Working Paper 84-1. Starkville, MS: Mississippi State University.

Snyder, C. (1978). *Alcohol and the Jews*. Carbondale, IL: Southern Illinois University Press.

Sokolovsky, J., Cohen, C., Berger, D., & Geiger, J. (1978). Personal networks of ex-mental patients in a Manhattan SRO hotel. *Human Organization, 37*, 5–15.

Sommer, R. (1965). The isolated drinker in the Edmonton beer parlor. *Quarterly Journal of Studies on Alcohol, 26*, 95–110.

Sommer, R. (1969). *Personal space*. Englewood Cliffs, NJ: Prentice-Hall.

Speck, R. V., & Attneave, C. L. (1973). *Family networks*. New York: Pantheon.

Spector, M., & Kitsuse, J. I. (1977). *Constructing social problems*. Menlo Park, CA: Cummings.

Speiglman, R., & Wittman, F. D. (1982, September). *Urban redevelopment and public drunkenness in Fresno: A California move toward decriminalization*. Paper presented at the Annual Meeting, Society for the Study of Social Problems, San Francisco.

Spencer, C., & Blades, M. (1986). Pattern and process: A review essay on the relationship between behavioral geography and environmental psychology. *Progress in Human Geography, 10*, 230–248.

Spergel, I. A., Reamer, F. G., & Lynch, J. P. (1981). Deinstitutionalization of status offenders: Individual outcome and system effects. *Journal of Research in Crime and Delinquency, 18*, 4–33.

Spitzer, S. (1975). Toward a Marxian theory of deviance. *Social Problems, 22*, 641–651.

Srole, L., Langner, T. S., Michael, S. T., Opler, M. K., & Rennie, T. A. C. (1962). *Mental health in the metropolis: The Midtown Manhattan Study*. New York: McGraw-Hill.

Srole, L., & Fischer, A. K. (Eds.). (1978). *Mental health in the metropolis: The Midtown Manhattan Study* (rev. ed.). New York: New York University Press.

Srole, L., & Fischer, A. K. (1980). The midtown Manhattan longitudinal study vs. "the mental paradise lost" doctrine. *Archives of General Psychiatry, 37*, 209–221.

Stack, S. (1981). Divorce and suicide: A time series analysis, 1933–1970. *Journal of Family Issues, 2*, 77–90.

Stanton, M. D. (1976). Drugs, Vietnam, and the Vietnamese veteran: An overview. *American Journal of Drug and Alcohol Abuse, 3*, 557–570.

Stark, E., Flitcraft, A., & Frazier, W. (1979). Medicine and patriarchal violence: The social construction of a "private" event. *International Journal of Health Services, 9*, 461–493.

Steadman-Jones, G. (1983). Class expression versus social control? A critique of recent trends in the social history of "Leisure." In S. Cohen & A. Scull (Eds.), *Social control and the state: Historical and comparative essays* (pp. 39–49). Oxford, England: Martin Robertson.

Steffensmeier, D. J. (1980). Sex differences in patterns of adult crimes, 1965–1977: A review and assessment. *Social Forces, 58*, 566–584.

Stein, L. I., & Test, M. A. (1980). Alternative to mental hospital treatment: I. Conceptual model, treatment program, and clinical evaluation. *Archives of General Psychiatry, 37*, 392–397.

Stein, L. I., Test, M. A., & Marx, A. J. (1975). Alternative to the hospital: A controlled study. *American Journal of Psychiatry, 132*, 517–532.

Stevens, S. R. (1976). *Loners, losers, and lovers: Elderly tenants in a slum hotel*. Seattle: University of Washington Press.

Stevenson, G. (1976, July/August). Social relations and consumption in the human service occupations. *Monthly Review*, 78–87.

Stoesz, D. (1981). A wake for the welfare state: Social welfare and the neoconservative challenge. *Social Service Review, 55*, 398–410.

Stokols, D. (1978). Environmental psychology. *Annual Review of Psychology, 29*, 253–295.

Strug, D. L., & Hyman, M. M. (1981). Social networks of alcoholics. *Journal of Studies on Alcohol, 42*, 855–884.

Struyk, R., & Soldo, B. (1980). *Improving the elderly's housing*. Cambridge, MA: Ballinger.

Sulkunen, P. (1976). Adjustment patterns and the level of alcohol consumption. In R. J. Gibbins (Ed.), *Research advances in alcohol and drug problems* (Vol. 3, pp. 223–282). New York: Wiley.

Sulkunen, P. (1983). Alcohol consumption and the transformation of living conditions. In R. G. Smart (Ed.) *Research Advances in Alcohol and Drug Problems* (Vol. 17, pp. 247–297). New York: Plenum.

Stutz, F. P. (1976). Adjustment and mobility of elderly poor amid downtown renewal. *The Geographical Review, 66:* 391–400.

Taeuber, K. (1965). Residential segregation. *Scientific American, 213:* 12–19.

Taylor, I., Walton, P., & Young, J. (1973). *The new criminology.* New York: Harper & Row.

Taylor, P. J., & Johnston, R. J. (1979). *Geography of elections.* Penguin: Harmondsworth.

Tessler, R. C., & Goldman, H. H. (1982). *The chronically mentally ill: Assessing community support programs.* Cambridge, MA: Ballinger.

Test, M. A., & Stein, L. I. (1980). Alternative to mental hospital treatment: III. Social cost. *Archives of General Psychiatry, 37:* 409–412.

Thoits, P. (1982). Conceptual, methodological, and theoretical problems in studying social support as a buffer against life stress. *Journal of Health and Social Behavior, 23,* 145–159.

Tonry, M. H. (1976). Juvenile justice and the national crime commissions. In M. K. Rosenheim (Ed.), *Pursuing justice for the child* (pp. 281–298). Chicago: University of Chicago Press.

Townsend, P., & Davidson, N. (Eds.). (1982). *Inequalities in health: The Black report.* Harmondsworth, England: Penguin.

Troyer, R. J., & Markle, G. E. (1983). *Cigarettes: The battle over smoking.* New Brunswick, NJ: Rutgers University Press.

Trute, B., & Segal, S. P. (1976). Census tract predictors and the social integration of sheltered care residents. *Social Psychiatry, 11,* 153–161.

Tuan, Y. F. (1974). *Topophilia: A study of environmental perception, attitudes, and values.* Englewood Cliffs, NJ: Prentice-Hall.

Tuck, M. (1980). *Alcoholism and social policy: Are we on the right lines?* (Home Office Research Study No. 65). London: HMSO.

Turk, A. T. (1969). *Criminality and the legal order.* Chicago: Rand McNally.

Turner, J. C., & TenHoor, W. J. (1978). The NIMH community support program: Pilot approach to a needed social reform. *Schizophrenia Bulletin, 4,* 319–348.

Tyrrell, I. R. (1979). *Sobering-up: From temperance to prohibition in ante-bellum America, 1800–1860.* Westport, CT: Greenwood Press.

Vanderkooi, R. (1973). The main stem: Skid row revisited. *Society, 10,* 64–71.

Van Dusen, K. T. (1981). Net widening and relabeling: Some consequences of deinstitutionalization. *American Behavioral Scientist, 24,* 801–810.

Vanicelli, M., Washburn, S. L. & Scheff, B. J. (1980). Family attitudes toward mental illness: Immutable with respect to time, treatment setting, and outcome. *Amercian Journal of Orthopsychiatry, 50,* 151–155.

Van Valey, T. L., Roof, W. C. & Wilcox, J. E. (1977). Trends in residential segregation. *American Journal of Sociology, 82,* 824–844.

Vischi, T. R., Jones, K. R., Shank, E. L., & Lima, L. H. (1980). *The alcohol, drug abuse, and mental health national data book.* Rockville, MD: NIAAA.

Vold, G. B. (1958). *Theoretical criminology.* New York: Oxford University Press.

Vold, G. B. (1979). *Theoretical criminology: Second edition* (Prepared by T. J. Bernard). New York: Oxford University Press.

Walker, A. (1981). Community care and the elderly in Britain: Theory and practice. *International Journal of Health Services, 11,* 541–557.

Walker, A. (1983). Social policy and elderly people in Great Britain: The construction of dependent social and economic status in old age. In A. M. Guillemard (Ed.). *Old age and the welfare state* (pp. 143–167). Beverly Hills, CA: Sage.

Walker, R. A. (1981). A theory of suburbanization: capitalism and the construction of urban space in the United States. In M. Dear & A. J. Scott (Eds.), *Urbanization and urban planning in capitalist society* (pp. 383–430). London: Methuen.

Walsh, J. (1985). Are city shelters now open asylums? *In These Times,* January 23–29, p. 3.

Ward, D. (1980). Environs and neighbors in the "two nations": Residential differentiation in mid-nineteenth-century Leeds. *Journal of Historical Geography, 6,* 133–162.

Warren, R. B., & Warren, D. I. (1977). *The neighborhood organizer's handbook.* Notre Dame, IN: University of Notre Dame Press.

Warren, D. I. (1978, March). *The neighborhood factor in problem coping, help seeking and social support: Research findings and suggested policy implications.* Paper presented at the 55th Annual Meeting of the American Orthopsychiatric Association, San Francisco.

Watts, T. D. (1981). The uneasy triumph of a concept: The "disease" conception of alcoholism. *Journal of Drug Issues, 11,* 451–460.

Webb, S. D. (1978). Mental health in rural and urban environments. *Ekistics, 266,* 37–42.

Weisbrod, B. A., Test, M. A., Stein, L. I. (1980). Alternative to mental hospital treatment: II. Economic benefit-cost analysis. *Archives of General Psychiatry, 37,* 400–405.

Weisner, C. (1983). The alcohol treatment system and social control: A study in institutional change. *Journal of drug issues, 13,* 117–133.

Weisner, C., & Room, R. (1984). Financing and ideology in alcohol treatment. *Social Problems, 32,* 167–184.

Wellman, B., & Leighton, B. (1979). Networks, neighborhoods, and communities: Approaches to the study of the community question. *Urban Affairs Quarterly, 14,* 363–390.

Whitehead, P. C. (1979). Public policy and alcohol related damage: Media campaigns or social controls. *Addictive Behaviors, 4,* 83–89.

Wicker, A. W. (1972). Processes which mediate behavior–environment congruence. *Behavioral Science, 17,* 265–277.

Wiener, C. L. (1981). *The politics of alcoholism: Building an arena around a social problem.* New Brunswick, NJ: Transaction Books.

Williams, M. (1984). Alcohol and the elderly: An overview. *Alcohol, Health and Research World, 8,* 3–9.

Wilkins, L. T. (1964). *Social deviance.* London: Tavistock.

Wilsnack, S. C. (1982). Prevention of alcohol problems in women. In *Special population issues* (Alcohol and Health Monograph No. 4, pp. 77–108). Rockville, MD: NIAAA.

Wilsnack, S. C., Wilsnack, R. W., & Klassen, A. D. (1985). Drinking and problem drinking among women in a U. S. national survey. *Alcohol Health and Research World, 9,* 3–13.

Wilson, J. Q. (1975). *Thinking about crime.* New York: Basic Books.

Winsborough, H., Taeuber, K. E., & Sorensen, A. (1975). *Models of change in residential segregation* (Working Paper No. 75-26). Madison: Center for Demography and Ecology, University of Wisconsin.

Winslow, W. W. (1982). Changing trends in CMHC's: Keys to survival in the Eighties. *Hospital and Community Psychiatry, 33,* 273–277.

Wirth, L. (1938). Urbanism as a way of life. *American Journal of Sociology, 44,* 3–24.

Wiseman, J. P. (1970). *Stations of the lost: The treatment of skid-row alcoholics.* Englewood Cliffs, NJ: Prentice-Hall.

Wiseman, R. F. (1978). *Spatial aspects of aging* (Resource Publication No. 78-4). Washington, DC: Association of American Geographers, Commission on College Geography.

Witkin, M. J. (1980). *Trends in patient care episodes in mental health facilities, 1955–1977.* (Statistical Note No. 154). Rockville, MD: NIAAA.

Wittman, F. D. (1982). *Zoning ordinances, alcohol outlets, and planning; Prospects for local control of alcohol problems.* Unpublished Manuscript, Alcohol Research Group, Medical Research Institute of San Francisco, Berkeley, CA.

Wittman, F. D. (1983). The environment debate. In M. Grant & B. Ritson (Eds.), *Alcohol: The prevention debate* (pp. 134–140). London: Croom-Helm.

Wolch, J. (1979). Residential location and the provision of human services. *The Professional Geographer, 31,* 271–276.

Wolch, J., Nelson, C. A., & Rubalcaba, A. (1987). Back to back wards: Prospects for reinstitutionalization of the mentally disabled. In C. J. Smith & J. A. Giggs (Eds.), *Location and stigma:* Emerging themes in the study of mental health and mental illness. London: George, Allen & Unwin.

Wolfe, A. (1981). *America's impasse: The rise and fall of the politics of growth.* Boston: South End Press.

Wolpert, J., & Wolpert, E. (1976). The relocation of released mental hospital patients into residential communities. *Policy Sciences, 7,* 31–51.

Yeates, M., & Garner, B. (1980). *The North American city.* San Francisco: Harper & Row.

Young, J. (1971). The role of the police as amplifier of deviancy, negotiators of reality and translators of fantasy: Some consequences of our present system of drug control as seen in Notting Hill. In S. Cohen (Ed.), *Images of deviance* (pp. 27–61). London: Pelican.

Young, J. (1976). Introduction. In F. Pearce (Au.), *Crimes of the powerful* (pp. i–iv). London: Pluto Press.

Zimmerman, S. L. (1978). Reassessing the effect of public policy on family functioning. *Social Casework, 59,* 451–457.

Zucker, R. A. (1979). Developmental aspects of drinking through the young adult years. In H. T. Blane & M. E. Chafetz (Eds.), *Youth, alcohol, and social policy* (pp. 91–146). New York: Plenum.

Zunz, O. (Ed.). (1985). *Reliving the past: The worlds of social history.* Chapel Hill: University of North Carolina Press.

Index

A

Abandonment of neighborhoods, 45, 46
Action for Mental Health, 197
Adolescents
  drinking behavior
    frequency of drunkenness, 96
    groups of drinkers, 97
    manipulation of teenage drinking
      problem, 186, 187
    peer pressure, 97
    prevention, 185
    setting in, 95, 96
  as special population, 185, 186
Age factors, drinking behavior, 97
Aggression, bars and drunkenness, 94
Alcohol
  availability and drinking levels, 171,
    172
  consumption, trends in, 171, 172
  federal taxes on, lowering of, 166
Alcoholic Beverage Control (ABC), 166
Alcoholics Anonymous, 123
Alcoholism
  disease model, 145, 146
  drop in, 172
  etiology
    historical view, 8, 9
    social geographic context, 9
  incidence rate, 171
  positivist view, 146
  preventive measures, 99
  special populations, 183–188
    adolescents, 185, 186
    elderly, 183–185

    and reverse discrimination, 187
    women, 183
Alcoholism treatment services
  availability of, 129, 131
  classification of, 125
  components of, 125, 128
  comprehensiveness of service delivery,
    128, 129
  distribution of programs, 128
    equality in, 129
  failure of, 127
  focus of, change in, 165, 166
  goals of, 123, 126
  individuals treated
    characteristics of, 125, 126, 127
    number of, 123, 126
  legislation related to, 120, 123, 124–132
  misuse by skid-row types, 126, 127
  and Native American geographic areas,
    131, 132
  NIAAA requirements, 123, 124, 165
  outlay from federal government, 166
  and physician supply, 132
  recidivism and, 126
  in state mental hospitals, 123, 165
  stresses of staff, 127
  surplus of programs, 187
Alcohol policies, 166–172
  conflict perspective, 166, 167
  goals of, 166
  media attention to problem, 171
  and profit motives, 167–172
    historical perspective, 167–172
  taxation, 166
  (*See also* Economic interests, alcohol.)

Alcohol use. (*See* Drinking behavior;
   Public drunkenness)
Almshouse, 105
Anslinger, Henry J., 148
Antipoverty programs, 207
Antiurbanism, 21, 22
Arena building, 179–181
   by social service agencies, 180
   by universities, 180, 181
   homelessness, 232–235
   (*See also* Special populations, alcohol-
      ism.)
Asylum
   and "disappearance of madness," 211
   as social control, 211
Attachment, to neighborhoods, 44

B

Barker, Roger, 93
Behavior setting approach
   behavior setting, characteristics of, 93
   drinking behavior, 93, 94
Breeder hypothesis, 54
Budget cuts, results of, 156
Bureau of Narcotics and Dangerous
      Drugs (BNDD), 189, 191

C

Capitalist societies
   alcohol policies
      overproduction, 168
      production/consumption aspect, 167,
         168
      prohibition movements, 170
   mass education, 154
   and public problems, 152, 153
   and self-help groups, 155, 156
   surplus population, 153, 154
      dependency on state, 154
   and worker stress, 152, 153
   (*See also* Economic interests, alcohol;
      Welfare state.)

Chicago School, 26, 80
   studies as "natural histories," 33
City living, 21–50
   ambivalence about, 22, 23
      historical view, 23
   environmentalism, positive/negative,
      25
   negative view of, 21
   preferences for, 21, 22, 24
      economic factors, 24
   reform issues, 22–25
      alcohol use, 23
      categorization of population, 23, 24
      high density living, 23
      immigration, 24, 25
      mental health, 24
      visibility of vice/crime, 23
   spatial patterns and public problems
      city size, 26–29
      density, 29–33
      location, 35–37
      and public problems, 25–37
      segregation, 33–35
      study of, 25, 26
   spatial processes and public problems,
      37–48
      neighborhood types, 41–45
      residential mobility, 37–41
      structural changes, 45–48
   (*See also* Residential satisfaction.)
City size, 26–29
   and crime rates, 26–28
      explanations for, 28
   and mental health, 28, 29
      mental paradise lost doctrine, 28, 29
Commercial brewing, 167, 168
Community, versus neighborhood, 52,
      53
Community care, 211
   historical view, 196
   ideological forces in, 196, 197
   mental illness, goal of, 108
Community Mental Health Centers
      (CMHC) Act (1963), 11, 110,
      111, 116
Community mental health (CMH) move-
      ment, 74, 110–118, 195–204
   basic premise of, 115

community mental health centers, 197, 198
  services of, 197, 198
contributions of, 202–204
cost/benefit studies, 163
criticisms of, 110, 115, 116, 199
and federal intervention, 118
funding of, 198, 199
  proportionate allocation, 201
goals of, 113, 115
and growth of welfare states, 111, 112
hospitalization rates, 115, 116
impact on inpatient services, 115
as liberal expansionary sign, 198, 199
precursors to, 197, 198
presidential support, 201
and psychiatrization of society, 202, 203
redistribution of resources and, 117, 118
services offered, 113, 114
and social consumption expenditures, 114
and social expenses, 114
and social investments, 114
survival of, 196, 199
  reasons for, 199–202
Community Support Program (CSP), 73, 74, 76
Community Support System (CSS), 73–76
goals of, 73–75
implementation of, 74
  projects, 76
target population, 73
Comprehensive Alcohol Abuse and Alcoholism Prevention Treatment and Rehabilitation Act, 123
Comprehensive Drug Abuse Prevention and Control Act (1970), 189
Conflict perspective, 15
alcoholism treatment, 166, 167
focus of, 15
public problems, 150–160
  of crime, 151
  of current economic circumstances, 156–158

Marxist versus non-Marxist views, 152
  "new criminology" school, 151
  of population characteristics, 159, 160
  prevalence of problems, reducing, 155, 156
  problems and capitalist society, 152–154
social control, 205
Consensus model, public problems, 150, 151
Contextual approach, 51–77
early work, 51
neighborhood effects, 52–59
social networks, 59–76
Cradle of the Middle Class, The (Ryan), 236
Crime
conflict theory of, 151
fear of, and residential satisfaction, 84–87
Criminology, "new criminology" school, 151

D

Data collection, weaknesses of, 176, 177
Deinstitutionalization, 64–66, 108–119
and community care resources, 65, 70
community mental health (CMH) movement, 110–118
  basic premise of, 115
  criticism of, 110, 115, 116, 199
  and federal intervention, 118
  goal of, 113, 115
  and growth of welfare state, 111, 112
  hospitalization rates, 115, 116
  impact on inpatient services, 115
  redistribution of resources and, 117, 118
  services offered, 113, 114
  and social consumption expenditures, 114
  and social expenses, 114
  and social investments, 114

Deinstitutionalization (*Continued*)
  economic rationale, 160, 161
    economic benefits, 161
  and family care, 64–67
  homelessness, 229
  in 1950s, 109, 110
  reasons for, 108, 109
    fiscal advantages, 109
  and Social Security Act (1935), 109,
    110
Density (urban), 23
  density–pathology relationship, 30–32
    effects of density, 31, 32
    indicators of, 30
    persons-per-room measure, 32
Deviance
  label of, 147
  reinforcement of, 147, 148
  social control of, 148
Disappearance of madness, 211
Distribution of consumption model, alco-
    hol use, 99
Diversion
  components of, 133
  definition of, 133
  goals of, 135, 137
  (*See also* Youthful offenders, diversion
    of.)
Drinking behavior
  contextual approach, dry versus wet
    areas, 56–59
  environmental approach, 90–102
    interpersonal influences, 91, 92
    research goals, 91
    rise in research, 90, 91
    situational influences, 92, 93–97
    social availability factors, 100–102
    social geography of drinking, 91,
      97–99
    spatial context variables, 93
    subjective availability factors, 99,
      100
  public drinking, historical view, 236,
    237
  reasons for drinking, 100
  socially integrated drinking, 102
  (*See also* specific influences/variables.)

Driving while intoxicated (DWI), 5, 159
Drunk tanks, 121

E

Ecological studies, 25, 26
  Chicago school, 26
  ecological fallacy, 26
Economic interests (alcohol), 167–172
  African colonies, 168, 169
    drinking, reasons for, 169
    import substitution strategy, 168,
      169
    liquor revenues, importance of, 168
  capitalist societies
    market expansion, 168
    production/consumption aspect, 167,
      168
    prohibition movements, 170
  less developed countries, 169, 170
Economic loss hypothesis, homelessness,
    227
Eighteenth Amendment (1919), 148
Elderly
  alcoholism among, 183–185
    underestimation of, 184, 185
  institutionalization of, 115, 116
  residential mobility, 38–41
    adjustment factors, 39, 40
    reasons for moving, 39
  residential satisfaction, 82, 83
  segregation, 35
Eligibility laws, 210
Enduring Asylum, The (Morrissey, Gold-
    man, & Klerman), 115
Environmental approach, 78–102
  drinking behavior, 90–102, 91–102
    interpersonal influences, 91, 92
    research goals, 91
    rise in research, 90, 91
    situational influences, 92, 93–97
    social availability factors, 100–102
    social geography of drinking, 91,
      97–99
    spatial context variables, 93

subjective availability factors, 99, 100
overview of field, 78–82
  areas of study, 78, 80
  classification of studies, 81, 82
  contributions of study, 80
  multi-paradigmatic approach, 79
  quantification methods, 79, 80
  research areas, 80, 81
residential satisfaction, 82–90
  elderly, 82, 83
  fear of crime, 84–87
  physical environment, 83, 84
  quality of life, 87, 89, 90
  safety factors, 84
  State Stress Index (SSI), 87–89
(*See also* specific influences/variables.)
Environmentalism, positive/negative, 25
Epidemiology of public problems
  definition of, 7, 8
  geographical focus of, 7
  goals of, 8
  political context, 10–13
  service delivery context, 9, 10
  social geographic context, 8, 9
Ethnic density, and mental health/mental health services, 54, 56
Ethnic groups, drinking behavior, 100, 102
Etiology, theories, change over time, 6

F

Family care and mental illness
  coping by family, 67
  decision to seek treatment, 69–73
  deinstitutionalized patients, 64, 65
  family burden concept, 66–68
  recognition of problem, 69
  support systems, 67, 68
Family influences, drinking behavior, 91, 92
Family Networks (Speck & Attneave), 61
Federal Bureau of Narcotics, 189
Federal Housing Act (1949), 218

Feminization of poverty, 176
Fischer, Claude, 60
Fromm, Erich, 24
Functionalist perspective, social control, 206

G

Gentrification of neighborhoods, homelessness, 228
Ghettoization
  mental patient ghettos, 47, 48
  of neighborhoods, 46–48
Great Society, 206–208
  interpretation of programs, 206–208
  strategies for programs, 207

H

Heroin addiction, 188–195
  legal sanctions, results of, 188
  medical care of, 188, 194, 195
    and "drug-abuse industrial complex," 195
  methadone maintenance, 190–194
    criticism of, 191, 193, 194
    growth of cli
    racial aspects,
    social control
    194
  1960s, status of abuse, 189
  Nixon administration
    Bureau of Narcotics and Dangerous Drugs (BNDD), 189, 191
    federal budget, 191
    law enforcement, changes in, 189
    methadone maintenance, 190–194
    National Institute of Drug Abuse (NIDA), 193
    Office of Drug Abuse Law Enforcement (ODALE), 191, 192
    Operation Intercept, 192
    Special Action Office for Drug

Heroin addiction (*Continued*)
　　Abuse Prevention (SAODAP),
　　　190, 193
　　states responsibilities, 192, 193
　　"turning the corner" speech, 192
Homelessness, 17, 225–238
　　arena building, 232–235
　　epidemic nature of, 226–230
　　historical view, 235–238
　　media coverage of, 231, 232, 238
　　neighborhood shelters, reactions to,
　　　232, 233
　　and new social service providers, 234
　　political implications of, 233, 234
　　reasons for
　　　admission procedures, change in,
　　　　229
　　　deinstitutionalization, 229
　　　economic loss hypothesis, 227
　　　gentrification of neighborhoods, 228
　　　utilization of downtown areas, 228
　　　welfare, shift in, 227, 228
　　statistical information, 226
　　and welfare state, 230, 231
　　(*See also* Skid row.)
Hospitalization of mental patients, 69–73
　　family decision making
　　　precipitating circumstances, 70, 71
　　　recognition of problem, 69
　　　social network perspective, 69–73
Human service paradox, 52

I

Immigration, 24, 25
Institutions
　　historical view, 105
　　　criticisms of institutions, 106, 107
　　　18th century, 105
　　　19th century, 106
　　　public institutions, 106
　　　reasons for development of, 106–
　　　　108
　　　20th century, 108
Interactionist view
　　deviance, 147, 148

public problems, 147–150
Interpersonal influences
　　drinking behavior, 91, 92
　　　family, 91, 92
　　　secondary groups, 92
Intervention, and exacerbation of prob-
　　lems, 16
Inverse care law, and psychotherapy, 214
Is There no Place on Earth for Me?
　　(Sheehan), 64

J

Jewish drinking behavior, 101, 102
　　low alcoholism rate
　　　protective mechanisms, 102
　　　reasons for, 101, 102
Joint Commission on Mental Illness and
　　Health, 197
Juvenile Justice and Delinquency Preven-
　　tion Act (1974), 136

K

Koch, Mayor, 232

L

Labeling theory, 15
　　and admission to psychiatric facilities,
　　　54
　　focus of, 15
　　juvenile offenders, 134
　　　reinforcement of delinquent acts,
　　　　134, 135
　　proponents of, 15
　　secondary deviance phenomenon, 134,
　　　135, 147
Law Enforcement Assistance Administra-
　　tion (LEAA), 135
Legal factors, opinions, change over
　　time, 6

Location effects, 35–37
  famous study of, 35
  issues in, 37

M

Manchester School, 60
Marijuana Tax Act, 148
Marxism, conflict theories of crime, 152
Media, coverage of homelessness, 231,
    232, 238
Medical model, 8, 14, 15
  as "objectivist" view, 14, 15
  status of, 8
  weakness of, 14
Mental health
  and city living, 24
  and size of city, 28, 29
Mental health care
  as giant industry, 114
  outcome of, 114
  (*See also* Community mental health
    (CMH) movement.)
Mental health services, 52–56
  contextual approach
    ethnic density factors, 54, 56
    race factors, 54, 56
Mental Health Study Act (1955), 197
Mental illness
  disappearance of madness, 211
  early terms used, 211
  new chronics, 113
  social class and, 115
  SSI payments, 164
Mental paradise lost doctrine, 28, 29
Mental Treatment Act (1930), 211
Methadone maintenance, 190–194
  criticism of, 191, 193, 194
  growth of clinics, 194, 195
  racial aspects, 193
  social control interpretation, 193, 194
Middle-class home/family, historical
    view, 236, 237
Milgram, Stanley, 60
Mitchell, J. Clyde, 60
Moral entrepreneurs, 148

Moving. (*See* Residential mobility)
Mutual aid movement, 63

N

National Health Service, 154
National Institute on Alcohol Abuse and
    Alcoholism (NIAAA), 123, 124,
    131, 165, 166
  funding, 181, 183
  special populations, 183–188
National Institute of Mental Health
    (NIMH), 199
National Teenage Alcohol Education Pro-
    gram, 186
Natural Helping Networks (Collins &
    Pancoast), 61
Negative environmentalism, 25
Neighborhood, use of term, 52
Neighborhood effects, 52–59
  climate of opinion, 52, 53
    human service paradox, 52
  drinking behavior, 56–59
  mental health services, 52–56
    ethnic density factors, 54, 56
    race factors, 54, 56
Neighborhoods
  abandonment of, 45, 46
    contagious nature of, 45, 46
    positive aspects, 46
    and public problems, 46
    reasons for, 45
  attachment to, 44
    group differences, 44
    physical rootedness, 44
    social bonding, 44
  categories of residents, 53
    resource exploiters, 53
    resource identifiers, 53
    resource isolates, 53
    resource underutilizers, 53
  change process in, 41, 42
  classification of, 42, 43
  ghettoization, 46–48
    advantages for people, 47, 48
    and "public city" concept, 46, 47

Neighborhoods (*Continued*)
  reasons for, 46
  "healthy" neighborhoods, 52
  social networks of, 43, 44
  versus community, 52, 53
Net widening, and diversion of youthful
    offenders, 139, 140
"Network City, The" (Craven & Well-
    man), 61
"New chronic" patients, 113, 163
New Class War, 162
"New criminology" school, 151
"New federalism," 192
"New Prohibition, The," 171
Nixon administration
  heroin addiction
    Bureau of Narcotics and Dangerous
      Drugs (BNDD), 189, 191
    changes in, 189
    federal budget, 191
    methadone maintenance, 190–194
    National Institute of Drug Abuse
      (NIDA), 193
    Office of Drug Abuse Law Enforce-
      ment (ODALE), 191, 192
    Operation Intercept, 192
    Special Action Office for Drug
      Abuse Prevention (SAODAP),
      190, 193
    states responsibilities, 192, 193
    "turning the corner" speech, 192

O

Objectivist view, medical model as, 14,
    15
Office of Drug Abuse Law Enforcement
    (ODALE), 191, 192
Operation Intercept, 192
Outdoor relief, 106
Overproduction, capitalist societies, 168

P

Panoptic vision, 211, 212
Persistence over time, public problems, 6

Physical environment, residential satisfac-
    tion, 83, 84
Pluralists, 148
Political factors
  and homelessness, 233, 234
  and public problems, 10–13
    distribution of services, 11, 13
    outcome of legislation, 10, 11
Positive environmentalism, 25
Positivist view
  public problems, 145–147
    of alcoholism, 146
    basis of, 145
Production/consumption aspect, capitalist
    societies, 167, 168
Prohibition, 8, 148, 149, 236
  as "status politics" exercise, 149
  success of anti-drinking groups, 149
Psychiatrization of society, 202, 203
Psychotherapy, 212–215
  Freudian analysis, 215
  high status/low status groups, 214
  and inverse care law, 214
  jargon of, 213
  and social control, 212
    voluntary social control, 213
  types of patients, 214, 215
Public consensus, and public problems,
    149, 150
Public drunkenness, 120–132
  Comprehensive Alcohol Abuse and Al-
    coholism Prevention Treatment
    and Rehabilitation Act, 123
  decriminalization of, 120–132
    and alcoholism treatment facilities,
      121, 122
    analogy to deinstitutionalization,
      122, 123
    goal of, 121
    historical view, 121
    reasons for, 121–123
  drunk tanks, 121
  incarceration of drunks, 120
  responses to (1950s–1960s), 120
    and revolving door syndrome, 120,
      121, 147
  Uniform Alcoholism and Intoxication
    Treatment Act (1971), 120, 124–
    132

(*See also* Alcoholism treatment services.)
Public issues
  evolution of, 174, 175
  recognition as social problem, 181
Public problems
  areas of public concern (1974–1982), 5
  arena building, 179–181
    by social service agencies, 180
    by universities, 180, 181
  categories of, 3
  characteristics of, 4–7
    etiological aspect, 6
    interrelatedness, 6
    persistence over time, 6
    relativity, 4–6
    service dependence, 4
    stigma, 4
  conflict perspective, 150–160
    of crime, 151
    of current economic circumstances, 156–158
    Marxist versus non-Marxist views, 152
    "new criminology" school, 151
    of population characteristics, 159, 160
    prevalence of problems, reducing, 155, 156
    problems and capitalist society, 152–154
  consensus model, 150, 151
  contextual approach, 51–77
    early work, 51
    neighborhood effects, 52–59
    social networks, 59–76
  definition of, 3
    changing definitions, 5
  environmental approach, 78–102
    drinking behavior, 90–102
    overview of field, 78–82
    residential satisfaction, 82–90
  epidemiology of, 7–13
    political context, 10–13
    service delivery context, 9, 10
    social geographic context, 8, 9
  exacerbation, by official intervention, 16
  fascination with, 178, 179

  interactionist view, 147–150
    deviance, 147, 148
  positivist view, 145–147
    of alcoholism, 146
    basis of, 145
  prevalence of, 175–179
    and data collection, 176, 177
    and interpretation of facts, 177, 178
  and public consensus, 149, 150
  public issues
    evolution of, 174, 175
    recognition as social problem, 181
  social problems as, 4
  theories of
    conflict perspective, 15
    labeling theories, 15
    medical model, 8, 14, 15
  unemployment and, 158
  (*See also* individual topics.)

Q

Quality of life, residential satisfaction, 87, 89, 90
Quantification methods, environmental approach, 79, 80

R

Race, and mental health/mental health services, 54, 56
Reagan administration, cutbacks, 162, 164
Reform issues
  city living, 22–25
    alcohol use, 23
    categorization of population, 23, 24
    high density living, 23
    immigration, 24, 25
    mental health, 24
    visibility of vice/crime, 23
Rehabilitative social control, 215–222
  skid row, 215–222
Relabeling, and diversion of youthful offenders, 139, 140

Relativity, of public problems, 4–6
Residential mobility
  elderly, 38–41
    adjustment factors, 39, 40
    reasons for moving, 39
  involuntary relocation, problems of, 41
  stress model, 37, 38
Residential satisfaction, 82–90
  elderly, 82, 83
  fear of crime, 84–87
  physical environment, 83, 84
  quality of life, 87, 89, 90
  safety factors, 84
  State Stress Index (SSI), 87–89
Residents of neighborhoods, categories
    of, 53
Resource exploiters, 53
Resource identifiers, 53
Resource isolates, 53
Resource underutilizers, 53
Reverse discrimination, and special alco-
    holism populations, 187
Revisionist perspective, social control,
    205, 206, 208–210
Revolving door syndrome, 120, 121, 147
Ryan, Mary, 236

S

Safety factors, residential satisfaction, 84
Secondary deviance, 147
  juvenile offenders, 134, 135
Segregation
  categorization of urban dwellers, 23,
    24
  elderly, 35
  19th century, 33
  segregation index, 33, 34
  "service-dependent" groups, 34, 35
Self-awareness theory, drinking behavior,
    100
Self-help groups, 155, 156
Service delivery, and public problems, 9,
    10
"Service-dependent" groups, segregation
    and, 34, 35
Setting, drinking behavior, 92–95, 100

Silver, Sheldon, 232
Situational influences
  drinking behavior, 92, 93–97
    adolescent drinking, 95–97
    age factors, 97
    bars and aggression, 94
    behavior setting approach, 93, 94
    setting, 92–95, 100
Size of city. (*See* City size)
Skid row, 215–222
  definitions of, 216, 222
  as human condition, 222
  humanizing skid row, 217
    facilities needed, 217
  institutions/agencies related to, 216
  location of
    managerial interpretation, 218
    zone of transition, 218
  natural decline of, 218–221
  perceptions of, 216, 217
  predicting future geographical reloca-
    tion of, 219, 220
  residents, types of, 215, 216
  skid row-ness, measure of, 220
  (*See also* Homelessness.)
Social availability factors
  drinking behavior, 100–102
    ethnic subgroups, 101, 102
    and quantity of consumption, 101
    social norms in, 101
Social class, and mental illness, 115
Social consumption expenditures, and
    community mental health, 114
Social control
  adjudicatory, 213
  categories of, 209
  conciliatory, 213
  conflict perspective, 205
  as dependent variable, 206
  functionalist perspective, 206
  Great Society, 206–208
    interpretation of programs, 206–208
    strategies for programs, 207
  indoctrinatory, 213
  methadone maintenance and, 193, 194
  panoptic vision, 211, 212
  refinement of concept, 208, 209
  rehabilitative social control, 215–222

skid row, 215–222
revisionist perspective, 205, 206, 208–210
therapeutic social control, 210–215
asylum, 211
community care, 211
nonrepressive methods, 211, 212
psychotherapy, 212–215
and social structure, 214
uses of term, 205
(*See also* Skid row.)
Social expenses, and community mental health, 114
Social geographic context, public problems, 8, 9
Social geography of drinking, 91, 97–99
availability factors, 97, 99
distribution of consumption model, 99
Social investments, and community mental health, 114
Socially integrated drinking, 102
Social networks, 59–76
Community Support System (CSS), 73–76
definition of, 60
early work, 60
function of, 61–64
and mental health, 64–68
community care and, 64
decision making and hospitalization, 69–73
deinstitutionalization, 64–66
family burden concept, 66–68
importance of, 64
neighborhoods, 43, 44
research uses of, 60, 61
advantages to use, 61–64
Social Networks and Urban Situations (Mitchell), 60
Social Security Act (1935), 109, 110
Social Security income, 164
eligibility for, 164, 165
to mentally ill, 164
Social service agencies
arena building by, 180
functions of, 180
Social structure, and psychiatric social control, 214

Spatial context variables
drinking behavior, 93
availability/consumption patterns, 93
support factors, 93
Spatial patterns and public problems, 25–37
city size, 26–29
density, 29–33
location, 35–37
study of, 25, 26
(*See also* specific topics.)
Spatial processes and public problems, 37–48
neighborhood types, 41–45
residential mobility, 37–41
structural changes, 45–48
(*See also* specific topics.)
Special Action Office for Drug Abuse Prevention (SAODAP), 190, 193
Special populations, 183–188
adolescents, 185, 186
elderly, 183–185
and reverse discrimination, 187
women, 183
State mental hospitals, alcoholism treatment, 123, 165
State Stress Index (SSI), 87–89
Stigma
juvenile offenders, 134, 137
of public problems, 4
''Strength of Weak Ties, The'' (Granovetter), 61
Stress model, residential mobility, 37, 38
Subjective availability factors
drinking behavior, 99, 100
costs/benefits of drinking, 99, 100
reasons for drinking, 100
self-awareness theory, 100
Suburbanization, 21
Support systems. (*See* Social networks)

T

Temperance movement, 174, 175, 178, 179
(*See also* Prohibition.)

Territorial imperative, 30
Therapeutic social control, 210–215
  asylum, 211
  community care, 211
  nonrepressive methods, 211, 212
  psychotherapy, 212–215
  and social structure, 214
Tilly, Charles, 60
Transinstitutionalization, 140

U

Unemployment, and public problems,
    158
Uniform Alcoholism and Intoxication
    Treatment Act (1971), 120, 124–
    132
Universities, arena building, 180, 181
Urban study methods, 25, 26
  ecological studies, 25, 26
  urban/rural comparison, 25

W

Welfare services
  cuts, results of, 156–158, 162, 164
  factors for provision of, 158
  groups dependent on, 156, 157
  slash and burn approach, 156
Welfare state
  and community mental health centers,
    113
  development of, 111, 112
    and capitalist system, 112
    expansion of state, 111, 112
  and fiscal crisis, 160, 163
  and homelessness, 230, 231
  prevalence of problems, management
    of, 155
  and reproduction of labor power, 112
  social service cuts, 162

Wellman, Barry, 60
White, Harrison, 60
Women
  alcoholism among, 183
  female crime, rise of, 176, 177

Y

Youthful offenders
  categories of, 134
  court processing, effects of, 134
  labeling theory, 134
    reinforcement of delinquent acts,
      134, 135
    secondary deviance, 134, 135
  stigma of, 134, 137
  (*See also* Youthful offenders, diversion
    of.)
Youthful offenders, diversion of, 133–
    141
  components of diversion, 133
  criticism of, 136
  definition of diversion, 133
  direct outcomes, 137–139
    cost saving, 138, 139
    perception of stigma, 137
    recidivism, 138
    social control aspects, 138, 139
  evaluation of, problems related to,
    136, 137, 140
  goals of diversion, 135, 137
  historical view, 133–136
    beginning of movement, 134
    Juvenile Justice and Delinquency
      Prevention Act (1974), 136
    President's Commission (1967), 134,
      135
  indirect outcomes, 139, 140
    net widening, 139, 140
    relabeling, 139, 140
  motivations for, 134, 135
Youth Service Bureaus, 135